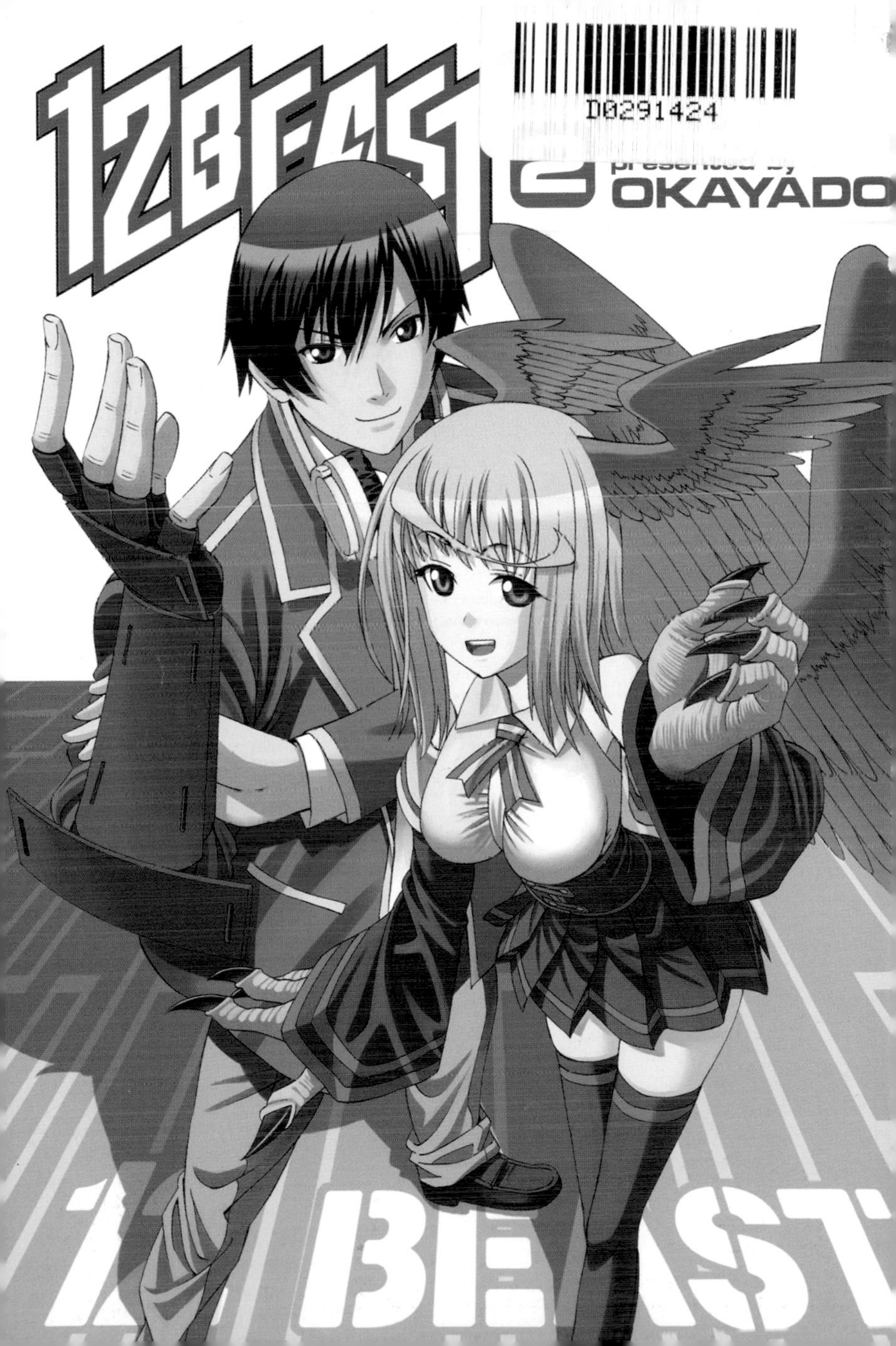
OKAYADO
BEAST

12 BEAST

presented by
OKAYADO 2

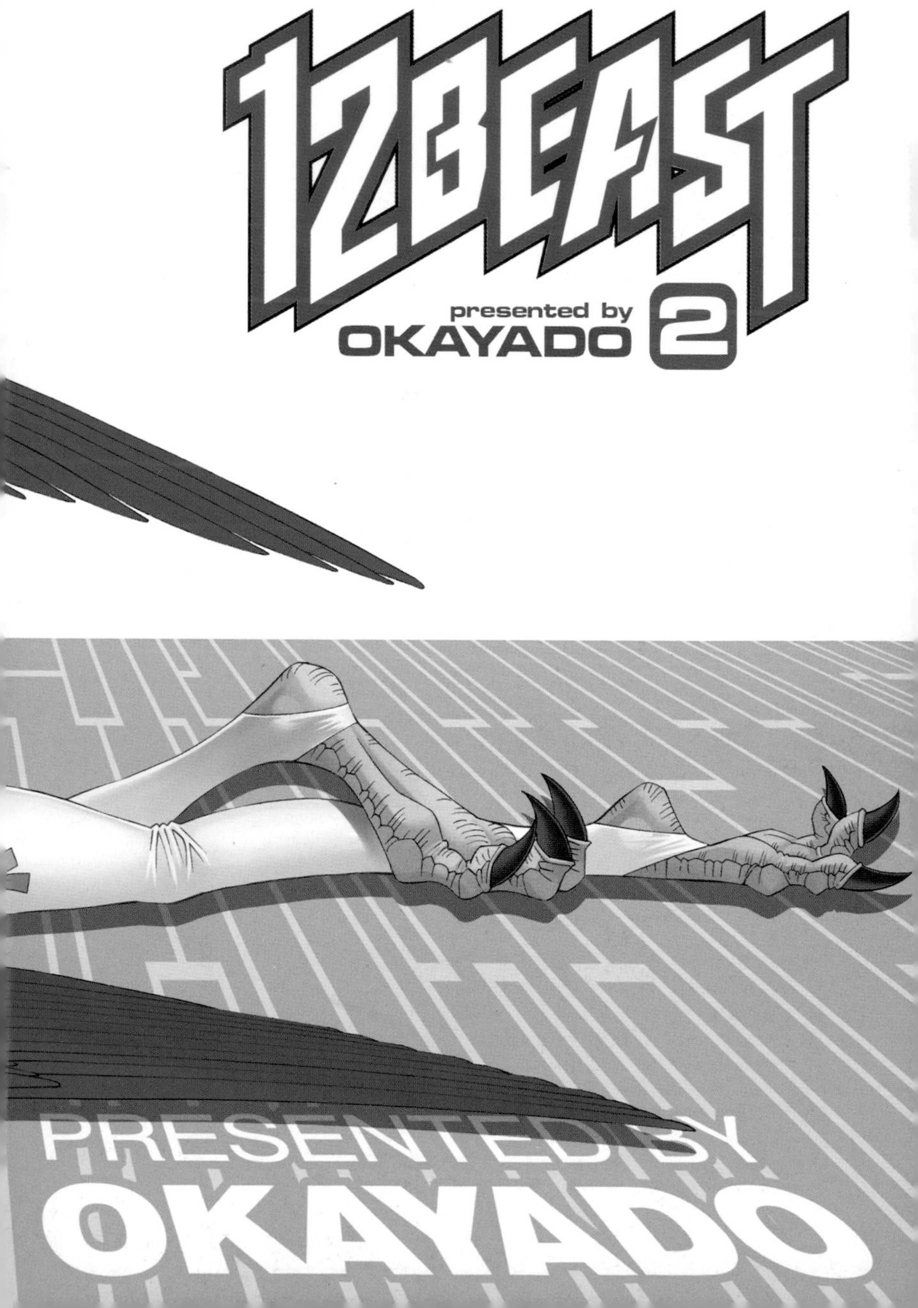
PRESENTED BY
OKAYADO

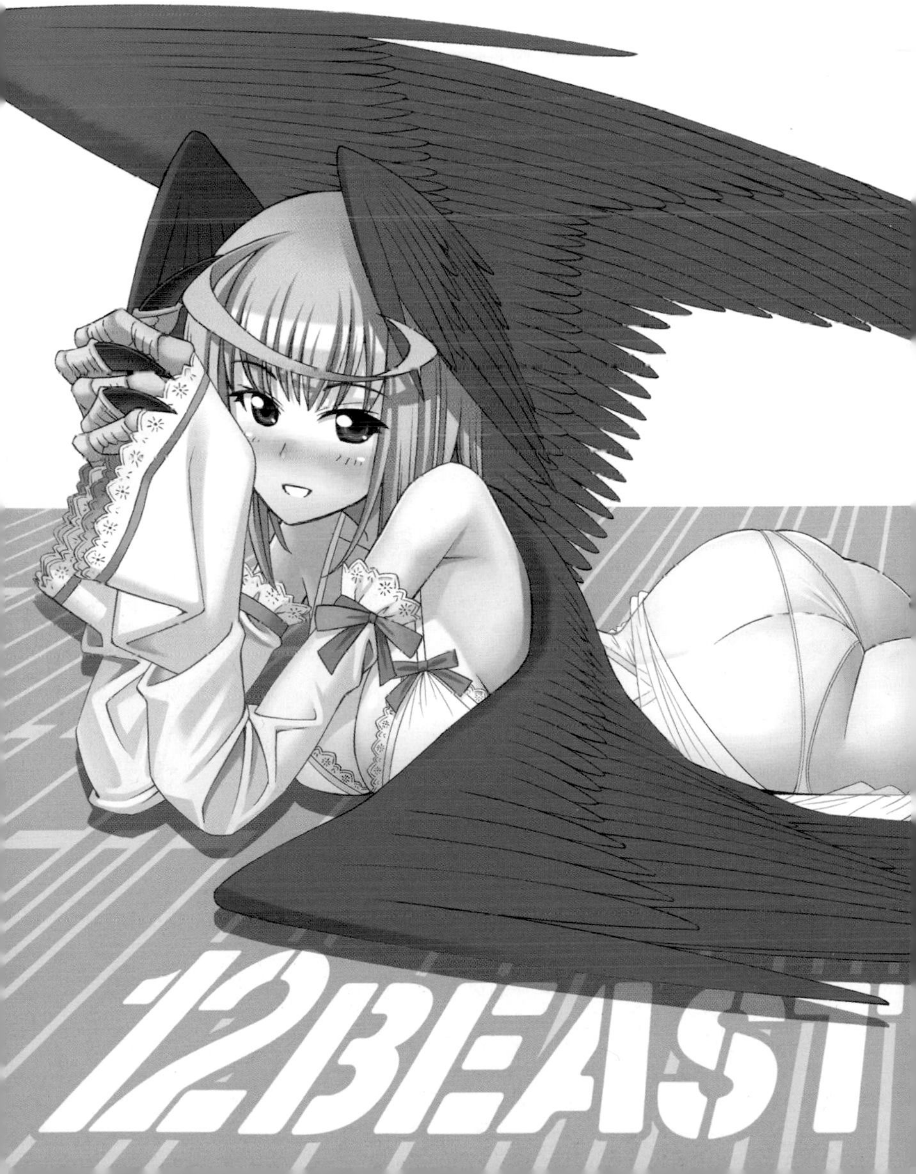
12BEAST

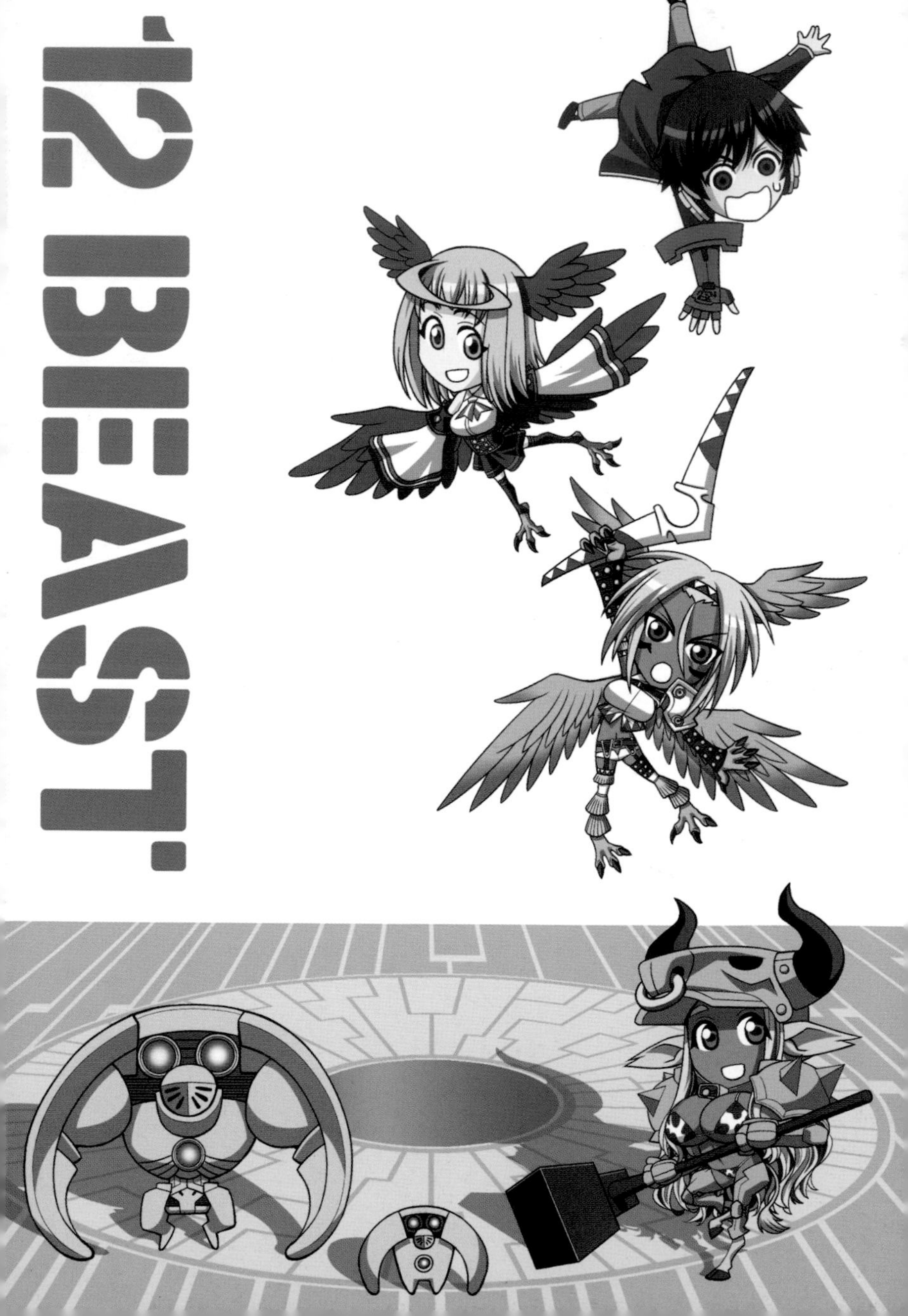
12 BEAST

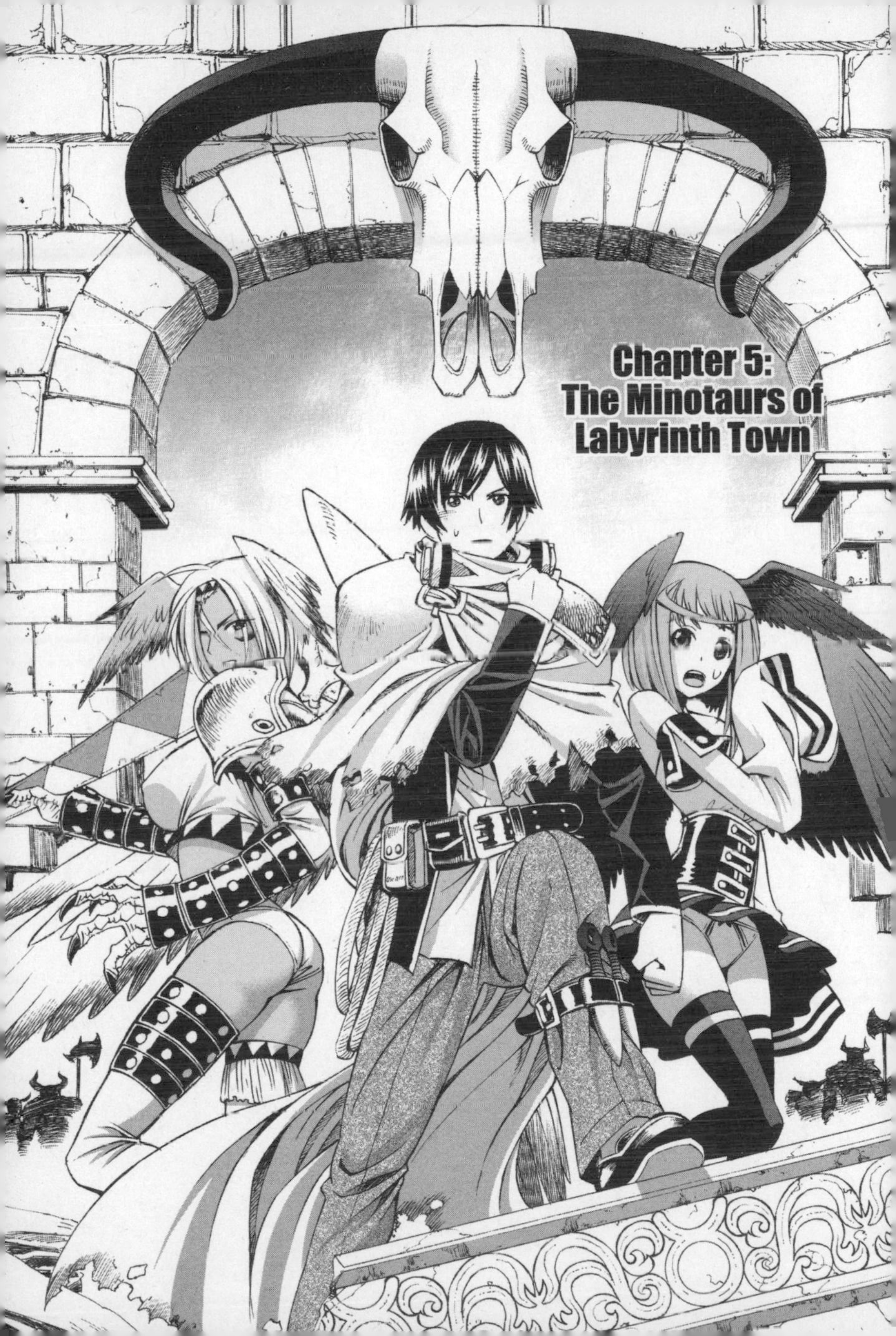
Chapter 5:
The Minotaurs of
Labyrinth Town

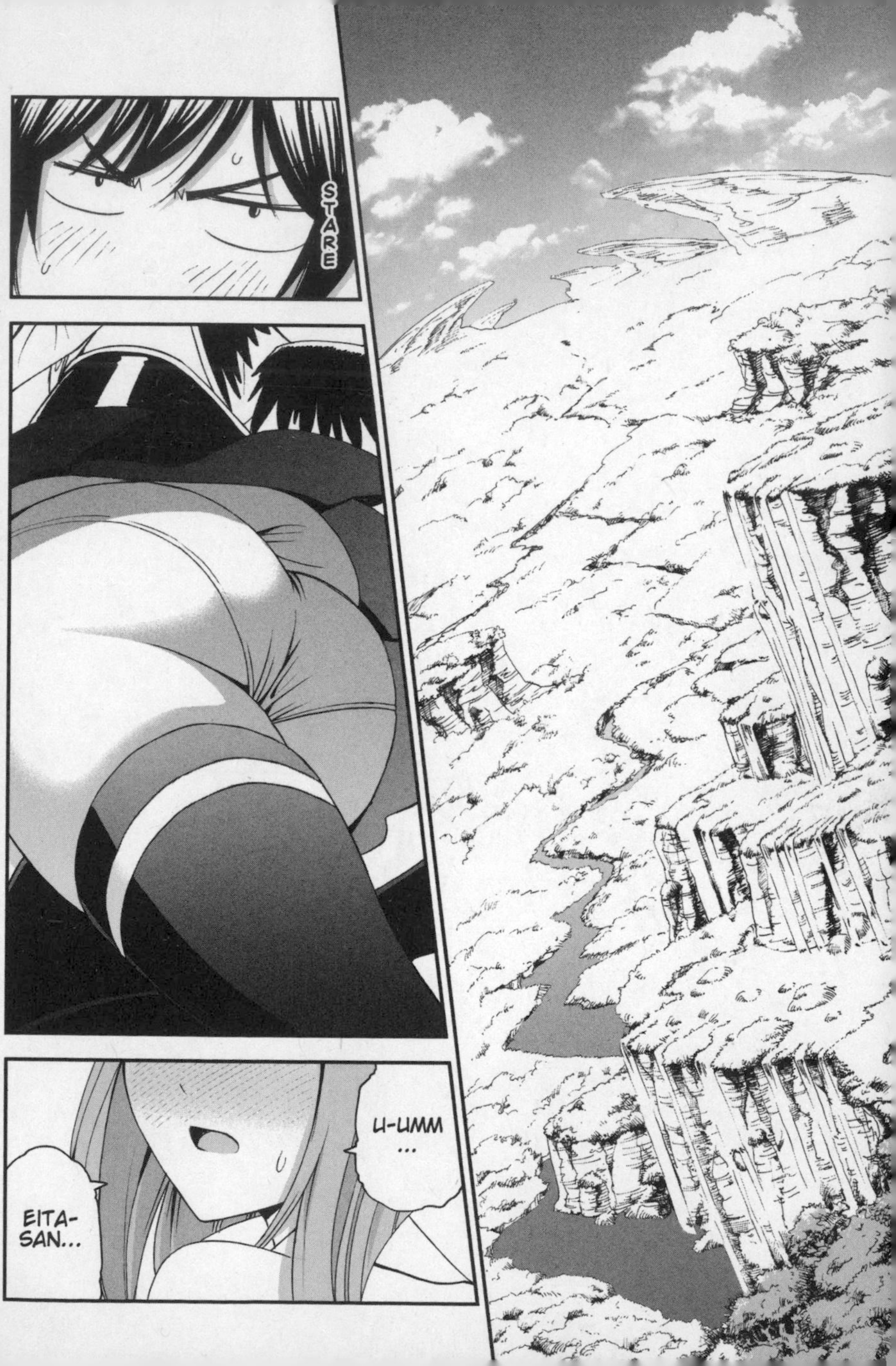
STARE
U-UMM ...
EITA-SAN...

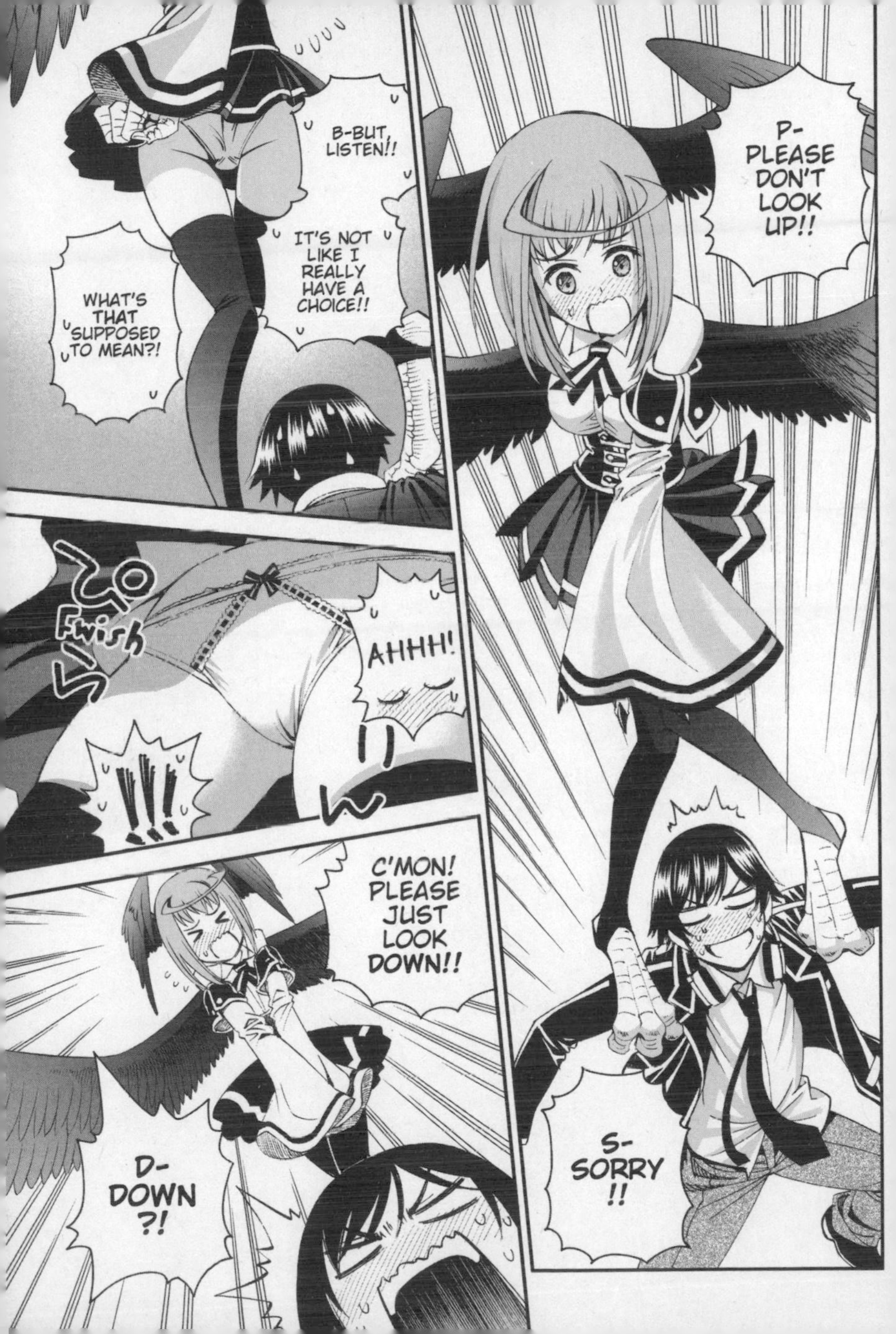
P-PLEASE DON'T LOOK UP!!
S-SORRY!!
B-BUT, LISTEN!!
IT'S NOT LIKE I REALLY HAVE A CHOICE!!
WHAT'S THAT SUPPOSED TO MEAN?!
AHHH!
Fwish
!!!
C'MON! PLEASE JUST LOOK DOWN!!
D-DOWN?!

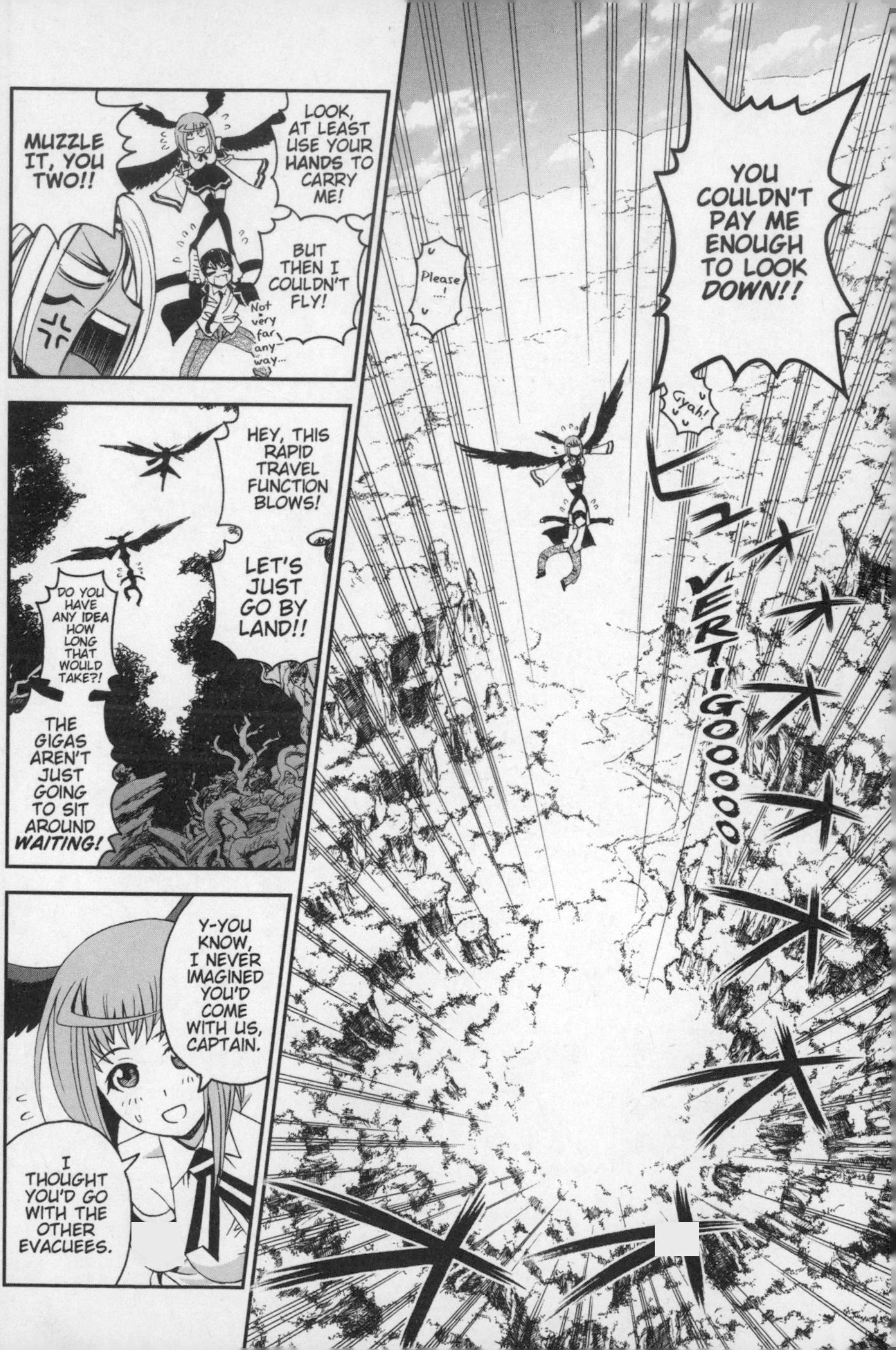
YOU COULDN'T PAY ME ENOUGH TO LOOK DOWN!!
Please...!
Gyah!
VERTIGOOOOOO
LOOK, AT LEAST USE YOUR HANDS TO CARRY ME!
MUZZLE IT, YOU TWO!!
BUT THEN I COULDN'T FLY!
Not very far anyway...
HEY, THIS RAPID TRAVEL FUNCTION BLOWS!
LET'S JUST GO BY LAND!!
DO YOU HAVE ANY IDEA HOW LONG THAT WOULD TAKE?!
THE GIGAS AREN'T JUST GOING TO SIT AROUND WAITING!
Y-YOU KNOW, I NEVER IMAGINED YOU'D COME WITH US, CAPTAIN.
I THOUGHT YOU'D GO WITH THE OTHER EVACUEES.

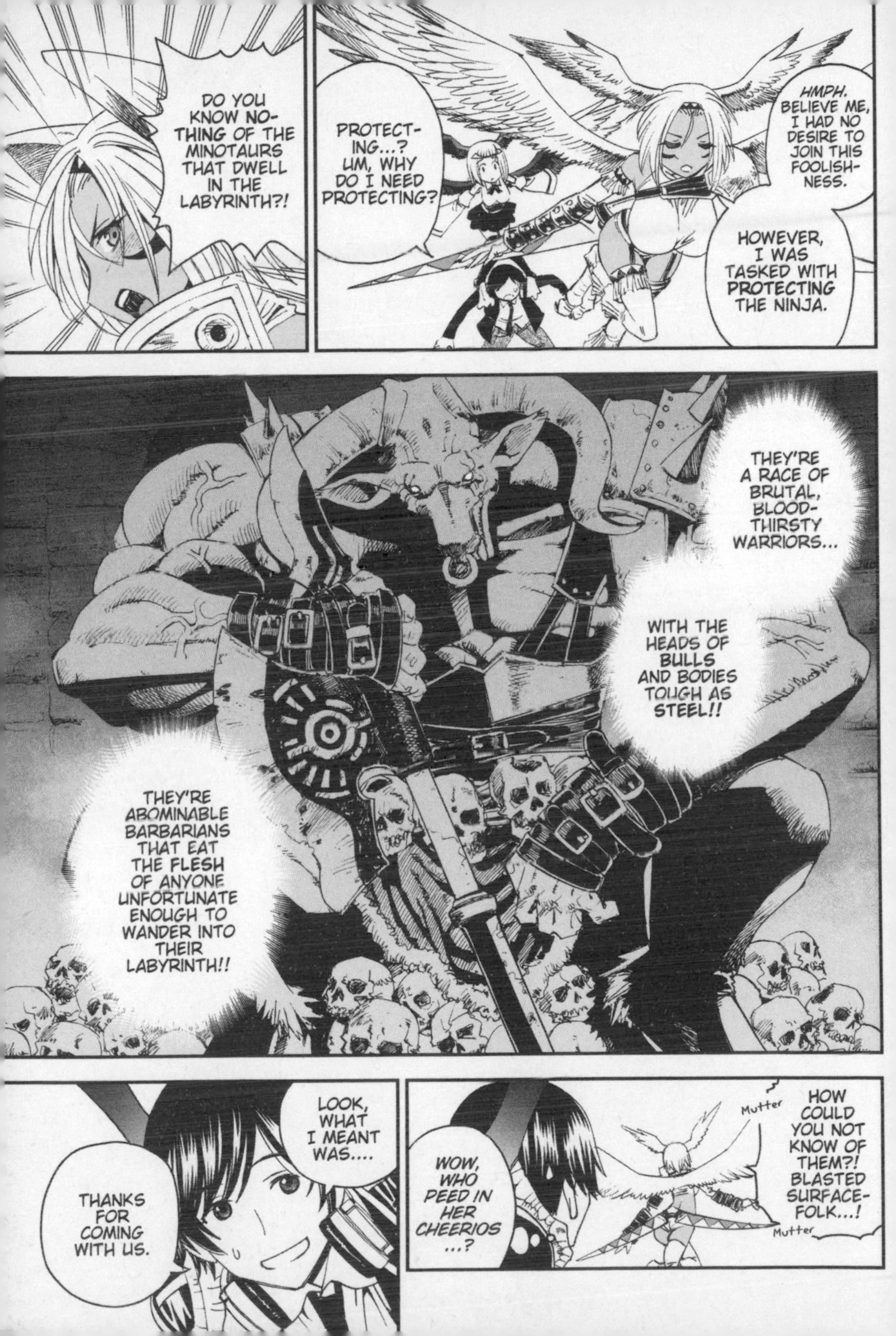
HMPH. BELIEVE ME, I HAD NO DESIRE TO JOIN THIS FOOLISHNESS.
HOWEVER, I WAS TASKED WITH PROTECTING THE NINJA.
PROTECTING...? UM, WHY DO I NEED PROTECTING?
DO YOU KNOW NOTHING OF THE MINOTAURS THAT DWELL IN THE LABYRINTH?!
THEY'RE A RACE OF BRUTAL, BLOODTHIRSTY WARRIORS...
WITH THE HEADS OF BULLS AND BODIES TOUGH AS STEEL!!
THEY'RE ABOMINABLE BARBARIANS THAT EAT THE FLESH OF ANYONE UNFORTUNATE ENOUGH TO WANDER INTO THEIR LABYRINTH!!
HOW COULD YOU NOT KNOW OF THEM?! BLASTED SURFACE-FOLK...!
Mutter
Mutter
WOW, WHO PEED IN HER CHEERIOS...?
LOOK, WHAT I MEANT WAS....
THANKS FOR COMING WITH US.

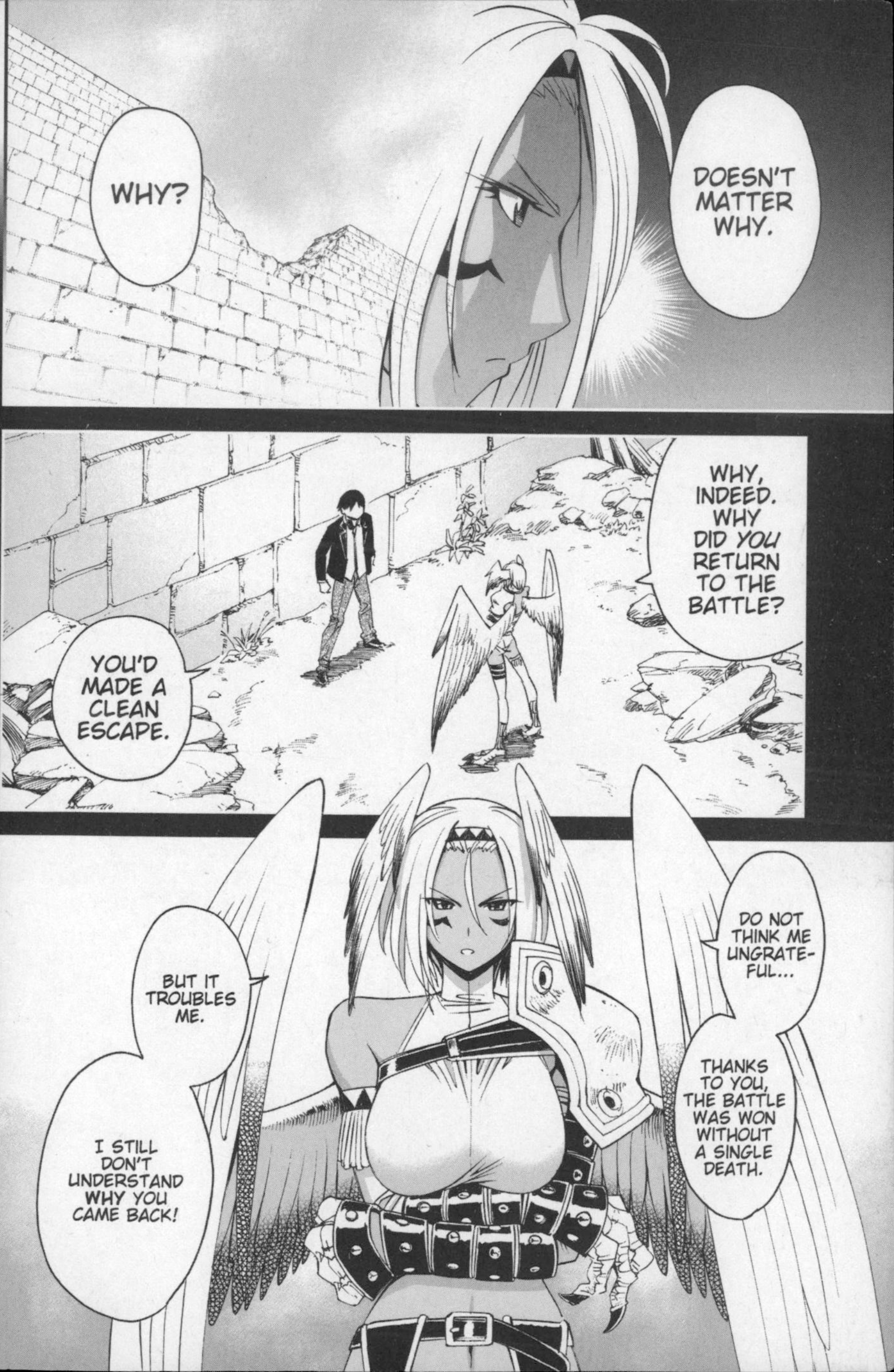

DOESN'T MATTER WHY.
WHY?
WHY, INDEED. WHY DID *YOU* RETURN TO THE BATTLE?
YOU'D MADE A CLEAN ESCAPE.
DO NOT THINK ME UNGRATE-FUL...
BUT IT TROUBLES ME.
THANKS TO YOU, THE BATTLE WAS WON WITHOUT A SINGLE DEATH.
I STILL DON'T UNDERSTAND WHY YOU CAME BACK!

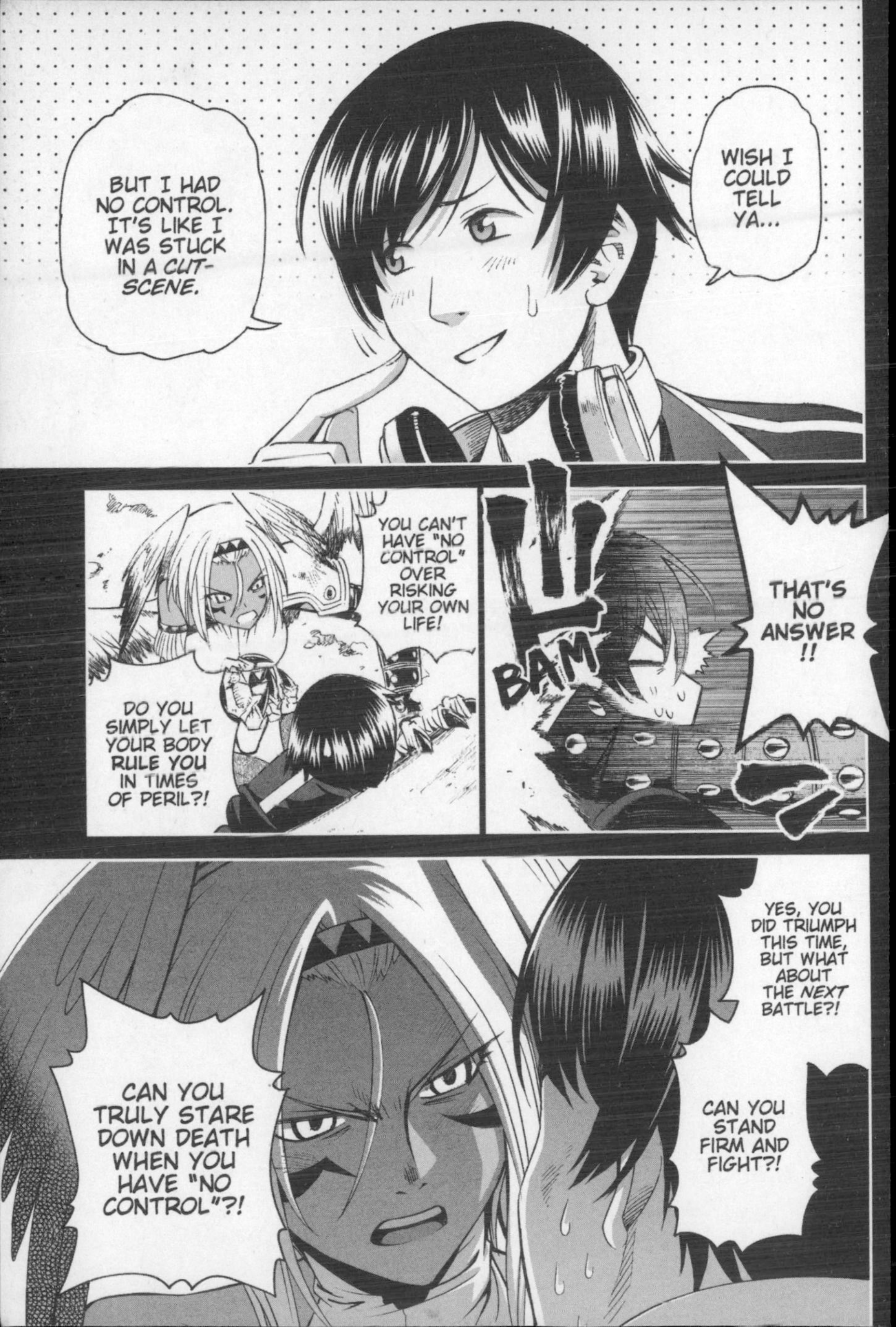
WISH I COULD TELL YA...
BUT I HAD NO CONTROL. IT'S LIKE I WAS STUCK IN A *CUT-SCENE*.
!!
BAM
THAT'S NO ANSWER!!
YOU CAN'T HAVE "NO CONTROL" OVER RISKING YOUR OWN LIFE!
DO YOU SIMPLY LET YOUR BODY RULE YOU IN TIMES OF PERIL?!
YES, YOU DID TRIUMPH THIS TIME, BUT WHAT ABOUT THE *NEXT* BATTLE?!
CAN YOU STAND FIRM AND FIGHT?!
CAN YOU TRULY STARE DOWN DEATH WHEN YOU HAVE "NO CONTROL"?!

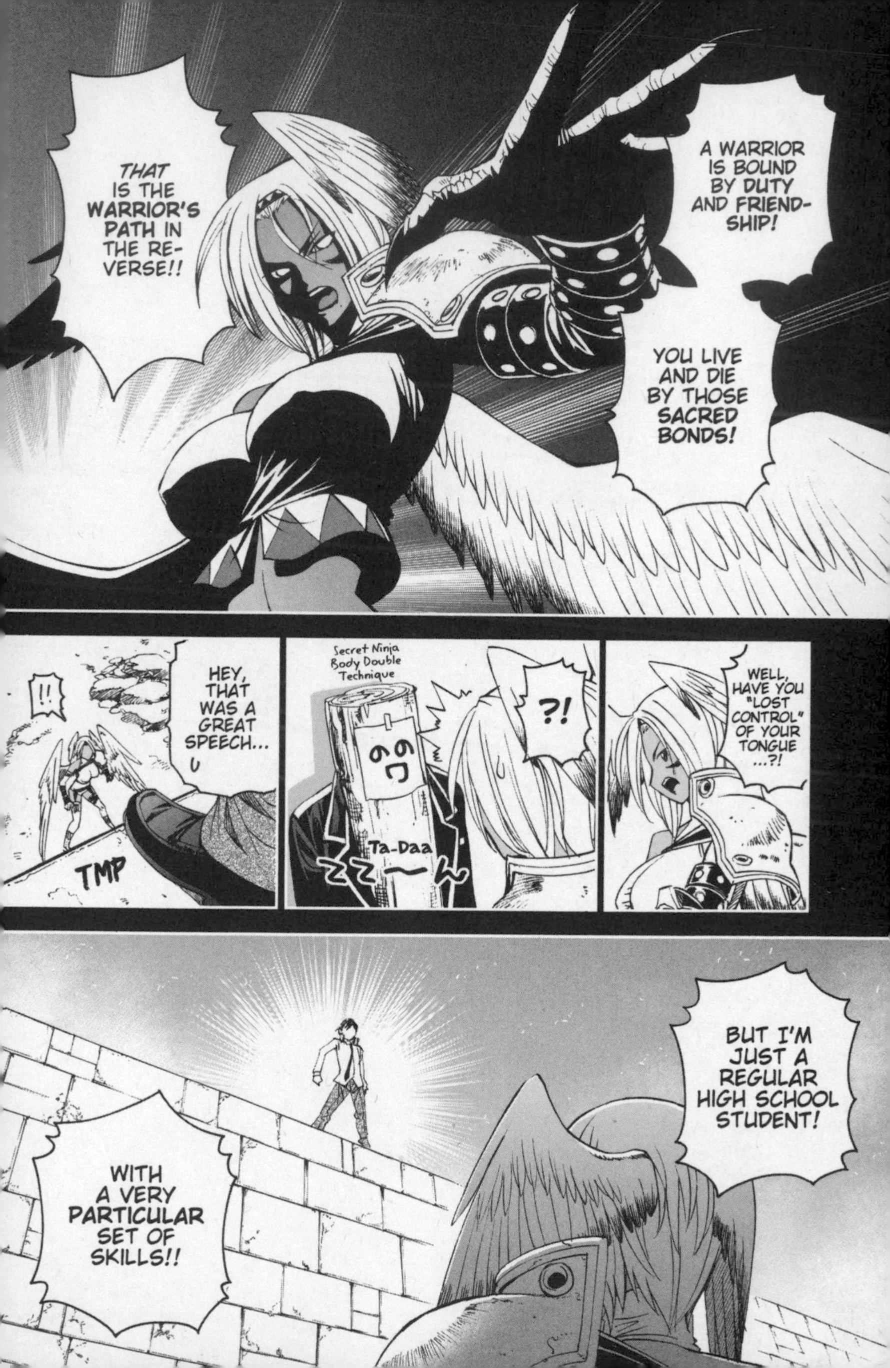
A WARRIOR IS BOUND BY DUTY AND FRIEND-SHIP!
YOU LIVE AND DIE BY THOSE SACRED BONDS!
THAT IS THE WARRIOR'S PATH IN THE RE-VERSE!!
WELL, HAVE YOU "LOST CONTROL" OF YOUR TONGUE ...?!
?!
Secret Ninja Body Double Technique
Ta-Daa
HEY, THAT WAS A GREAT SPEECH...
!!
TMP
BUT I'M JUST A REGULAR HIGH SCHOOL STUDENT!
WITH A VERY PARTICULAR SET OF SKILLS!!

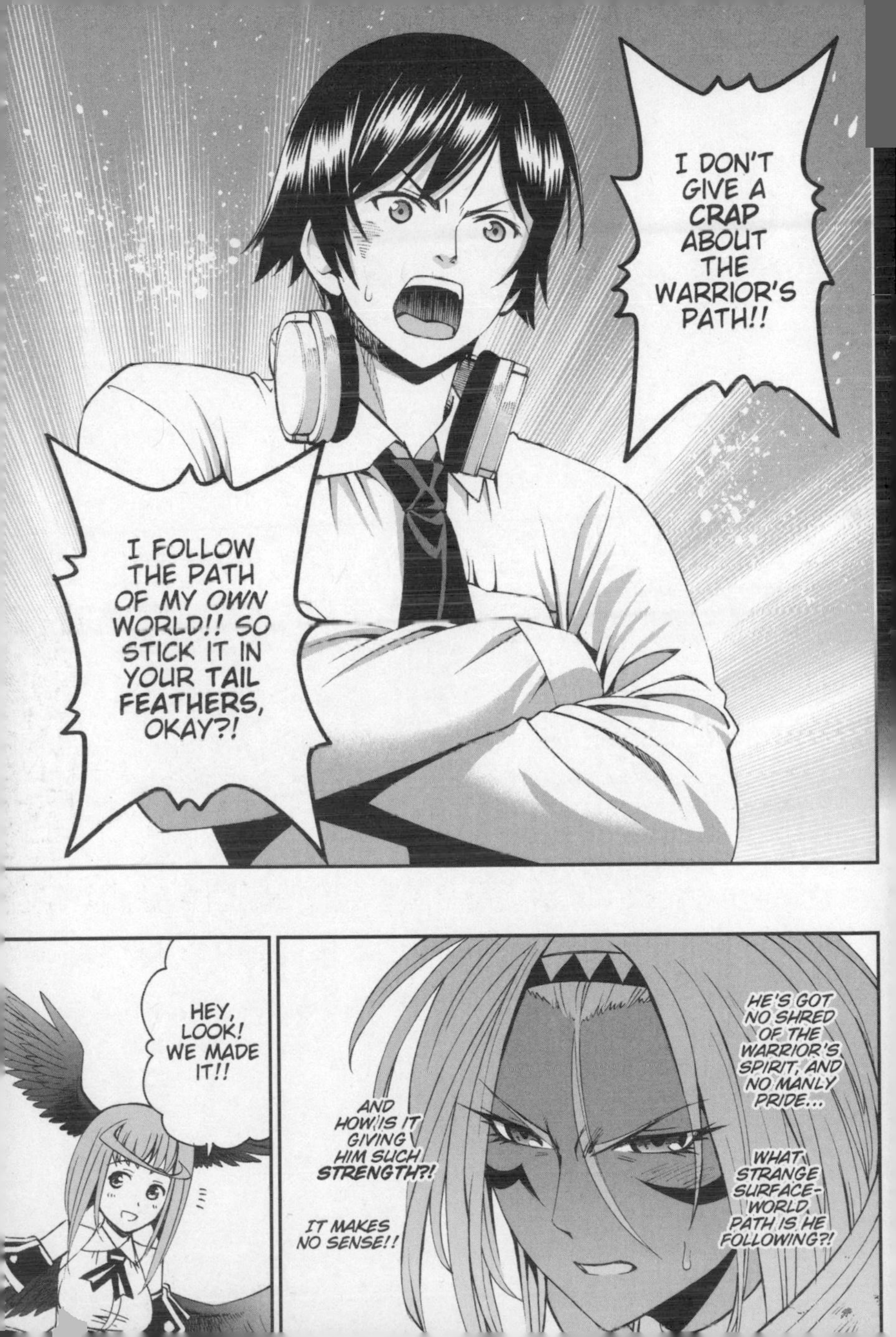
I DON'T GIVE A CRAP ABOUT THE WARRIOR'S PATH!!
I FOLLOW THE PATH OF MY OWN WORLD!! SO STICK IT IN YOUR TAIL FEATHERS, OKAY?!
HE'S GOT NO SHRED OF THE WARRIOR'S SPIRIT, AND NO MANLY PRIDE...
AND HOW IS IT GIVING HIM SUCH STRENGTH?!
WHAT STRANGE SURFACE-WORLD PATH IS HE FOLLOWING?!
IT MAKES NO SENSE!!
HEY, LOOK! WE MADE IT!!

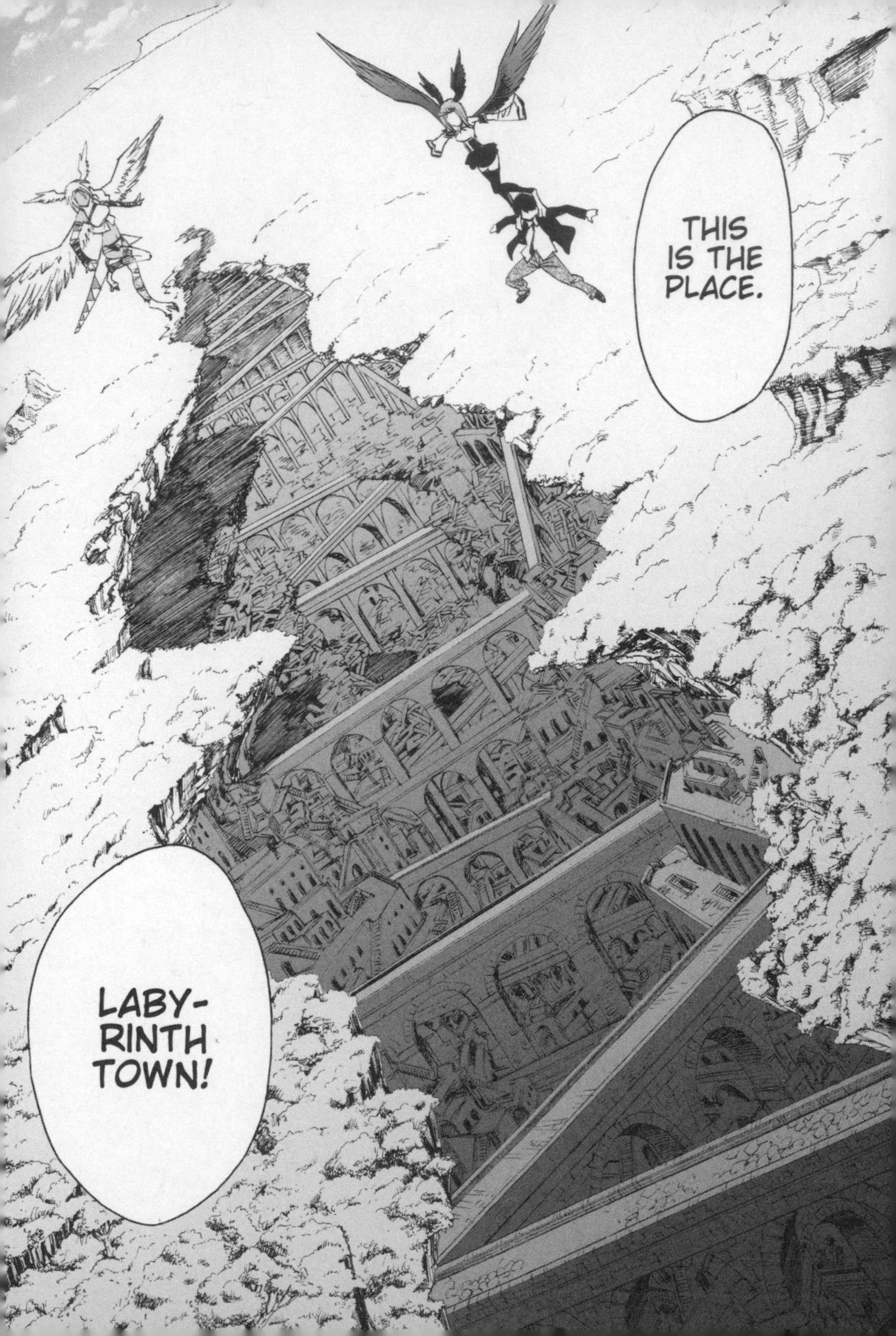
THIS IS THE PLACE.
LABY-RINTH TOWN!

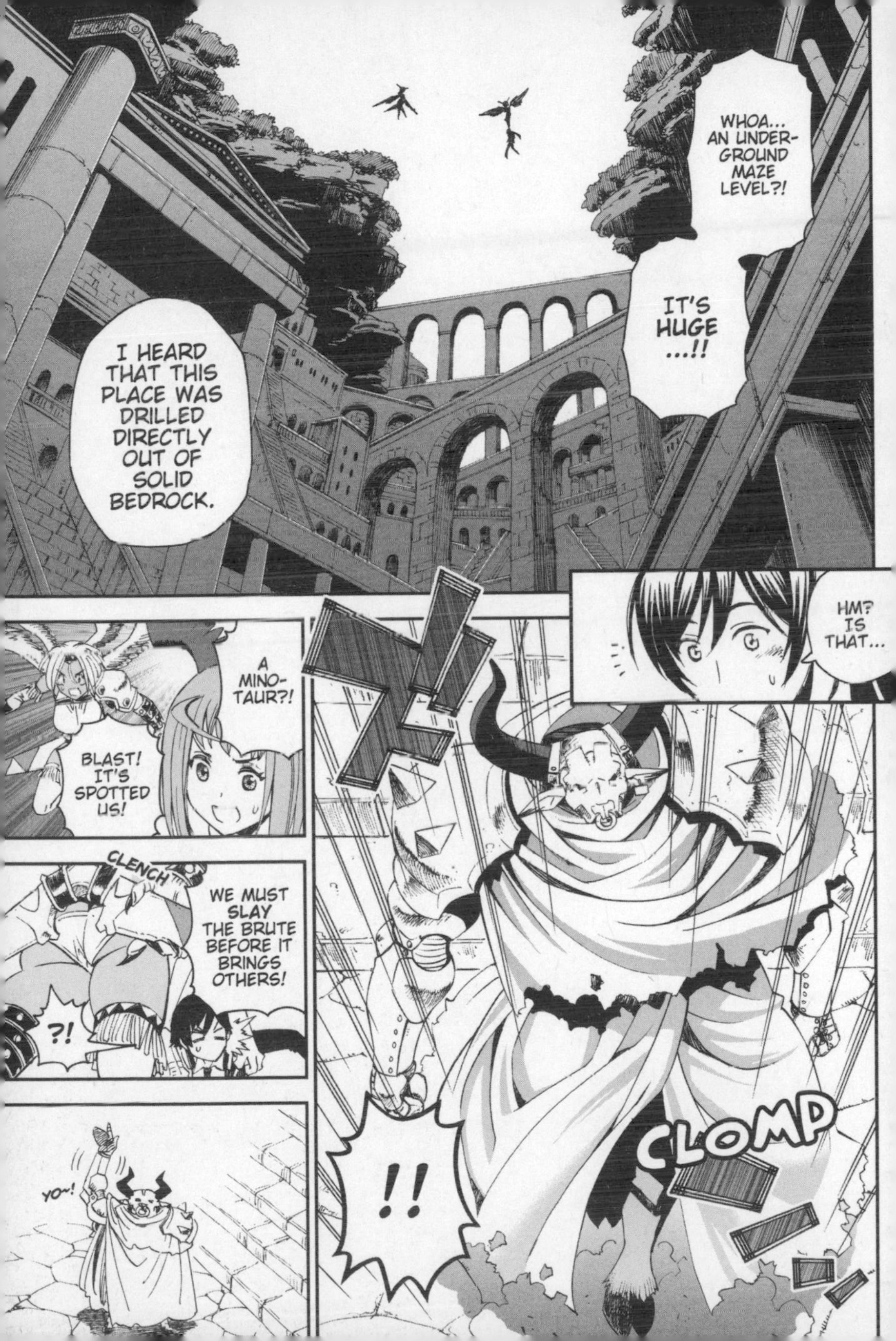
WHOA... AN UNDER-GROUND MAZE LEVEL?!
IT'S HUGE ...!!
I HEARD THAT THIS PLACE WAS DRILLED DIRECTLY OUT OF SOLID BEDROCK.
HM? IS THAT...
CLOMP
!!
A MINO-TAUR?!
BLAST! IT'S SPOTTED US!
CLENCH
WE MUST SLAY THE BRUTE BEFORE IT BRINGS OTHERS!
?!
YO~!

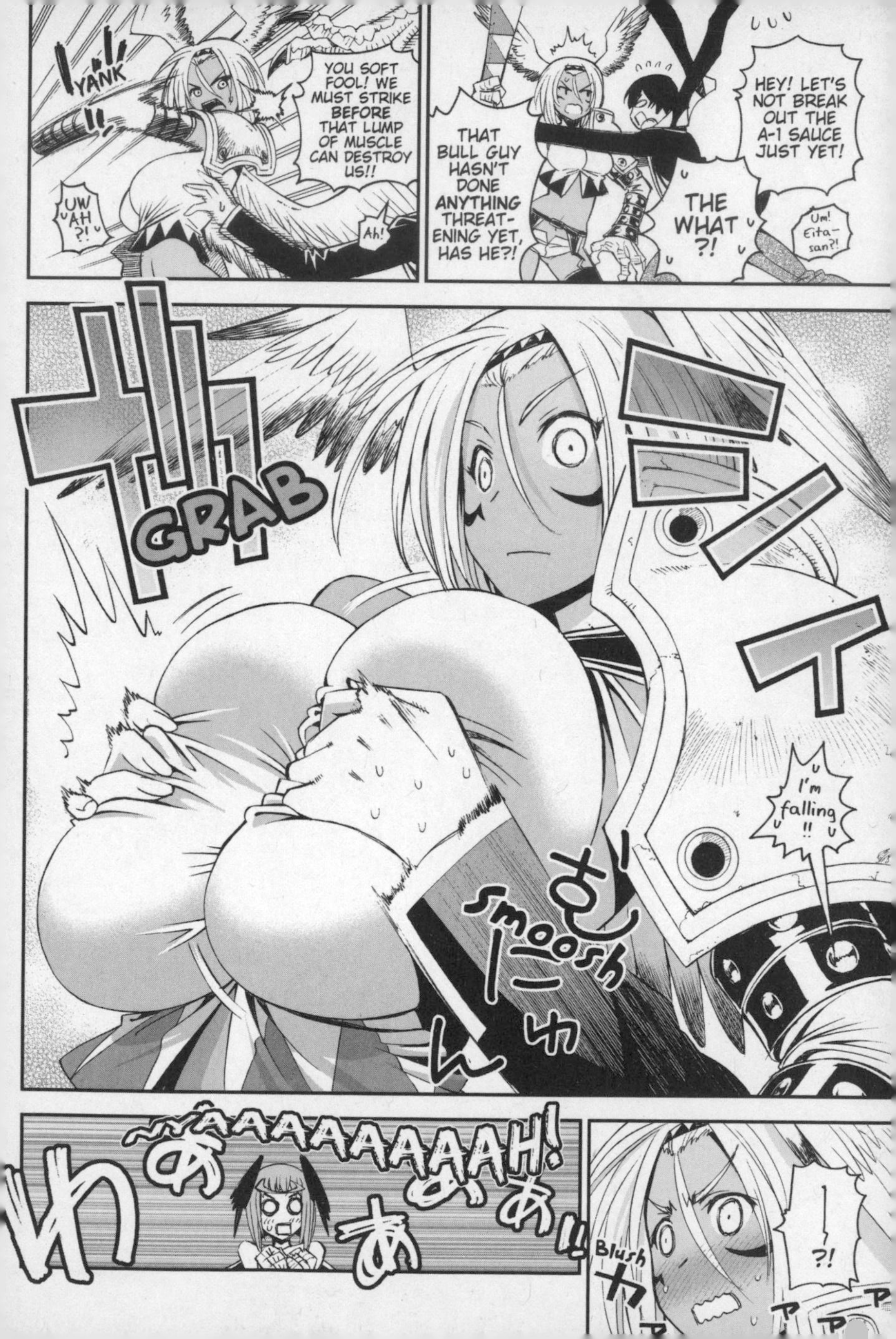

HEY! LET'S NOT BREAK OUT THE A-1 SAUCE JUST YET!
THE WHAT?!
Um! Eita-san?!
THAT BULL GUY HASN'T DONE ANYTHING THREAT-ENING YET, HAS HE?!
YANK
YOU SOFT FOOL! WE MUST STRIKE BEFORE THAT LUMP OF MUSCLE CAN DESTROY US!!
UWAH?!
Ah!
GRAB
I'm falling!!
smoosh
Blush
!?!
YAAAAAAAAAAAH!
わあああ!!

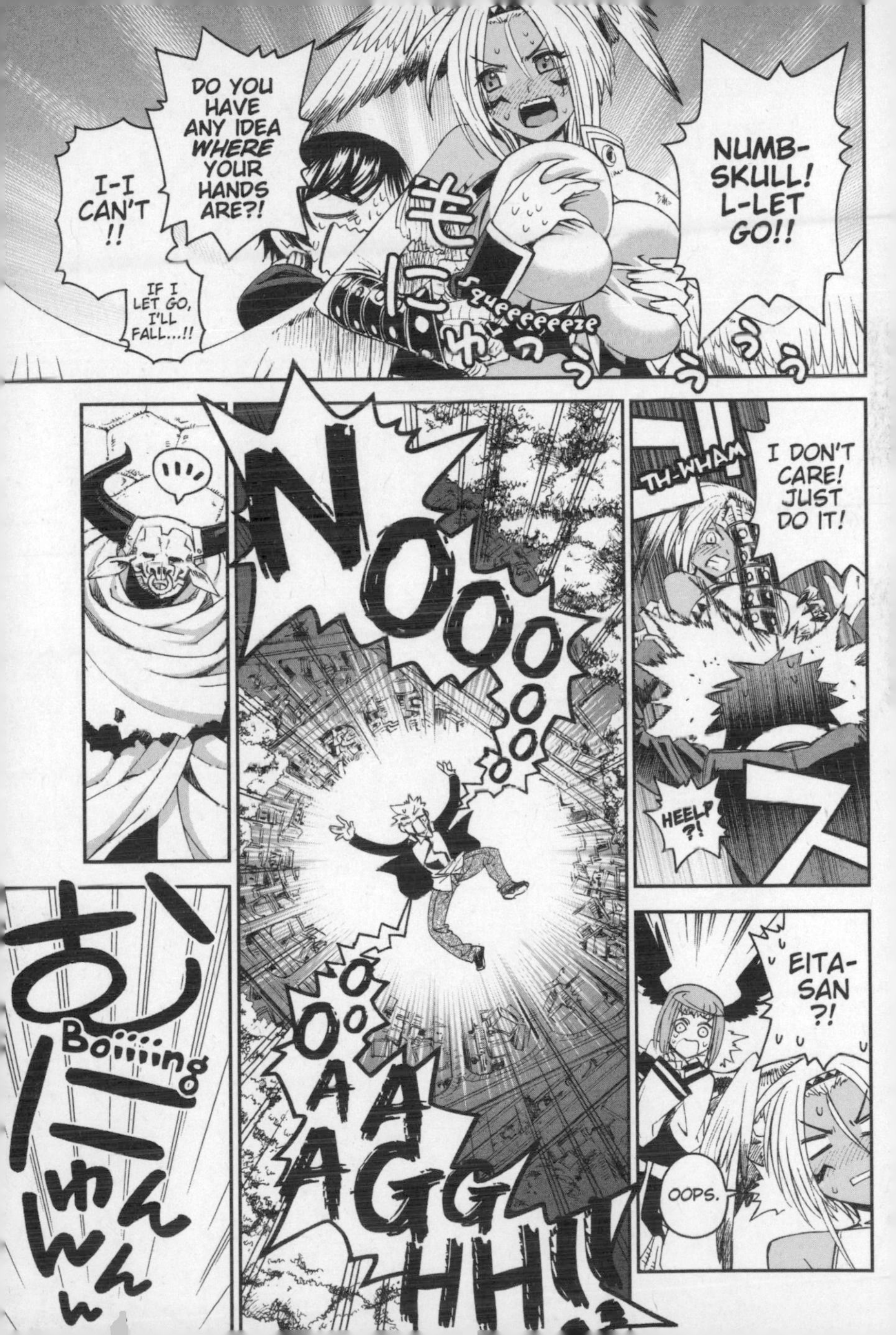
NUMB-SKULL! L-LET GO!!
DO YOU HAVE ANY IDEA WHERE YOUR HANDS ARE?!
I-I CAN'T !!
IF I LET GO, I'LL FALL...!!
squeeeeeeeze
TH-WHAM
I DON'T CARE! JUST DO IT!
HEELP ?!
EITA-SAN ?!
OOPS.
NOOOOOOOOOOOOAAAGGHH!!
Boiiiing

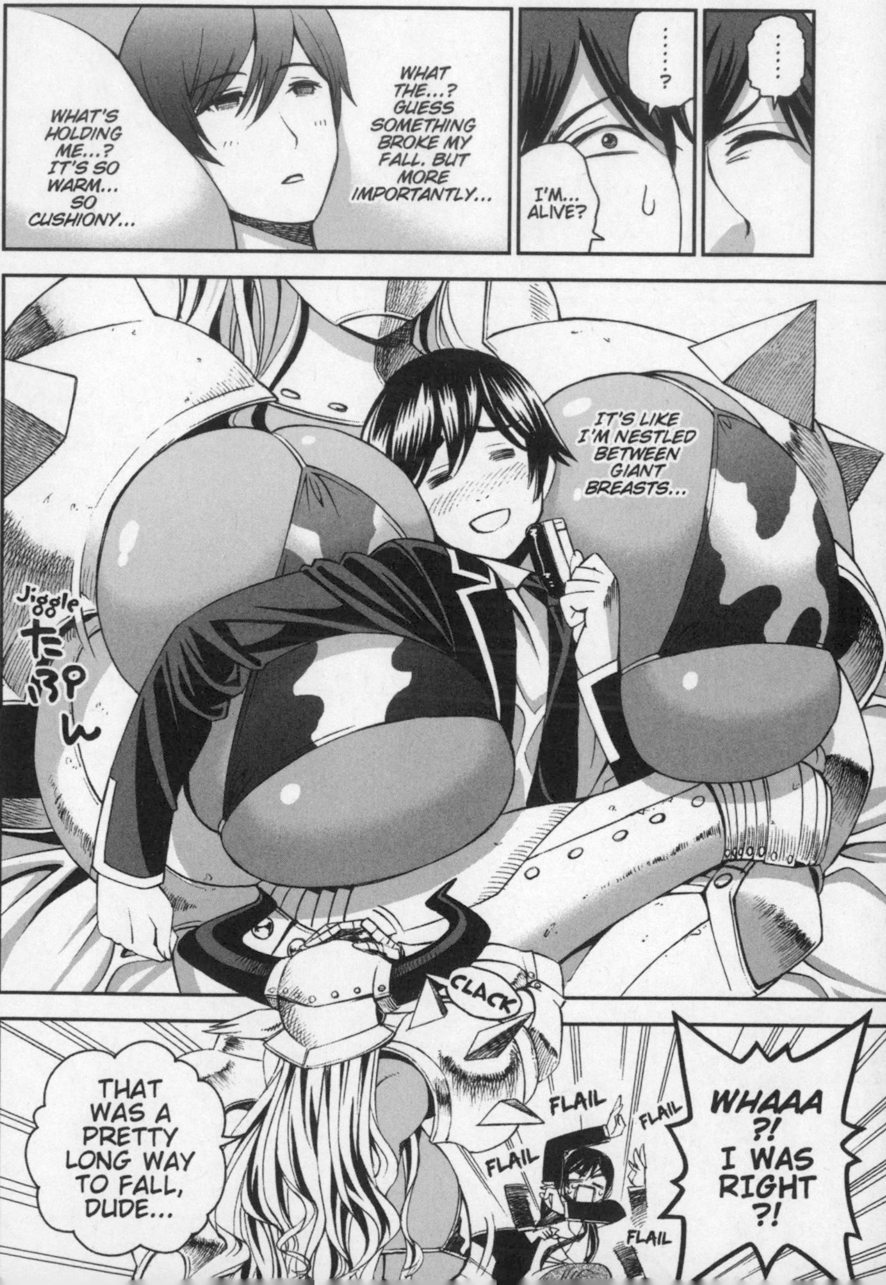
......
......?
I'M... ALIVE?
WHAT THE...? GUESS SOMETHING BROKE MY FALL. BUT MORE IMPORTANTLY...
WHAT'S HOLDING ME...? IT'S SO WARM... SO CUSHIONY...
IT'S LIKE I'M NESTLED BETWEEN GIANT BREASTS...
Jiggle
たぷん
CLACK
WHAAA?! I WAS RIGHT?!
FLAIL
FLAIL
FLAIL
FLAIL
THAT WAS A PRETTY LONG WAY TO FALL, DUDE...

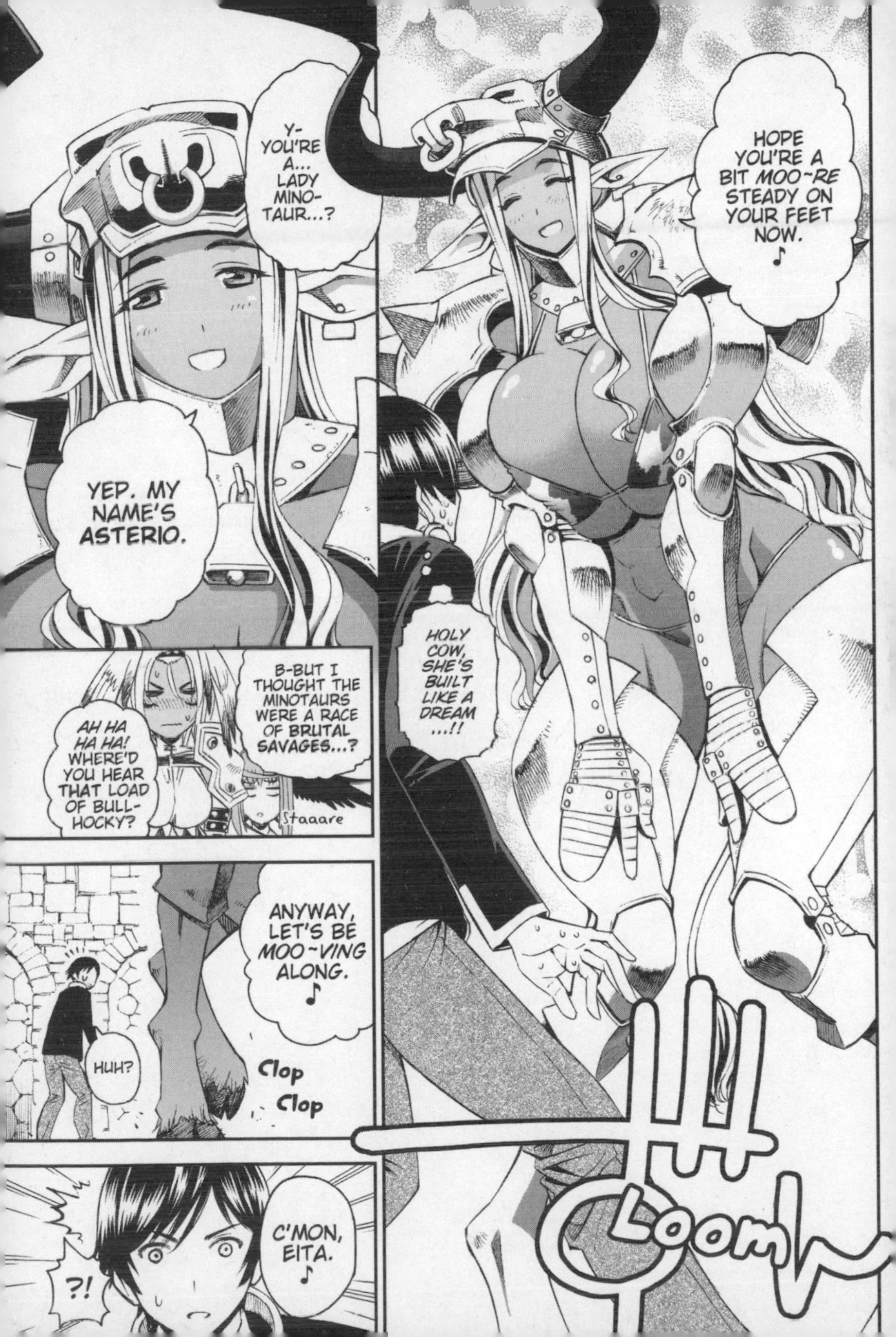
HOPE YOU'RE A BIT MOO~RE STEADY ON YOUR FEET NOW. ♪
HOLY COW, SHE'S BUILT LIKE A DREAM ...!!
Loom
Y-YOU'RE A... LADY MINO-TAUR...?
YEP. MY NAME'S ASTERIO.
B-BUT I THOUGHT THE MINOTAURS WERE A RACE OF BRUTAL SAVAGES...?
AH HA HA HA! WHERE'D YOU HEAR THAT LOAD OF BULL-HOCKY?
Staaare
ANYWAY, LET'S BE MOO~VING ALONG. ♪
HUH?
Clop
Clop
C'MON, EITA. ♪
?!

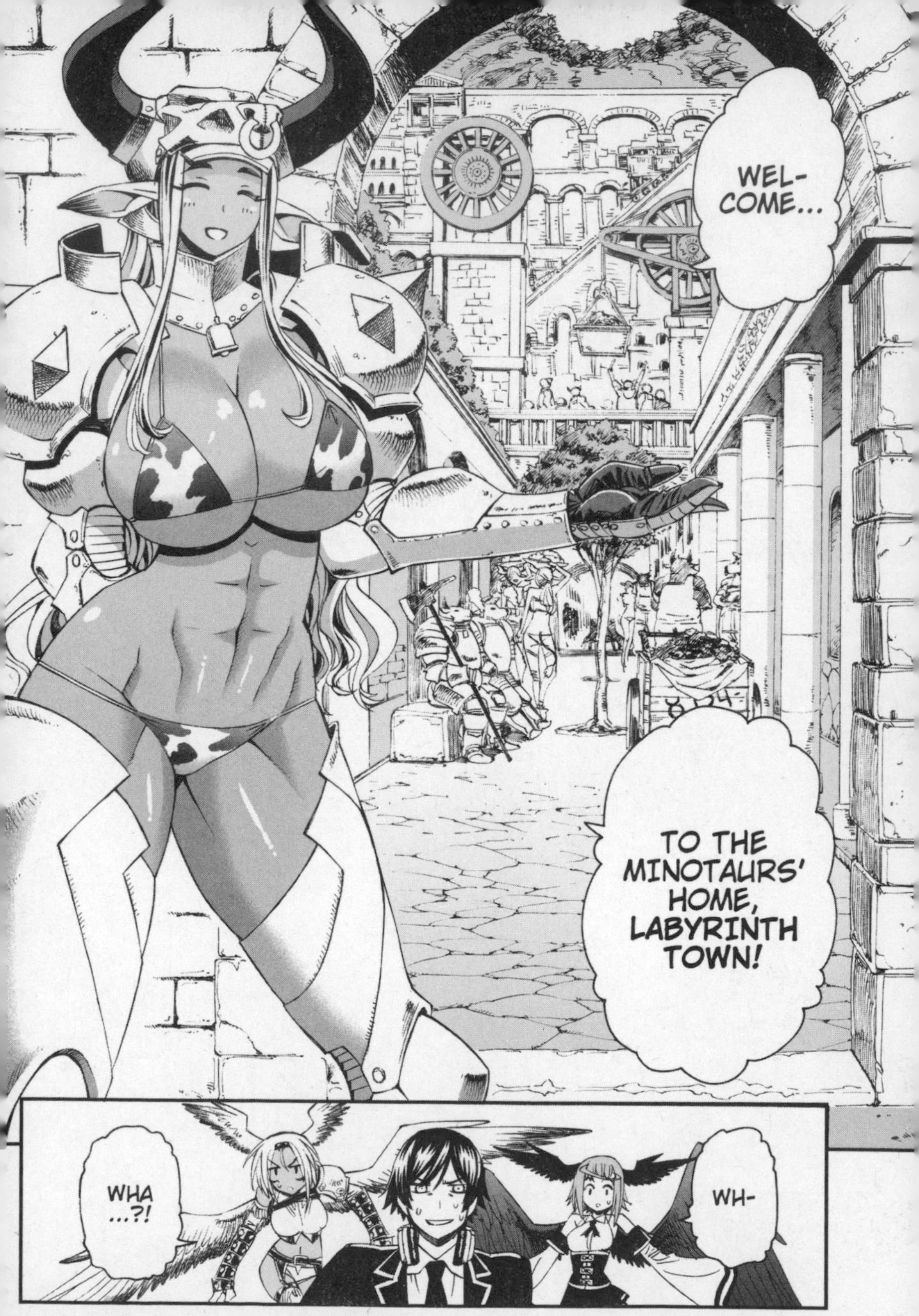
WEL-COME...
TO THE MINOTAURS' HOME, LABYRINTH TOWN!
WH-
WHA ...?!

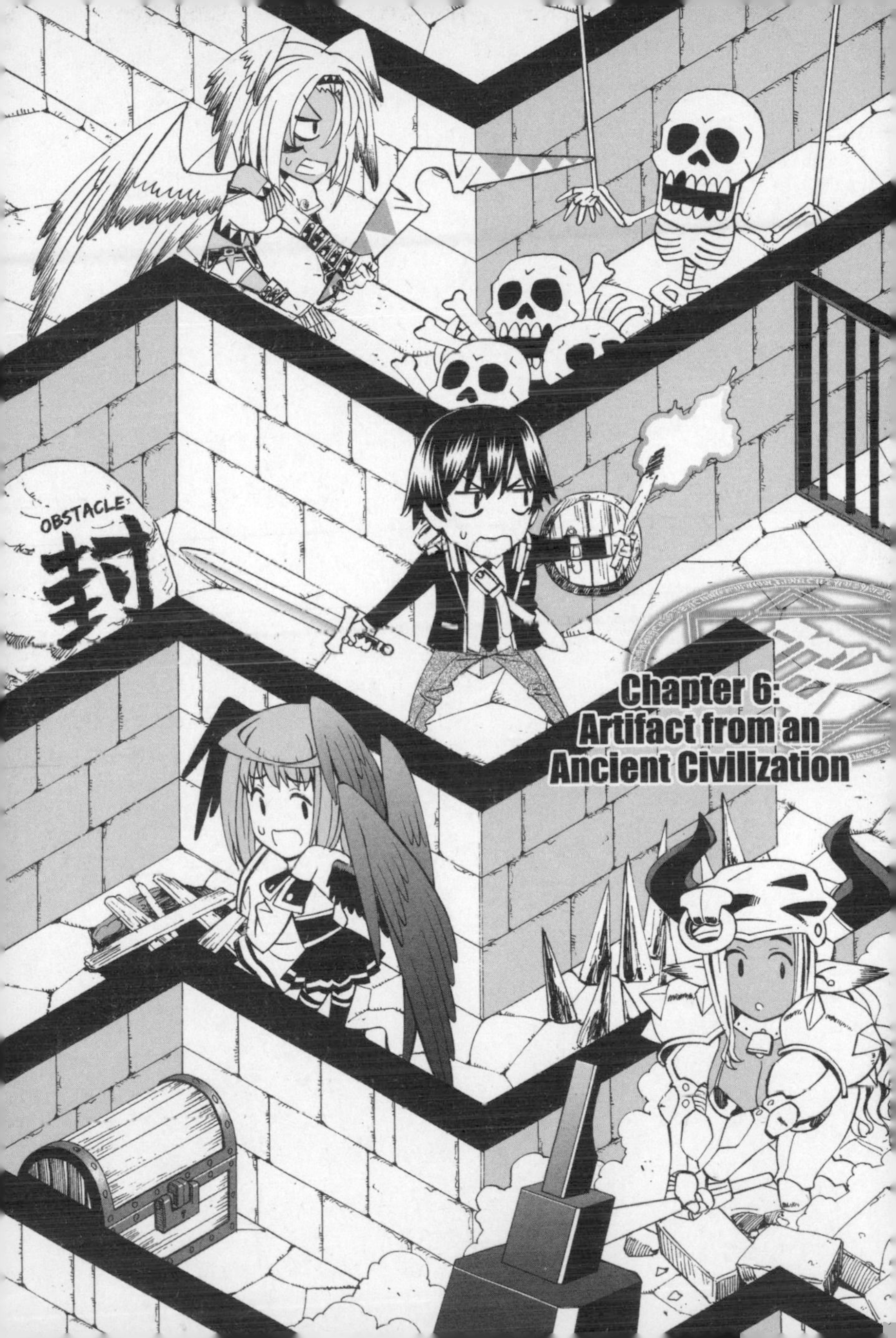
OBSTACLE:
封
Chapter 6:
Artifact from an
Ancient Civilization

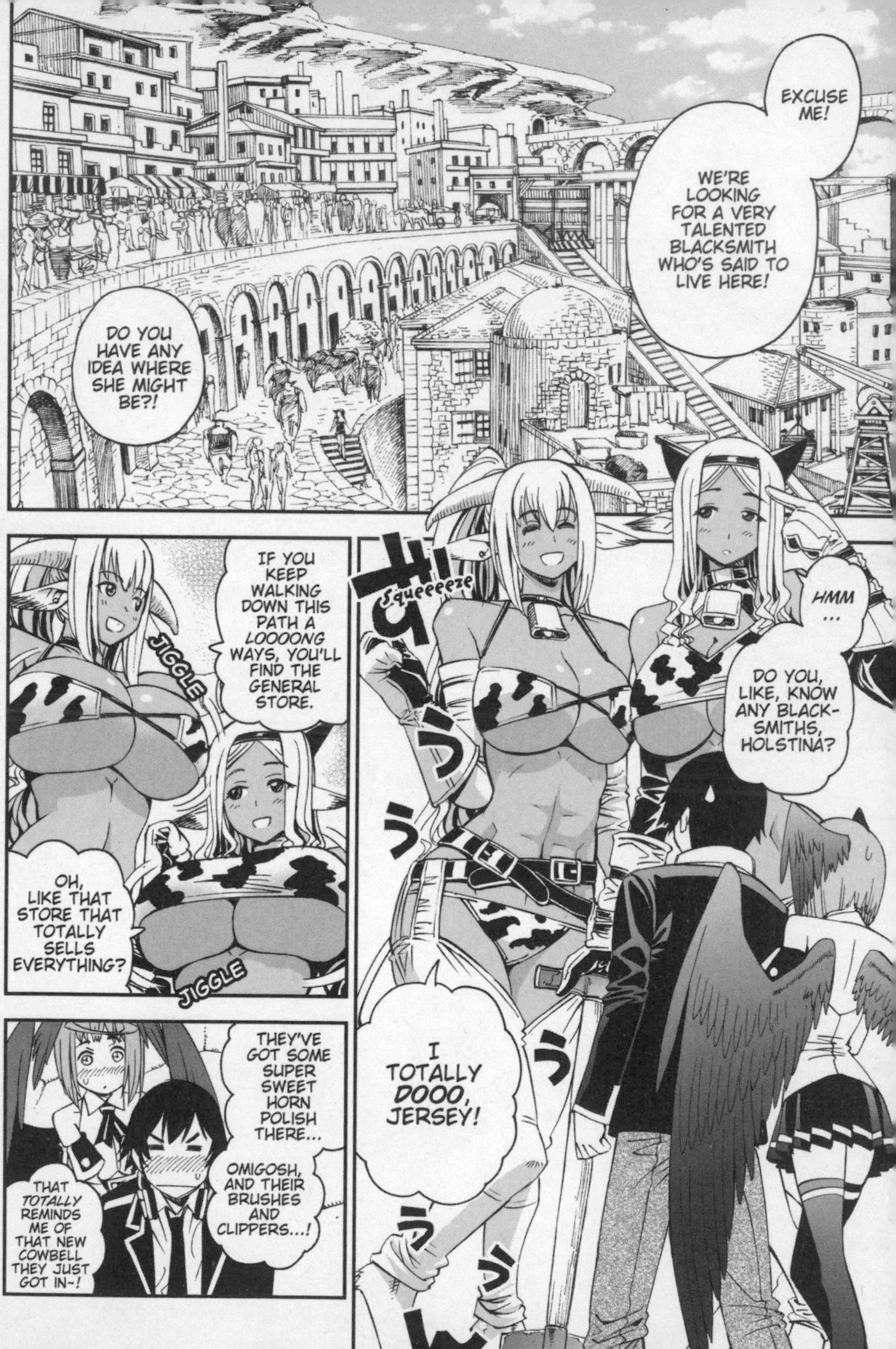
EXCUSE ME!
WE'RE LOOKING FOR A VERY TALENTED BLACKSMITH WHO'S SAID TO LIVE HERE!
DO YOU HAVE ANY IDEA WHERE SHE MIGHT BE?!
HMM...
DO YOU, LIKE, KNOW ANY BLACKSMITHS, HOLSTINA?
Squeeeeze
I TOTALLY *DOOO*, JERSEY!
IF YOU KEEP WALKING DOWN THIS PATH A *LOOOONG* WAYS, YOU'LL FIND THE GENERAL STORE.
JIGGLE
OH, LIKE THAT STORE THAT TOTALLY SELLS EVERYTHING?
JIGGLE
THEY'VE GOT SOME SUPER SWEET HORN POLISH THERE...
OMIGOSH, AND THEIR BRUSHES AND CLIPPERS...!
THAT *TOTALLY* REMINDS ME OF THAT NEW COWBELL THEY JUST GOT IN~!

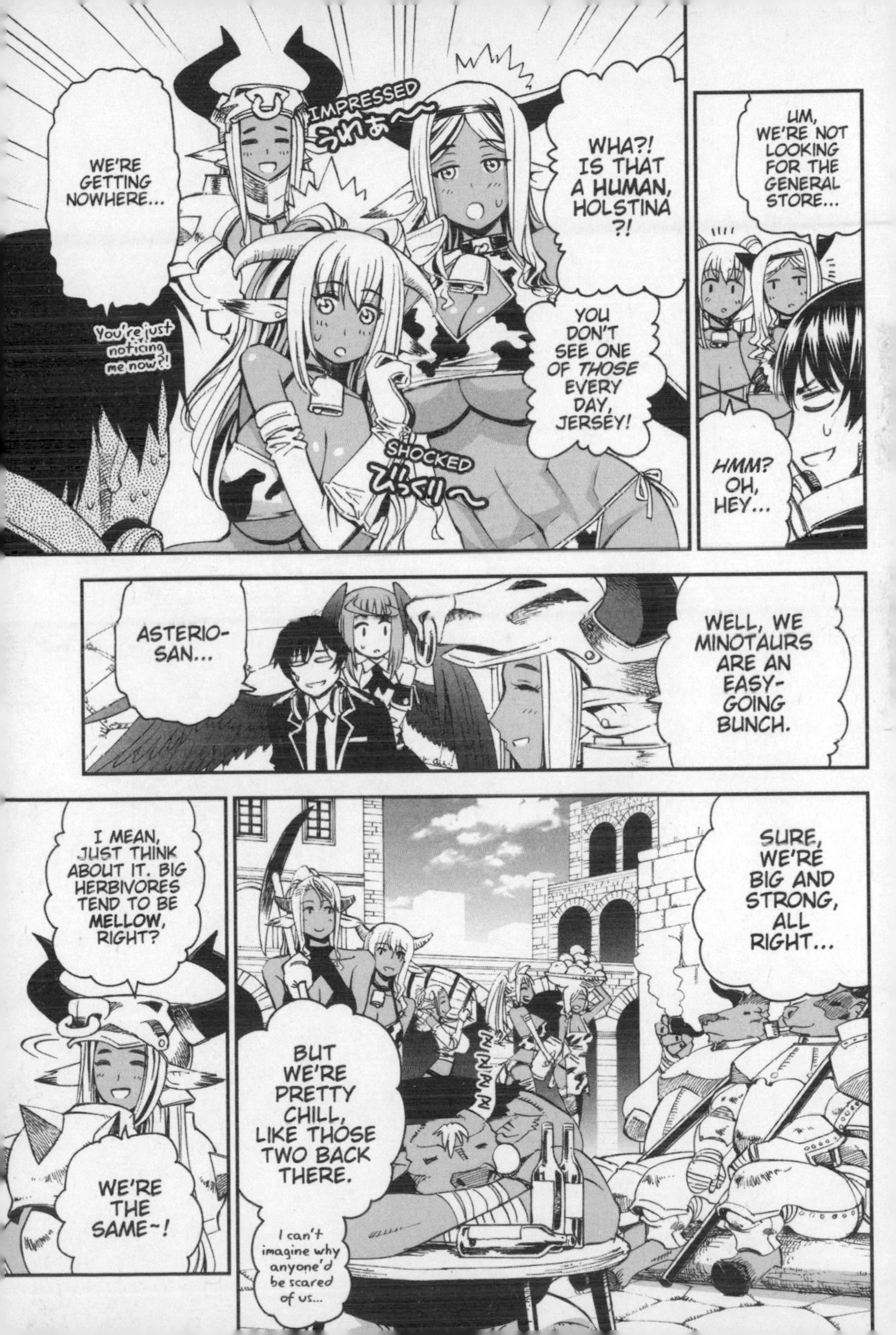
UM, WE'RE NOT LOOKING FOR THE GENERAL STORE...
HMM? OH, HEY...
WHA?! IS THAT A HUMAN, HOLSTINA?!
IMPRESSED
WE'RE GETTING NOWHERE...
YOU DON'T SEE ONE OF *THOSE* EVERY DAY, JERSEY!
SHOCKED
びっくり〜
You're just noticing me now?!
WELL, WE MINOTAURS ARE AN EASY-GOING BUNCH.
ASTERIO-SAN...
SURE, WE'RE BIG AND STRONG, ALL RIGHT...
BUT WE'RE PRETTY CHILL, LIKE THOSE TWO BACK THERE.
I can't imagine why anyone'd be scared of us...
I MEAN, JUST THINK ABOUT IT. BIG HERBIVORES TEND TO BE MELLOW, RIGHT?
WE'RE THE SAME~!

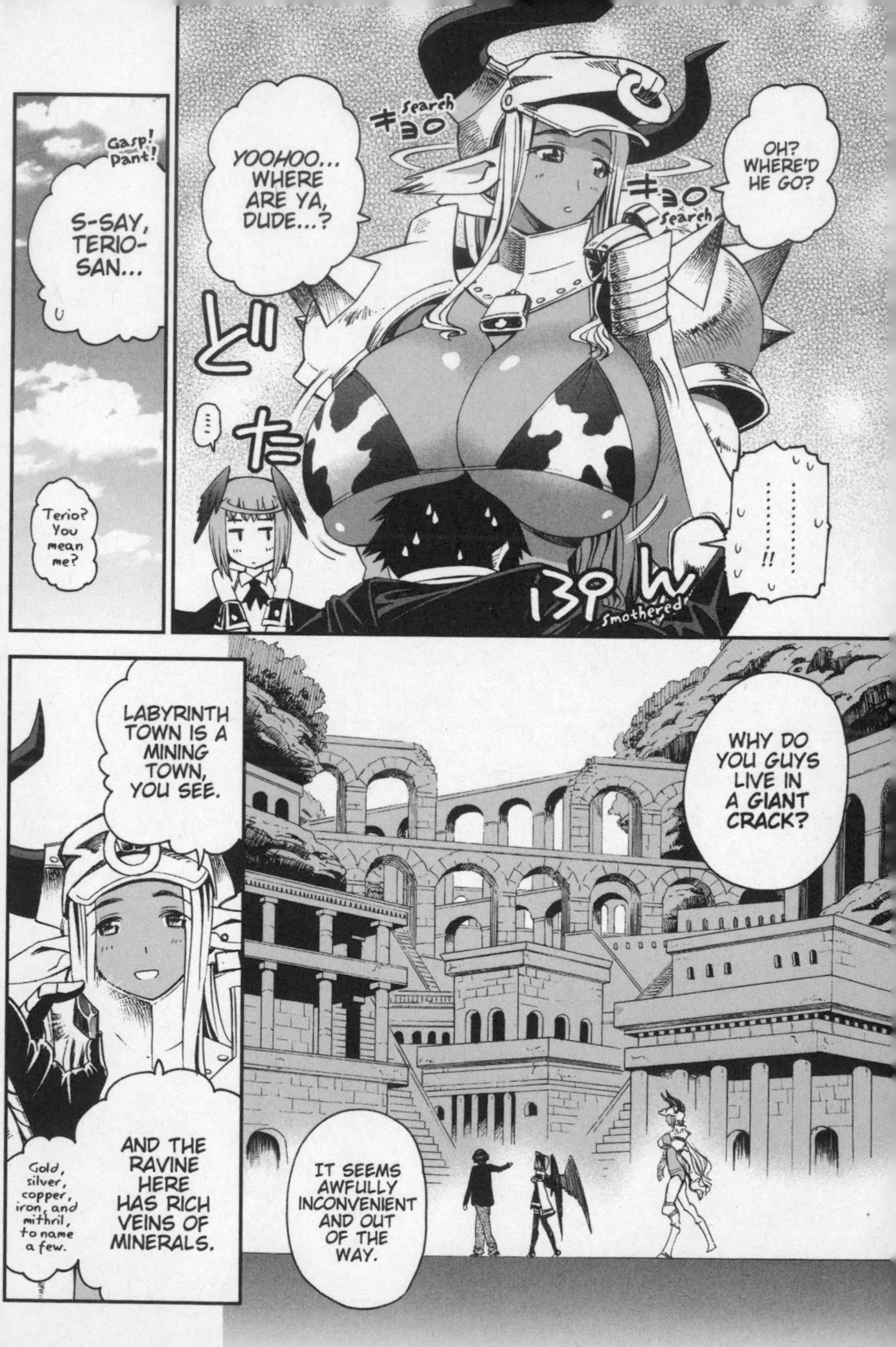
OH? WHERE'D HE GO?
キョロ
Search
キョロ
Search
YOOHOO... WHERE ARE YA, DUDE...?
どた
......
......!!
Smothered
Gasp! Pant!
S-SAY, TERIO-SAN...
Terio? You mean me?
WHY DO YOU GUYS LIVE IN A GIANT CRACK?
IT SEEMS AWFULLY INCONVENIENT AND OUT OF THE WAY.
LABYRINTH TOWN IS A MINING TOWN, YOU SEE.
AND THE RAVINE HERE HAS RICH VEINS OF MINERALS.
Gold, silver, copper, iron, and mithril, to name a few.

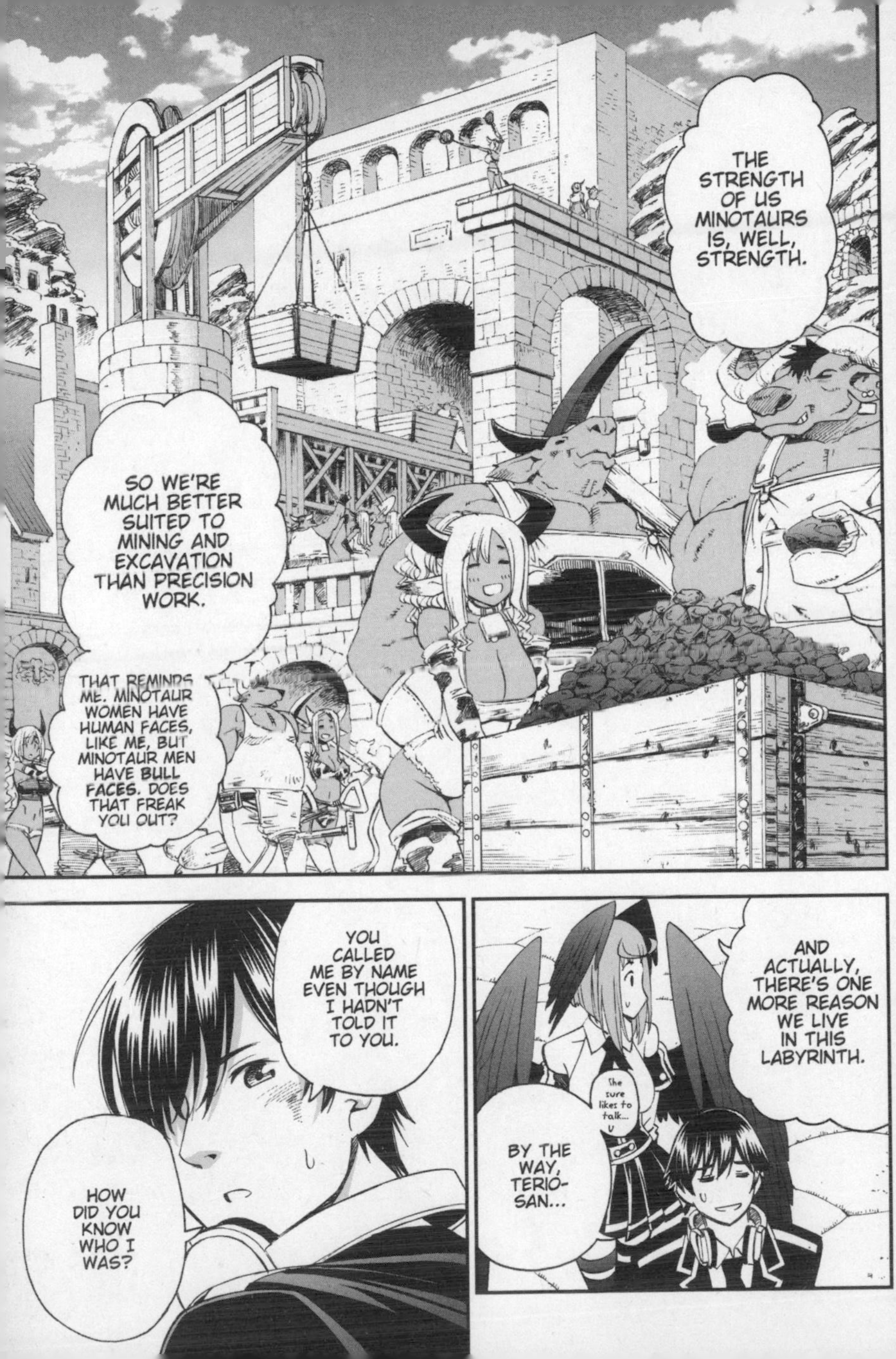
THE STRENGTH OF US MINOTAURS IS, WELL, STRENGTH.
SO WE'RE MUCH BETTER SUITED TO MINING AND EXCAVATION THAN PRECISION WORK.
THAT REMINDS ME. MINOTAUR WOMEN HAVE HUMAN FACES, LIKE ME, BUT MINOTAUR MEN HAVE BULL FACES. DOES THAT FREAK YOU OUT?
AND ACTUALLY, THERE'S ONE MORE REASON WE LIVE IN THIS LABYRINTH.
She sure likes to talk...
BY THE WAY, TERIO-SAN...
YOU CALLED ME BY NAME EVEN THOUGH I HADN'T TOLD IT TO YOU.
HOW DID YOU KNOW WHO I WAS?

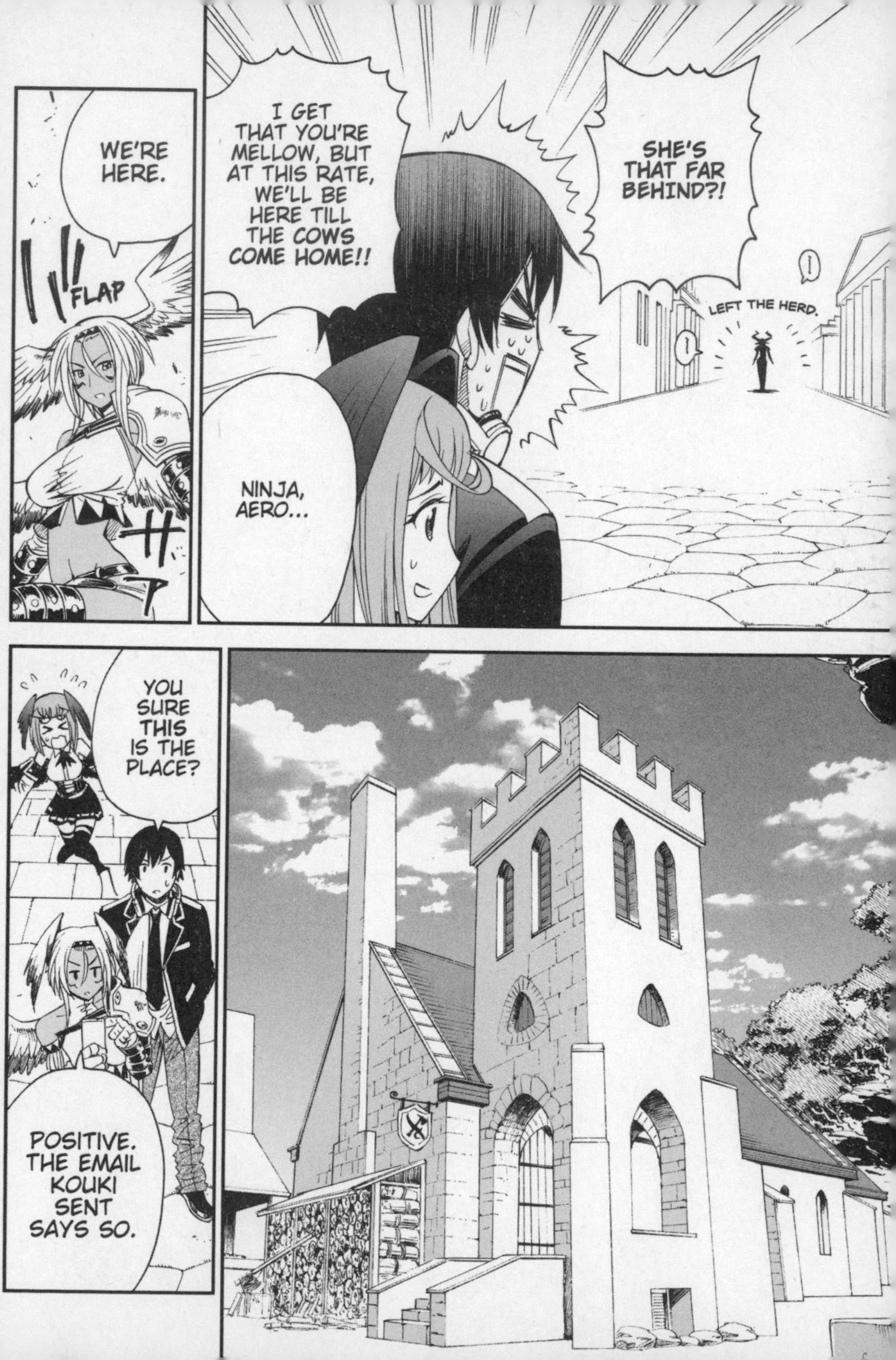
SHE'S THAT FAR BEHIND?!
LEFT THE HERD.
I GET THAT YOU'RE MELLOW, BUT AT THIS RATE, WE'LL BE HERE TILL THE COWS COME HOME!!
NINJA, AERO...
WE'RE HERE.
FLAP
YOU SURE THIS IS THE PLACE?
POSITIVE. THE EMAIL KOUKI SENT SAYS SO.

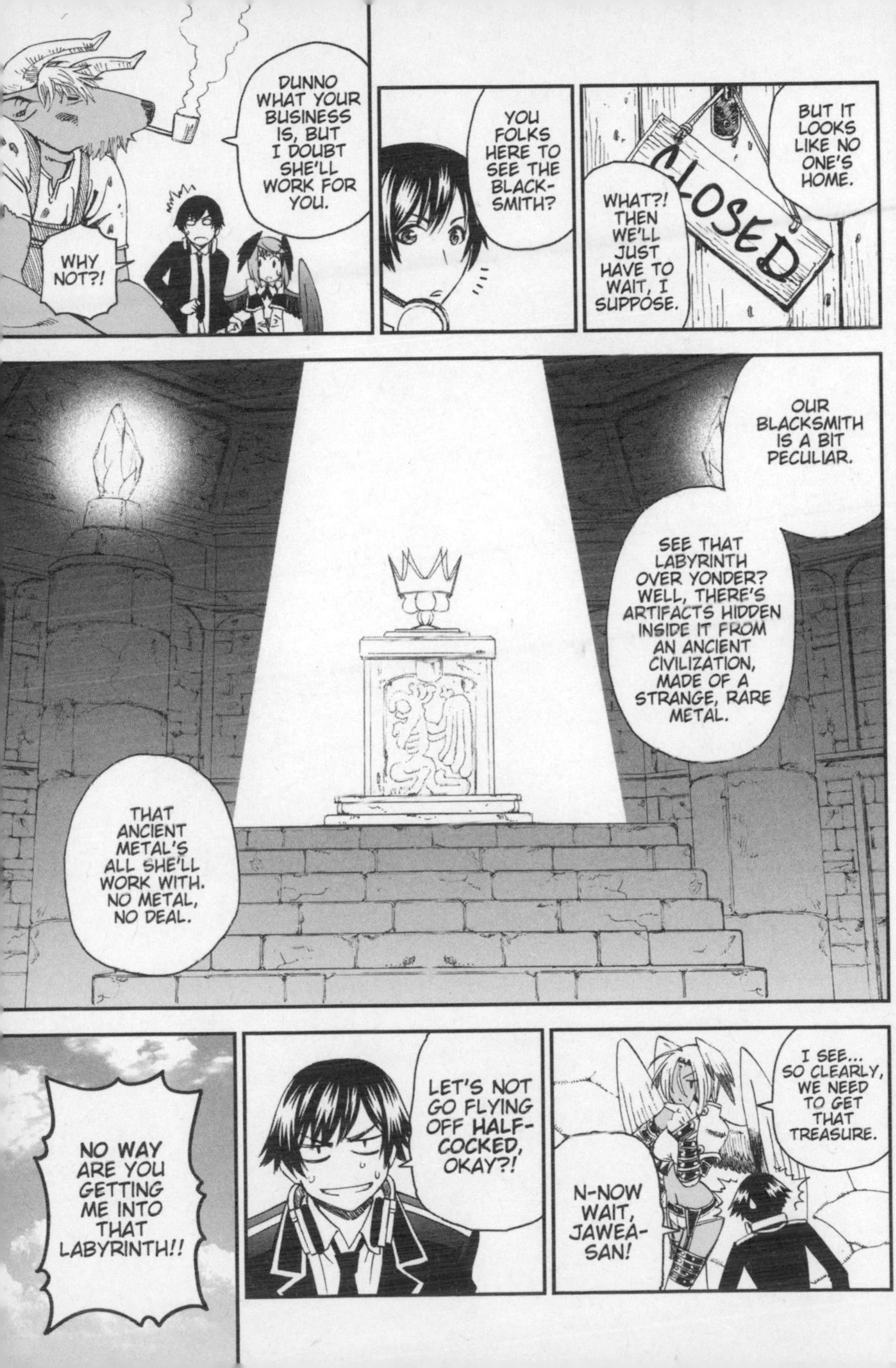
BUT IT LOOKS LIKE NO ONE'S HOME.
CLOSED
WHAT?! THEN WE'LL JUST HAVE TO WAIT, I SUPPOSE.
YOU FOLKS HERE TO SEE THE BLACK-SMITH?
DUNNO WHAT YOUR BUSINESS IS, BUT I DOUBT SHE'LL WORK FOR YOU.
WHY NOT?!
OUR BLACKSMITH IS A BIT PECULIAR.
SEE THAT LABYRINTH OVER YONDER? WELL, THERE'S ARTIFACTS HIDDEN INSIDE IT FROM AN ANCIENT CIVILIZATION, MADE OF A STRANGE, RARE METAL.
THAT ANCIENT METAL'S ALL SHE'LL WORK WITH. NO METAL, NO DEAL.
I SEE... SO CLEARLY, WE NEED TO GET THAT TREASURE.
N-NOW WAIT, JAWEA-SAN!
LET'S NOT GO FLYING OFF HALF-COCKED, OKAY?!
NO WAY ARE YOU GETTING ME INTO THAT LABYRINTH!!

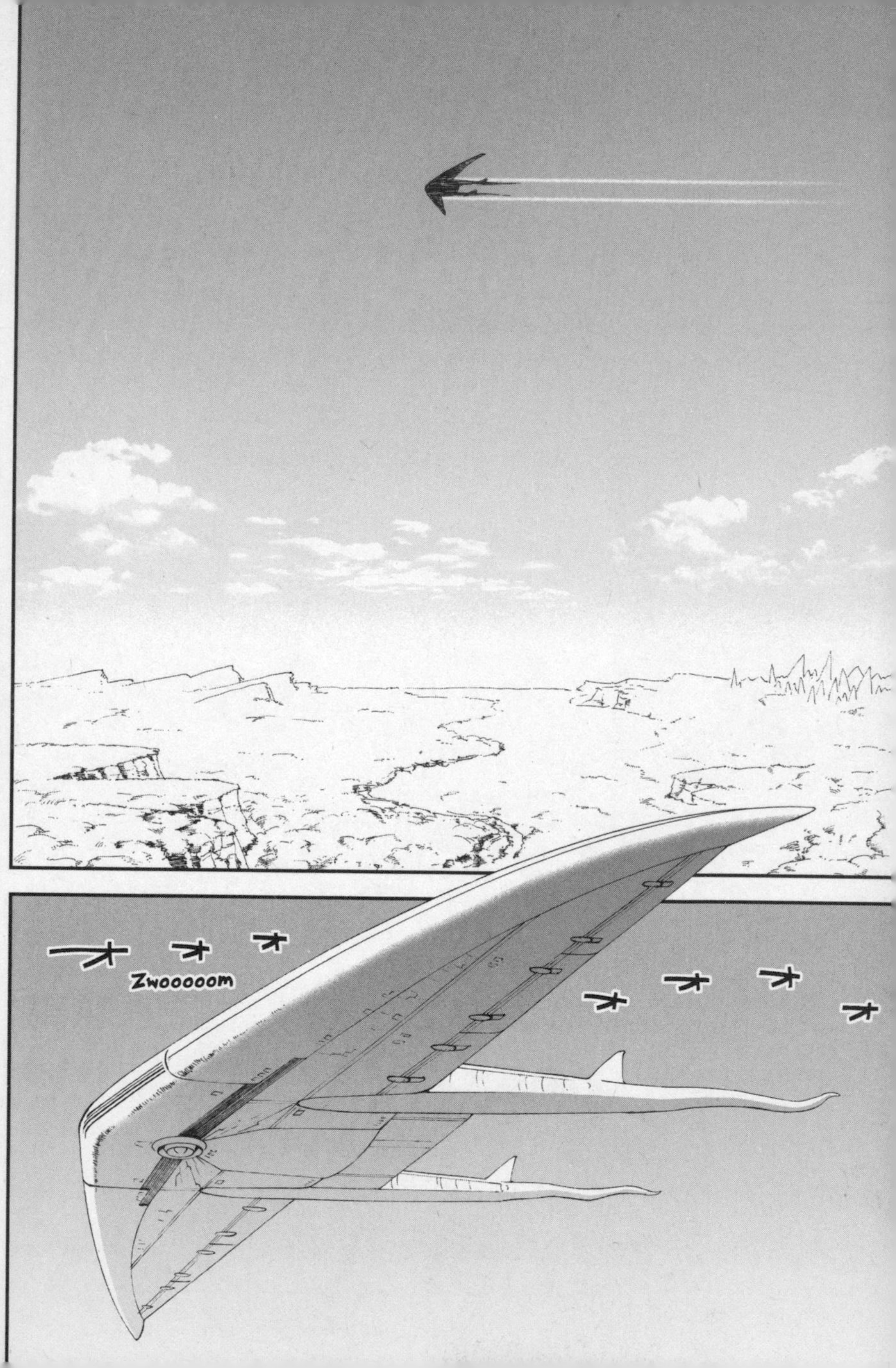

ーオオオ
Zwooooom
オオオオ

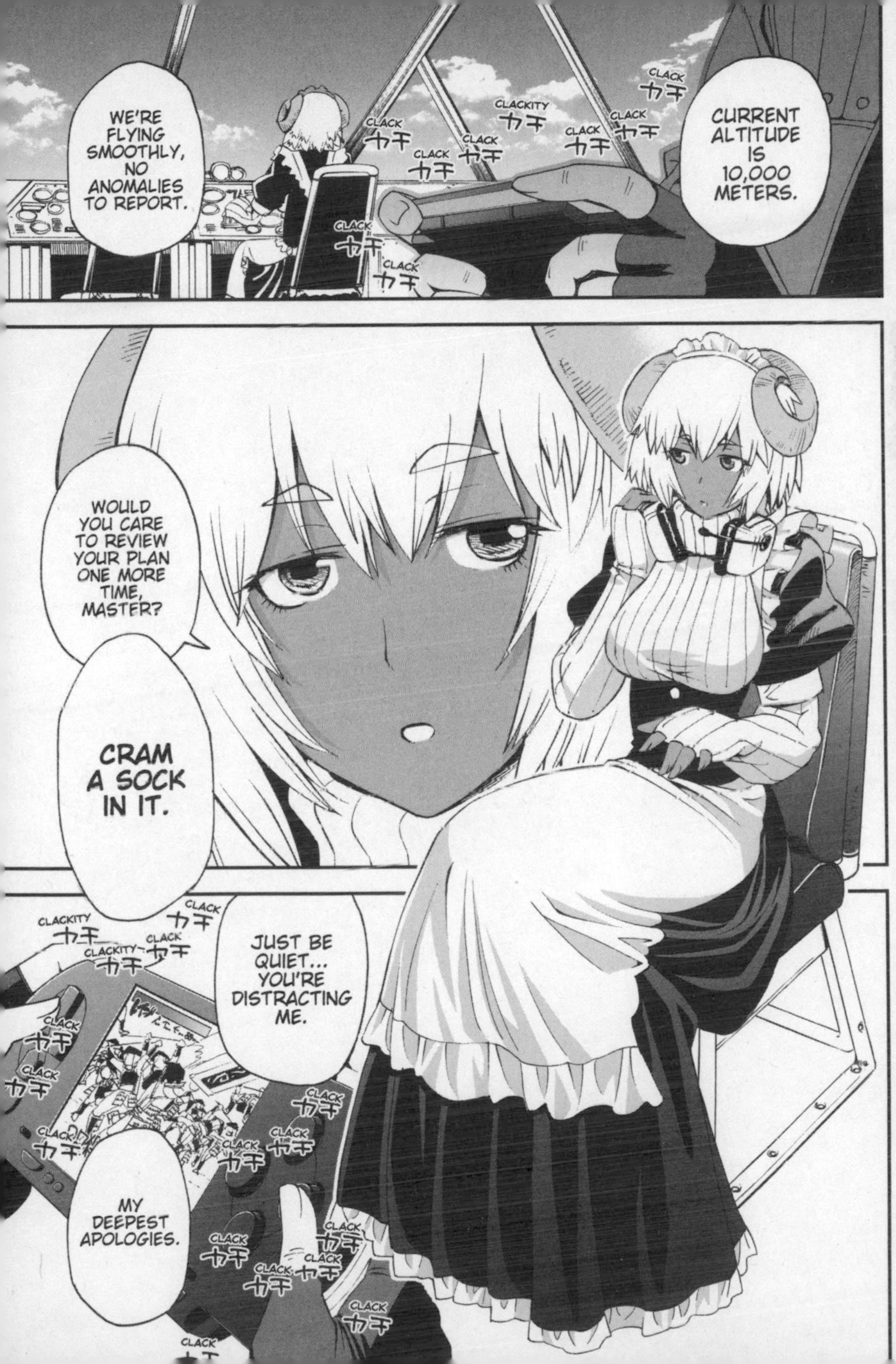
CLACK カチ
CURRENT ALTITUDE IS 10,000 METERS.
CLACK カチ
CLACKITY カチ
CLACK カチ
CLACK カチ
CLACK カチ
CLACK カチ
WE'RE FLYING SMOOTHLY, NO ANOMALIES TO REPORT.
CLACK カチ
CLACK カチ
WOULD YOU CARE TO REVIEW YOUR PLAN ONE MORE TIME, MASTER?
CRAM A SOCK IN IT.
JUST BE QUIET... YOU'RE DISTRACTING ME.
CLACK カチ
CLACK カチ
CLACKITY カチ
CLACKITY カチ
CLACK カチ
CLACK カチ
CLACK カチ
CLACK カチ
CLACK カチ
CLACK カチ
MY DEEPEST APOLOGIES.
CLACK カチ
CLACK カチ
CLACK カチ
CLACK カチ
CLACK カチ
CLACK

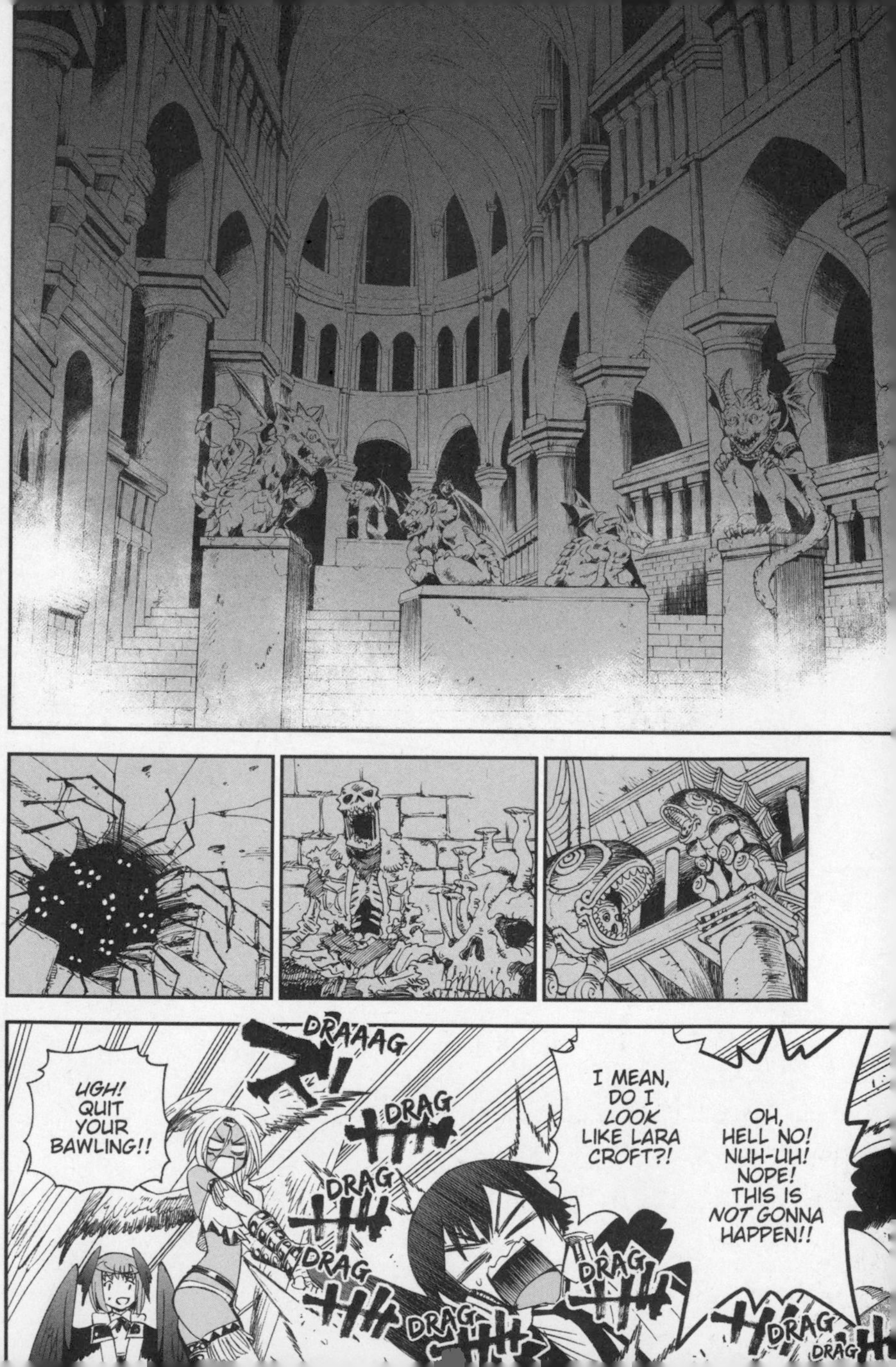
OH, HELL NO! NUH-UH! NOPE! THIS IS NOT GONNA HAPPEN!!
I MEAN, DO I LOOK LIKE LARA CROFT?!
DRAG DRAG
DRAG
DRAG
UGH! QUIT YOUR BAWLING!!
DRAAAG
DRAG
DRAG
DRAG
DRAG

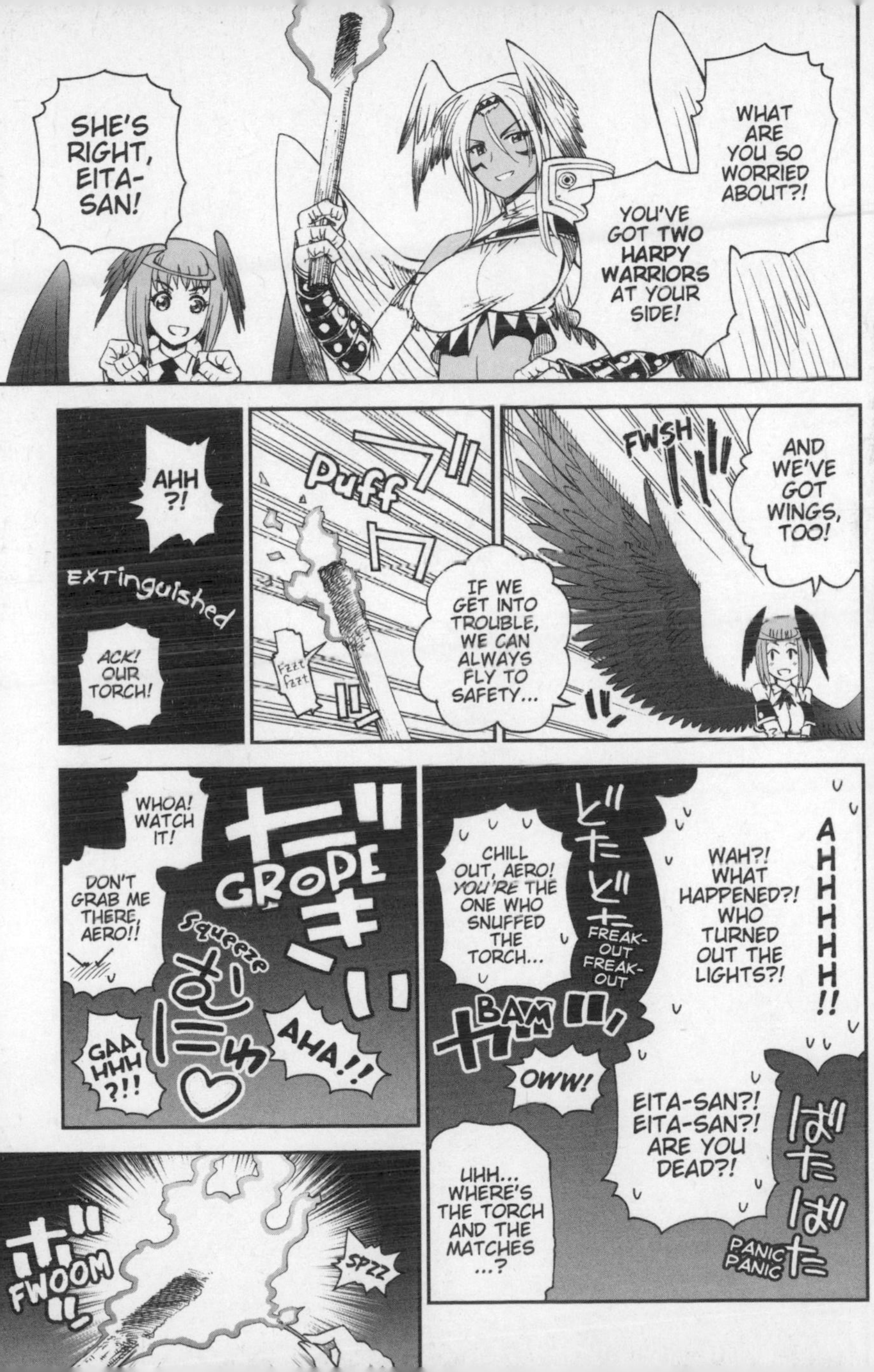
WHAT ARE YOU SO WORRIED ABOUT?!
YOU'VE GOT TWO HARPY WARRIORS AT YOUR SIDE!
SHE'S RIGHT, EITA-SAN!
FWSH
AND WE'VE GOT WINGS, TOO!
Puff
IF WE GET INTO TROUBLE, WE CAN ALWAYS FLY TO SAFETY...
Fzzt fzzt
AHH ?!
EXTinguished
ACK! OUR TORCH!
AHHHHHH!!
WAH?! WHAT HAPPENED?! WHO TURNED OUT THE LIGHTS?!
どたどた
FREAK-OUT FREAK-OUT
CHILL OUT, AERO! *YOU'RE* THE ONE WHO SNUFFED THE TORCH...
BAM
OWW!
ばたばた
PANIC PANIC
EITA-SAN?! EITA-SAN?! ARE YOU DEAD?!
UHH... WHERE'S THE TORCH AND THE MATCHES ...?
GROPE
WHOA! WATCH IT!
DON'T GRAB ME THERE, AERO!!
squeeze
AHA!!
GAAHHH?!!
SPZZ
FWOOM

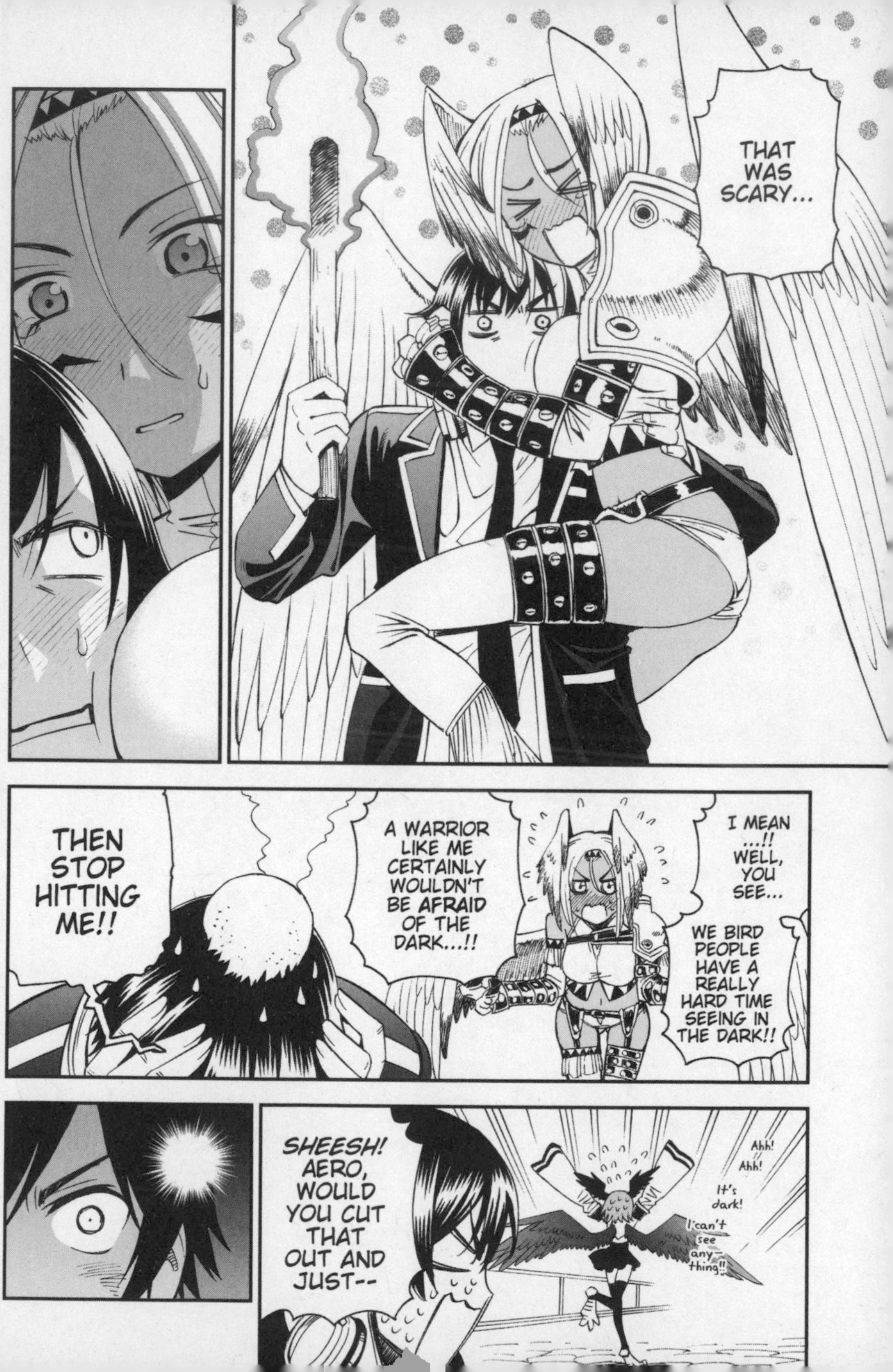
THAT WAS SCARY...
I MEAN ...!! WELL, YOU SEE...
WE BIRD PEOPLE HAVE A REALLY HARD TIME SEEING IN THE DARK!!
A WARRIOR LIKE ME CERTAINLY WOULDN'T BE AFRAID OF THE DARK...!!
THEN STOP HITTING ME!!
Ahh! Ahh!
It's dark!
I can't see any-thing!!
SHEESH! AERO, WOULD YOU CUT THAT OUT AND JUST--

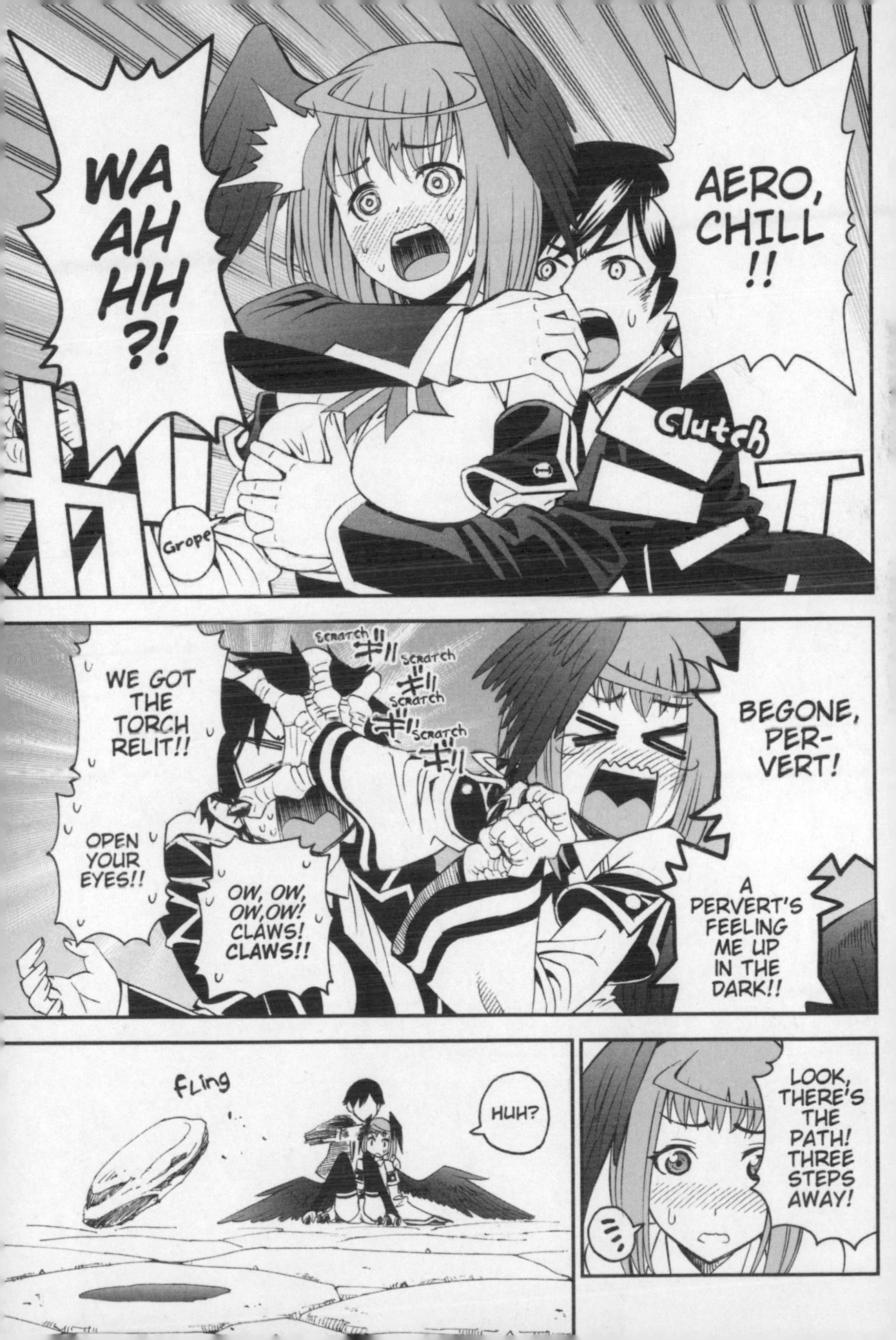
AERO, CHILL !!
WA AH HH ?!
Clutch
Grope
BEGONE, PER-VERT!
A PERVERT'S FEELING ME UP IN THE DARK!!
SCRATCH ギ!!
SCRATCH ギ!!
SCRATCH ギ!!
SCRATCH ギ!!
WE GOT THE TORCH RELIT!!
OPEN YOUR EYES!!
OW, OW, OW,OW! CLAWS! CLAWS!!
LOOK, THERE'S THE PATH! THREE STEPS AWAY!
HUH?
fLing

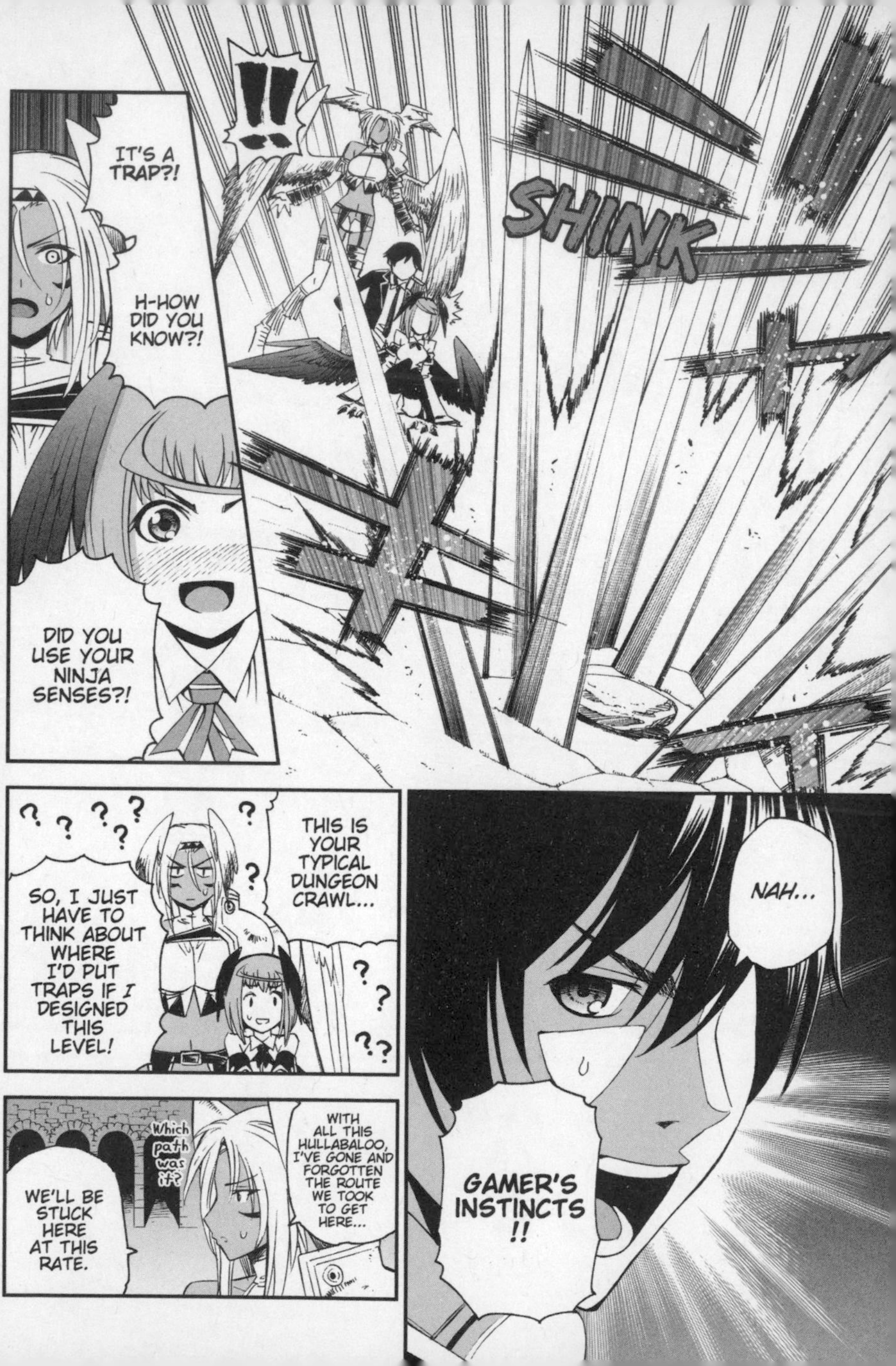
!!
SHINK
IT'S A TRAP?!
H-HOW DID YOU KNOW?!
DID YOU USE YOUR NINJA SENSES?!
NAH...
GAMER'S INSTINCTS !!
THIS IS YOUR TYPICAL DUNGEON CRAWL...
SO, I JUST HAVE TO THINK ABOUT WHERE I'D PUT TRAPS IF I DESIGNED THIS LEVEL!
WITH ALL THIS HULLABALOO, I'VE GONE AND FORGOTTEN THE ROUTE WE TOOK TO GET HERE...
Which path was it?
WE'LL BE STUCK HERE AT THIS RATE.

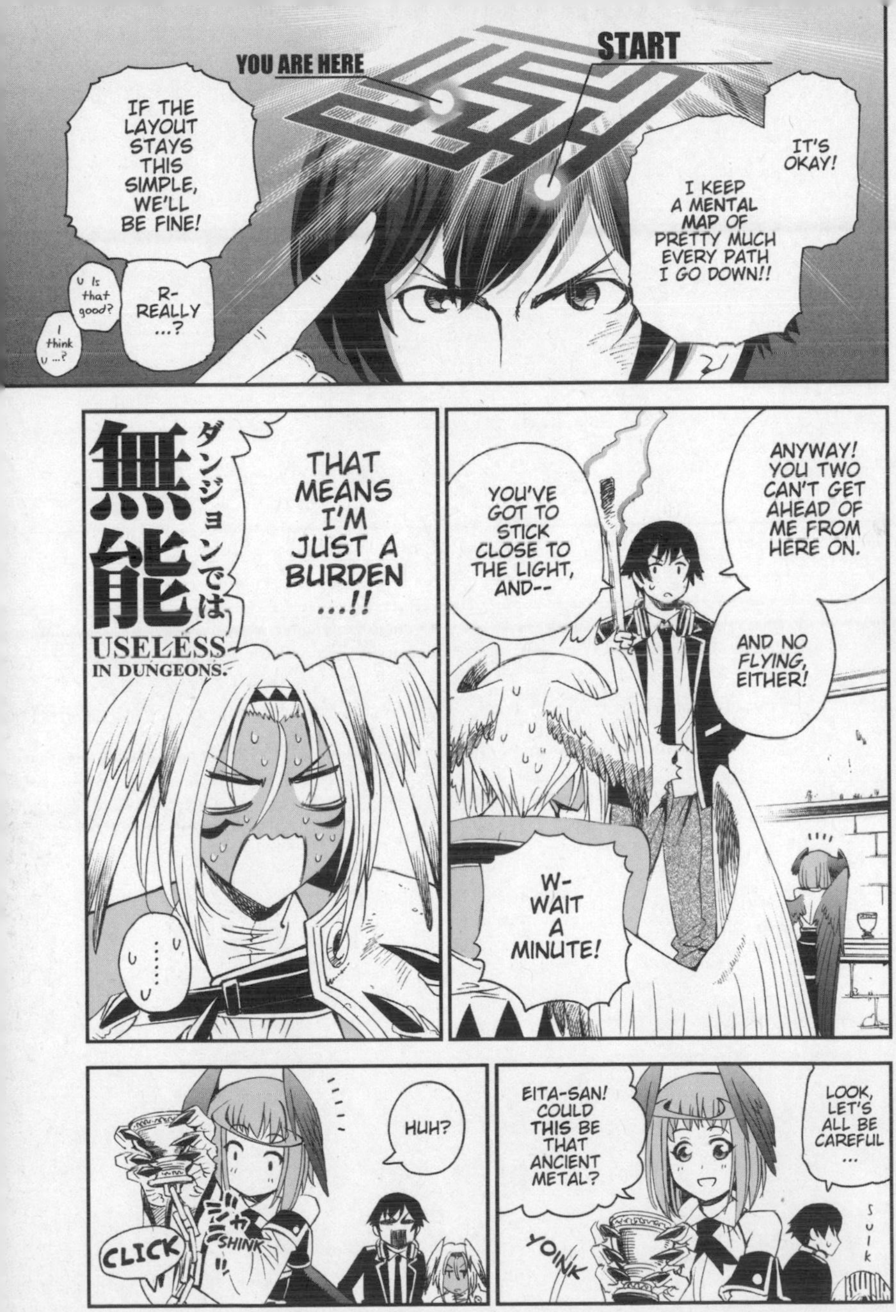
START
IT'S OKAY!
I KEEP A MENTAL MAP OF PRETTY MUCH EVERY PATH I GO DOWN!!
YOU ARE HERE
IF THE LAYOUT STAYS THIS SIMPLE, WE'LL BE FINE!
R-REALLY ...?
Is that good?
I think ...?
ANYWAY! YOU TWO CAN'T GET AHEAD OF ME FROM HERE ON.
AND NO FLYING, EITHER!
YOU'VE GOT TO STICK CLOSE TO THE LIGHT, AND--
W-WAIT A MINUTE!
ダンジョンでは無能
USELESS IN DUNGEONS.
THAT MEANS I'M JUST A BURDEN ...!!
......
LOOK, LET'S ALL BE CAREFUL ...
EITA-SAN! COULD THIS BE THAT ANCIENT METAL?
SULK
YOINK
HUH?
ジャ
SHINK
CLICK

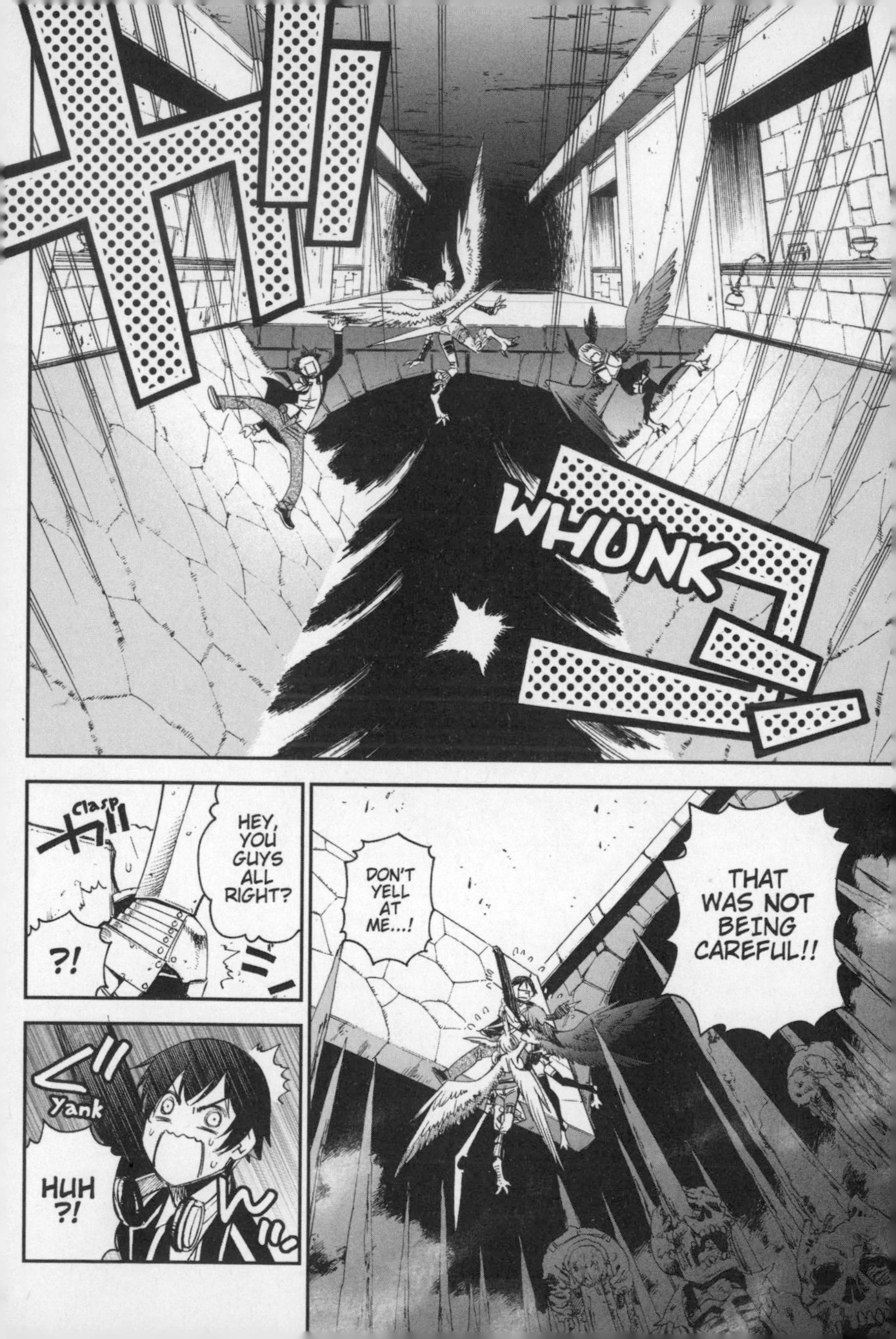
WHUNK
THAT WAS NOT BEING CAREFUL!!
DON'T YELL AT ME...!
Clasp
HEY, YOU GUYS ALL RIGHT?
?!
Yank
HUH ?!

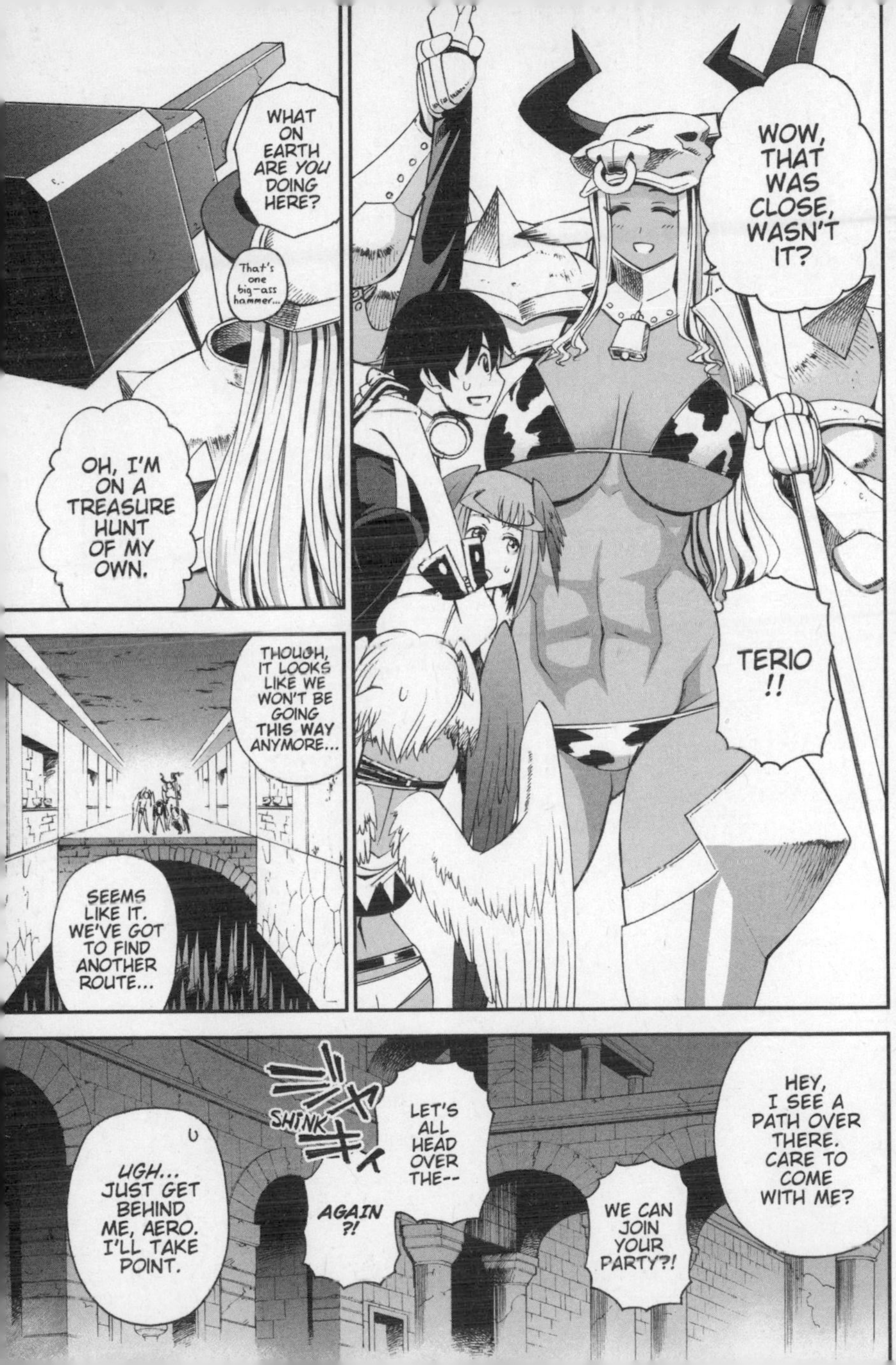
WOW, THAT WAS CLOSE, WASN'T IT?
TERIO!!
WHAT ON EARTH ARE *YOU* DOING HERE?
That's one big-ass hammer...
OH, I'M ON A TREASURE HUNT OF MY OWN.
THOUGH, IT LOOKS LIKE WE WON'T BE GOING THIS WAY ANYMORE...
SEEMS LIKE IT. WE'VE GOT TO FIND ANOTHER ROUTE...
HEY, I SEE A PATH OVER THERE. CARE TO COME WITH ME?
WE CAN JOIN YOUR PARTY?!
LET'S ALL HEAD OVER THE--
SHINK
AGAIN?!
UGH... JUST GET BEHIND ME, AERO. I'LL TAKE POINT.

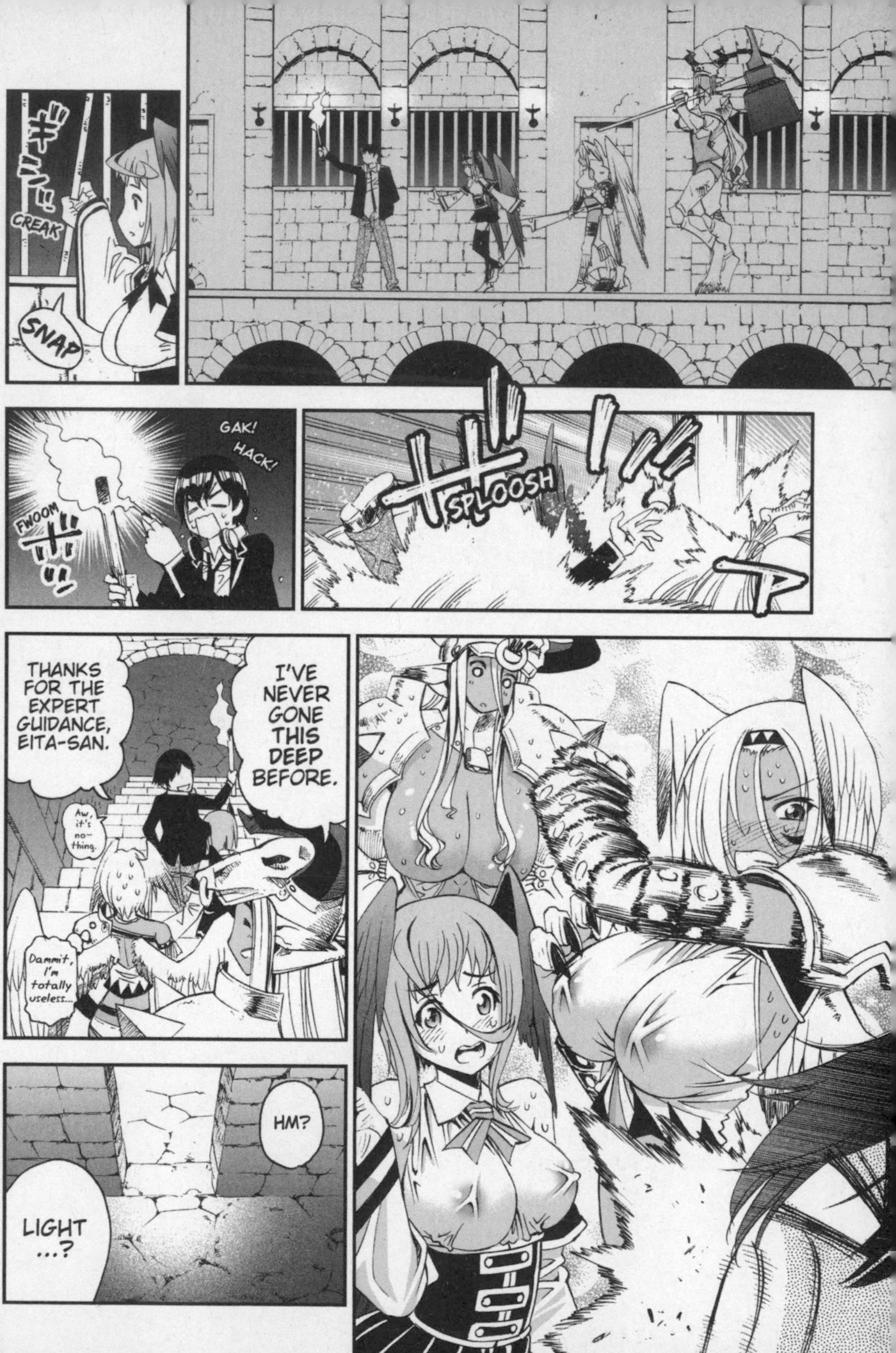
CREAK
SNAP
SPLOOSH
GAK!
HACK!
FWOOM
I'VE NEVER GONE THIS DEEP BEFORE.
THANKS FOR THE EXPERT GUIDANCE, EITA-SAN.
Aw, it's no-thing.
Dammit, I'm totally useless...
HM?
LIGHT ...?

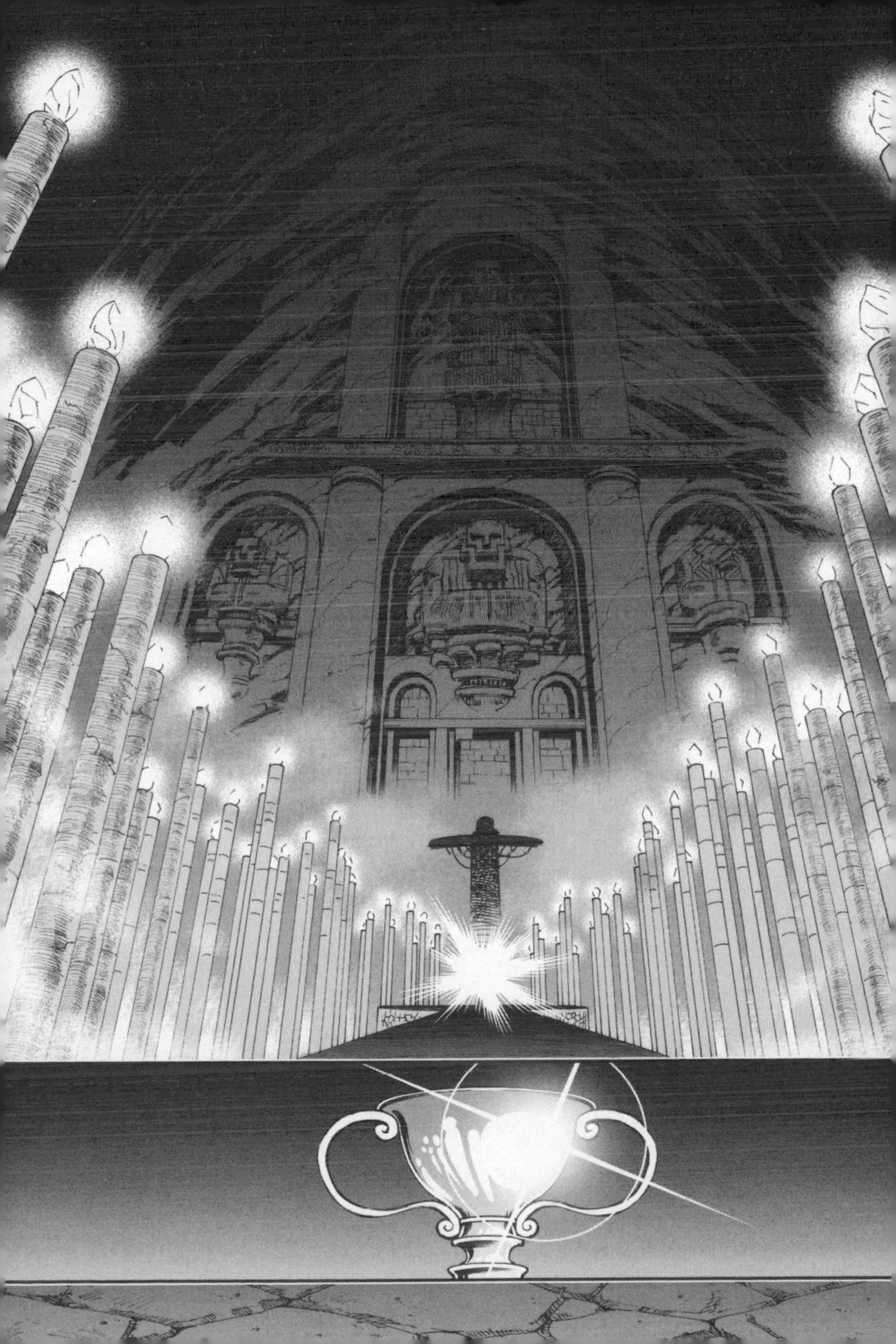

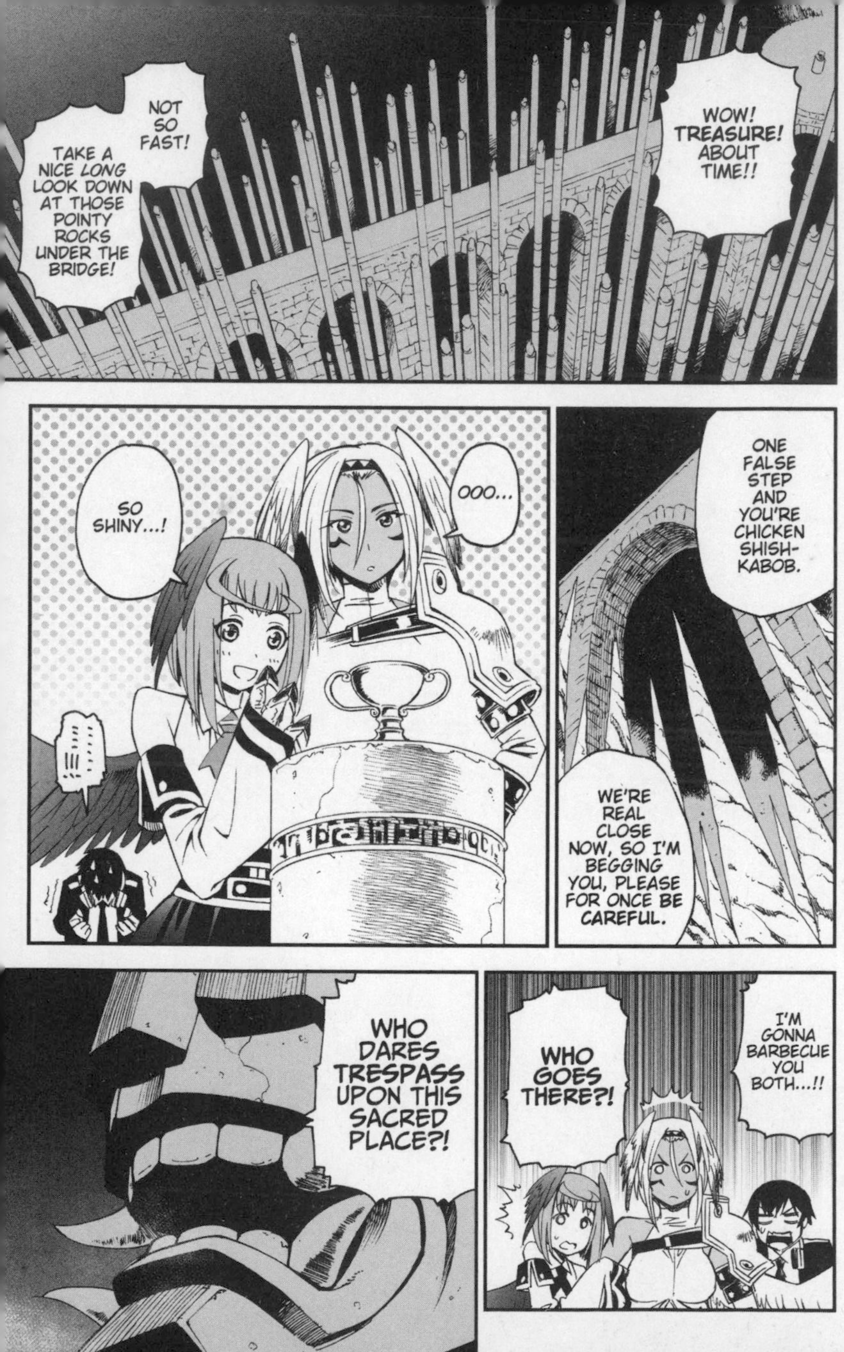
WOW! TREASURE! ABOUT TIME!!
NOT SO FAST!
TAKE A NICE LONG LOOK DOWN AT THOSE POINTY ROCKS UNDER THE BRIDGE!
ONE FALSE STEP AND YOU'RE CHICKEN SHISH-KABOB.
WE'RE REAL CLOSE NOW, SO I'M BEGGING YOU, PLEASE FOR ONCE BE CAREFUL.
OOO...
SO SHINY...!
...!!!
I'M GONNA BARBECUE YOU BOTH...!!
WHO GOES THERE?!
WHO DARES TRESPASS UPON THIS SACRED PLACE?!

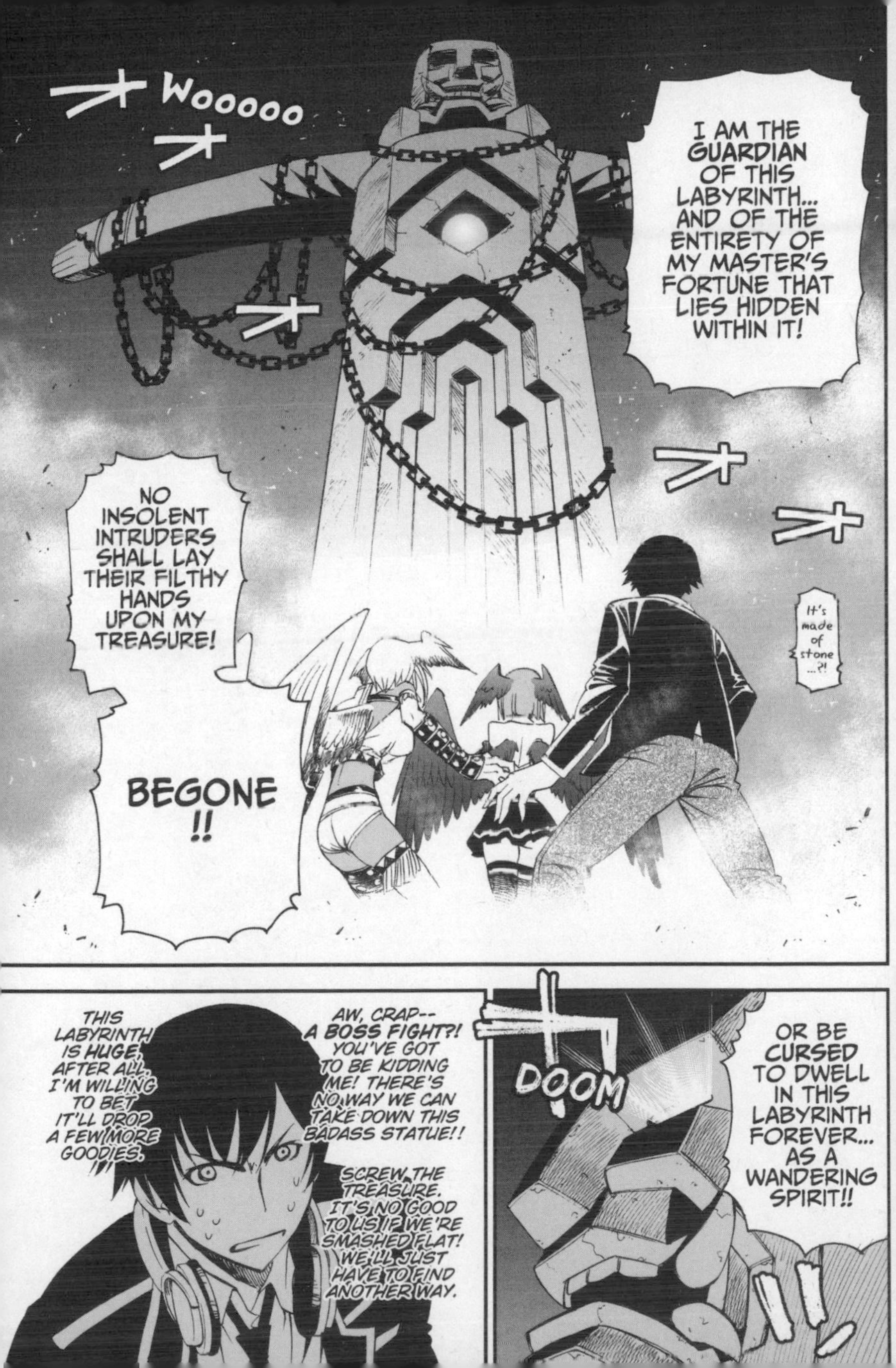
Woooooo
I AM THE GUARDIAN OF THIS LABYRINTH... AND OF THE ENTIRETY OF MY MASTER'S FORTUNE THAT LIES HIDDEN WITHIN IT!
It's made of stone ...?!
NO INSOLENT INTRUDERS SHALL LAY THEIR FILTHY HANDS UPON MY TREASURE!
BEGONE !!
DOOM
OR BE CURSED TO DWELL IN THIS LABYRINTH FOREVER... AS A WANDERING SPIRIT!!
AW, CRAP-- A BOSS FIGHT?! YOU'VE GOT TO BE KIDDING ME! THERE'S NO WAY WE CAN TAKE DOWN THIS BADASS STATUE!!
THIS LABYRINTH IS HUGE, AFTER ALL. I'M WILLING TO BET IT'LL DROP A FEW MORE GOODIES.
SCREW THE TREASURE. IT'S NO GOOD TO US IF WE'RE SMASHED FLAT! WE'LL JUST HAVE TO FIND ANOTHER WAY.

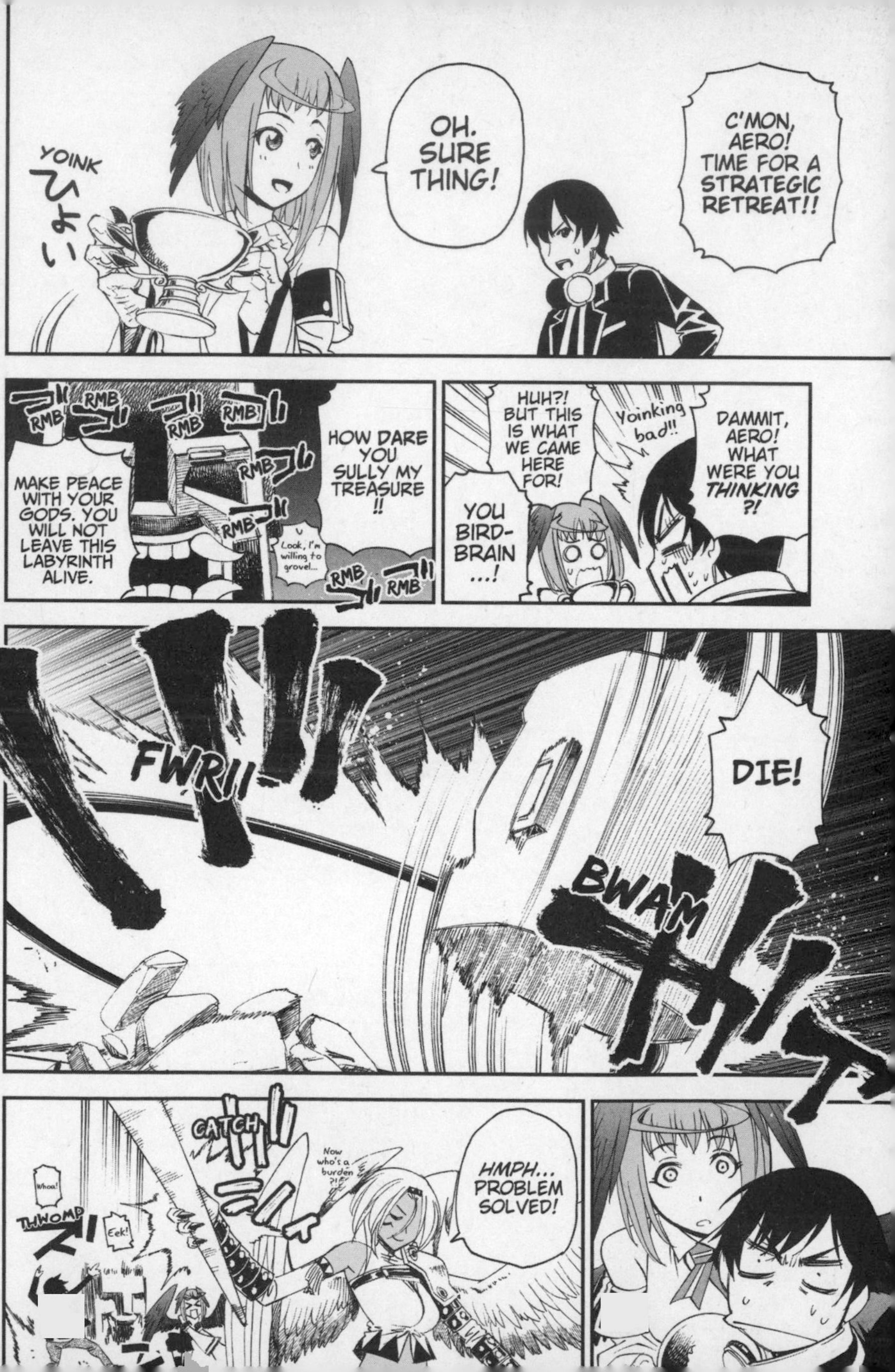
C'MON, AERO! TIME FOR A STRATEGIC RETREAT!!
OH. SURE THING!
YOINK
ひょい
DAMMIT, AERO! WHAT WERE YOU THINKING?!
Yoinking bad!!
HUH?! BUT THIS IS WHAT WE CAME HERE FOR!
YOU BIRD-BRAIN...!
RMB RMB RMB RMB
HOW DARE YOU SULLY MY TREASURE!!
RMB
MAKE PEACE WITH YOUR GODS. YOU WILL NOT LEAVE THIS LABYRINTH ALIVE.
RMB
Look, I'm willing to grovel...
RMB RMB
DIE!
BWAM
FWR
HMPH... PROBLEM SOLVED!
Now who's a burden?!
CATCH
Whoa!
Eek!
THWOMP

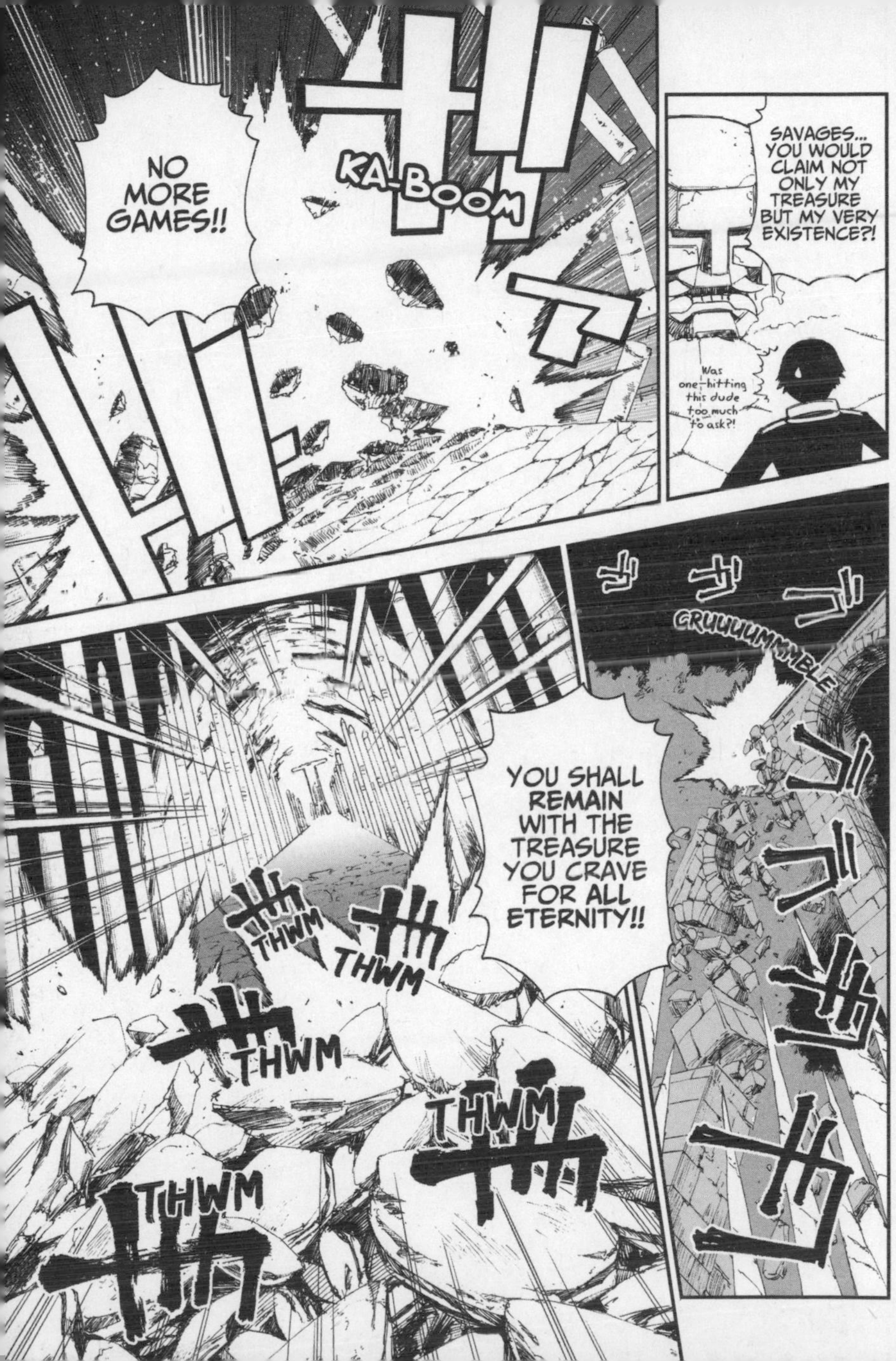
SAVAGES... YOU WOULD CLAIM NOT ONLY MY TREASURE BUT MY VERY EXISTENCE?!
Was one-hitting this dude too much to ask?!
NO MORE GAMES!!
KA-BOOM
GRUUUUMMMBLE
YOU SHALL REMAIN WITH THE TREASURE YOU CRAVE FOR ALL ETERNITY!!
THWM
THWM
THWM
THWM
THWM

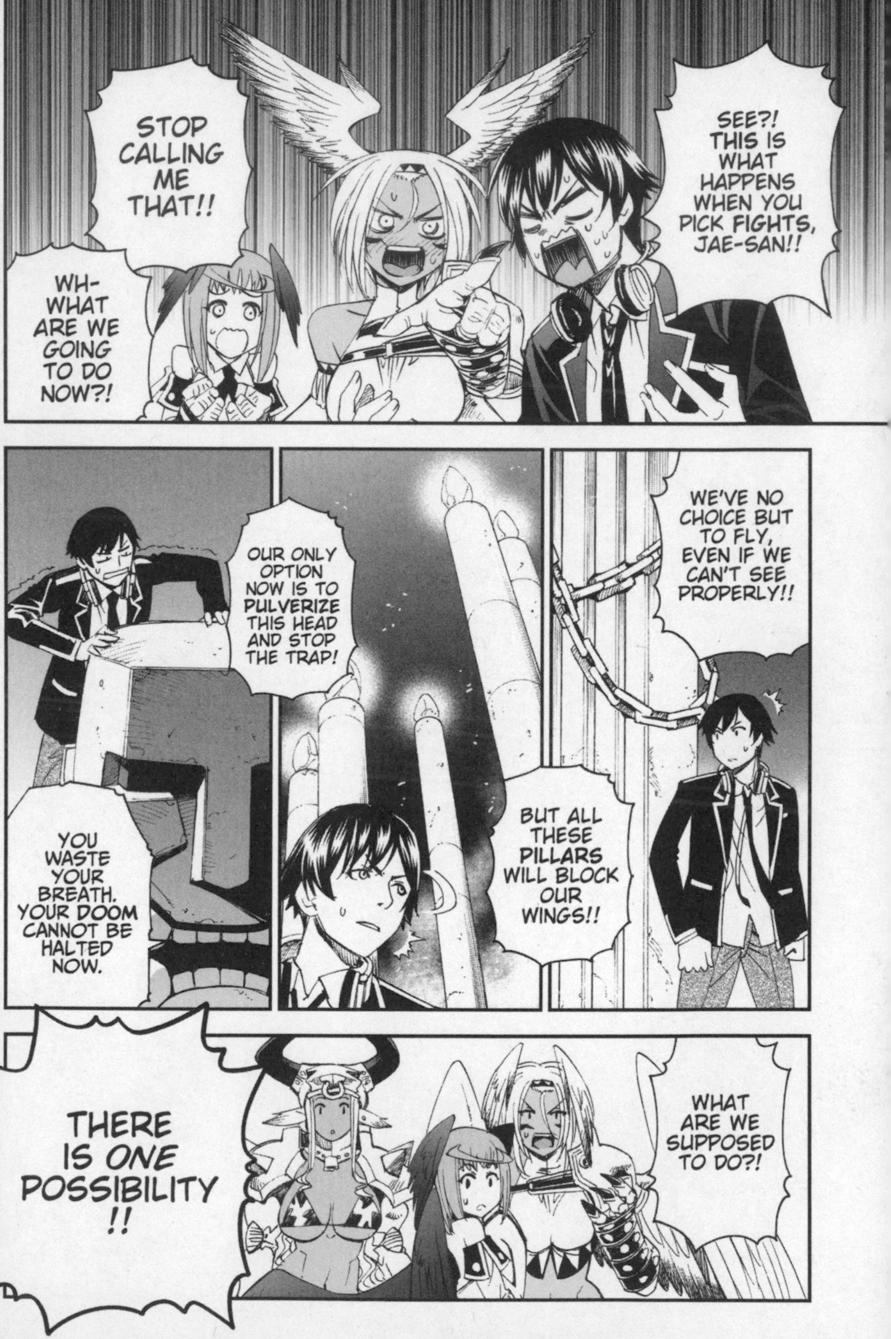
SEE?! THIS IS WHAT HAPPENS WHEN YOU PICK FIGHTS, JAE-SAN!!
STOP CALLING ME THAT!!
WH- WHAT ARE WE GOING TO DO NOW?!
WE'VE NO CHOICE BUT TO FLY, EVEN IF WE CAN'T SEE PROPERLY!!
BUT ALL THESE PILLARS WILL BLOCK OUR WINGS!!
OUR ONLY OPTION NOW IS TO PULVERIZE THIS HEAD AND STOP THE TRAP!
YOU WASTE YOUR BREATH. YOUR DOOM CANNOT BE HALTED NOW.
WHAT ARE WE SUPPOSED TO DO?!
THERE IS *ONE* POSSIBILITY!!

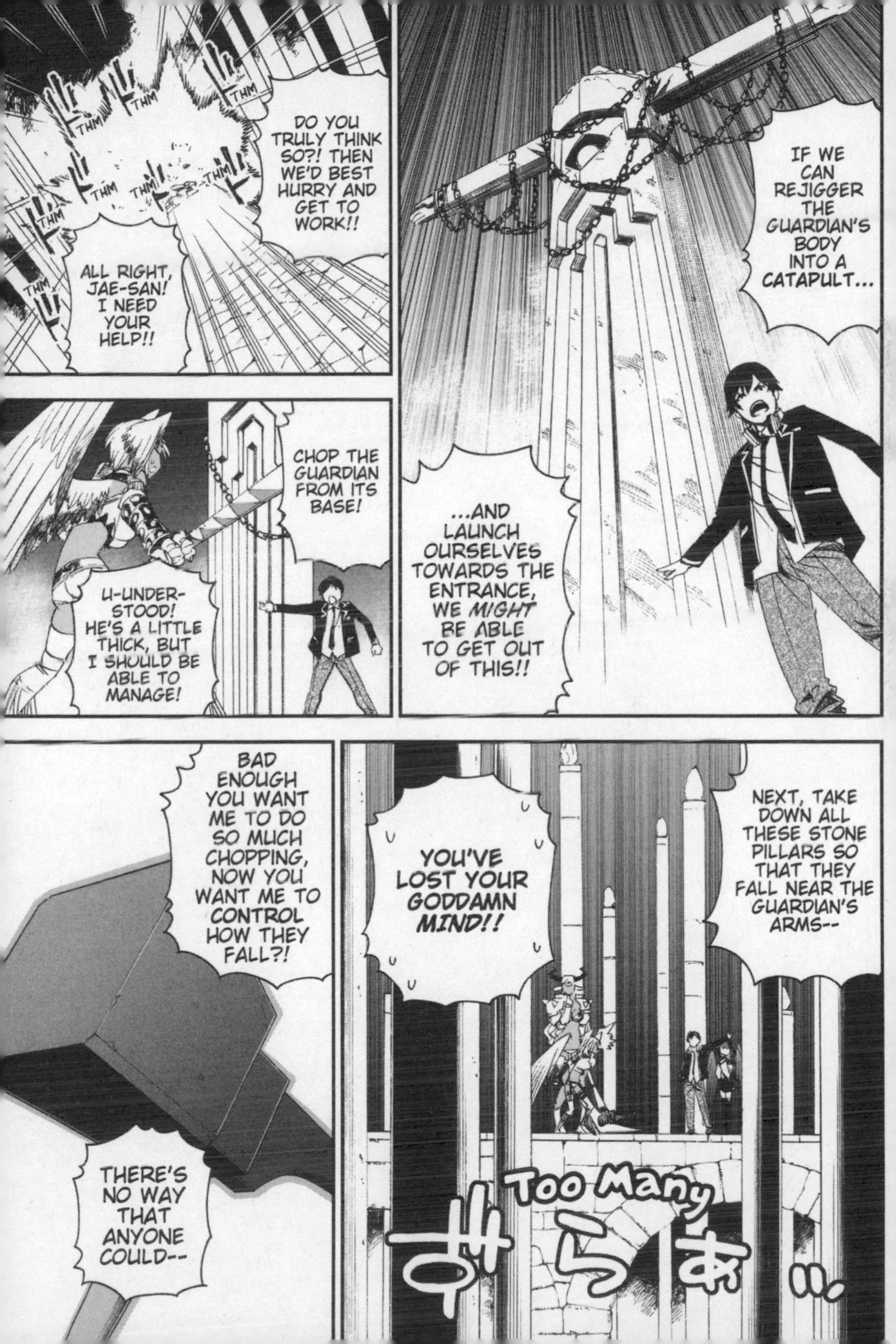
IF WE CAN REJIGGER THE GUARDIAN'S BODY INTO A CATAPULT...
...AND LAUNCH OURSELVES TOWARDS THE ENTRANCE, WE *MIGHT* BE ABLE TO GET OUT OF THIS!!
THM THM THM THM THM THM THM THM
DO YOU TRULY THINK SO?! THEN WE'D BEST HURRY AND GET TO WORK!!
ALL RIGHT, JAE-SAN! I NEED YOUR HELP!!
CHOP THE GUARDIAN FROM ITS BASE!
U-UNDERSTOOD! HE'S A LITTLE THICK, BUT I SHOULD BE ABLE TO MANAGE!
NEXT, TAKE DOWN ALL THESE STONE PILLARS SO THAT THEY FALL NEAR THE GUARDIAN'S ARMS--
YOU'VE LOST YOUR GODDAMN *MIND*!!
Too Many
ずらぁ..
BAD ENOUGH YOU WANT ME TO DO SO MUCH CHOPPING, NOW YOU WANT ME TO CONTROL HOW THEY FALL?!
THERE'S NO WAY THAT ANYONE COULD--

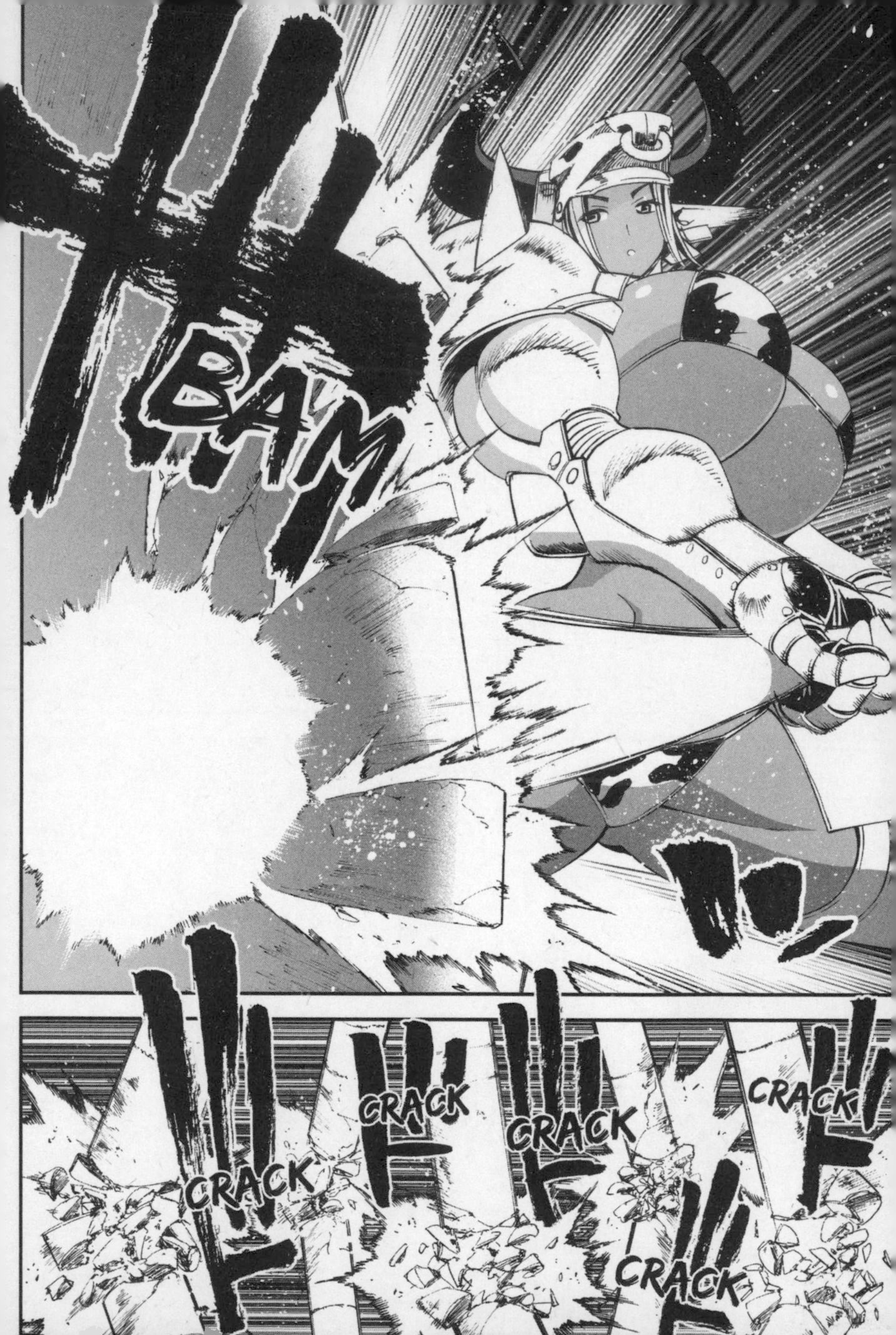
BAM
CRACK
CRACK
CRACK
CRACK
CRACK

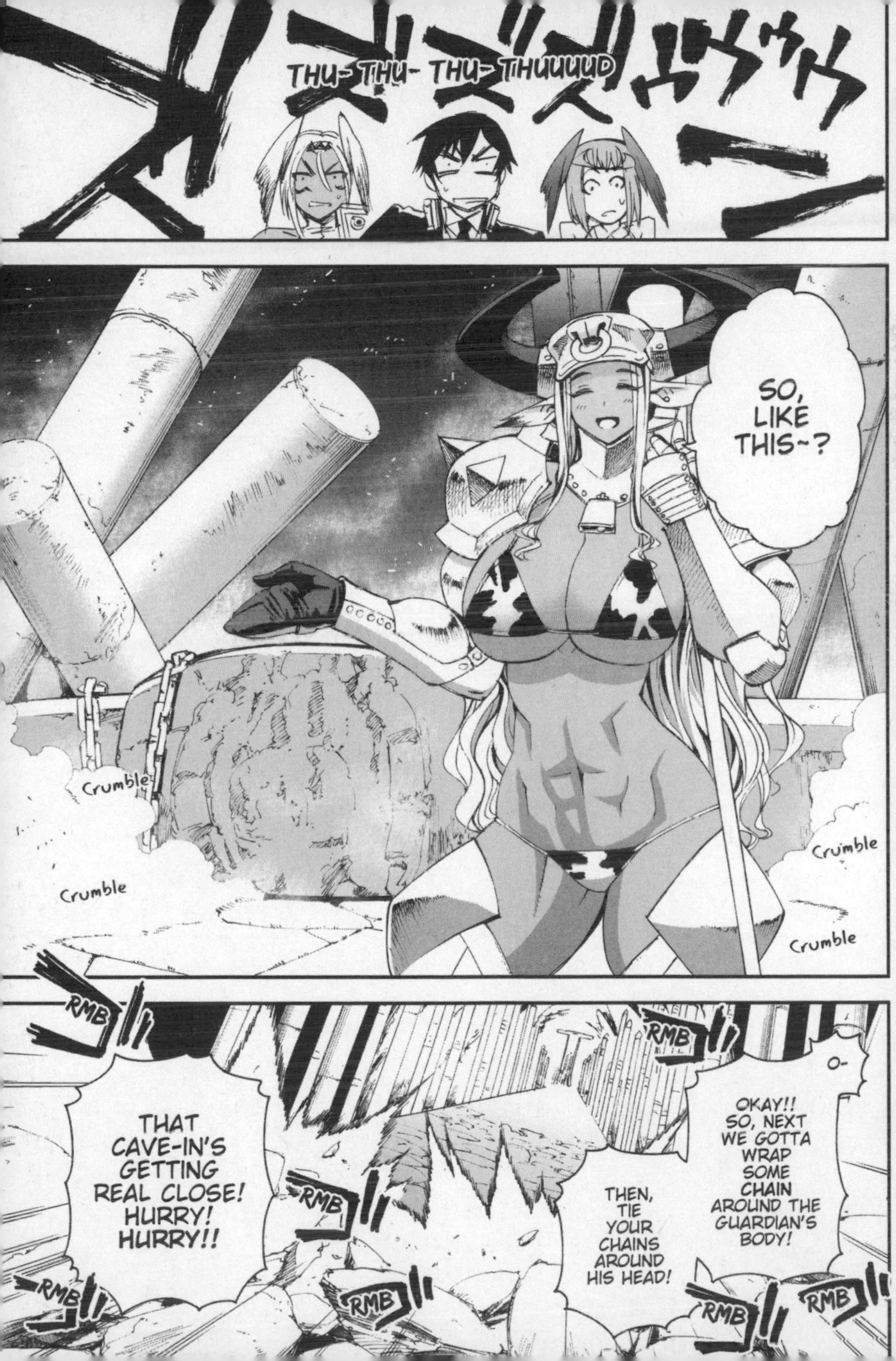
THU- THU- THU- THUUUUD
SO, LIKE THIS~?
Crumble
Crumble
Crumble
Crumble
RMB
RMB
O-
OKAY!! SO, NEXT WE GOTTA WRAP SOME CHAIN AROUND THE GUARDIAN'S BODY!
THEN, TIE YOUR CHAINS AROUND HIS HEAD!
THAT CAVE-IN'S GETTING REAL CLOSE! HURRY! HURRY!!
RMB
RMB
RMB
RMB
RMB

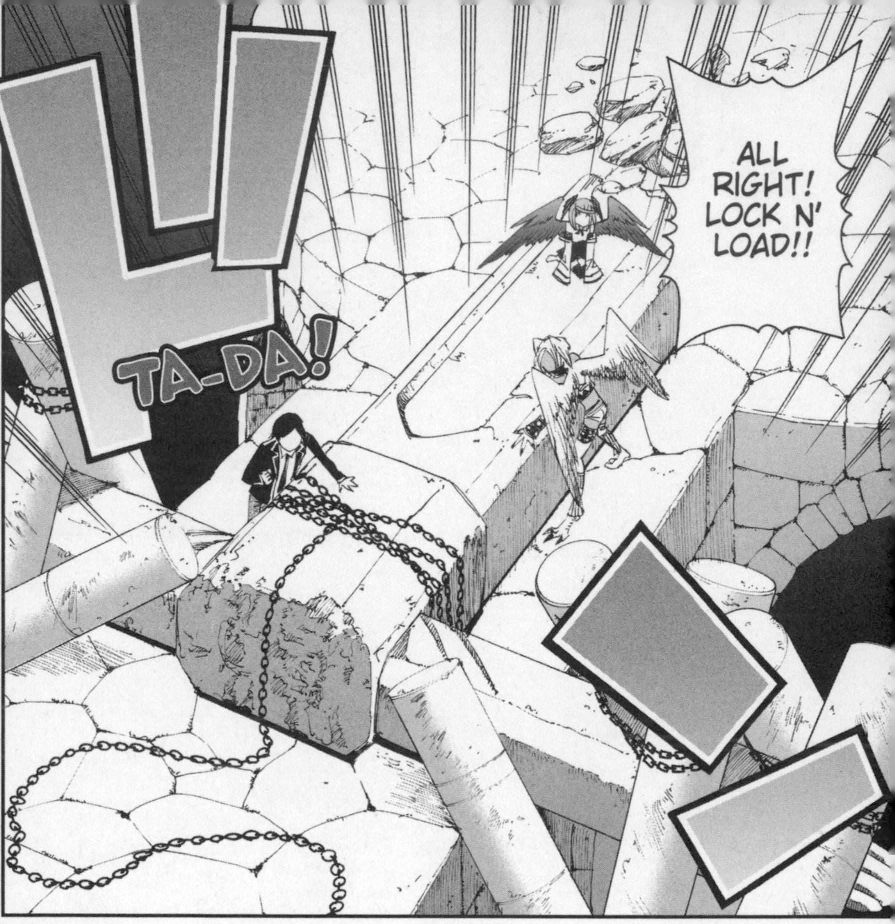
ALL RIGHT! LOCK N' LOAD!!
TA-DA!

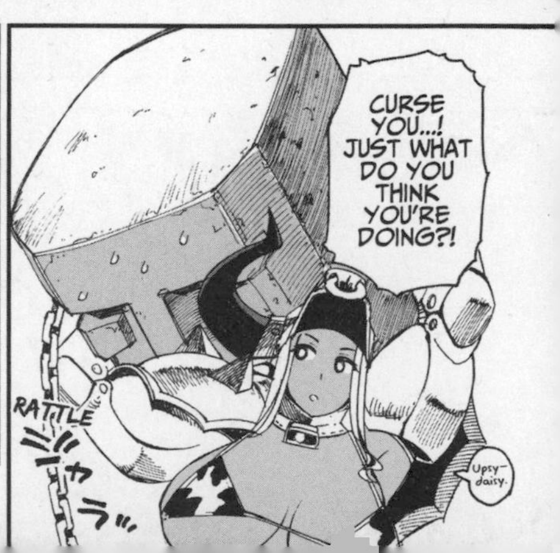
CURSE YOU...! JUST WHAT DO YOU THINK YOU'RE DOING?!
RATTLE
Upsy-daisy.

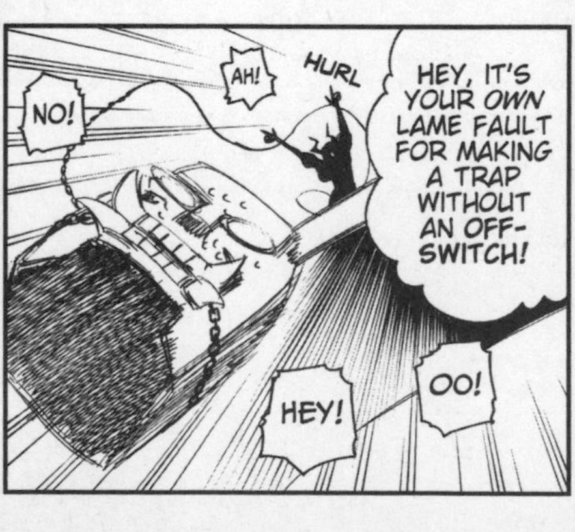
HEY, IT'S YOUR *OWN* LAME FAULT FOR MAKING A TRAP WITHOUT AN OFF-SWITCH!
HURL
AH!
NO!
OO!
HEY!

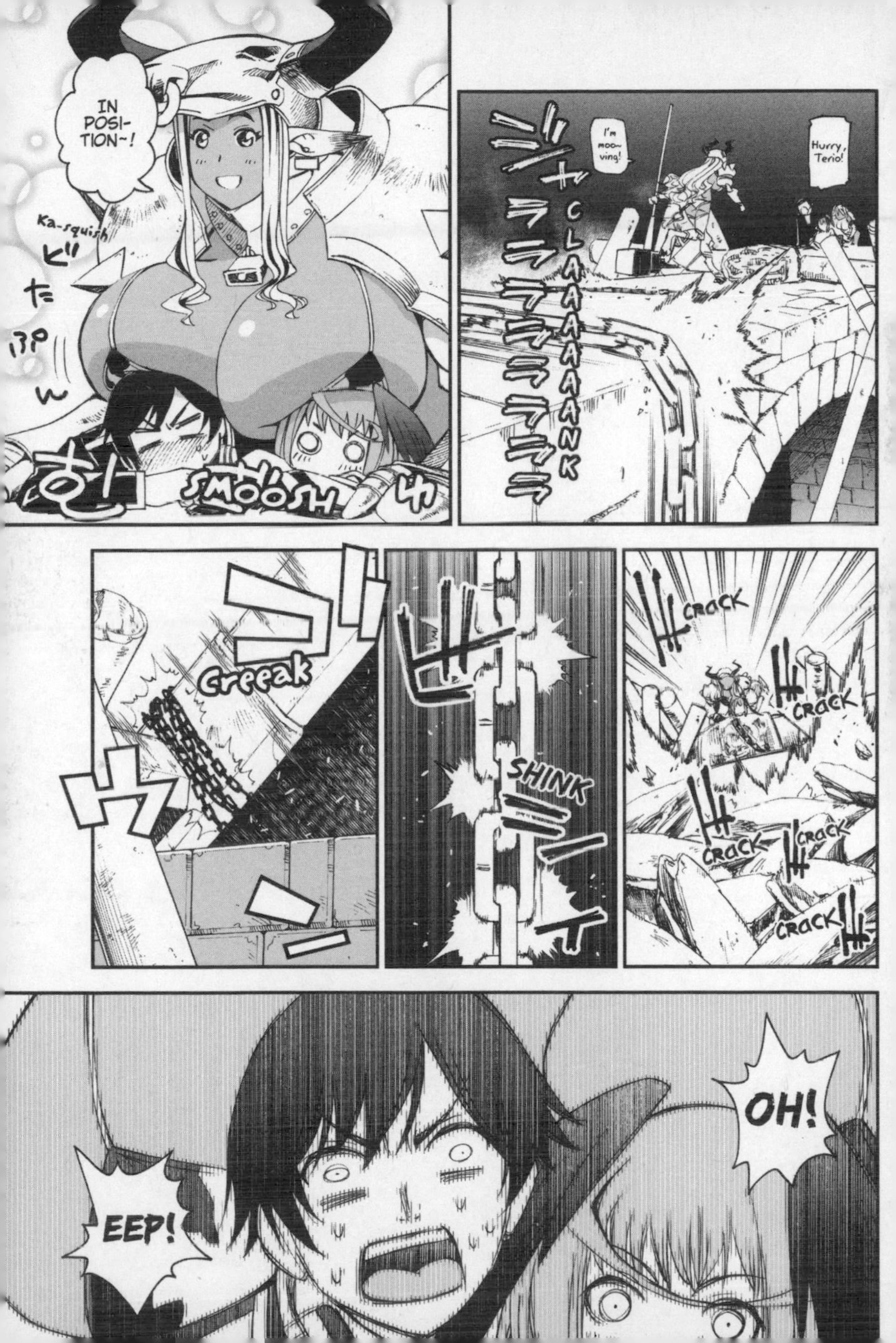
Hurry, Terio!
I'm moo~ving!
CLAAAAAAANK
IN POSI-TION~!
Ka-squish
SMOOSH
CRACK
CRACK
CRACK
CRACK
CRACK
SHINK
Creeak
OH!
EEP!

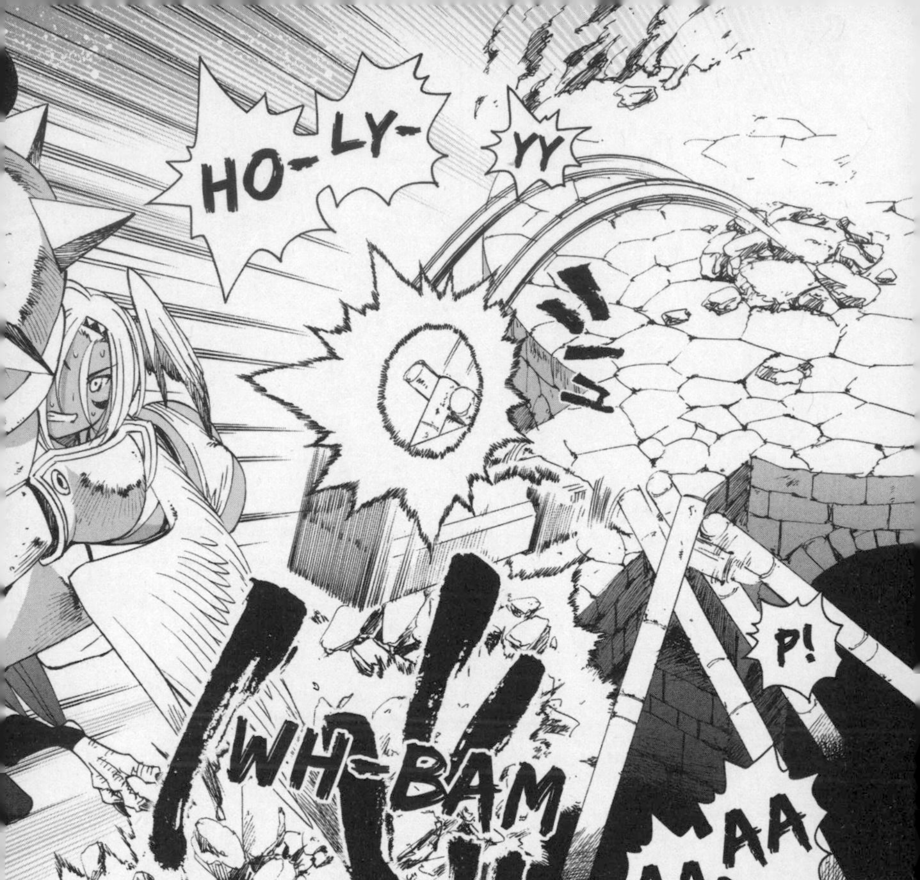
HO-LY-
YY
P!
WH-BAM
AA
AA
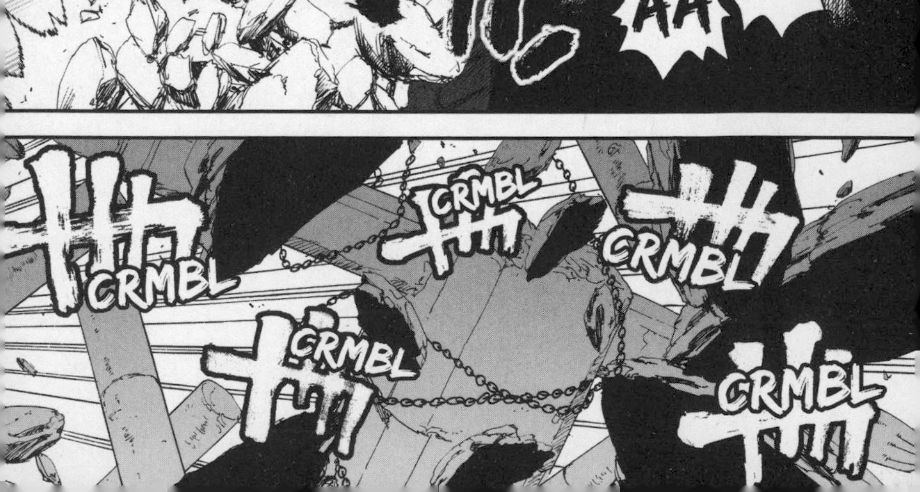
CRMBL
CRMBL
CRMBL
CRMBL
CRMBL

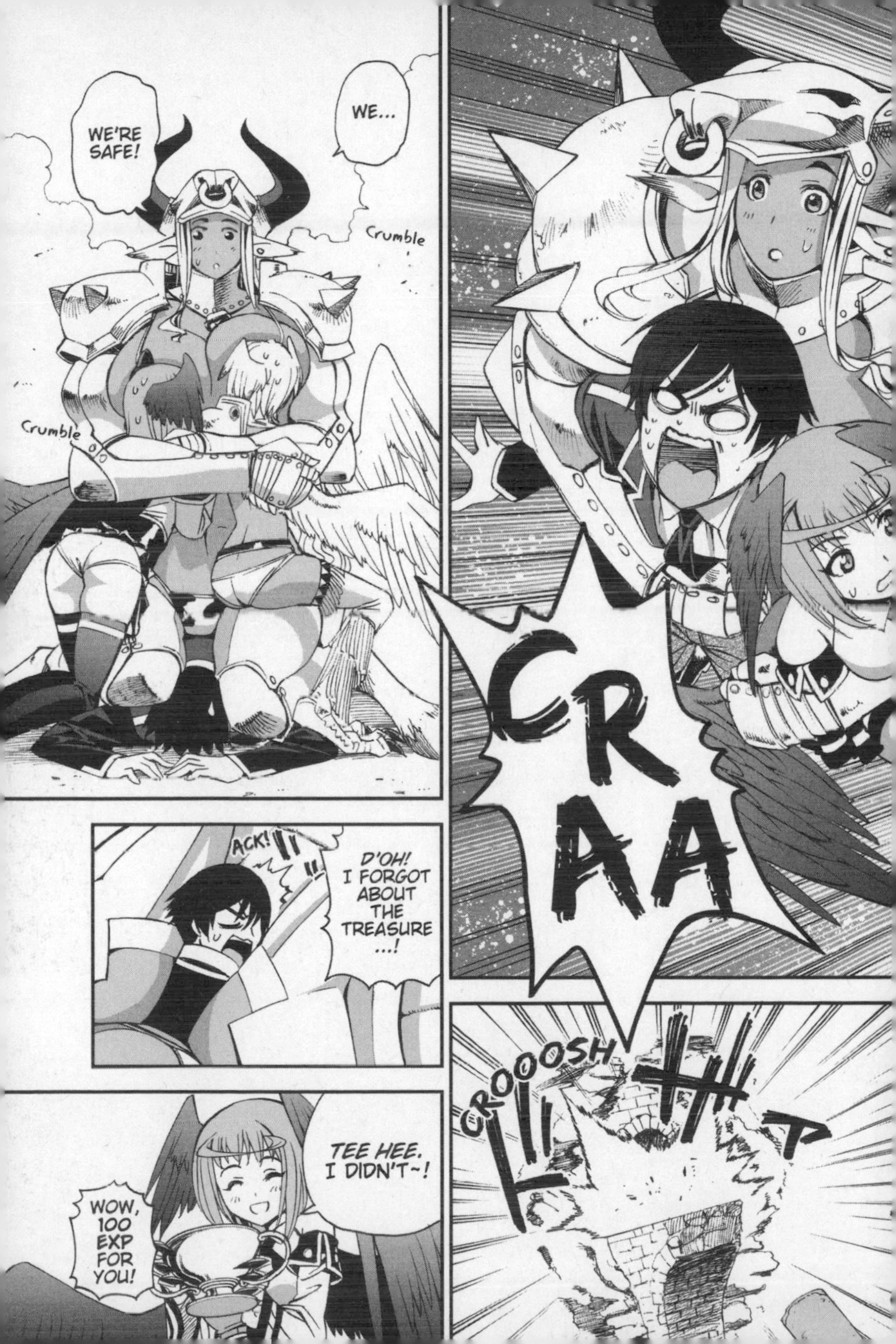

CRAA
WE...
WE'RE SAFE!
Crumble
Crumble
CROOOSH
ACK!
D'OH! I FORGOT ABOUT THE TREASURE ...!
TEE HEE. I DIDN'T~!
WOW, 100 EXP FOR YOU!

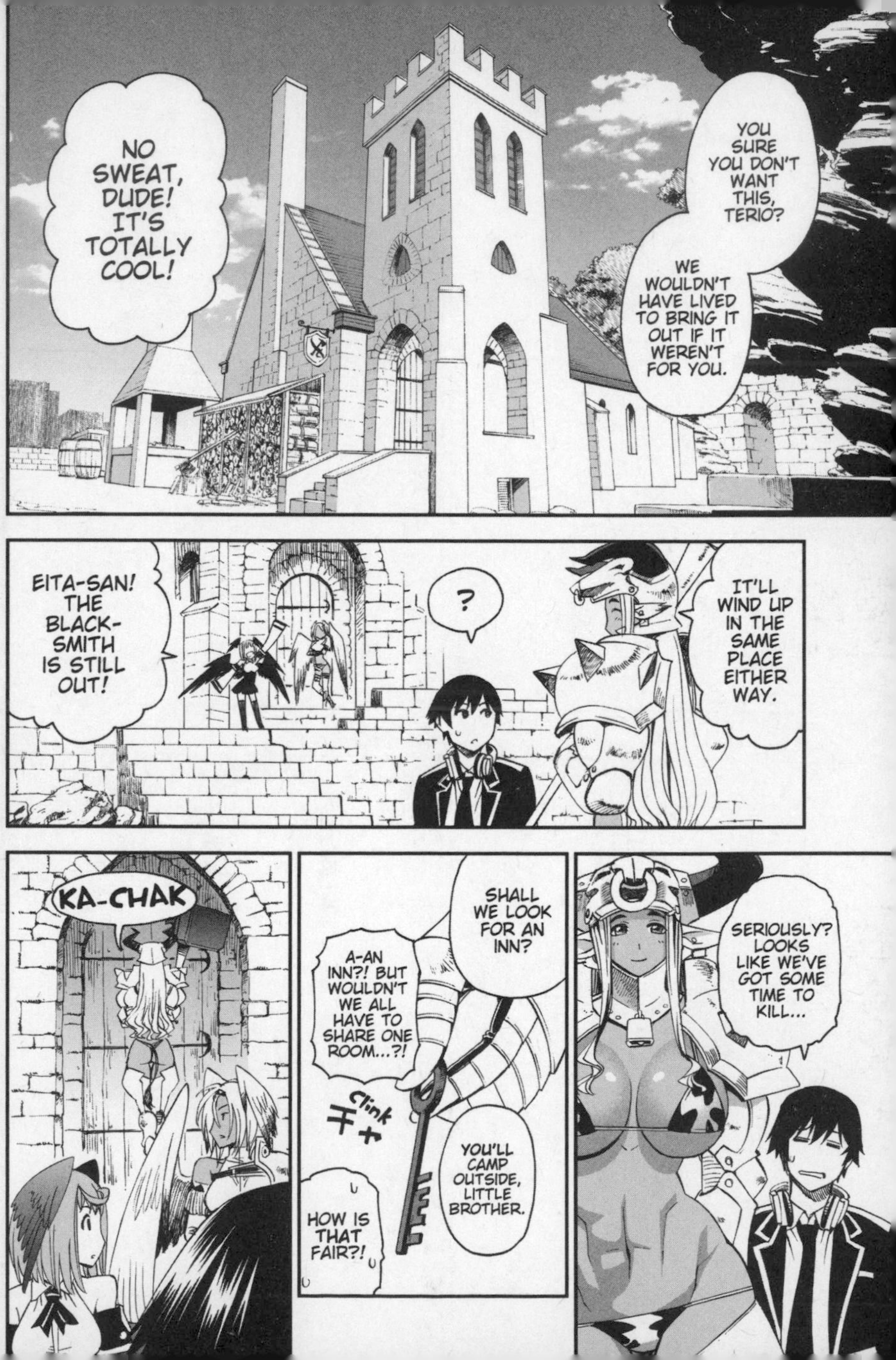
YOU SURE YOU DON'T WANT THIS, TERIO?
WE WOULDN'T HAVE LIVED TO BRING IT OUT IF IT WEREN'T FOR YOU.
NO SWEAT, DUDE! IT'S TOTALLY COOL!
IT'LL WIND UP IN THE SAME PLACE EITHER WAY.
?
EITA-SAN! THE BLACK-SMITH IS STILL OUT!
SERIOUSLY? LOOKS LIKE WE'VE GOT SOME TIME TO KILL...
SHALL WE LOOK FOR AN INN?
A-AN INN?! BUT WOULDN'T WE ALL HAVE TO SHARE ONE ROOM...?!
Clink
YOU'LL CAMP OUTSIDE, LITTLE BROTHER.
HOW IS THAT FAIR?!
KA-CHAK

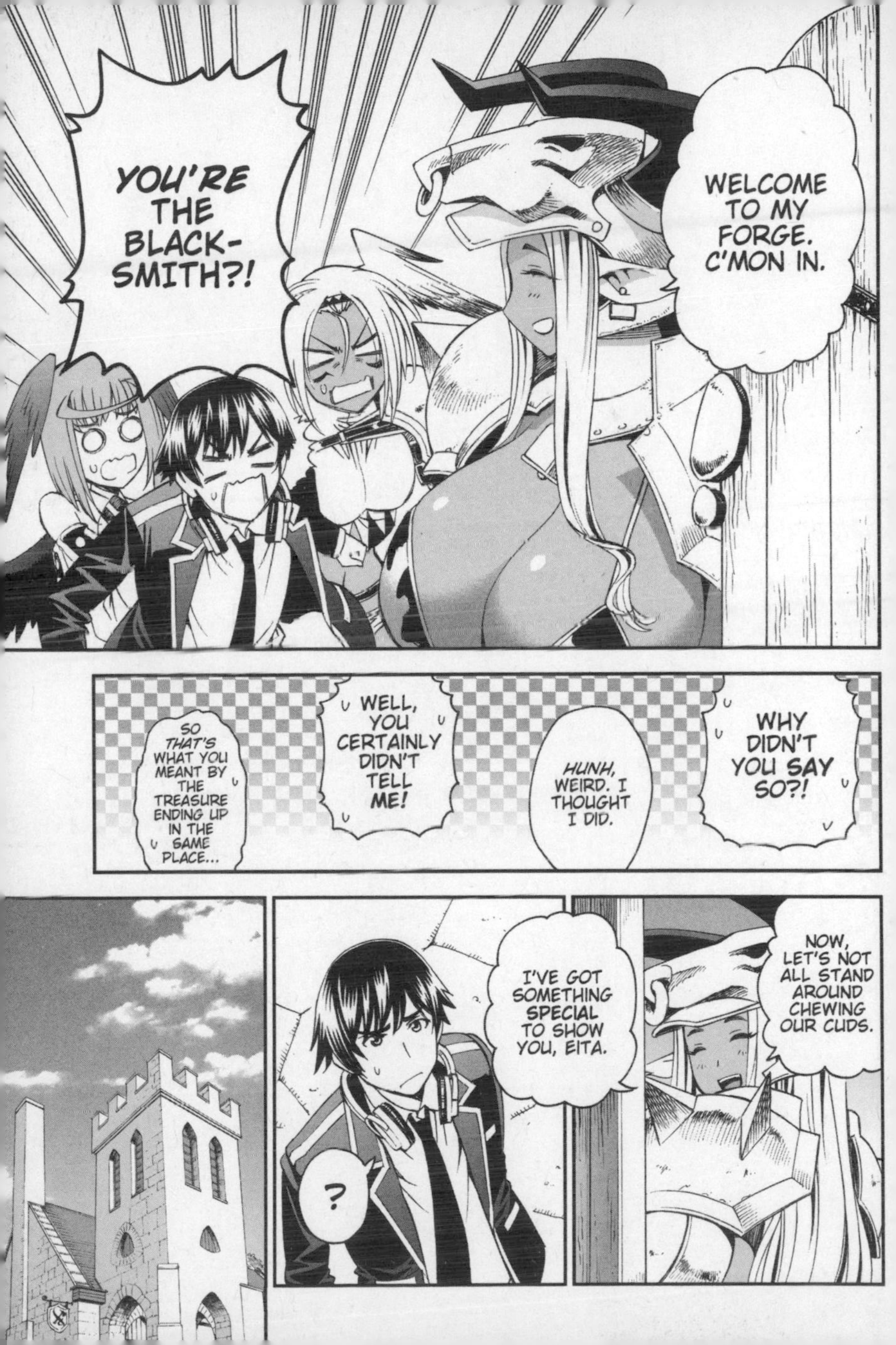
WELCOME TO MY FORGE. C'MON IN.
YOU'RE THE BLACK-SMITH?!
WHY DIDN'T YOU SAY SO?!
HUNH, WEIRD. I THOUGHT I DID.
WELL, YOU CERTAINLY DIDN'T TELL *ME!*
SO *THAT'S* WHAT YOU MEANT BY THE TREASURE ENDING UP IN THE SAME PLACE...
NOW, LET'S NOT ALL STAND AROUND CHEWING OUR CUDS.
I'VE GOT SOMETHING SPECIAL TO SHOW YOU, EITA.
?

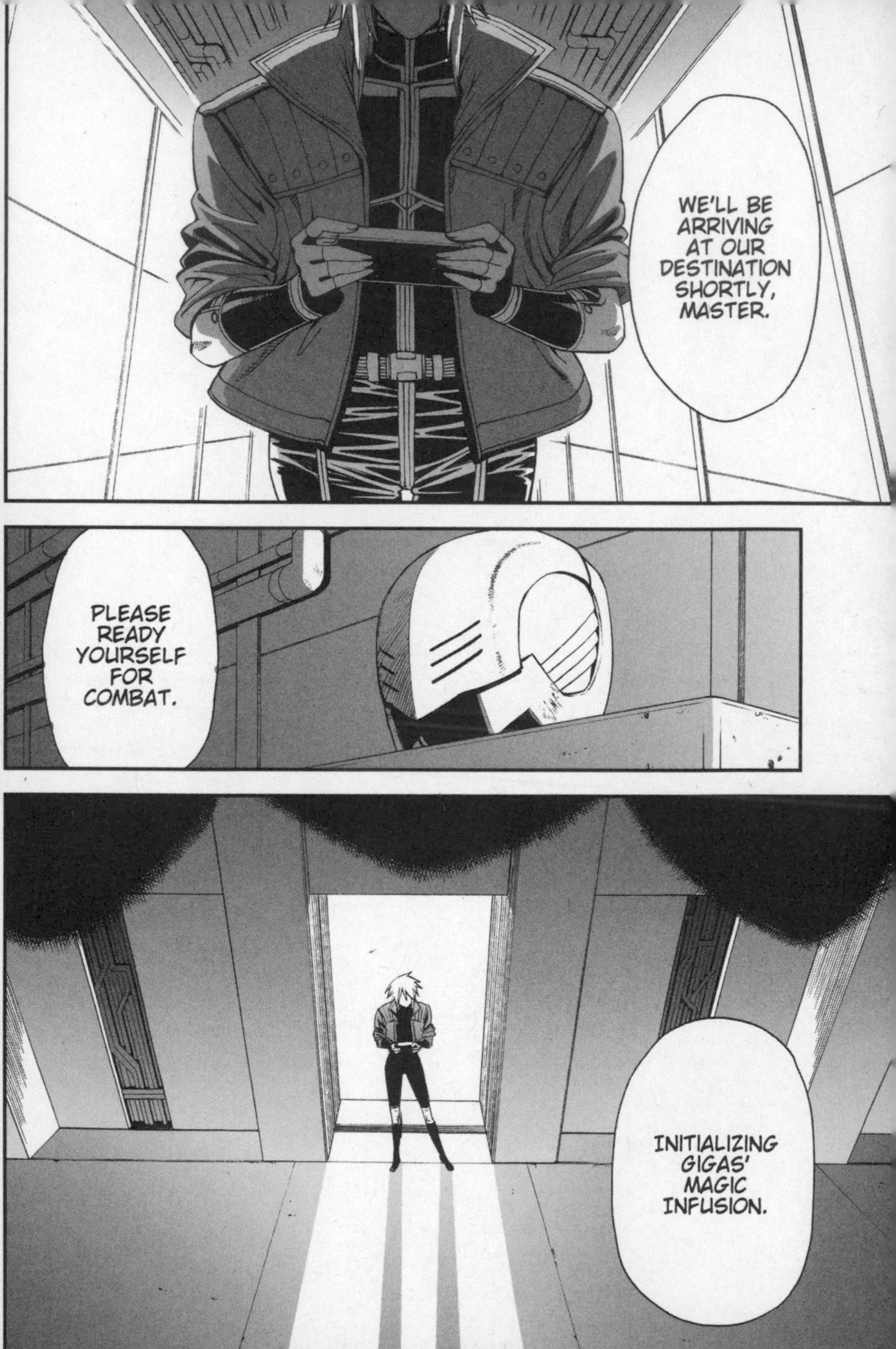
WE'LL BE ARRIVING AT OUR DESTINATION SHORTLY, MASTER.
PLEASE READY YOURSELF FOR COMBAT.
INITIALIZING GIGAS' MAGIC INFUSION.

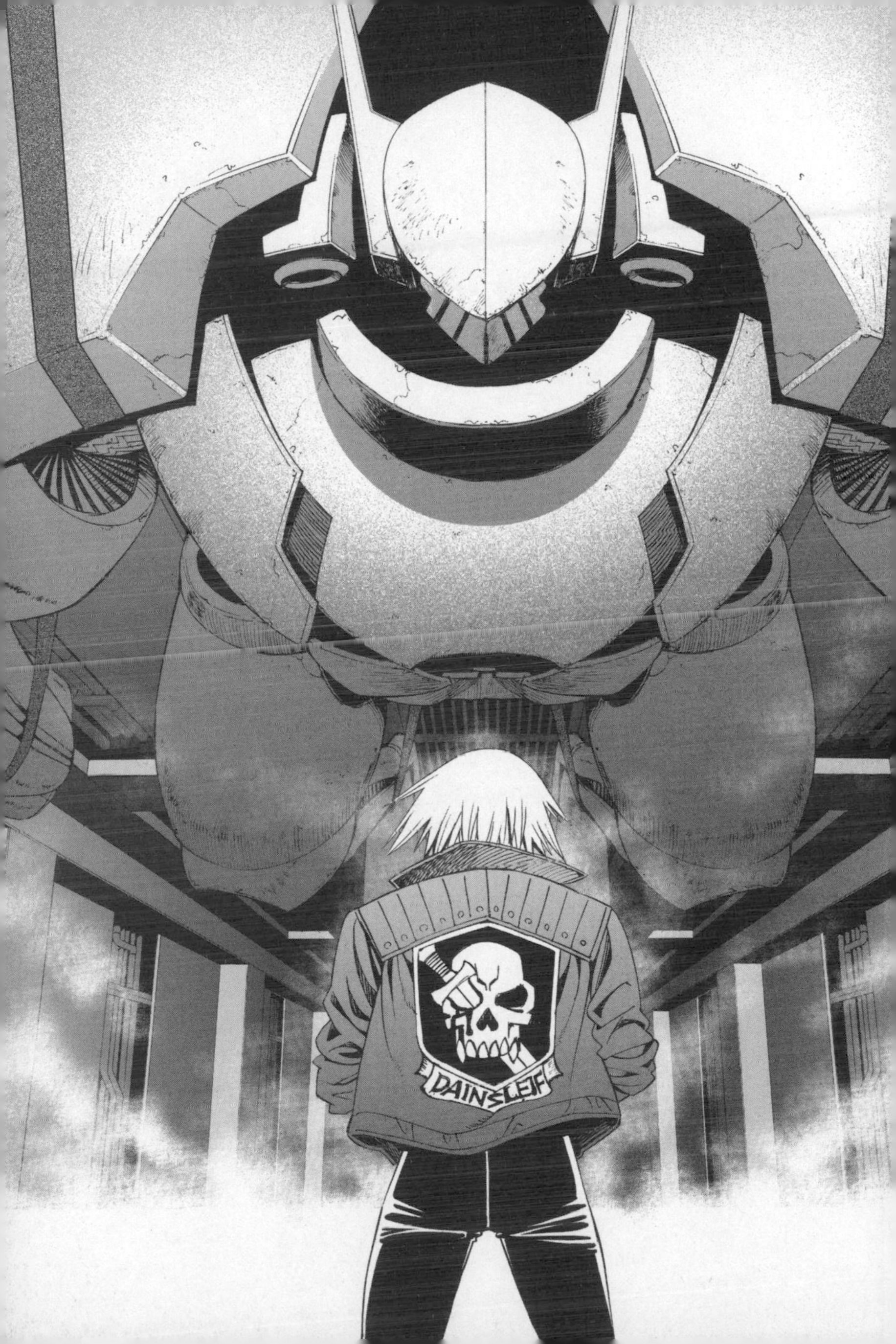
DAINSLEIF

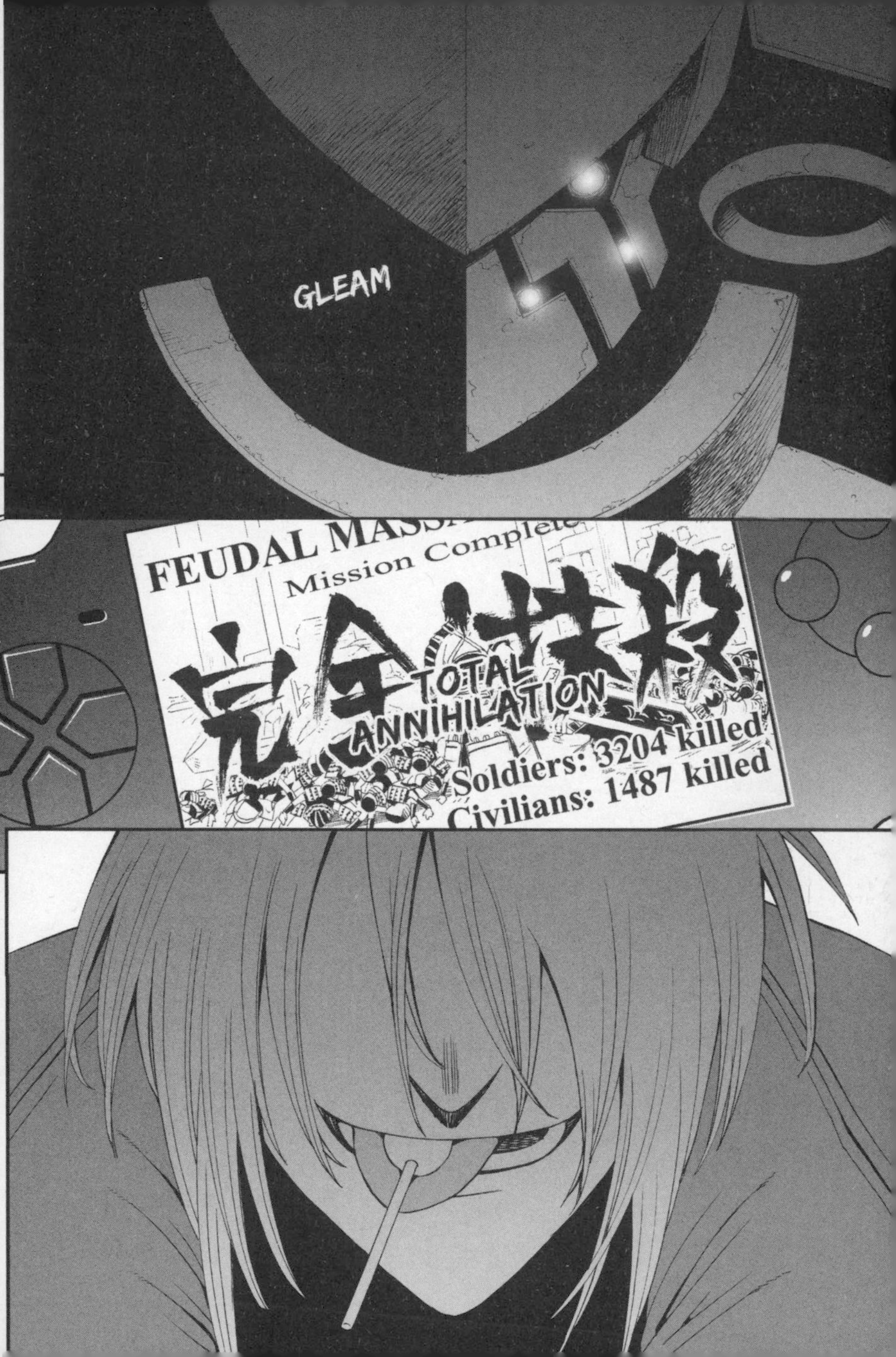
GLEAM
FEUDAL MASS
Mission Complete
完全抹殺
TOTAL ANNIHILATION
Soldiers: 3204 killed
Civilians: 1487 killed

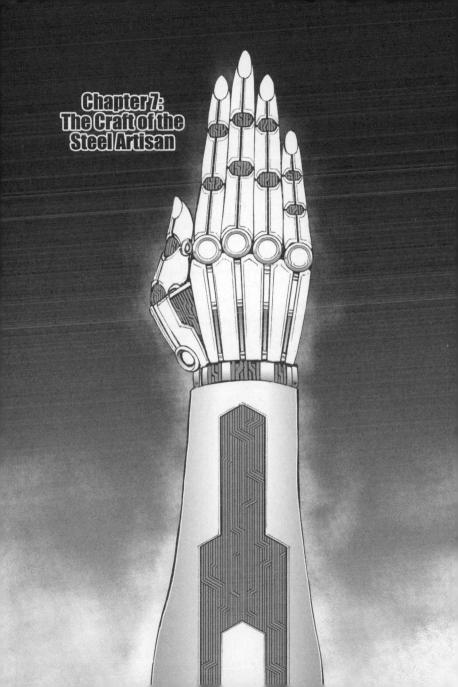

Chapter 7:
The Craft of the
Steel Artisan

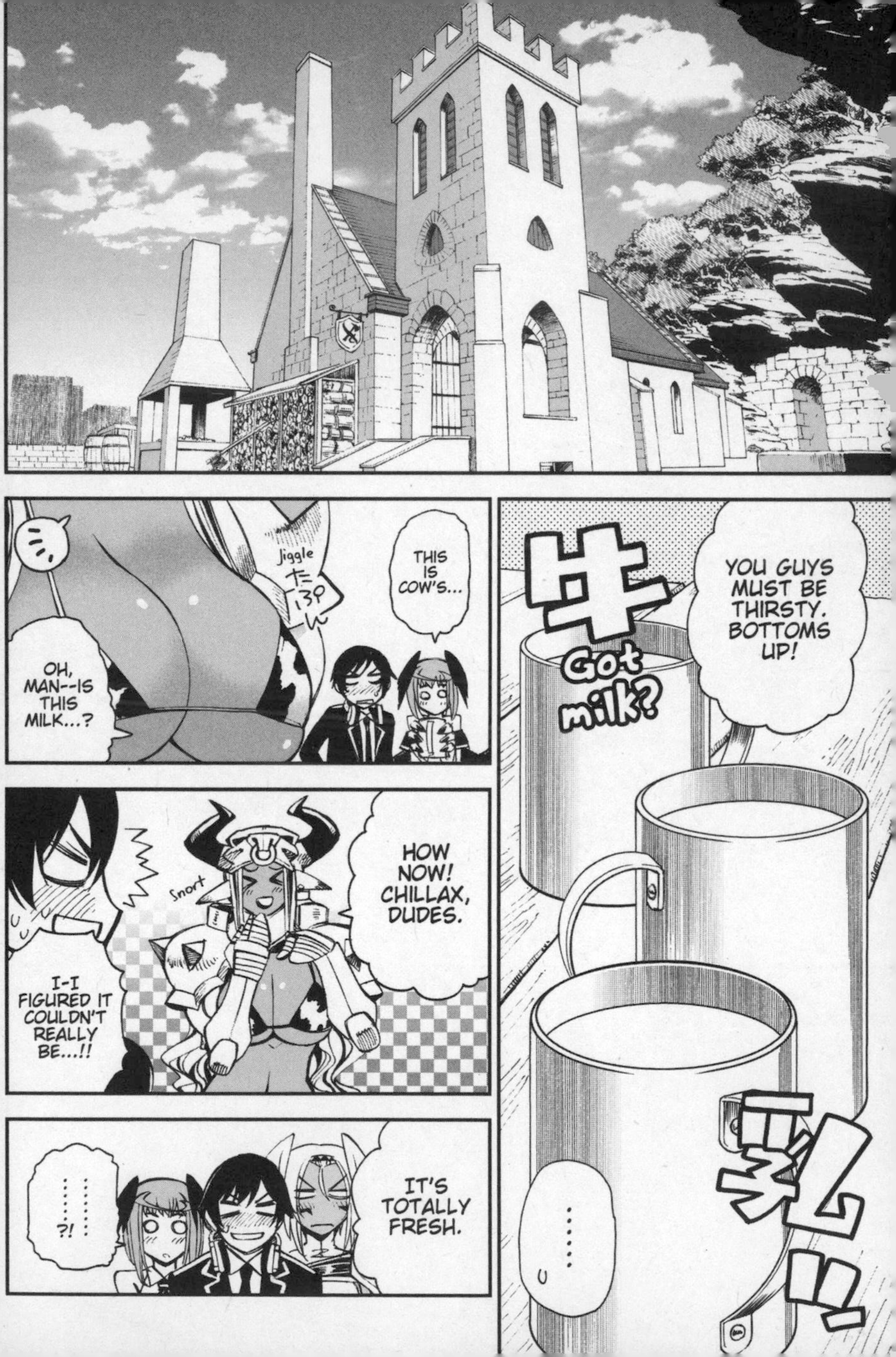
牛
YOU GUYS MUST BE THIRSTY. BOTTOMS UP!
Got milk?
乳
......
THIS IS COW'S...
Jiggle
OH, MAN--IS THIS MILK...?
HOW NOW! CHILLAX, DUDES.
Snort
I-I FIGURED IT COULDN'T REALLY BE...!!
IT'S TOTALLY FRESH.
......?!

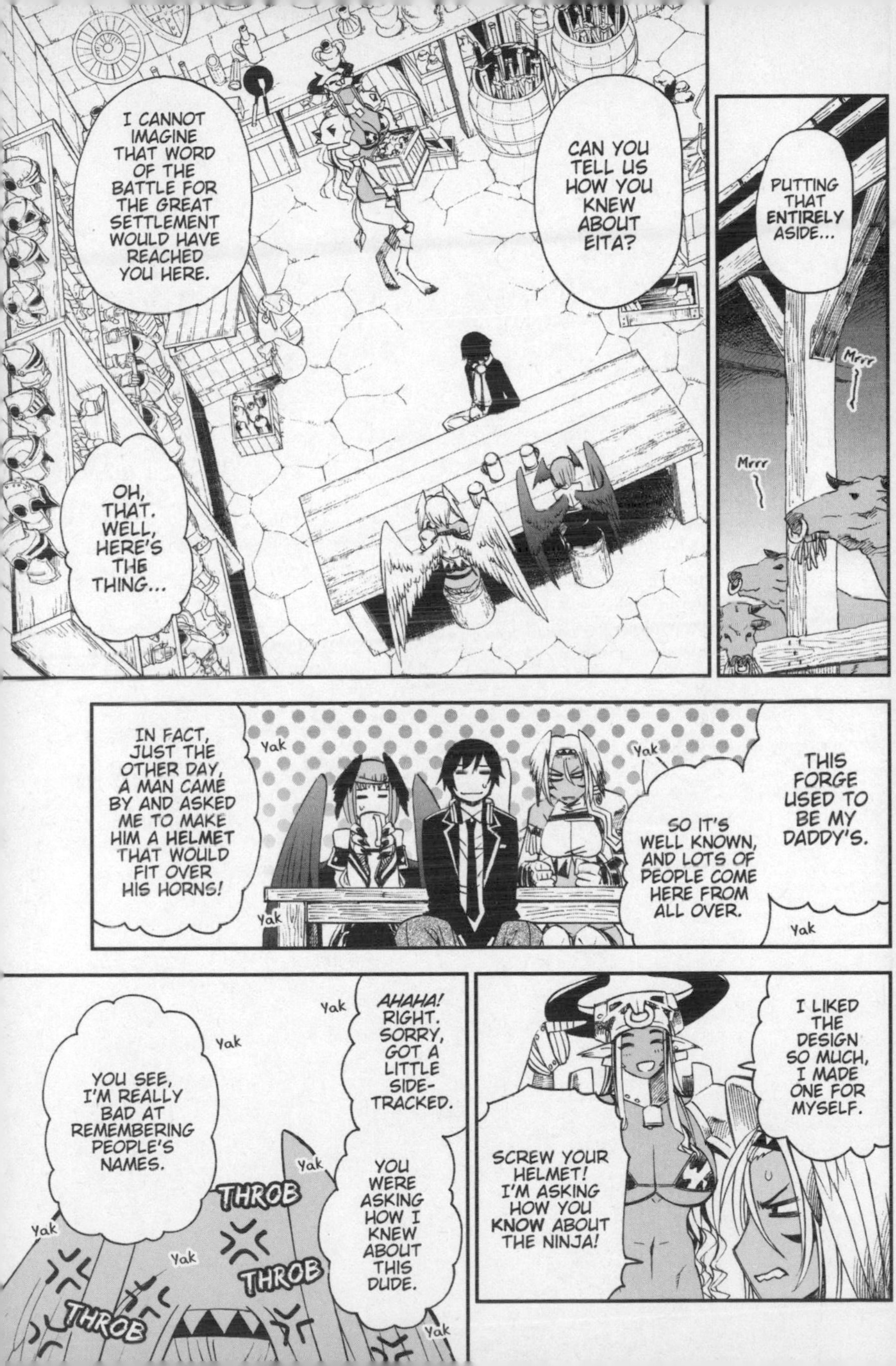
PUTTING THAT ENTIRELY ASIDE...
Mrrr
Mrrr
CAN YOU TELL US HOW YOU KNEW ABOUT EITA?
I CANNOT IMAGINE THAT WORD OF THE BATTLE FOR THE GREAT SETTLEMENT WOULD HAVE REACHED YOU HERE.
OH, THAT. WELL, HERE'S THE THING...
THIS FORGE USED TO BE MY DADDY'S.
Yak
SO IT'S WELL KNOWN, AND LOTS OF PEOPLE COME HERE FROM ALL OVER.
Yak
IN FACT, JUST THE OTHER DAY, A MAN CAME BY AND ASKED ME TO MAKE HIM A HELMET THAT WOULD FIT OVER HIS HORNS!
Yak
Yak
I LIKED THE DESIGN SO MUCH, I MADE ONE FOR MYSELF.
SCREW YOUR HELMET! I'M ASKING HOW YOU KNOW ABOUT THE NINJA!
AHAHA! RIGHT. SORRY, GOT A LITTLE SIDE-TRACKED.
Yak
Yak
YOU SEE, I'M REALLY BAD AT REMEMBERING PEOPLE'S NAMES.
YOU WERE ASKING HOW I KNEW ABOUT THIS DUDE.
Yak
THROB
Yak
Yak
THROB
THROB
Yak

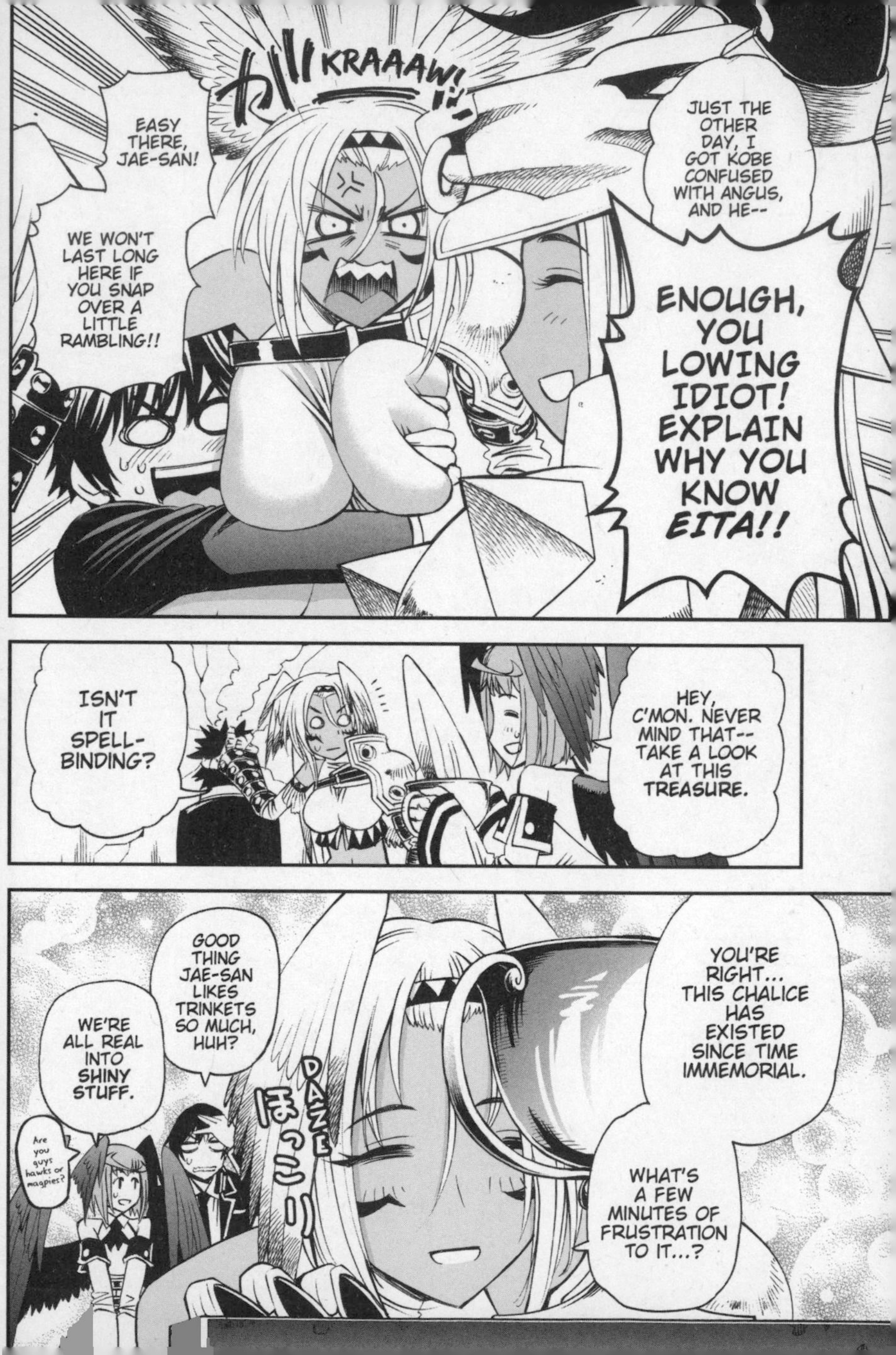
JUST THE OTHER DAY, I GOT KOBE CONFUSED WITH ANGUS, AND HE--
ENOUGH, YOU LOWING IDIOT! EXPLAIN WHY YOU KNOW *EITA!!*
KRAAAW!!
EASY THERE, JAE-SAN!
WE WON'T LAST LONG HERE IF YOU SNAP OVER A LITTLE RAMBLING!!
HEY, C'MON. NEVER MIND THAT-- TAKE A LOOK AT THIS TREASURE.
ISN'T IT SPELL-BINDING?
YOU'RE RIGHT... THIS CHALICE HAS EXISTED SINCE TIME IMMEMORIAL.
WHAT'S A FEW MINUTES OF FRUSTRATION TO IT...?
DAZE
GOOD THING JAE-SAN LIKES TRINKETS SO MUCH, HUH?
WE'RE ALL REAL INTO SHINY STUFF.
Are you guys hawks or magpies?

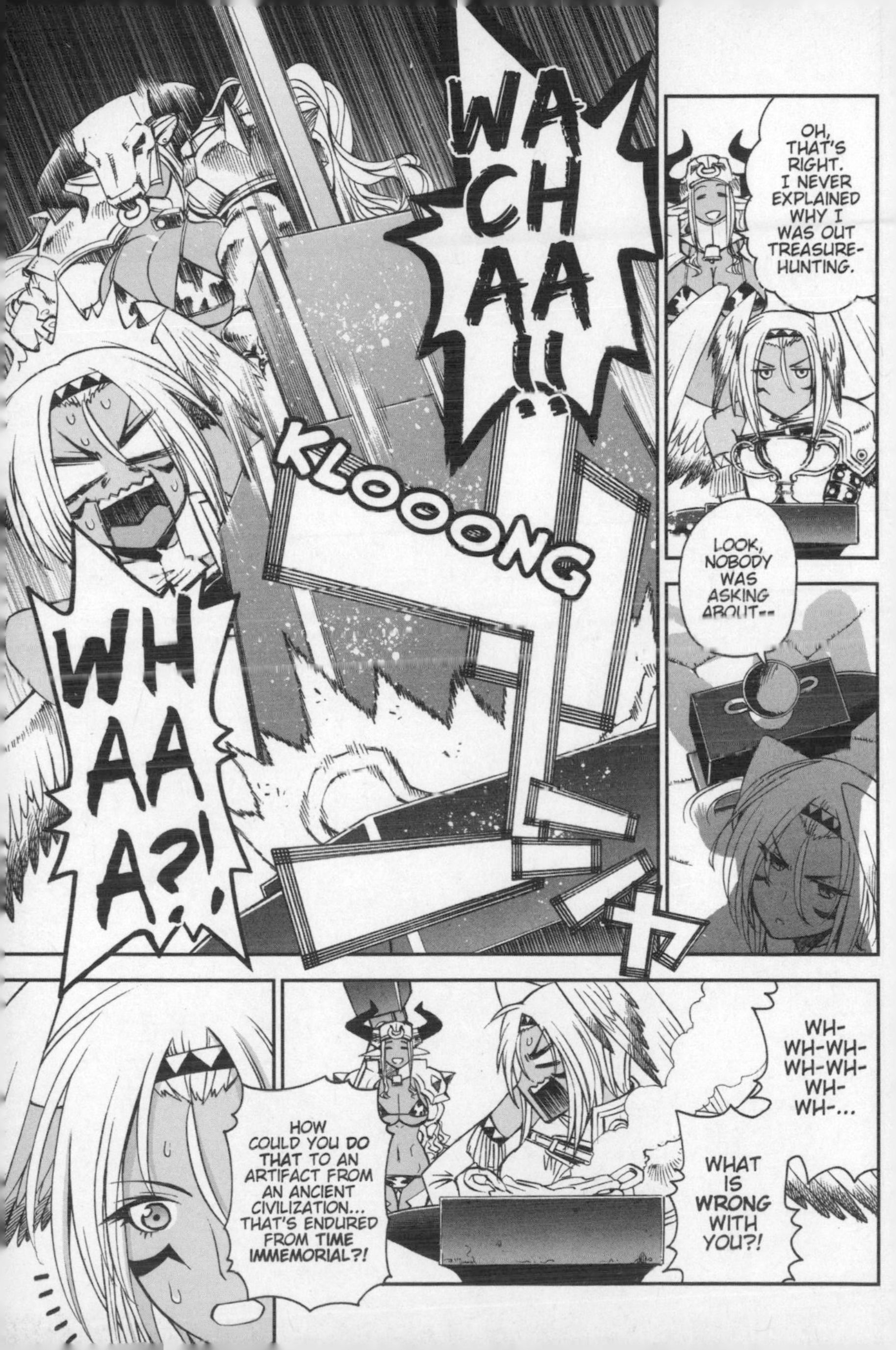
OH, THAT'S RIGHT. I NEVER EXPLAINED WHY I WAS OUT TREASURE-HUNTING.
LOOK, NOBODY WAS ASKING ABOUT--
WACHAAA!!
KLOOOONG
WHAAAA?!
WH-WH-WH-WH-WH-WH-WH-...
WHAT IS WRONG WITH YOU?!
HOW COULD YOU DO THAT TO AN ARTIFACT FROM AN ANCIENT CIVILIZATION... THAT'S ENDURED FROM TIME IMMEMORIAL?!

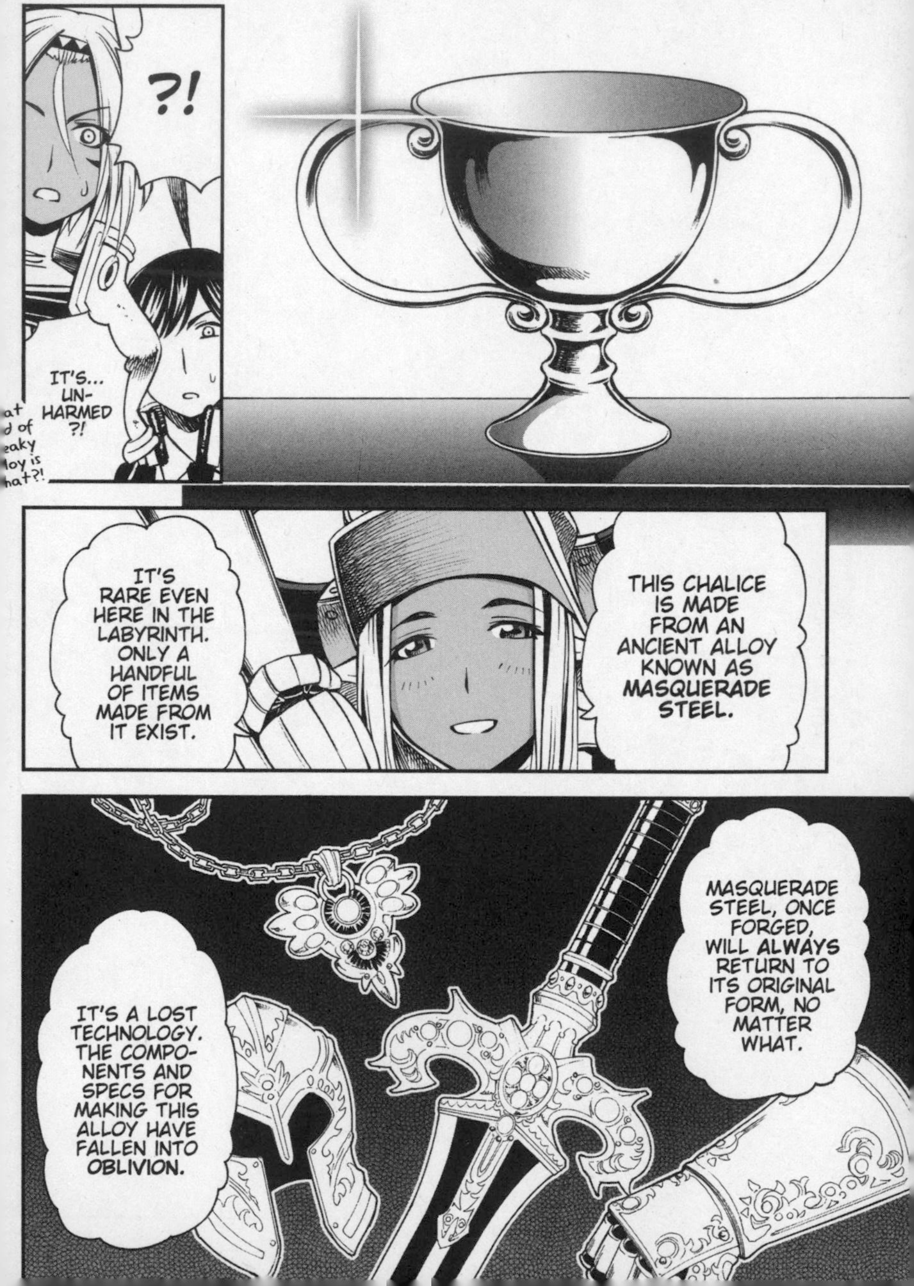
?!
IT'S... UN-HARMED ?!
THIS CHALICE IS MADE FROM AN ANCIENT ALLOY KNOWN AS MASQUERADE STEEL.
IT'S RARE EVEN HERE IN THE LABYRINTH. ONLY A HANDFUL OF ITEMS MADE FROM IT EXIST.
MASQUERADE STEEL, ONCE FORGED, WILL ALWAYS RETURN TO ITS ORIGINAL FORM, NO MATTER WHAT.
IT'S A LOST TECHNOLOGY. THE COMPO-NENTS AND SPECS FOR MAKING THIS ALLOY HAVE FALLEN INTO OBLIVION.

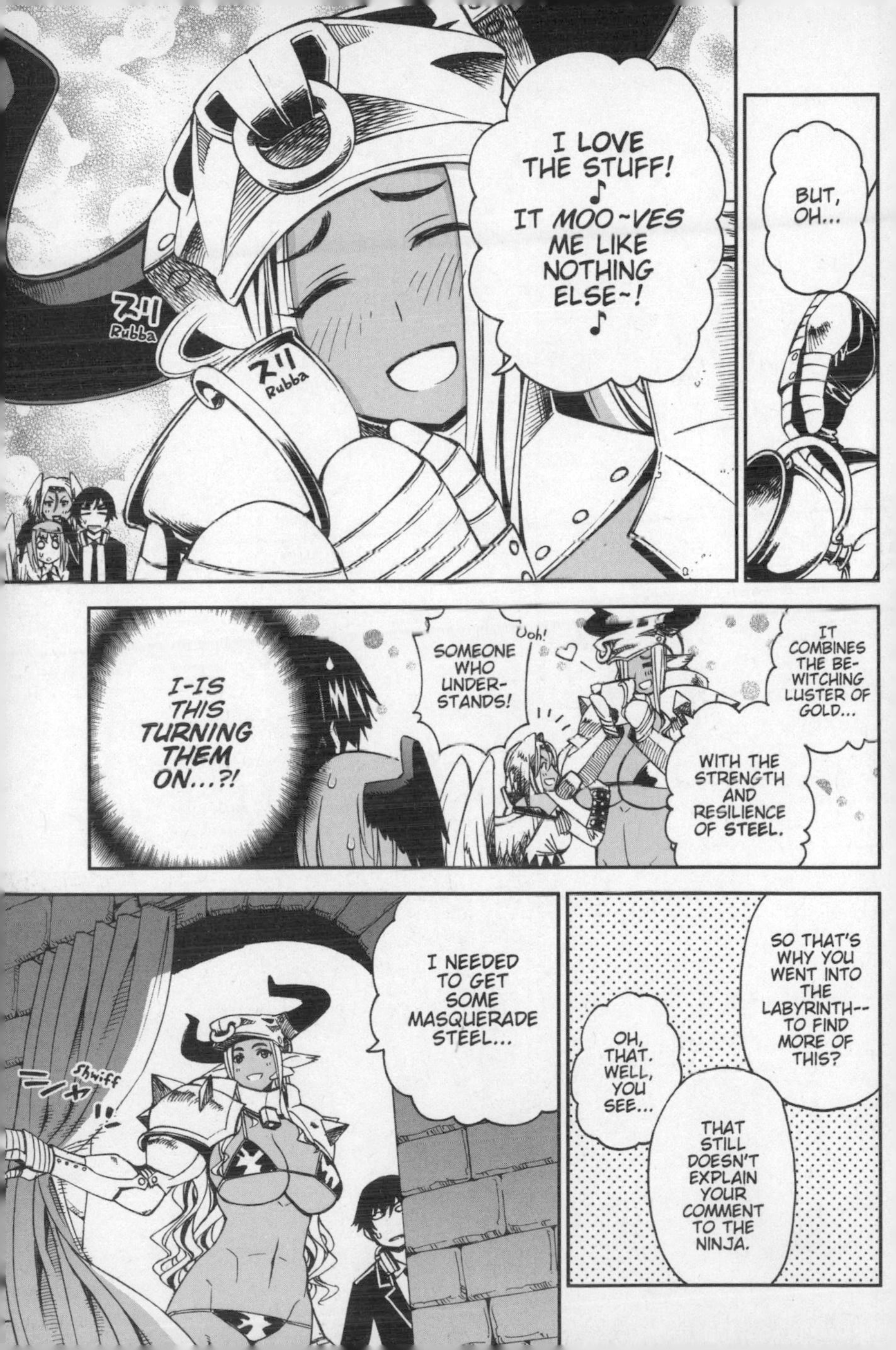
BUT, OH...
I LOVE THE STUFF! ♪ IT MOO~VES ME LIKE NOTHING ELSE~! ♪
Rubba
Rubba
IT COMBINES THE BE-WITCHING LUSTER OF GOLD...
WITH THE STRENGTH AND RESILIENCE OF STEEL.
Uoh!
SOMEONE WHO UNDER-STANDS!
I-IS THIS TURNING THEM ON...?!
SO THAT'S WHY YOU WENT INTO THE LABYRINTH-- TO FIND MORE OF THIS?
OH, THAT. WELL, YOU SEE...
THAT STILL DOESN'T EXPLAIN YOUR COMMENT TO THE NINJA.
I NEEDED TO GET SOME MASQUERADE STEEL...
Shwiff

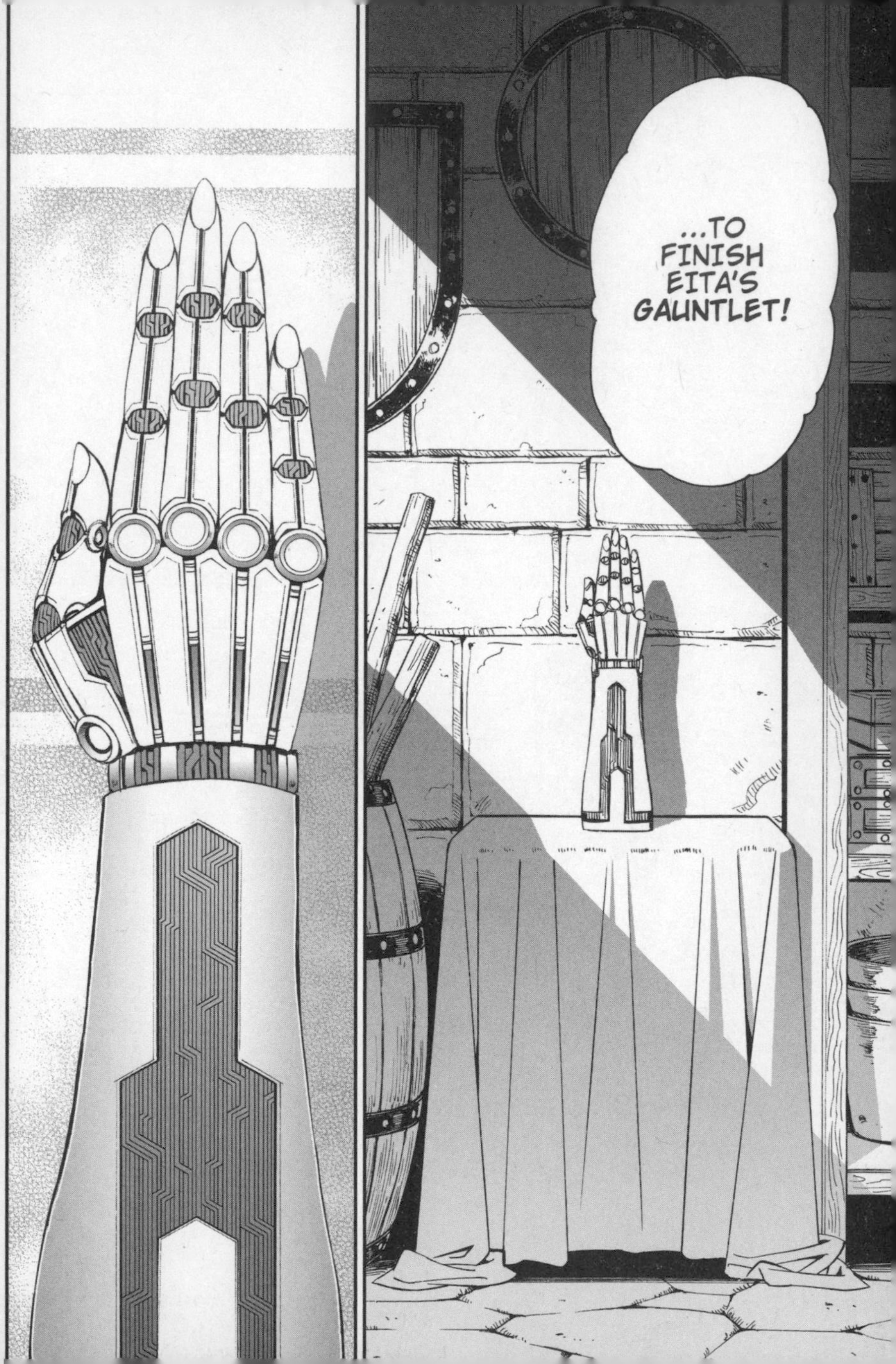
...TO FINISH EITA'S GAUNTLET!

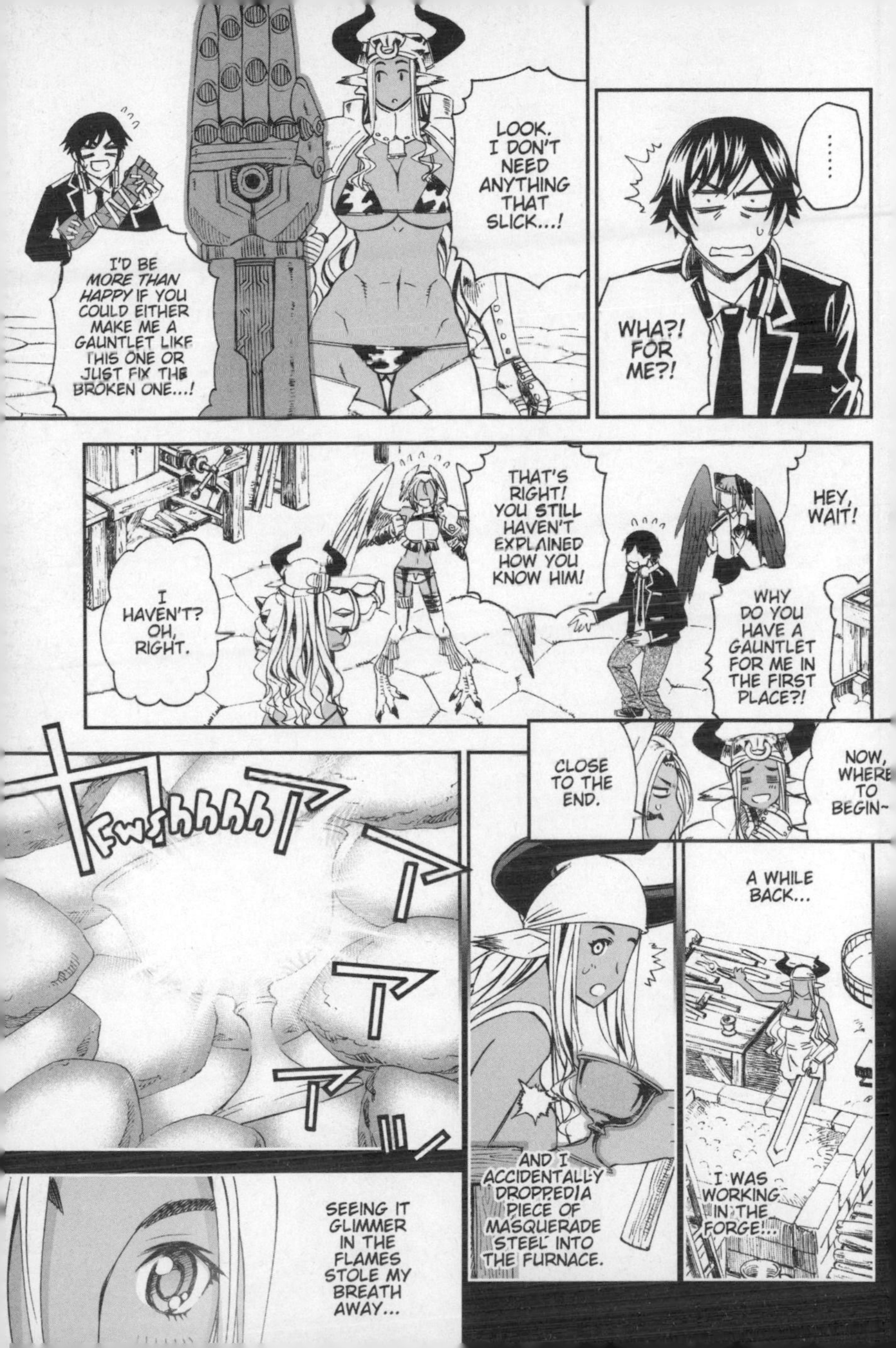
......
WHA?! FOR ME?!
LOOK. I DON'T NEED ANYTHING THAT SLICK...!
I'D BE MORE THAN HAPPY IF YOU COULD EITHER MAKE ME A GAUNTLET LIKE THIS ONE OR JUST FIX THE BROKEN ONE...!
HEY, WAIT!
WHY DO YOU HAVE A GAUNTLET FOR ME IN THE FIRST PLACE?!
THAT'S RIGHT! YOU STILL HAVEN'T EXPLAINED HOW YOU KNOW HIM!
I HAVEN'T? OH, RIGHT.
NOW, WHERE TO BEGIN~
CLOSE TO THE END.
A WHILE BACK...
I WAS WORKING IN THE FORGE!...
AND I ACCIDENTALLY DROPPED A PIECE OF MASQUERADE STEEL INTO THE FURNACE.
FWSHHHHH
SEEING IT GLIMMER IN THE FLAMES STOLE MY BREATH AWAY...

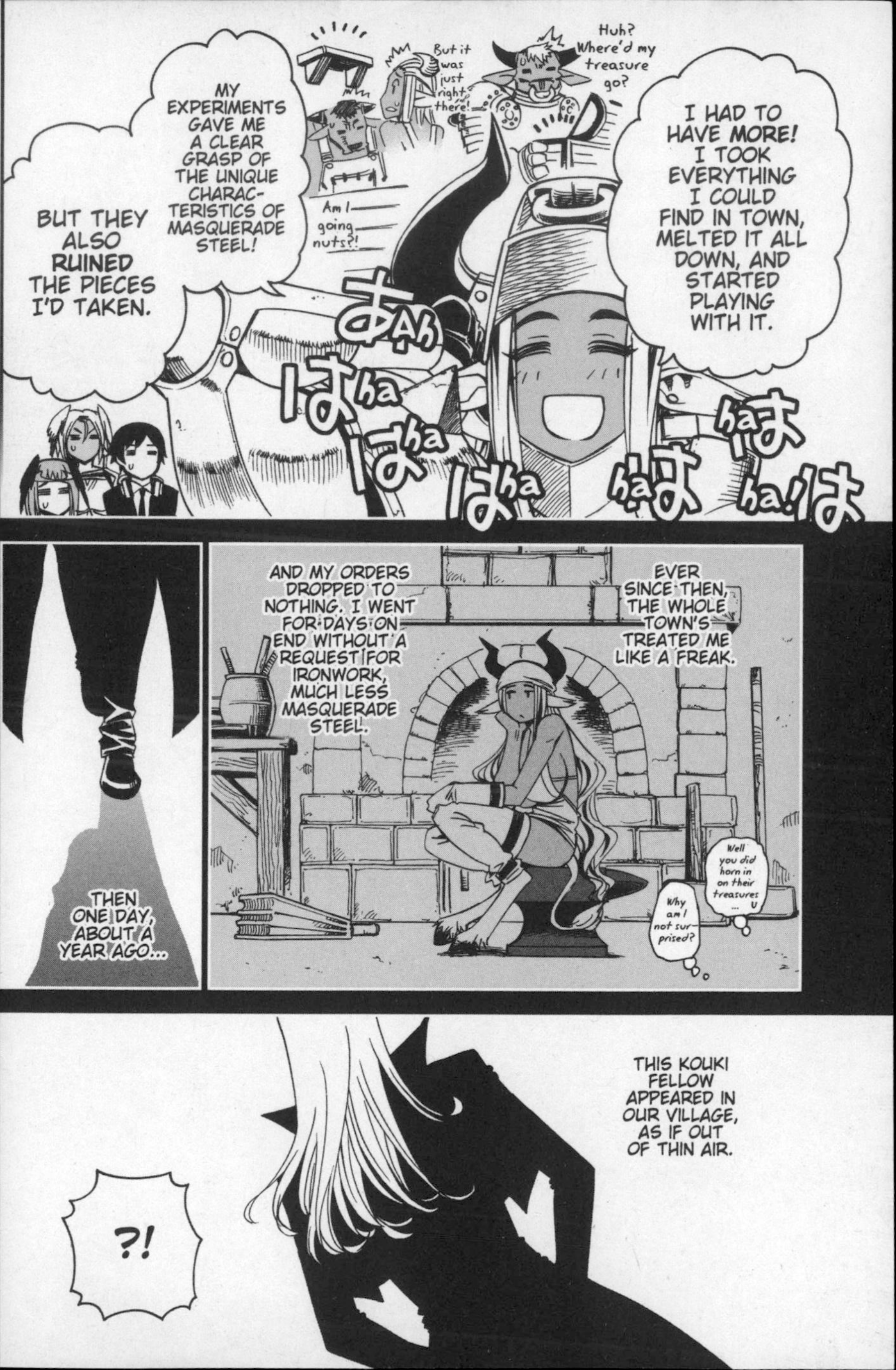
Huh? Where'd my treasure go?
I HAD TO HAVE MORE! I TOOK EVERYTHING I COULD FIND IN TOWN, MELTED IT ALL DOWN, AND STARTED PLAYING WITH IT.
But it was just right there!
MY EXPERIMENTS GAVE ME A CLEAR GRASP OF THE UNIQUE CHARAC-TERISTICS OF MASQUERADE STEEL!
Am I going nuts?!
BUT THEY ALSO RUINED THE PIECES I'D TAKEN.
あAh はha はha はha はha はha ha!は
EVER SINCE THEN, THE WHOLE TOWN'S TREATED ME LIKE A FREAK.
AND MY ORDERS DROPPED TO NOTHING. I WENT FOR DAYS ON END WITHOUT A REQUEST FOR IRONWORK, MUCH LESS MASQUERADE STEEL.
Well you did horn in on their treasures...
Why am I not sur-prised?
THEN ONE DAY, ABOUT A YEAR AGO...
THIS KOUKI FELLOW APPEARED IN OUR VILLAGE, AS IF OUT OF THIN AIR.
?!

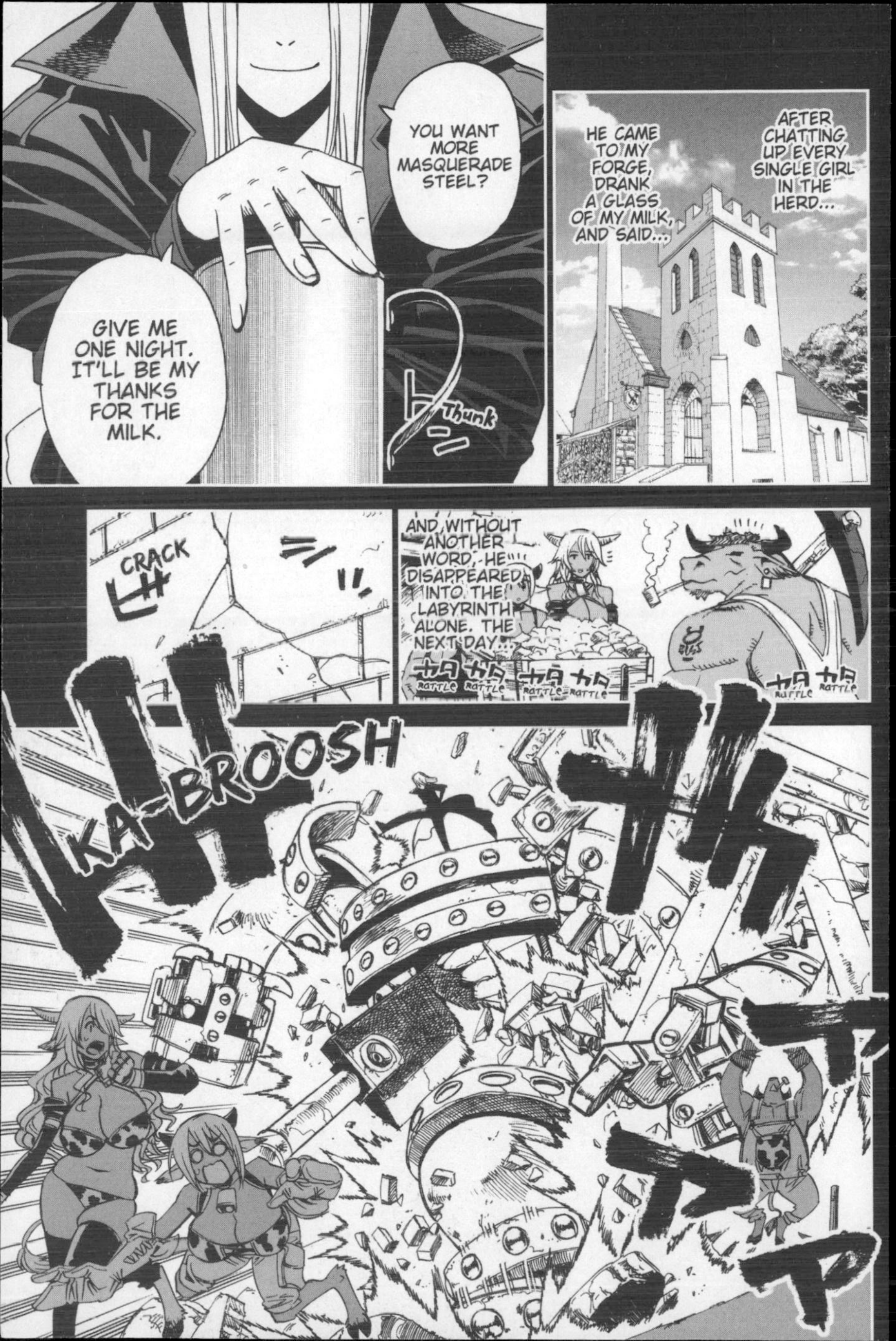
AFTER CHATTING UP EVERY SINGLE GIRL IN THE HERD...
HE CAME TO MY FORGE, DRANK A GLASS OF MY MILK, AND SAID...
YOU WANT MORE MASQUERADE STEEL?
GIVE ME ONE NIGHT. IT'LL BE MY THANKS FOR THE MILK.
Thunk
AND WITHOUT ANOTHER WORD, HE DISAPPEARED INTO THE LABYRINTH ALONE. THE NEXT DAY...
RATTLE RATTLE RATTLE RATTLE RATTLE RATTLE
CRACK
KA-BROOSH

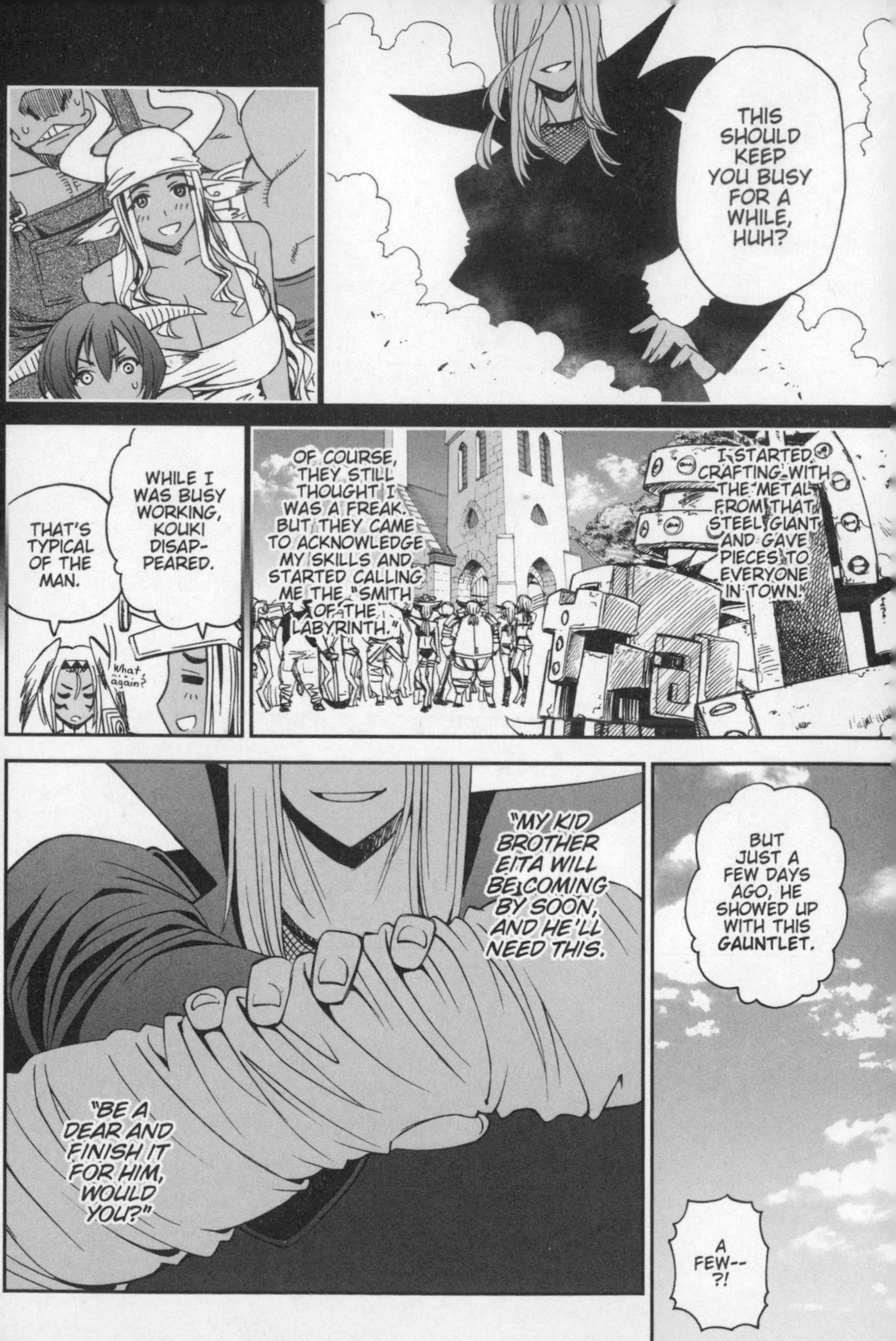

THIS SHOULD KEEP YOU BUSY FOR A WHILE, HUH?
I STARTED CRAFTING WITH THE METAL FROM THAT STEEL GIANT AND GAVE PIECES TO EVERYONE IN TOWN.
OF COURSE, THEY STILL THOUGHT I WAS A FREAK. BUT THEY CAME TO ACKNOWLEDGE MY SKILLS AND STARTED CALLING ME THE "SMITH OF THE LABYRINTH."
WHILE I WAS BUSY WORKING, KOUKI DISAPPEARED.
THAT'S TYPICAL OF THE MAN.
What, again?
BUT JUST A FEW DAYS AGO, HE SHOWED UP WITH THIS GAUNTLET.
A FEW--?!
"MY KID BROTHER EITA WILL BE COMING BY SOON, AND HE'LL NEED THIS.
"BE A DEAR AND FINISH IT FOR HIM, WOULD YOU?"

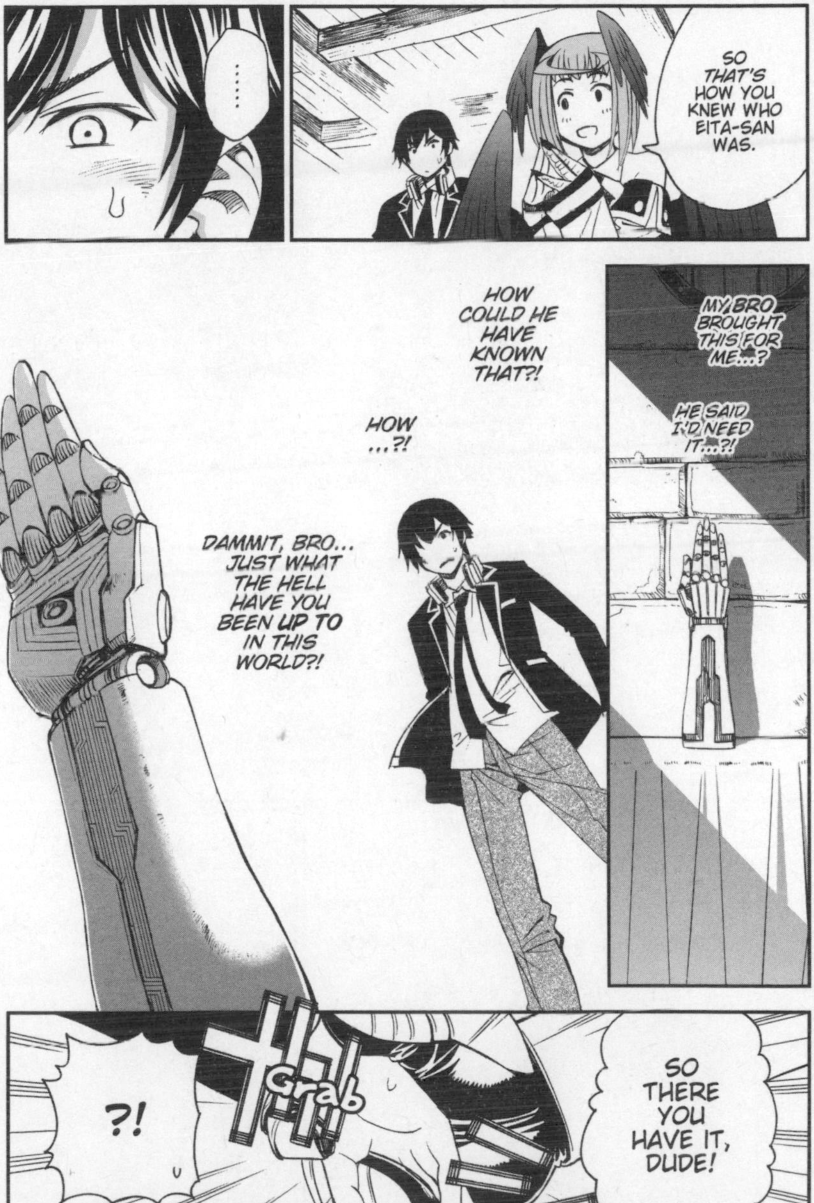
SO THAT'S HOW YOU KNEW WHO EITA-SAN WAS.
......
MY BRO BROUGHT THIS FOR ME...?
HE SAID I'D NEED IT...?!
HOW COULD HE HAVE KNOWN THAT?!
HOW ...?!
DAMMIT, BRO... JUST WHAT THE HELL HAVE YOU BEEN UP TO IN THIS WORLD?!
SO THERE YOU HAVE IT, DUDE!
Grab
?!

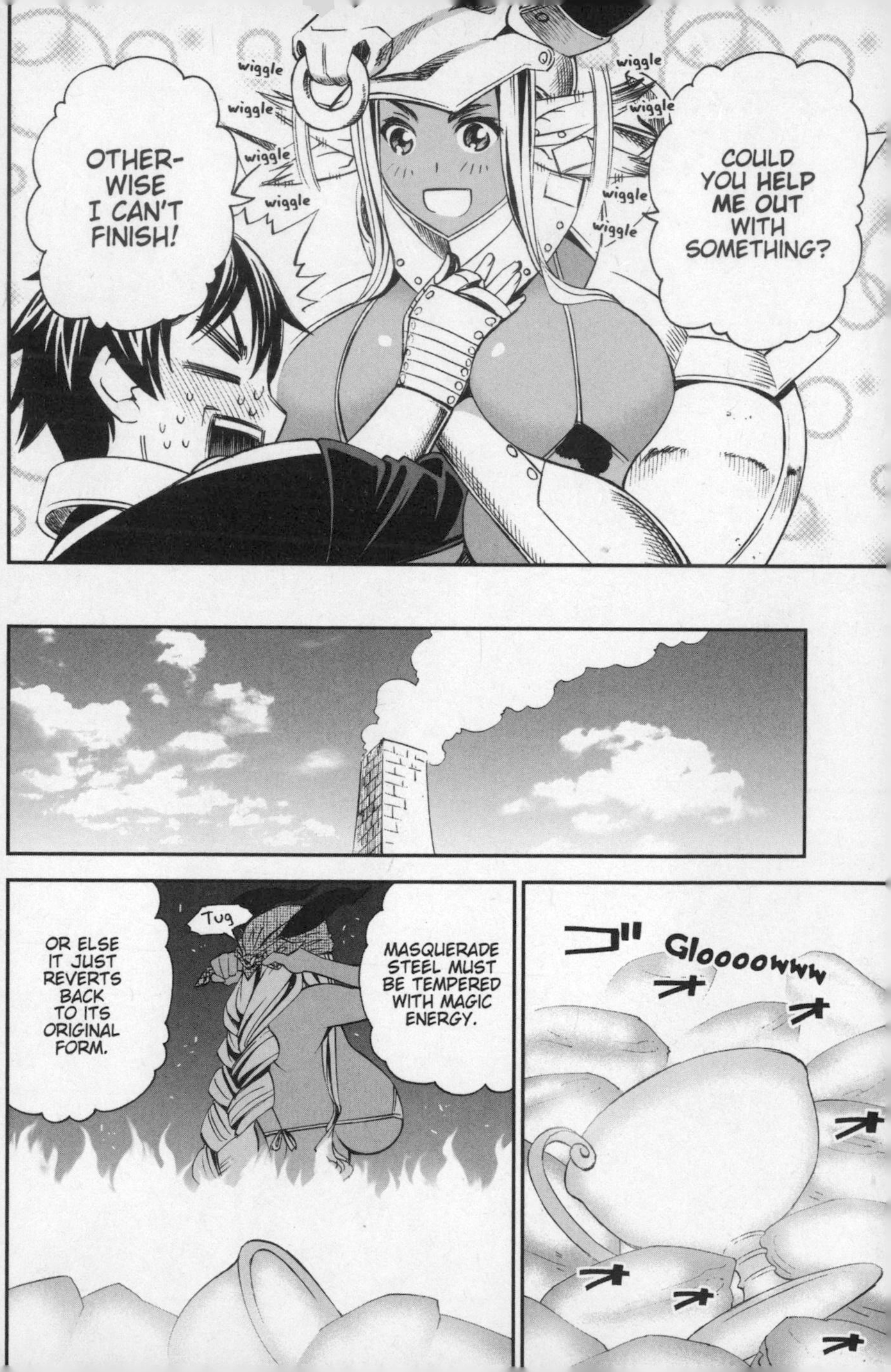
wiggle
wiggle
wiggle
COULD YOU HELP ME OUT WITH SOMETHING?
wiggle
wiggle
wiggle
wiggle
wiggle
OTHER-WISE I CAN'T FINISH!
ゴ
Gloooowww
オ
オ
オ
オ
オ
オ
MASQUERADE STEEL MUST BE TEMPERED WITH MAGIC ENERGY.
Tug
OR ELSE IT JUST REVERTS BACK TO ITS ORIGINAL FORM.

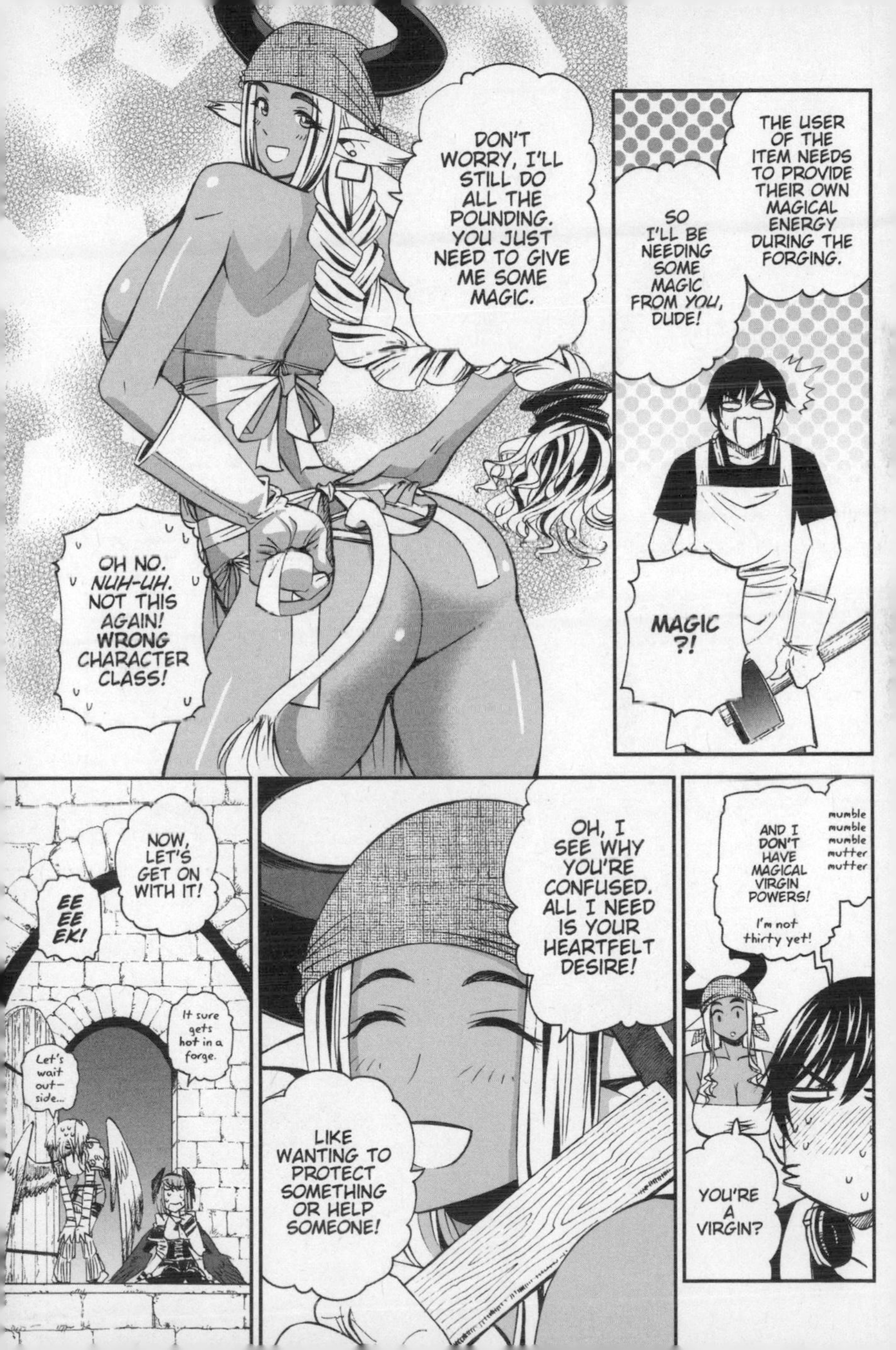
THE USER OF THE ITEM NEEDS TO PROVIDE THEIR OWN MAGICAL ENERGY DURING THE FORGING.
SO I'LL BE NEEDING SOME MAGIC FROM *YOU*, DUDE!
MAGIC?!
DON'T WORRY, I'LL STILL DO ALL THE POUNDING. YOU JUST NEED TO GIVE ME SOME MAGIC.
OH NO. *NUH-UH.* NOT THIS AGAIN! WRONG CHARACTER CLASS!
mumble mumble mumble mutter mutter
AND I DON'T HAVE MAGICAL VIRGIN POWERS!
I'm not thirty yet!
YOU'RE A VIRGIN?
OH, I SEE WHY YOU'RE CONFUSED. ALL I NEED IS YOUR HEARTFELT DESIRE!
LIKE WANTING TO PROTECT SOMETHING OR HELP SOMEONE!
NOW, LET'S GET ON WITH IT!
EE EE EK!
It sure gets hot in a forge.
Let's wait outside...

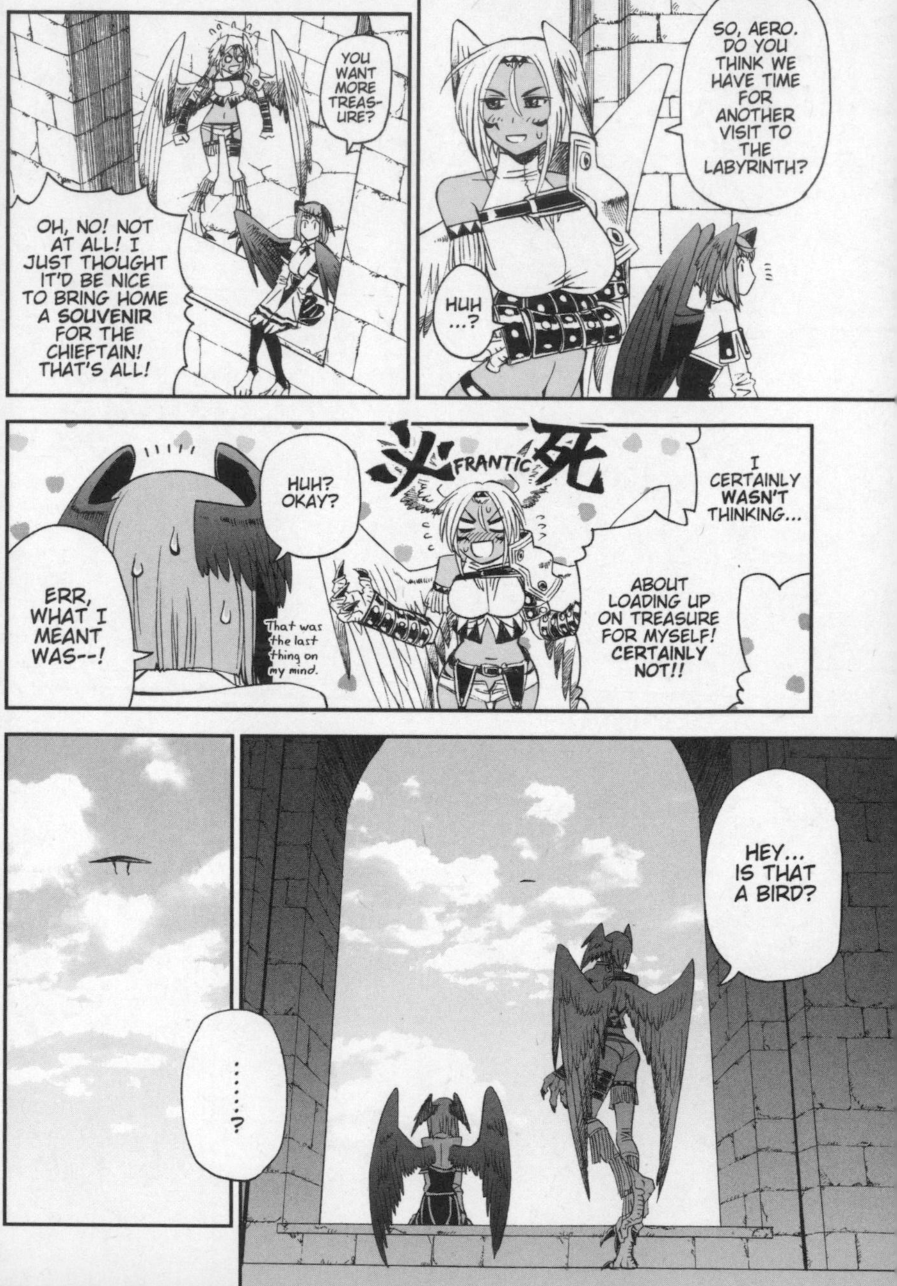
SO, AERO. DO YOU THINK WE HAVE TIME FOR ANOTHER VISIT TO THE LABYRINTH?
HUH ...?
YOU WANT MORE TREASURE?
OH, NO! NOT AT ALL! I JUST THOUGHT IT'D BE NICE TO BRING HOME A SOUVENIR FOR THE CHIEFTAIN! THAT'S ALL!
I CERTAINLY WASN'T THINKING...
ABOUT LOADING UP ON TREASURE FOR MYSELF! CERTAINLY NOT!!
FRANTIC
HUH? OKAY?
That was the last thing on my mind.
ERR, WHAT I MEANT WAS--!
HEY... IS THAT A BIRD?
......?

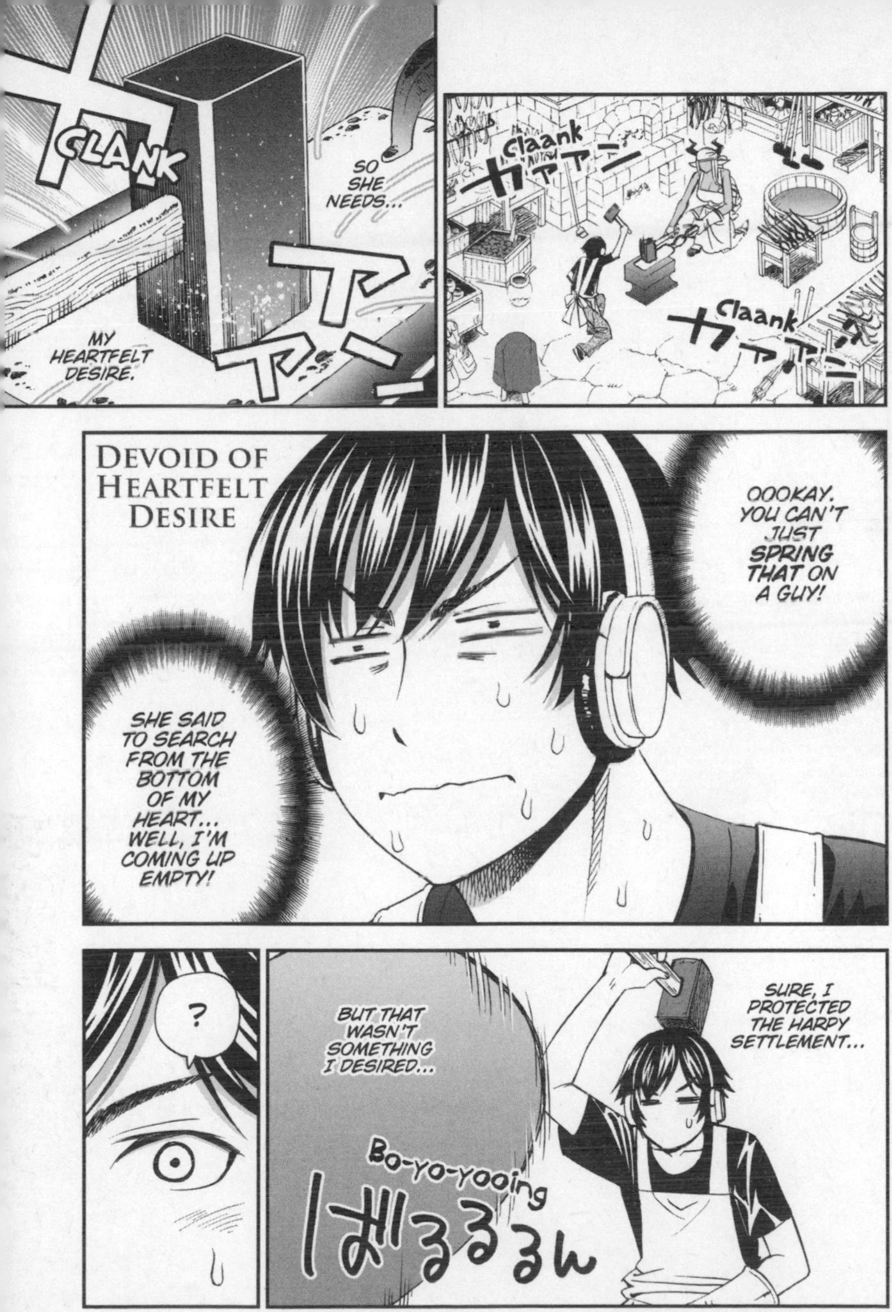
Claank
Claaank
CLANK
SO SHE NEEDS...
MY HEARTFELT DESIRE.
Devoid of Heartfelt Desire
OOOKAY. YOU CAN'T JUST SPRING THAT ON A GUY!
SHE SAID TO SEARCH FROM THE BOTTOM OF MY HEART... WELL, I'M COMING UP EMPTY!
SURE, I PROTECTED THE HARPY SETTLEMENT...
BUT THAT WASN'T SOMETHING I DESIRED...
Bo-yo-yooing
?

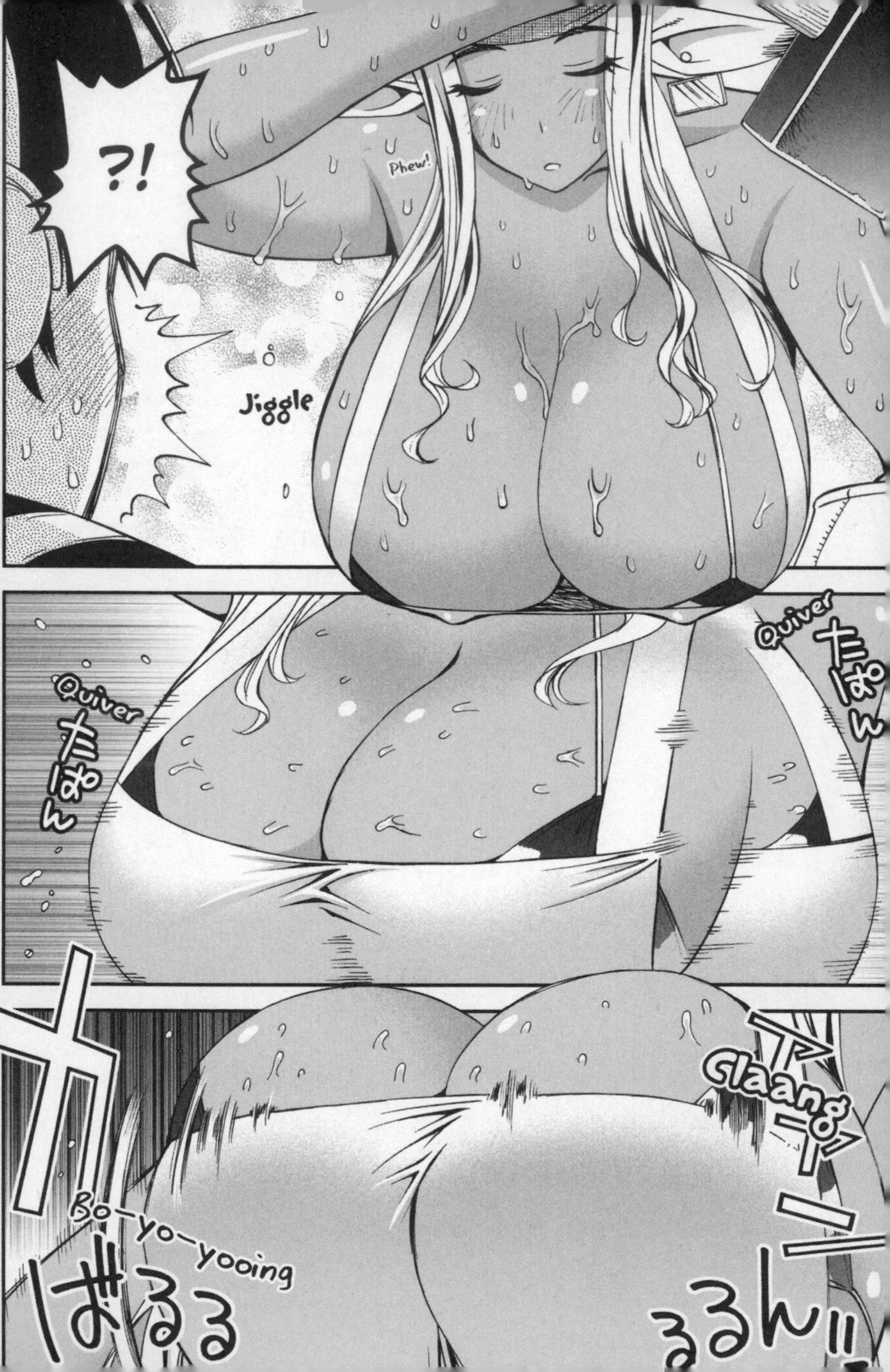
Phew!
?!
Jiggle
Quiver
たぽん
Quiver
たぽん
Claaang
るるん!!
Bo-yo-yooing
ぼるる

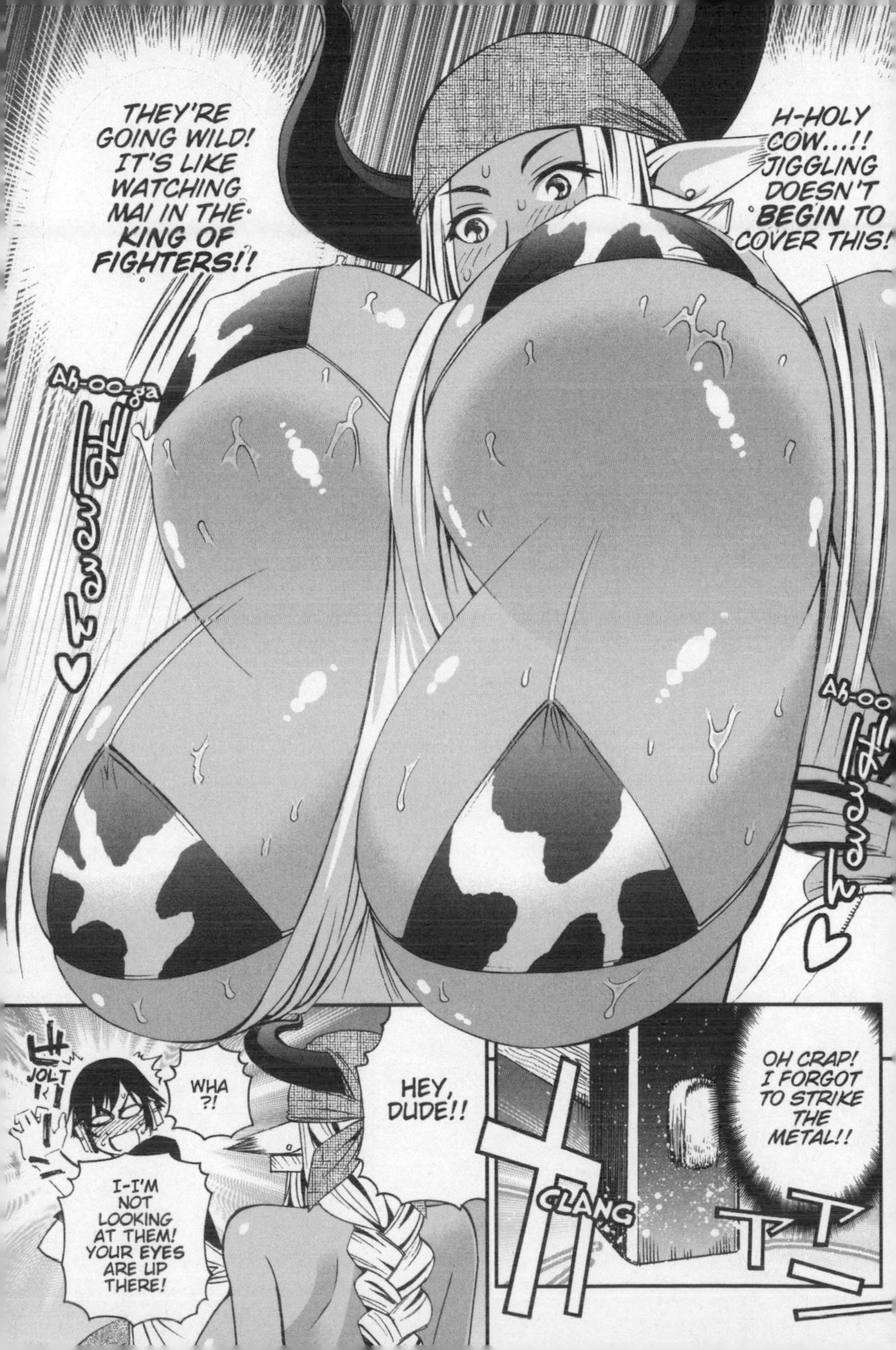
H-HOLY COW...!! JIGGLING DOESN'T BEGIN TO COVER THIS!
Ah-oo
THEY'RE GOING WILD! IT'S LIKE WATCHING MAI IN THE KING OF FIGHTERS!!
Ah-oo-ga
OH CRAP! I FORGOT TO STRIKE THE METAL!!
CLANG
HEY, DUDE!!
WHA ?!
JOLT
I-I'M NOT LOOKING AT THEM! YOUR EYES ARE UP THERE!

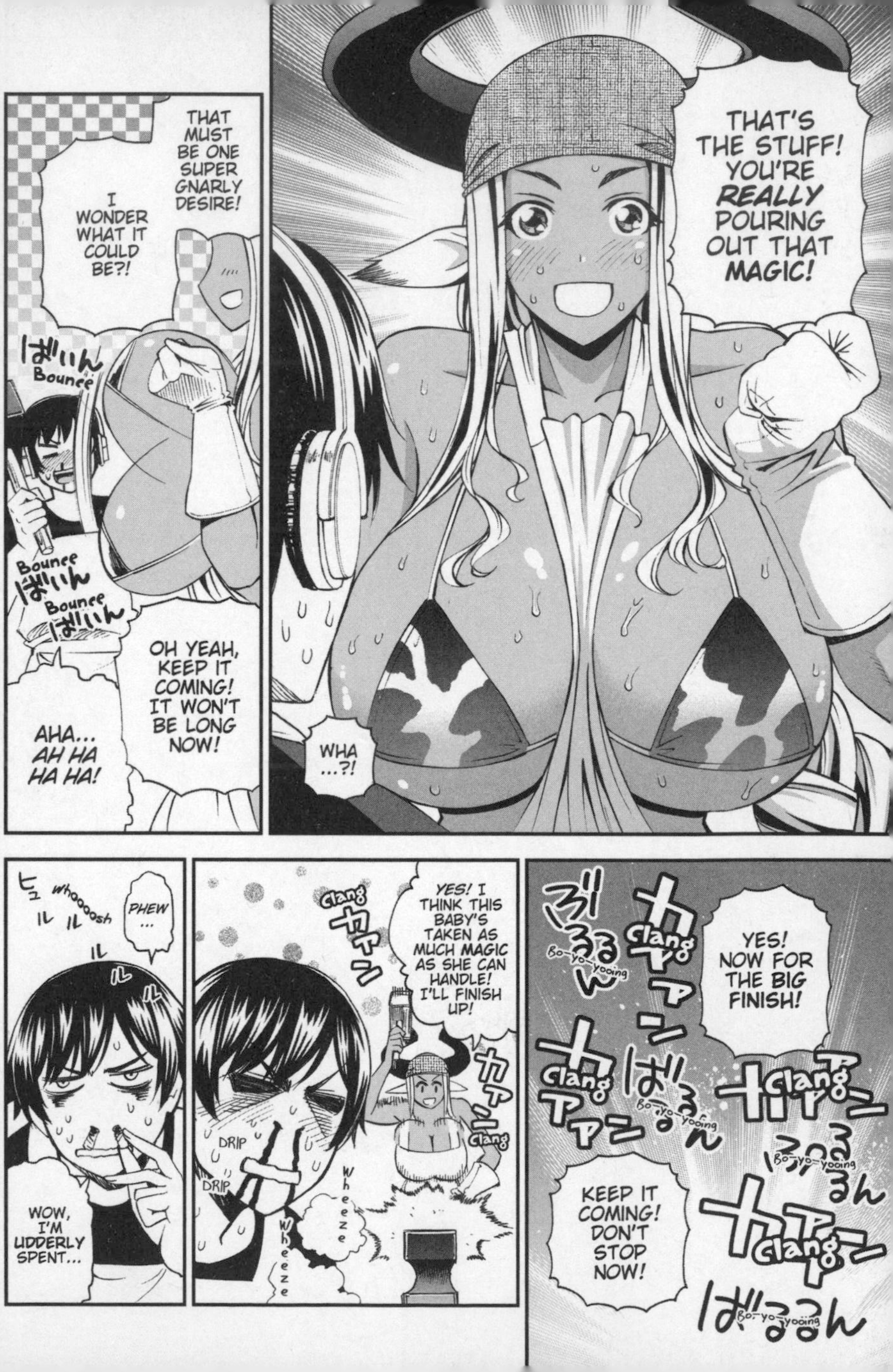
THAT'S THE STUFF! YOU'RE REALLY POURING OUT THAT MAGIC!
WHA ...?!
THAT MUST BE ONE SUPER GNARLY DESIRE!
I WONDER WHAT IT COULD BE?!
ばいん Bounce
Bounce ばいん
Bounce ばいん
OH YEAH, KEEP IT COMING! IT WON'T BE LONG NOW!
AHA... AH HA HA HA!
ぼるるん Bo-yo-yooing
カァン Clang
YES! NOW FOR THE BIG FINISH!
カァン Clang
ばるるん Bo-yo-yooing
カァン Clang
ぼるるん Bo-yo-yooing
KEEP IT COMING! DON'T STOP NOW!
カァン Clang
ばるるん Bo-yo-yooing
YES! I THINK THIS BABY'S TAKEN AS MUCH MAGIC AS SHE CAN HANDLE! I'LL FINISH UP!
Clang カァン
カァン Clang
DRIP
DRIP
Wheeze
Wheeze
ヒュルルル Whoooosh
PHEW ...
WOW, I'M UDDERLY SPENT...

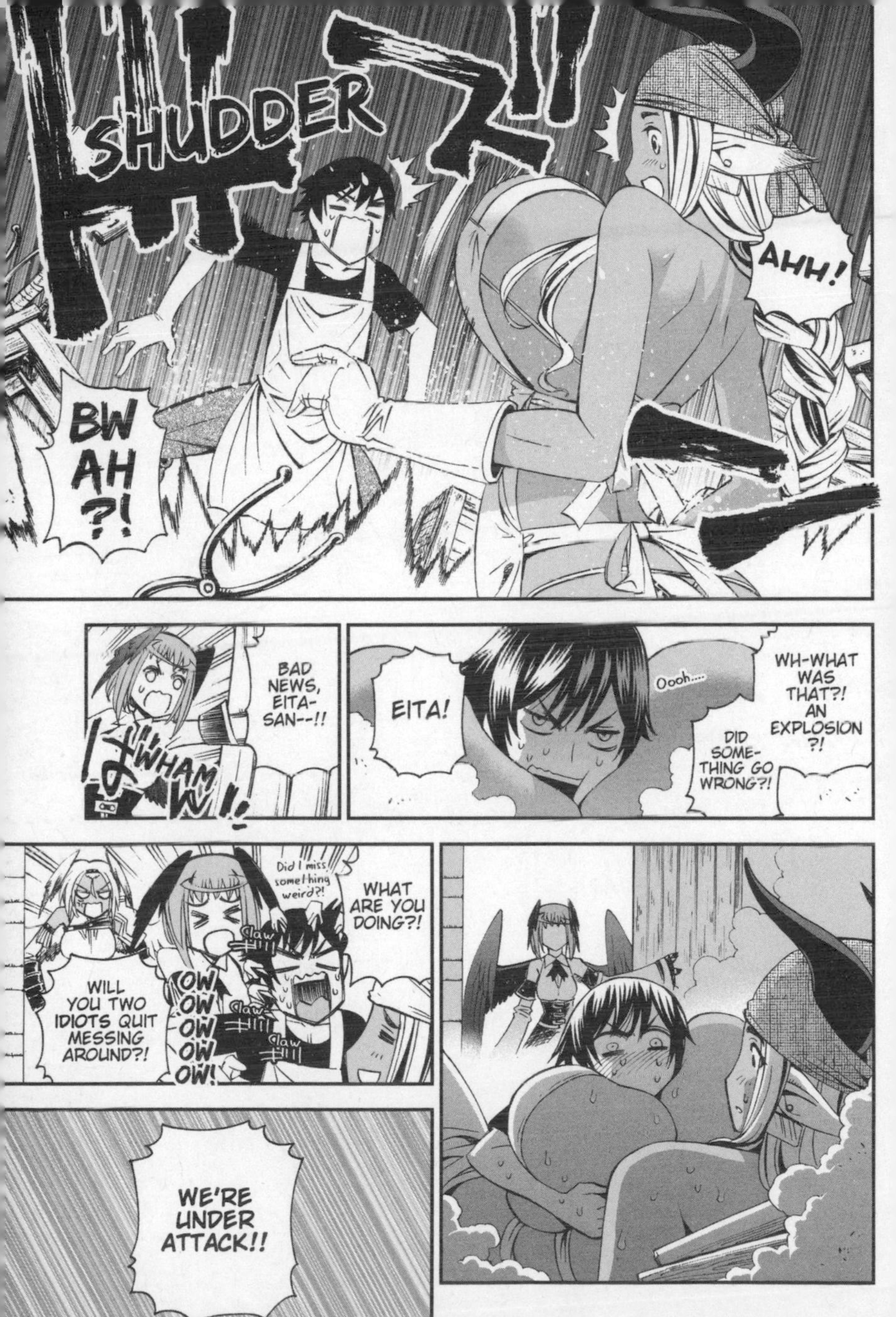
SHUDDER
AHH!
BWAH?!
WH-WHAT WAS THAT?! AN EXPLOSION?!
DID SOMETHING GO WRONG?!
Oooh....
EITA!
BAD NEWS, EITA-SAN--!!
WHAM
WHAT ARE YOU DOING?!
Did I miss something weird?!
claw
OW OW OW OW OW!
claw
claw
WILL YOU TWO IDIOTS QUIT MESSING AROUND?!
WE'RE UNDER ATTACK!!

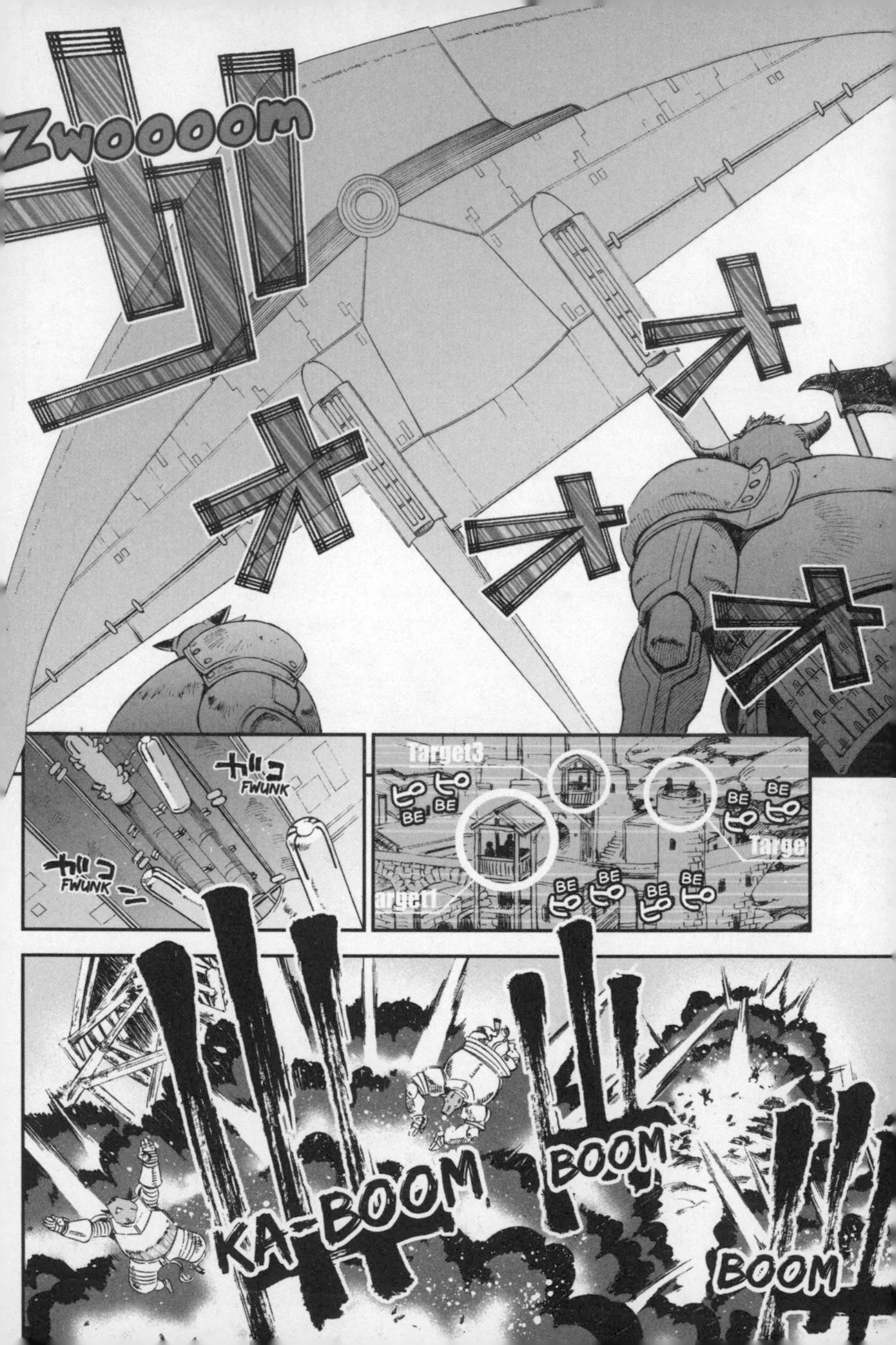
Zwoooom
Target3
ピ ピ
BE BE
BE BE
ピ ピ
Targe
arget1
BE BE
ピ ピ
BE BE
ピ ピ
FWUNK
FWUNK
KA-BOOM
BOOM
BOOM

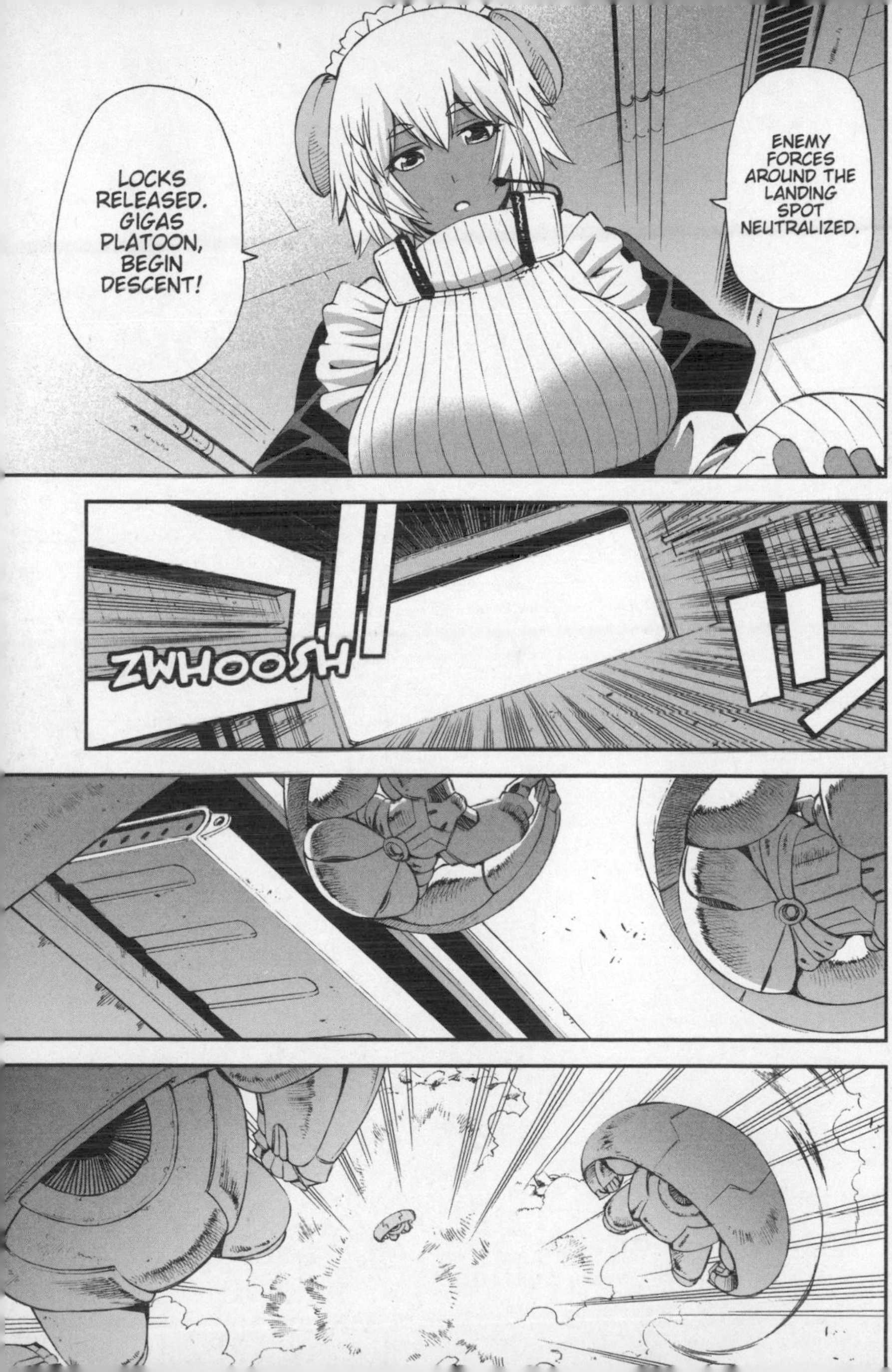
ENEMY FORCES AROUND THE LANDING SPOT NEUTRALIZED.
LOCKS RELEASED. GIGAS PLATOON, BEGIN DESCENT!
ZWHOOSH

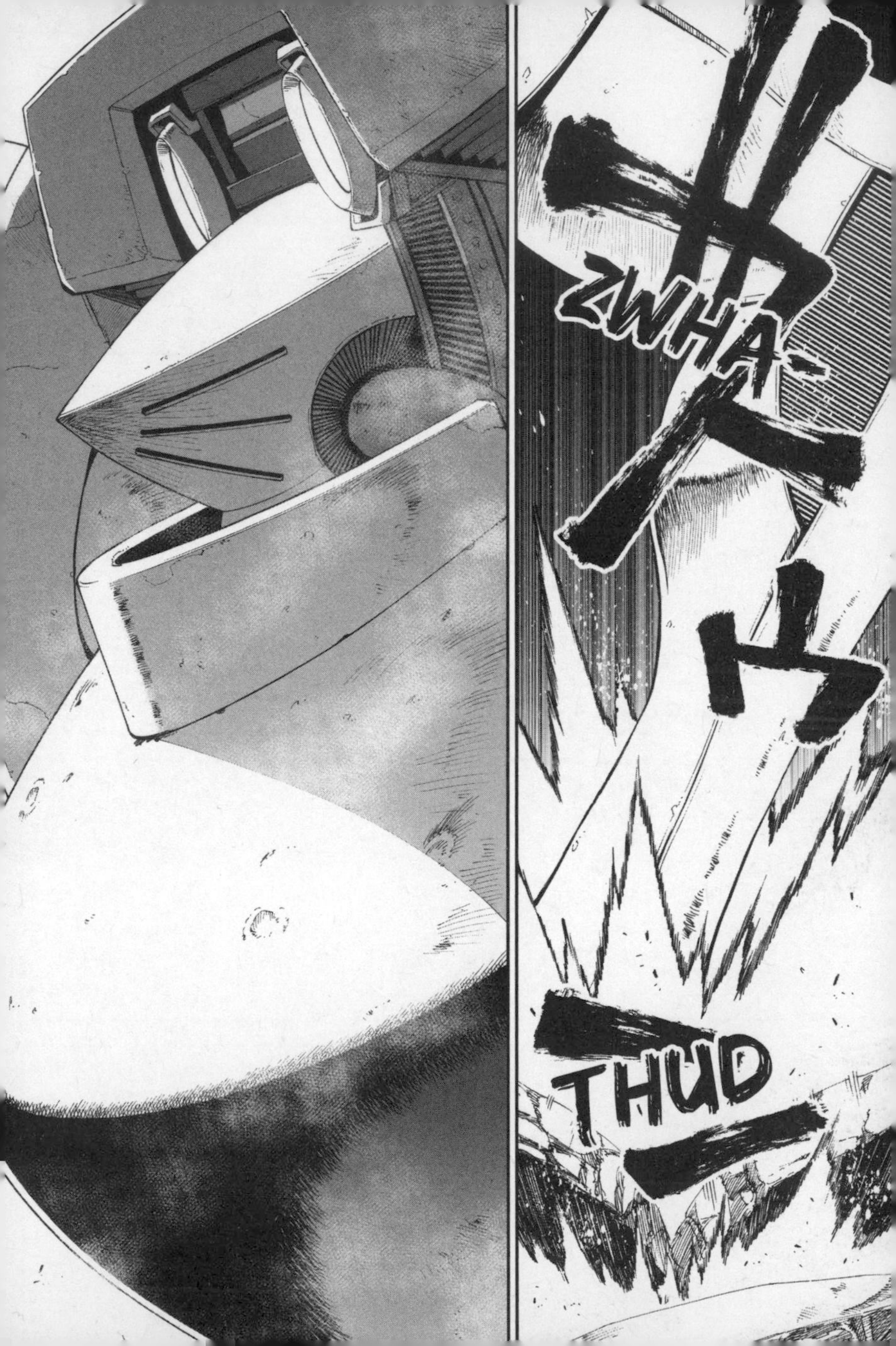
ZWHA-
THUD

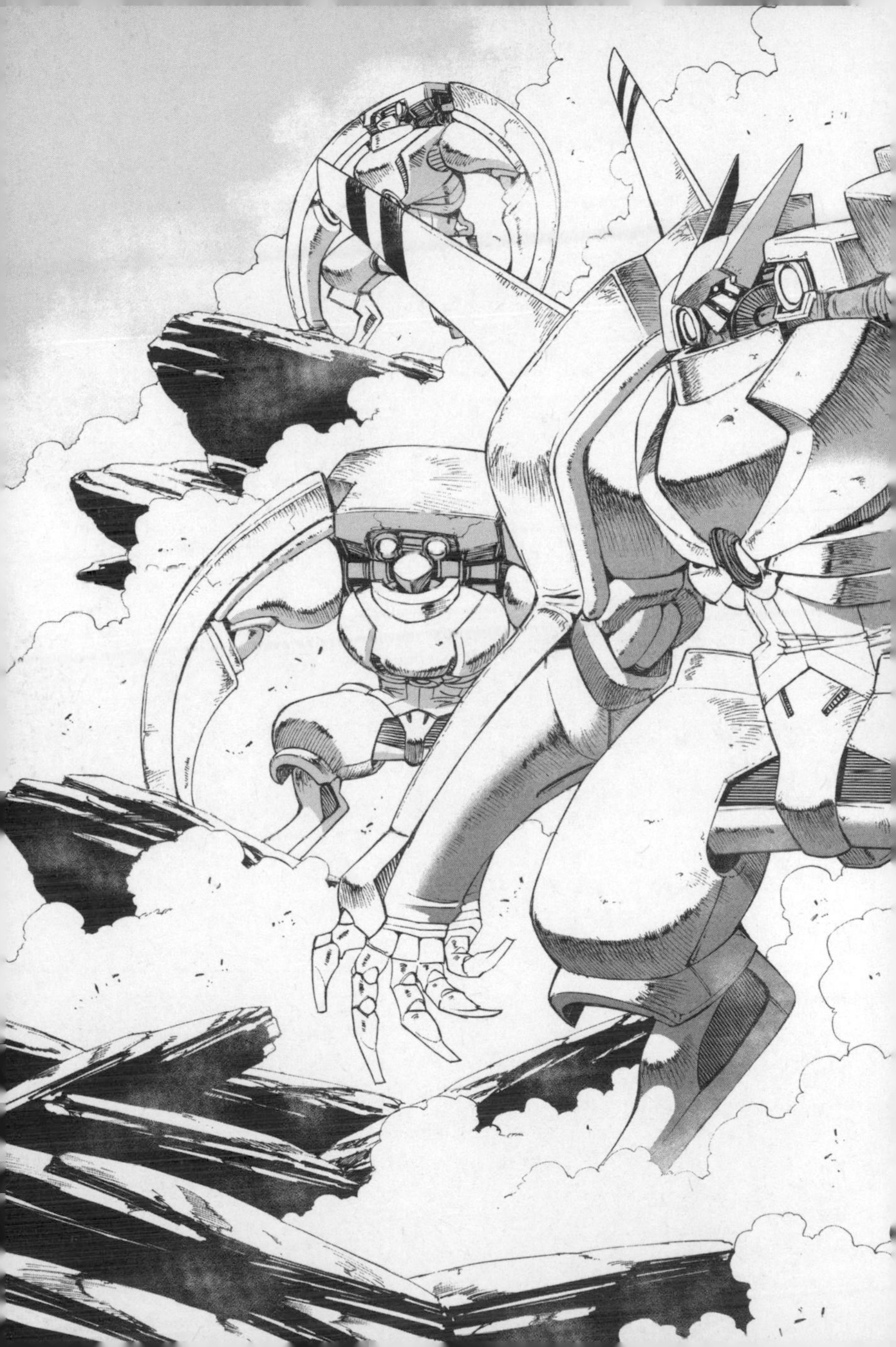

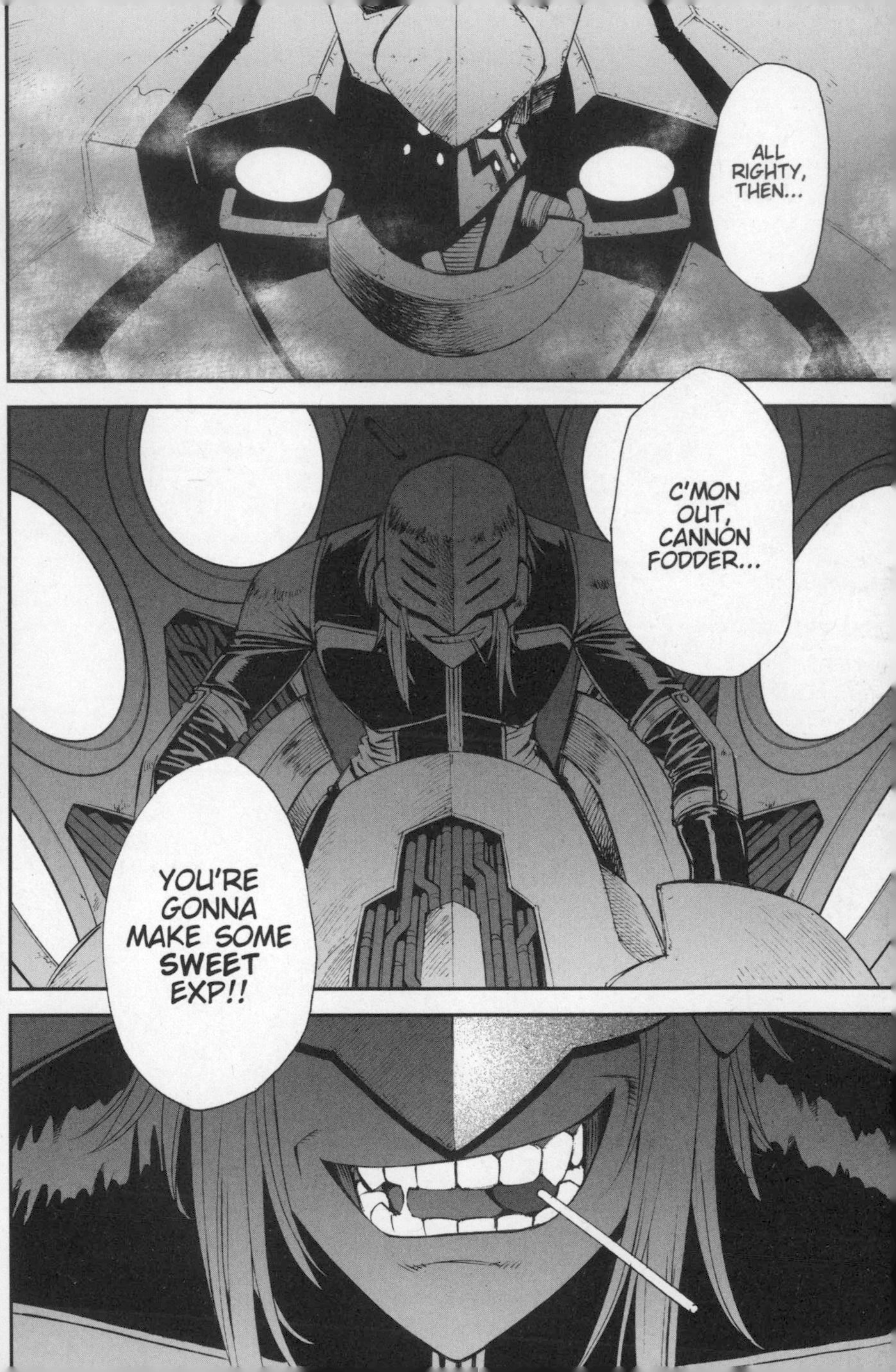
ALL RIGHTY, THEN...
C'MON OUT, CANNON FODDER...
YOU'RE GONNA MAKE SOME SWEET EXP!!

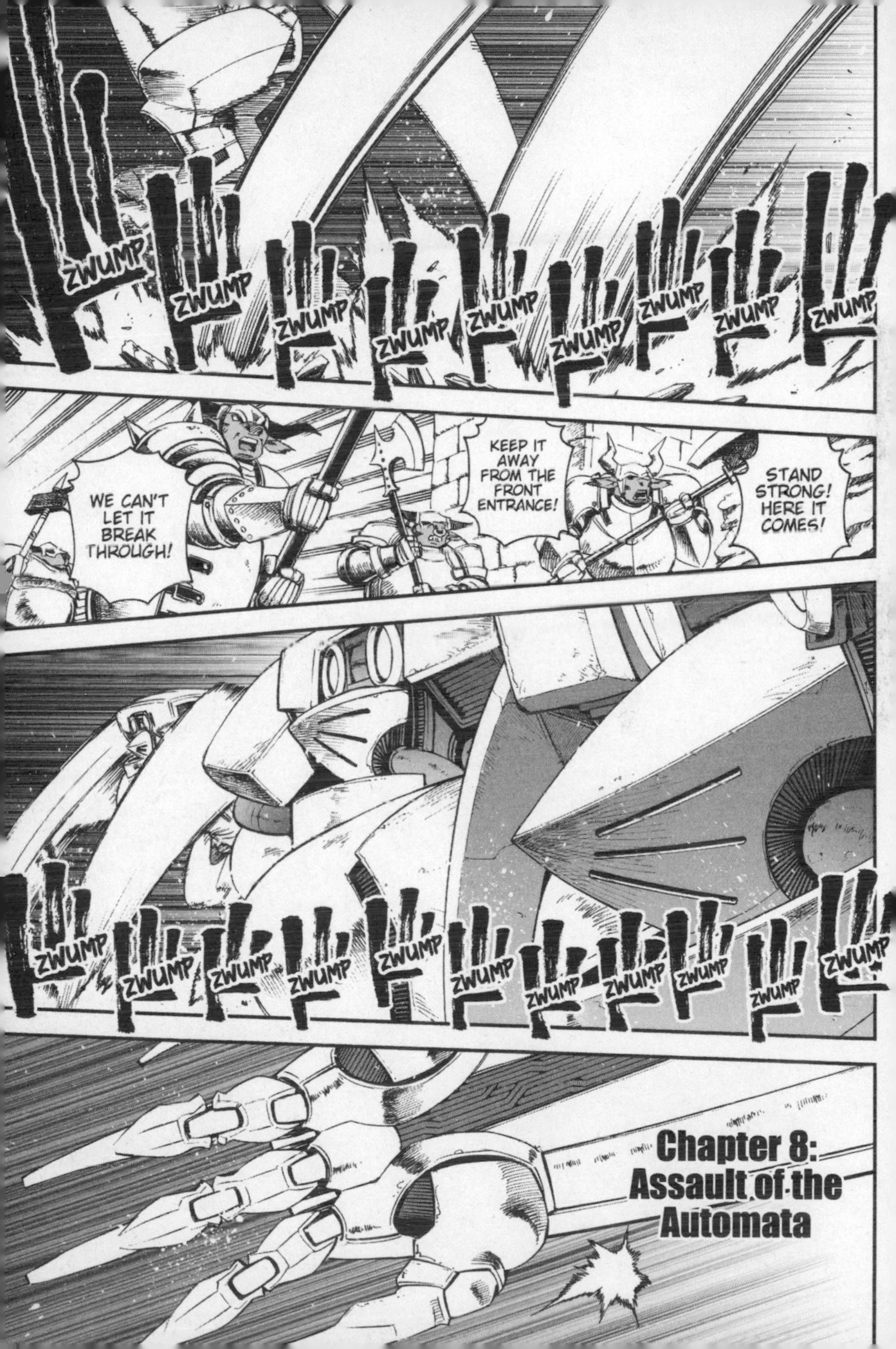
ZWUMP
ZWUMP
ZWUMP
ZWUMP
ZWUMP
ZWUMP
ZWUMP
ZWUMP
ZWUMP
STAND STRONG! HERE IT COMES!
KEEP IT AWAY FROM THE FRONT ENTRANCE!
WE CAN'T LET IT BREAK THROUGH!
ZWUMP
ZWUMP
ZWUMP
ZWUMP
ZWUMP
ZWUMP
ZWUMP
ZWUMP
ZWUMP
ZWUMP
ZWUMP
Chapter 8: Assault of the Automata

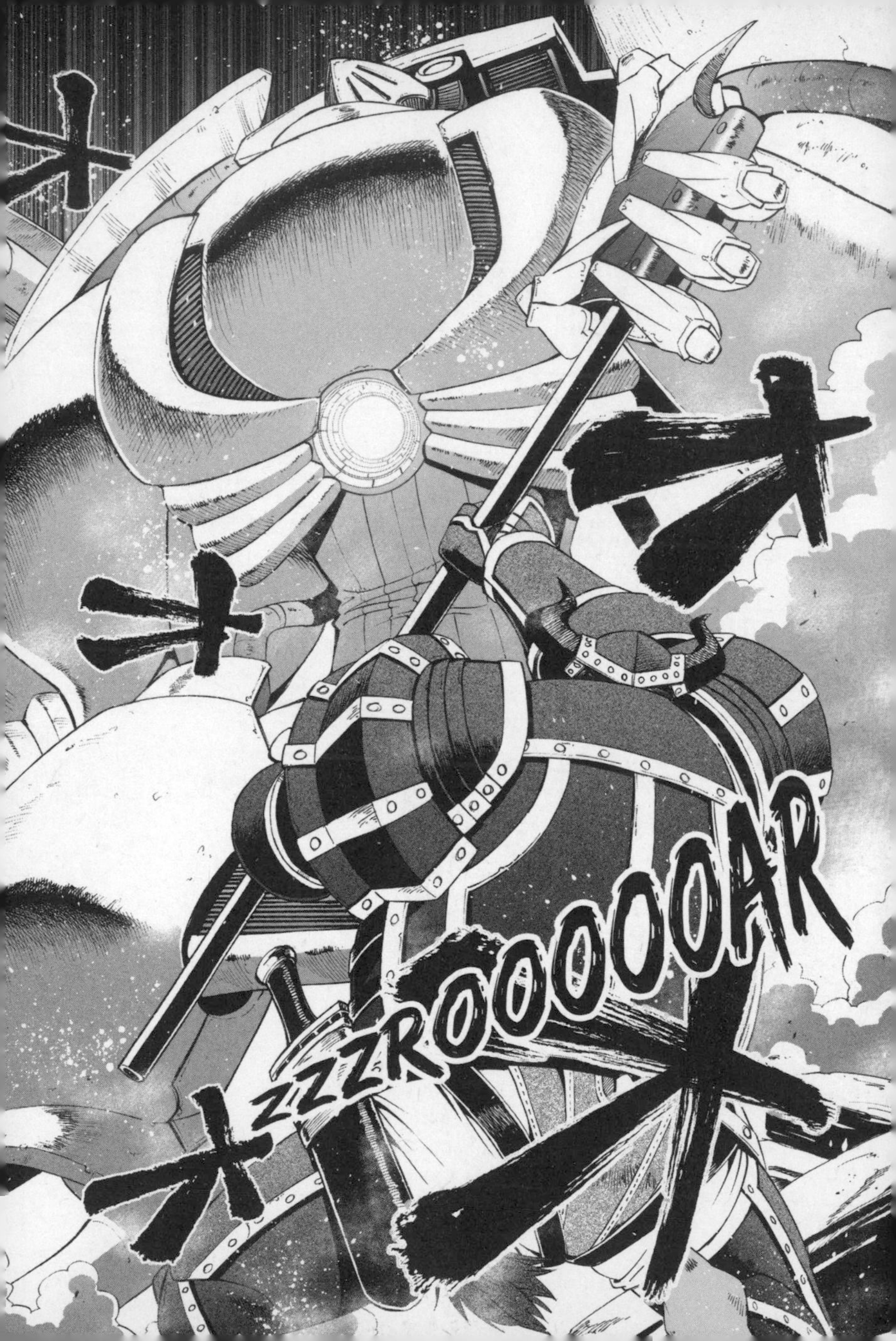
ZZZROOOOOOAR

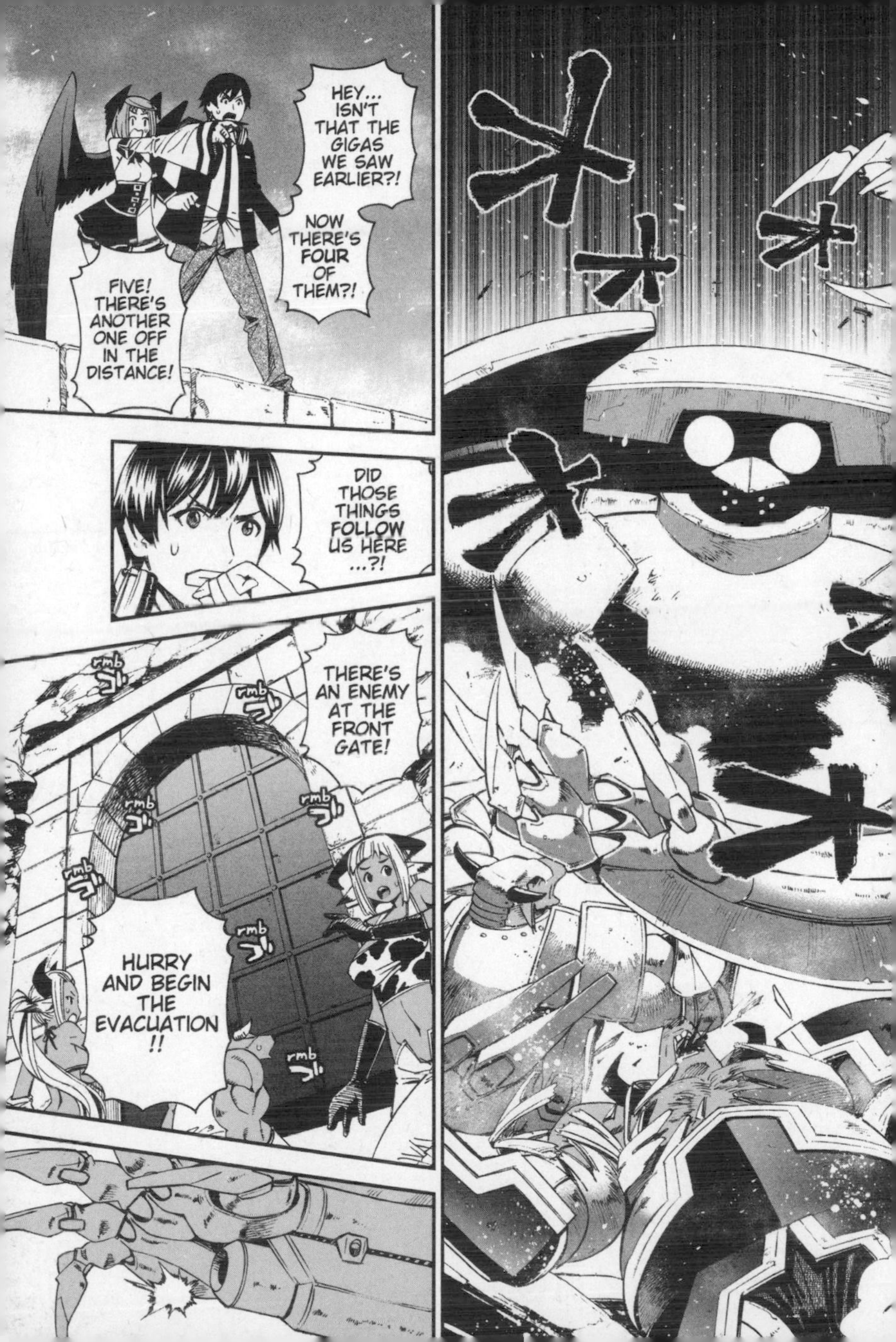

HEY... ISN'T THAT THE GIGAS WE SAW EARLIER?!
NOW THERE'S FOUR OF THEM?!
FIVE! THERE'S ANOTHER ONE OFF IN THE DISTANCE!
DID THOSE THINGS FOLLOW US HERE ...?!
THERE'S AN ENEMY AT THE FRONT GATE!
rmb
rmb
rmb
rmb
rmb
rmb
rmb
HURRY AND BEGIN THE EVACUATION !!

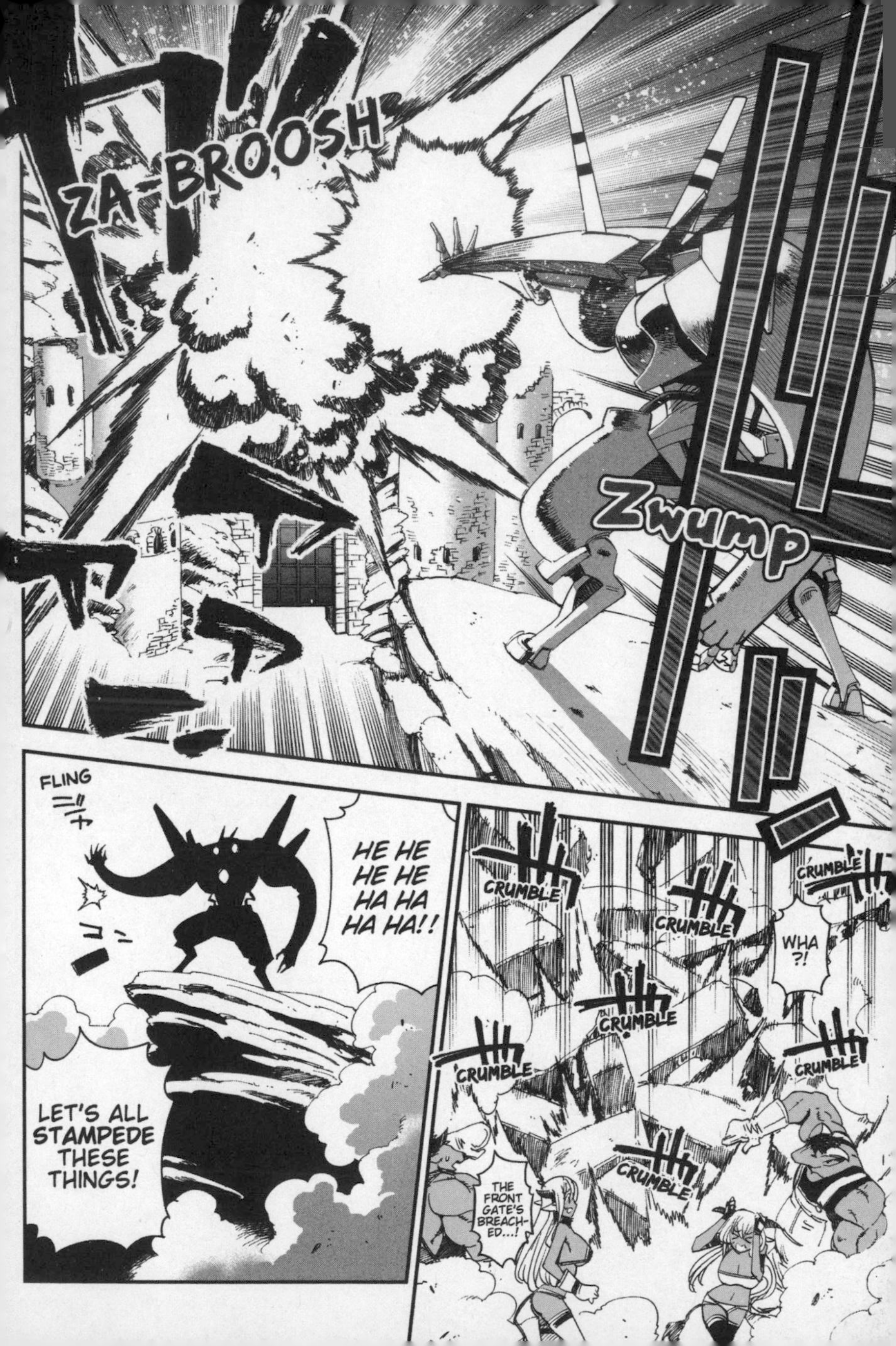
ZA-BROOSH
Zwump
CRUMBLE
CRUMBLE
CRUMBLE
WHA ?!
CRUMBLE
CRUMBLE
CRUMBLE
CRUMBLE
THE FRONT GATE'S BREACHED...!
FLING
HE HE HE HE HA HA HA HA!!
LET'S ALL STAMPEDE THESE THINGS!

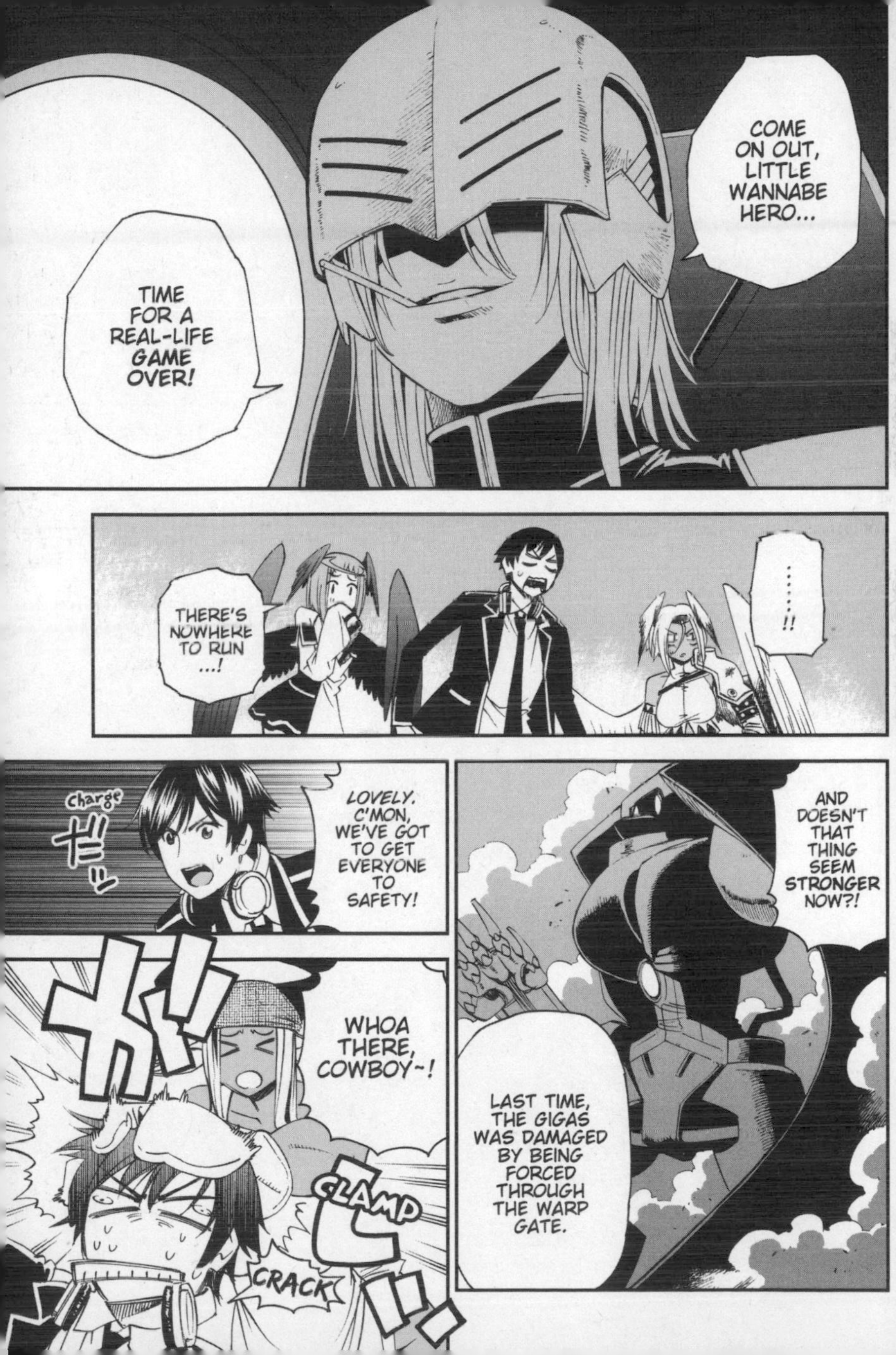
COME ON OUT, LITTLE WANNABE HERO...
TIME FOR A REAL-LIFE GAME OVER!
......!!
THERE'S NOWHERE TO RUN ...!
AND DOESN'T THAT THING SEEM STRONGER NOW?!
LAST TIME, THE GIGAS WAS DAMAGED BY BEING FORCED THROUGH THE WARP GATE.
LOVELY. C'MON, WE'VE GOT TO GET EVERYONE TO SAFETY!
Charge
ダッ
WHOA THERE, COWBOY~!
ガッ
CLAMP
CRACK

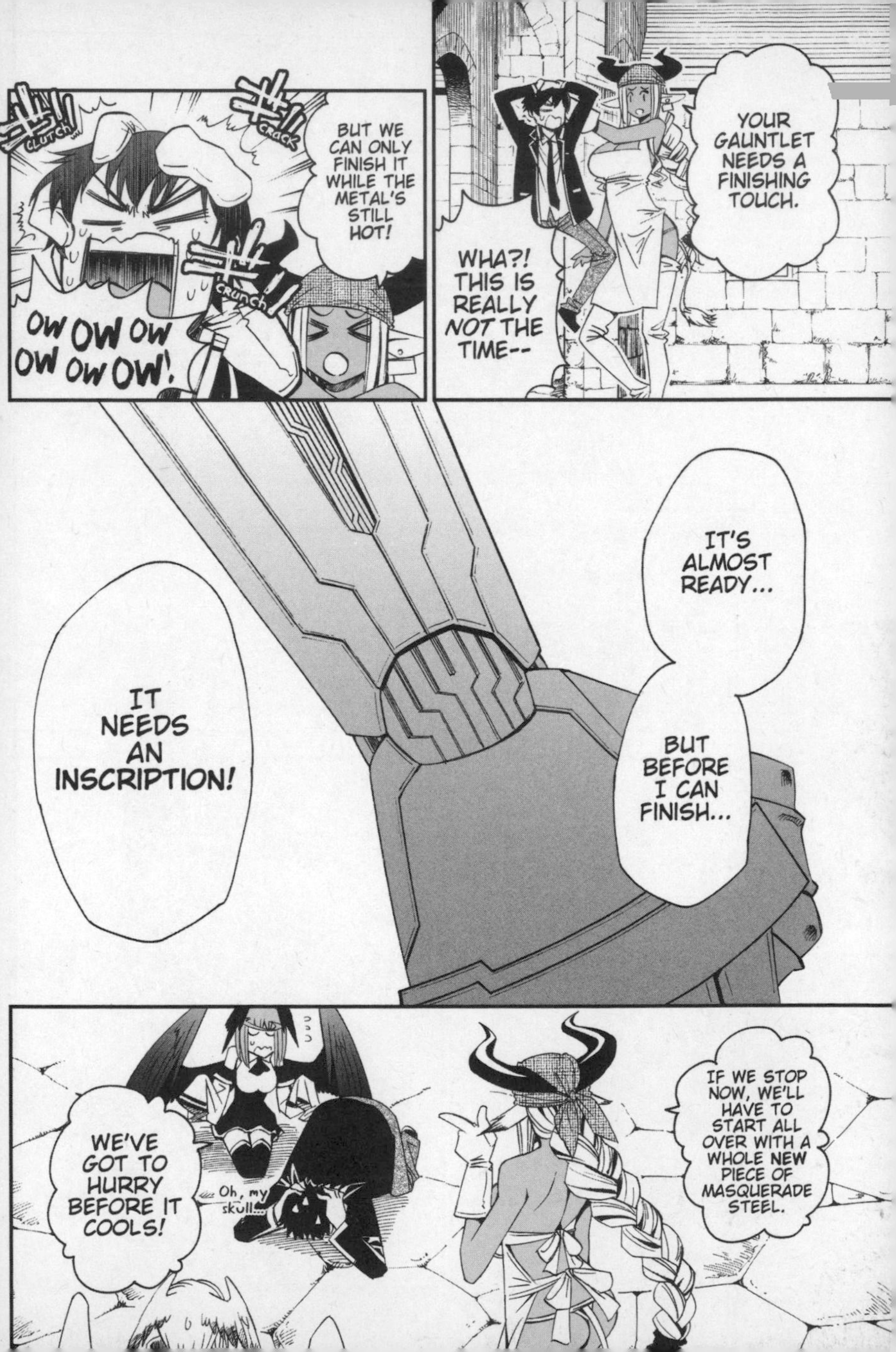
YOUR GAUNTLET NEEDS A FINISHING TOUCH.
WHA?! THIS IS REALLY *NOT* THE TIME--
CLUTCH
CRACK
BUT WE CAN ONLY FINISH IT WHILE THE METAL'S STILL HOT!
CRUNCH
OW OW OW OW OW OW!
IT'S ALMOST READY...
BUT BEFORE I CAN FINISH...
IT NEEDS AN INSCRIPTION!
IF WE STOP NOW, WE'LL HAVE TO START ALL OVER WITH A WHOLE NEW PIECE OF MASQUERADE STEEL.
Oh, my skull...
WE'VE GOT TO HURRY BEFORE IT COOLS!

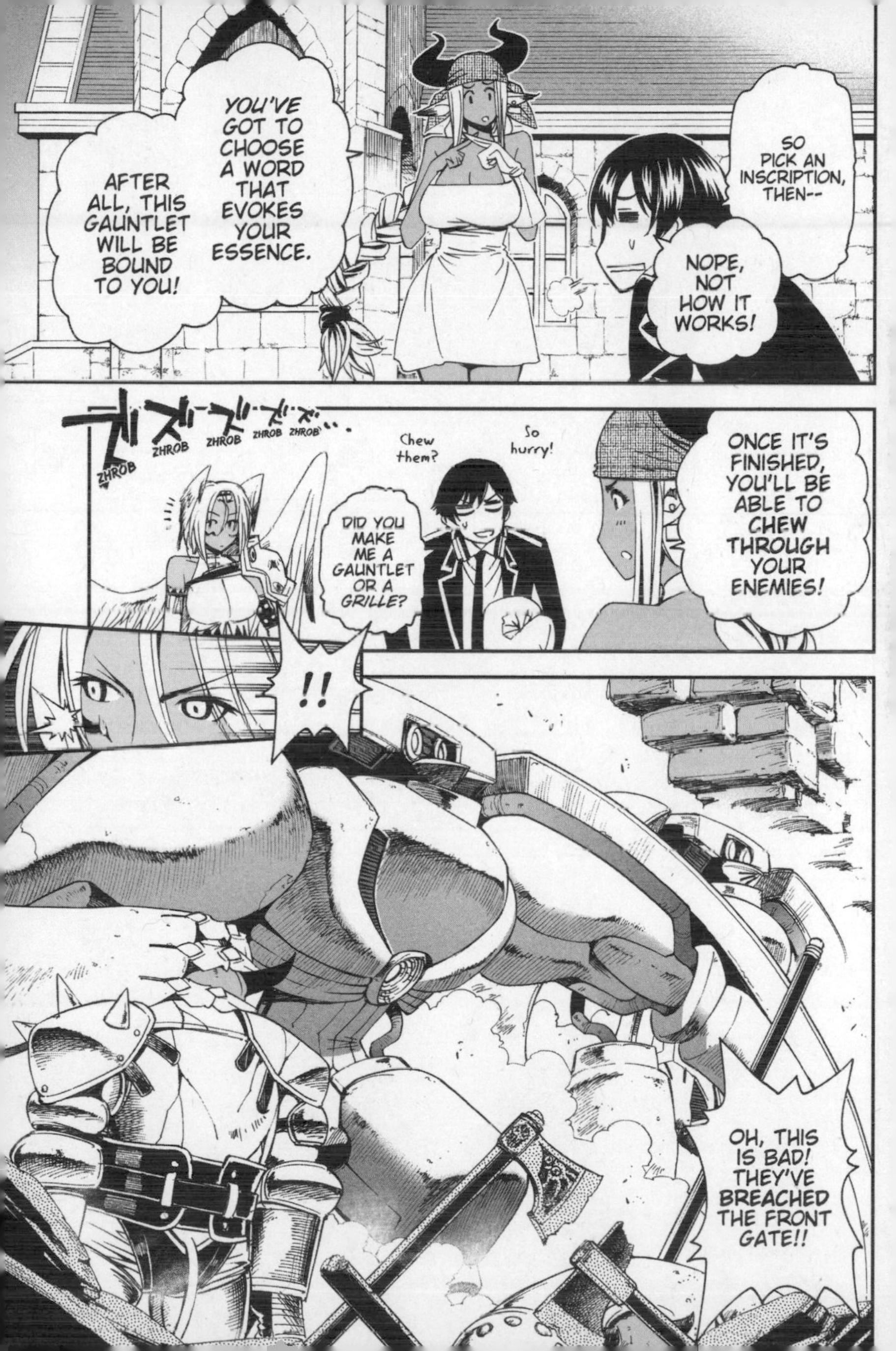
SO PICK AN INSCRIPTION, THEN--
NOPE, NOT HOW IT WORKS!
YOU'VE GOT TO CHOOSE A WORD THAT EVOKES YOUR ESSENCE.
AFTER ALL, THIS GAUNTLET WILL BE BOUND TO YOU!
ONCE IT'S FINISHED, YOU'LL BE ABLE TO CHEW THROUGH YOUR ENEMIES!
So hurry!
Chew them?
DID YOU MAKE ME A GAUNTLET OR A GRILLE?
ZHROB ZHROB ZHROB ZHROB ZHROB
!!
OH, THIS IS BAD! THEY'VE BREACHED THE FRONT GATE!!

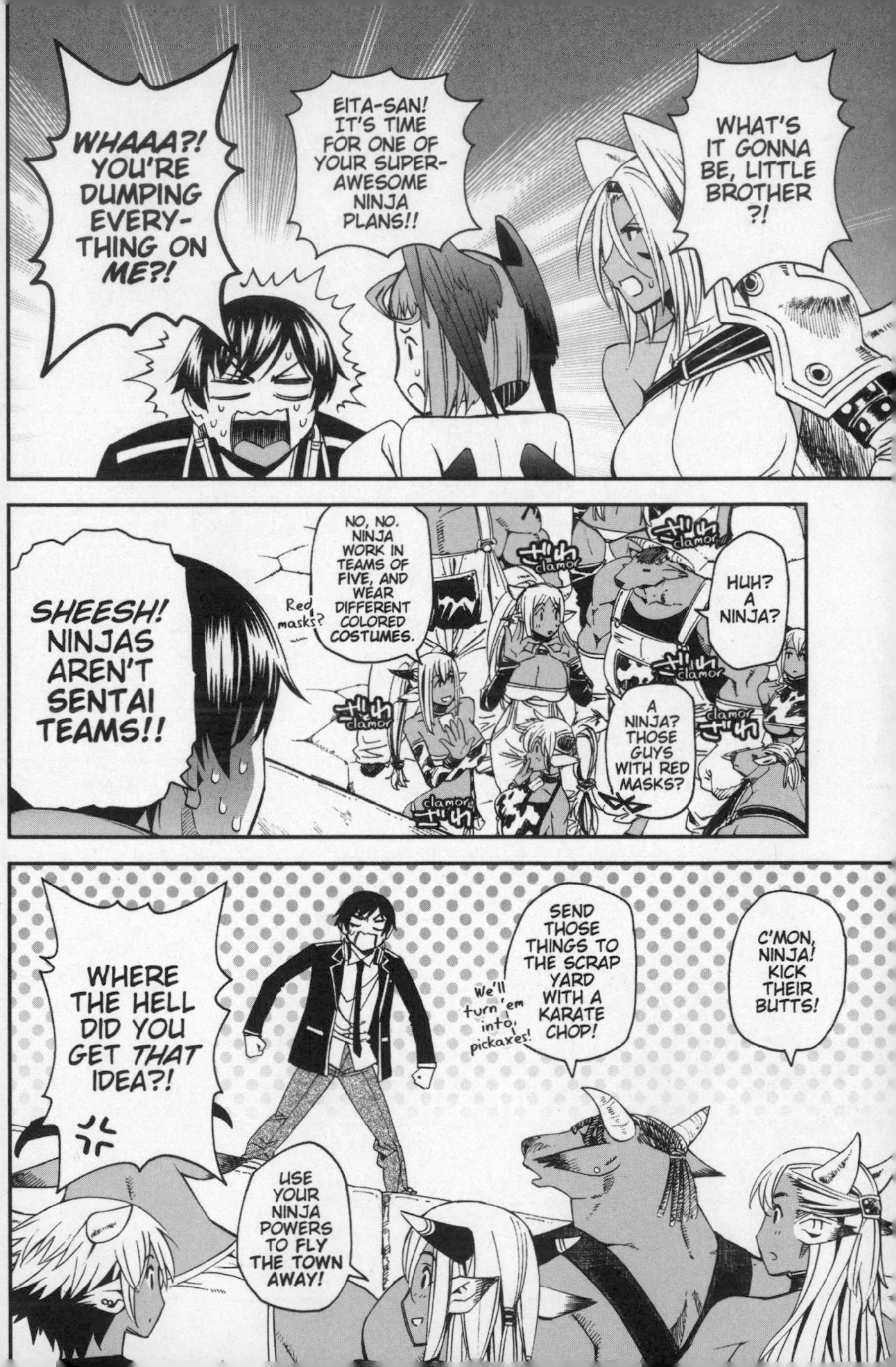
WHAT'S IT GONNA BE, LITTLE BROTHER?!
EITA-SAN! IT'S TIME FOR ONE OF YOUR SUPER-AWESOME NINJA PLANS!!
WHAAA?! YOU'RE DUMPING EVERY-THING ON ME?!
HUH? A NINJA?
A NINJA? THOSE GUYS WITH RED MASKS?
clamor
clamor
clamor
clamor
NO, NO. NINJA WORK IN TEAMS OF FIVE, AND WEAR DIFFERENT COLORED COSTUMES.
clamor
clamor
Red masks?
SHEESH! NINJAS AREN'T SENTAI TEAMS!!
C'MON, NINJA! KICK THEIR BUTTS!
SEND THOSE THINGS TO THE SCRAP YARD WITH A KARATE CHOP!
We'll turn 'em into pickaxes!
USE YOUR NINJA POWERS TO FLY THE TOWN AWAY!
WHERE THE HELL DID YOU GET THAT IDEA?!

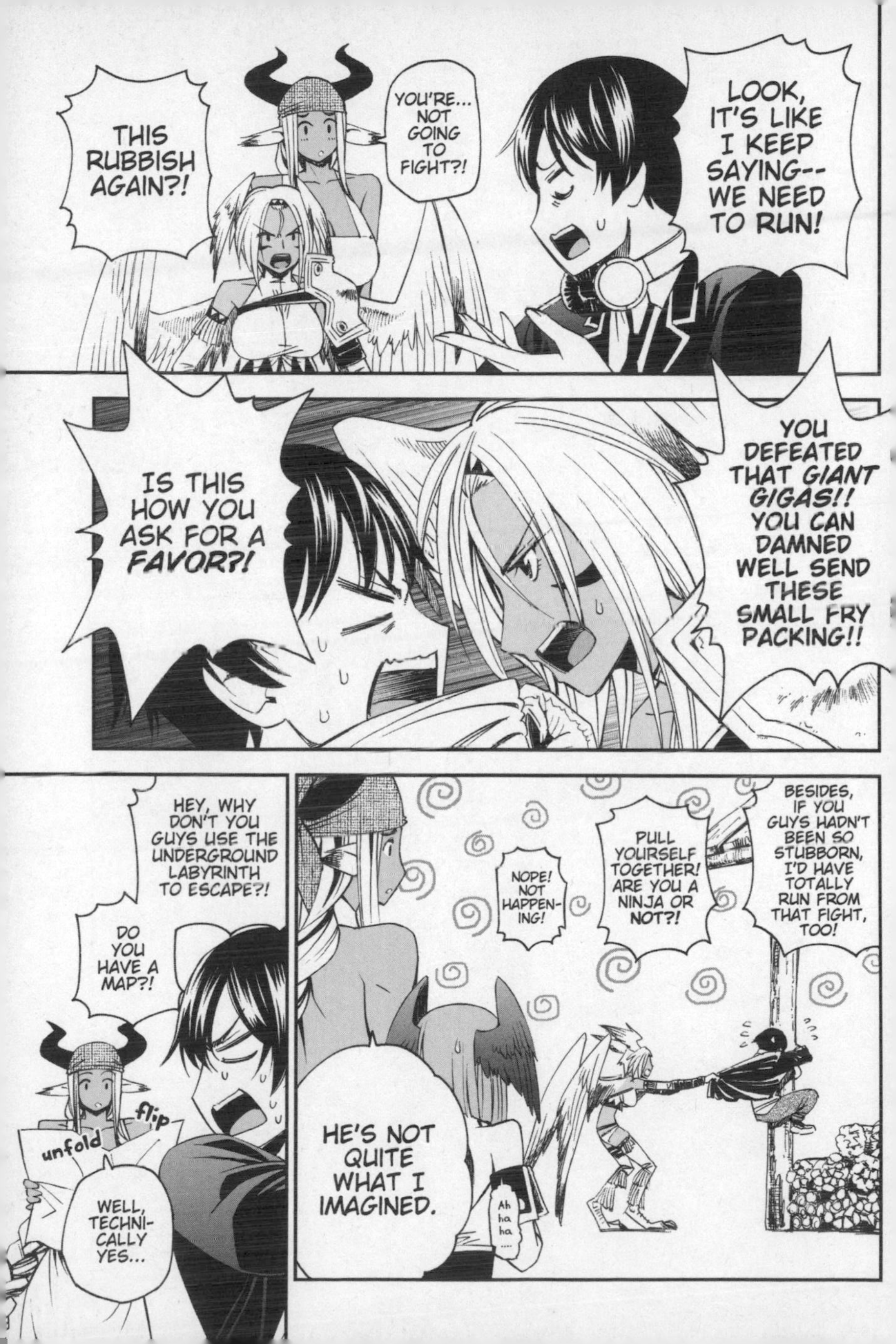
LOOK, IT'S LIKE I KEEP SAYING-- WE NEED TO RUN!
YOU'RE... NOT GOING TO FIGHT?!
THIS RUBBISH AGAIN?!
YOU DEFEATED THAT *GIANT GIGAS!!* YOU CAN DAMNED WELL SEND THESE SMALL FRY PACKING!!
IS THIS HOW YOU ASK FOR A *FAVOR?!*
BESIDES, IF YOU GUYS HADN'T BEEN SO STUBBORN, I'D HAVE TOTALLY RUN FROM THAT FIGHT, TOO!
PULL YOURSELF TOGETHER! ARE YOU A NINJA OR NOT?!
NOPE! NOT HAPPENING!
HE'S NOT QUITE WHAT I IMAGINED.
Ah ha ha....
HEY, WHY DON'T YOU GUYS USE THE UNDERGROUND LABYRINTH TO ESCAPE?!
DO YOU HAVE A MAP?!
flip
unfold
WELL, TECHNICALLY YES...

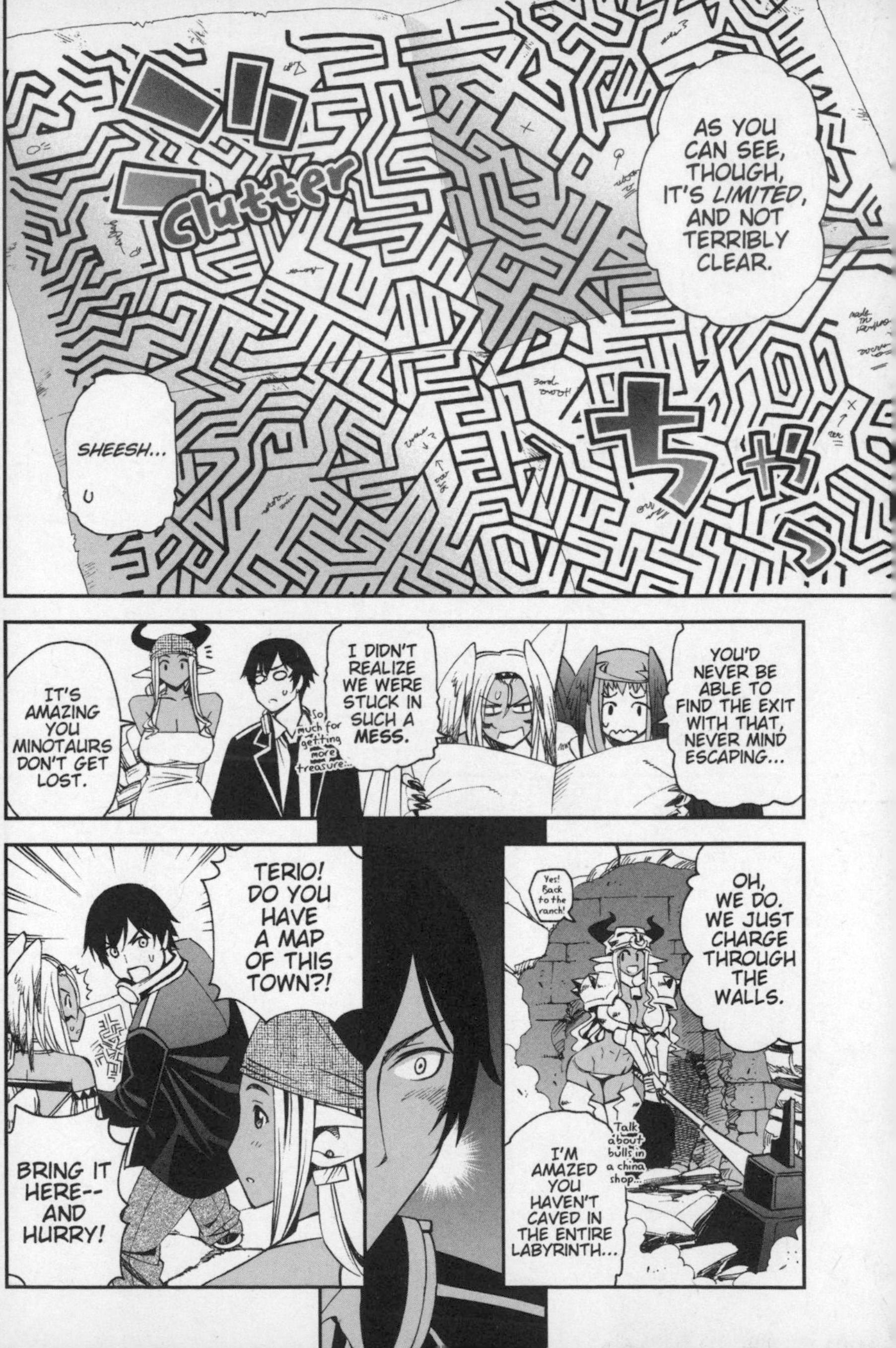

Clutter
AS YOU CAN SEE, THOUGH, IT'S *LIMITED*, AND NOT TERRIBLY CLEAR.
SHEESH...
YOU'D NEVER BE ABLE TO FIND THE EXIT WITH THAT, NEVER MIND ESCAPING...
I DIDN'T REALIZE WE WERE STUCK IN SUCH A MESS.
So much for getting more treasure...
IT'S AMAZING YOU MINOTAURS DON'T GET LOST.
OH, WE DO. WE JUST CHARGE THROUGH THE WALLS.
Yes! Back to the ranch!
Talk about bulls in a china shop...
I'M AMAZED YOU HAVEN'T CAVED IN THE ENTIRE LABYRINTH...
TERIO! DO YOU HAVE A MAP OF THIS TOWN?!
BRING IT HERE--AND HURRY!

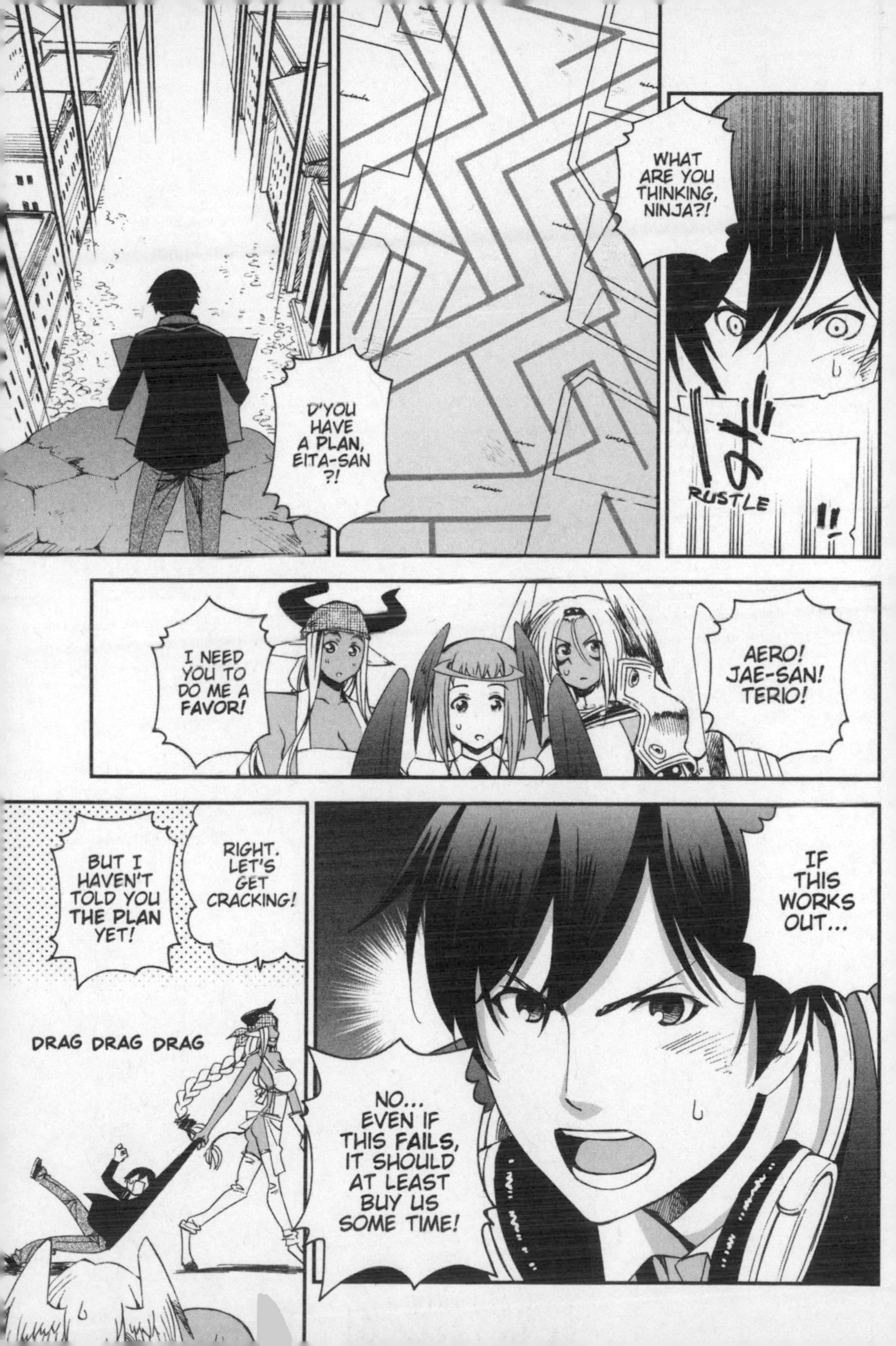
WHAT ARE YOU THINKING, NINJA?!
RUSTLE
D'YOU HAVE A PLAN, EITA-SAN?!
AERO! JAE-SAN! TERIO!
I NEED YOU TO DO ME A FAVOR!
IF THIS WORKS OUT...
NO... EVEN IF THIS FAILS, IT SHOULD AT LEAST BUY US SOME TIME!
RIGHT. LET'S GET CRACKING!
BUT I HAVEN'T TOLD YOU THE PLAN YET!
DRAG DRAG DRAG

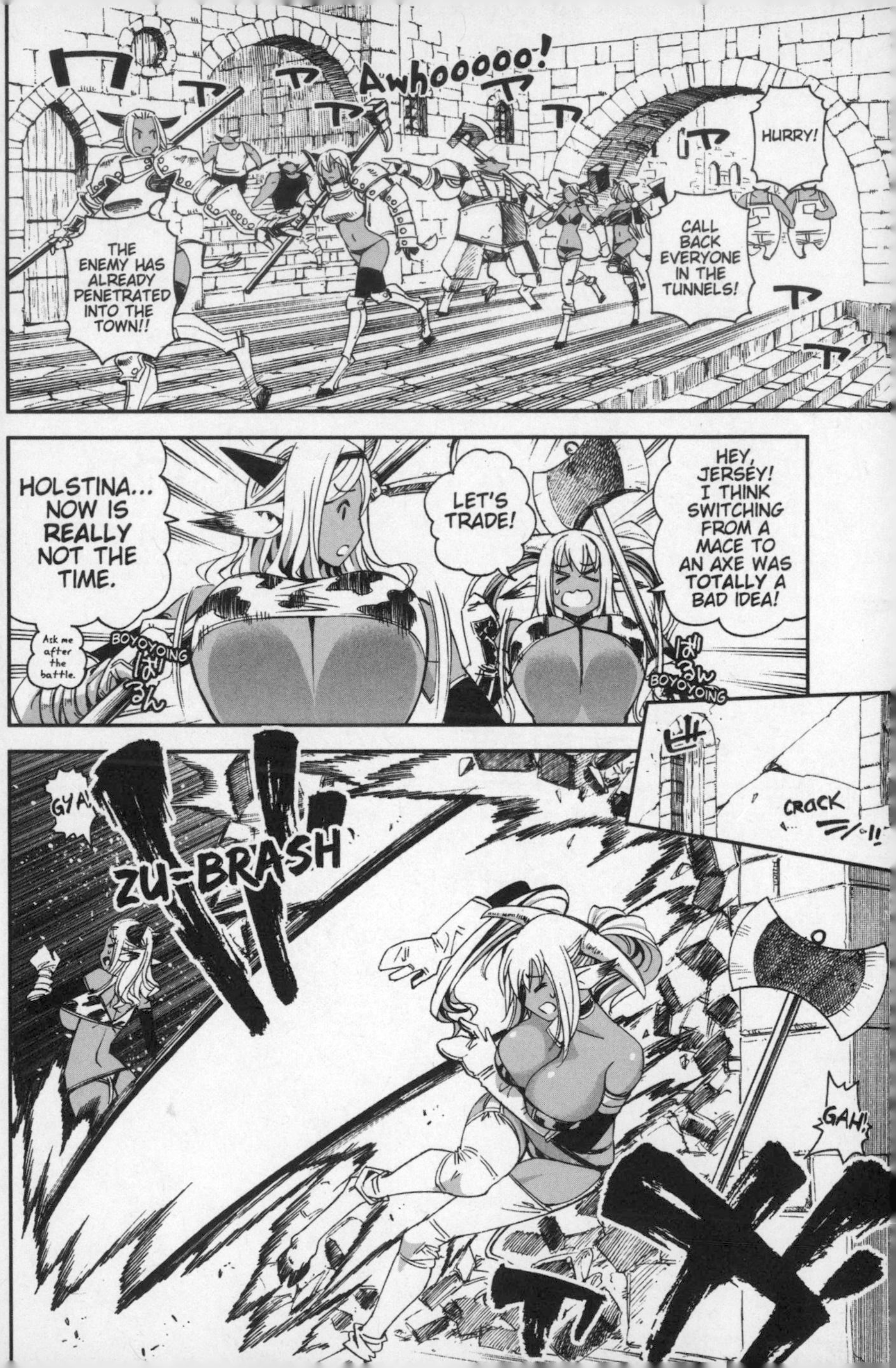

Awhooooo!
HURRY!
CALL BACK EVERYONE IN THE TUNNELS!
THE ENEMY HAS ALREADY PENETRATED INTO THE TOWN!!
HEY, JERSEY! I THINK SWITCHING FROM A MACE TO AN AXE WAS TOTALLY A BAD IDEA!
LET'S TRADE!
BOYOYOING
HOLSTINA... NOW IS REALLY NOT THE TIME.
BOYOYOING
Ask me after the battle.
CRACK
GAH!
ZU-BRASH
GYA!

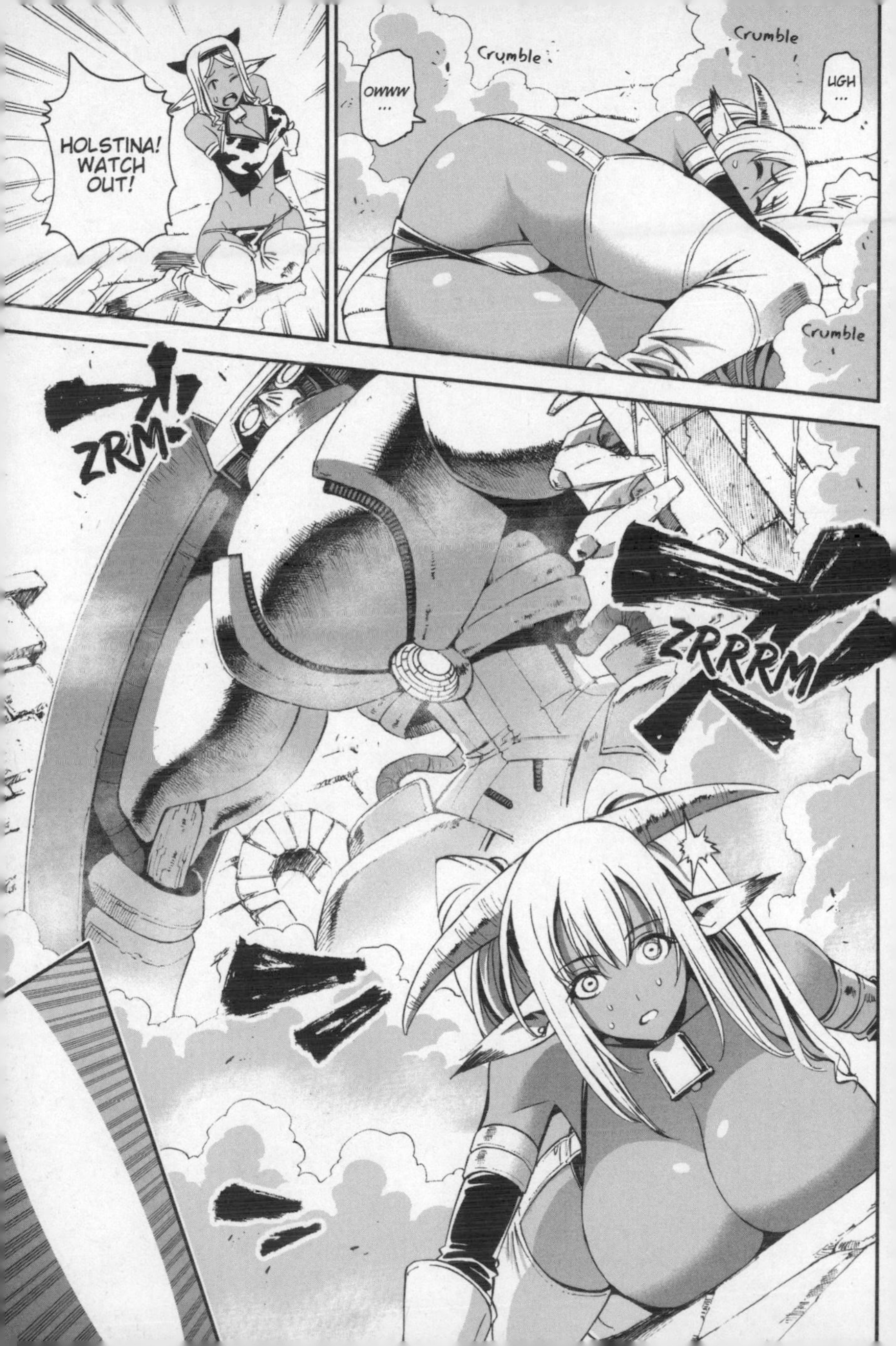
Crumble
UGH ...
Crumble
OWWW ...
Crumble
HOLSTINA! WATCH OUT!
ZRRRRM
ZRM

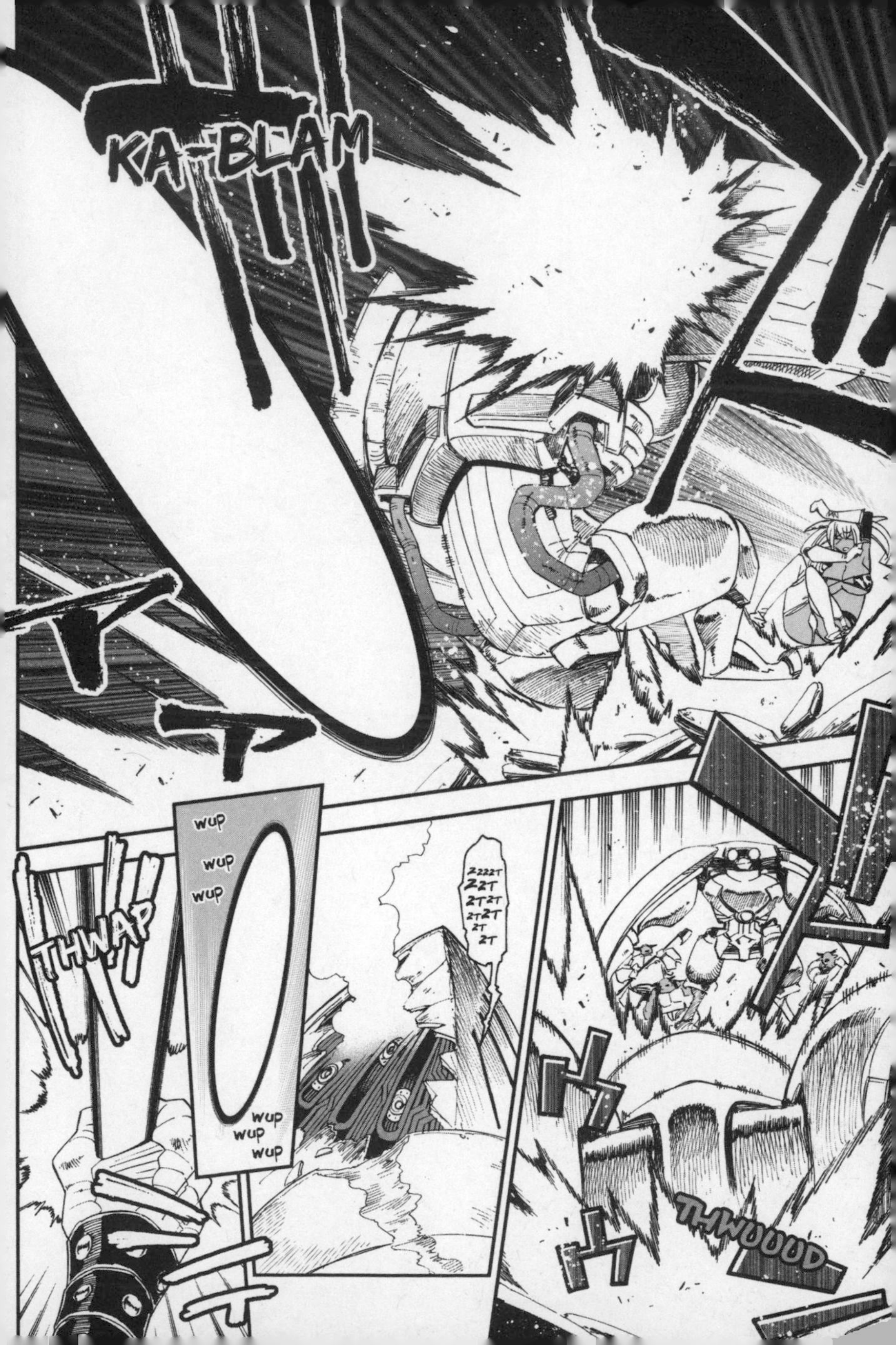
KA-BLAM
THWUUUD
ZZZZT ZZT ZT ZT ZT ZT ZT ZT
wup
wup
wup
wup
wup
wup
THWAP

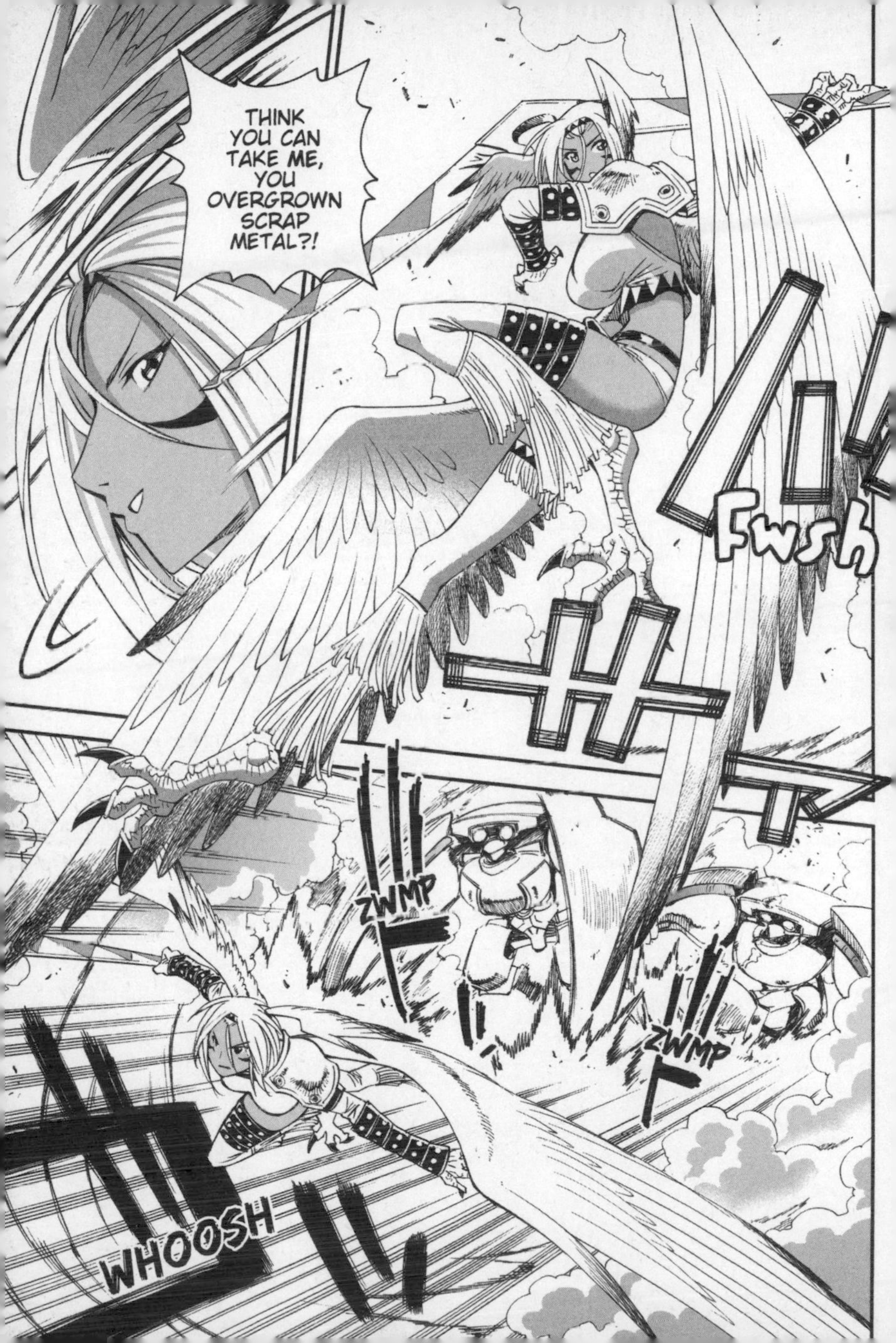
THINK YOU CAN TAKE ME, YOU OVERGROWN SCRAP METAL?!
Fwsh
ZWMP
ZWMP
WHOOSH

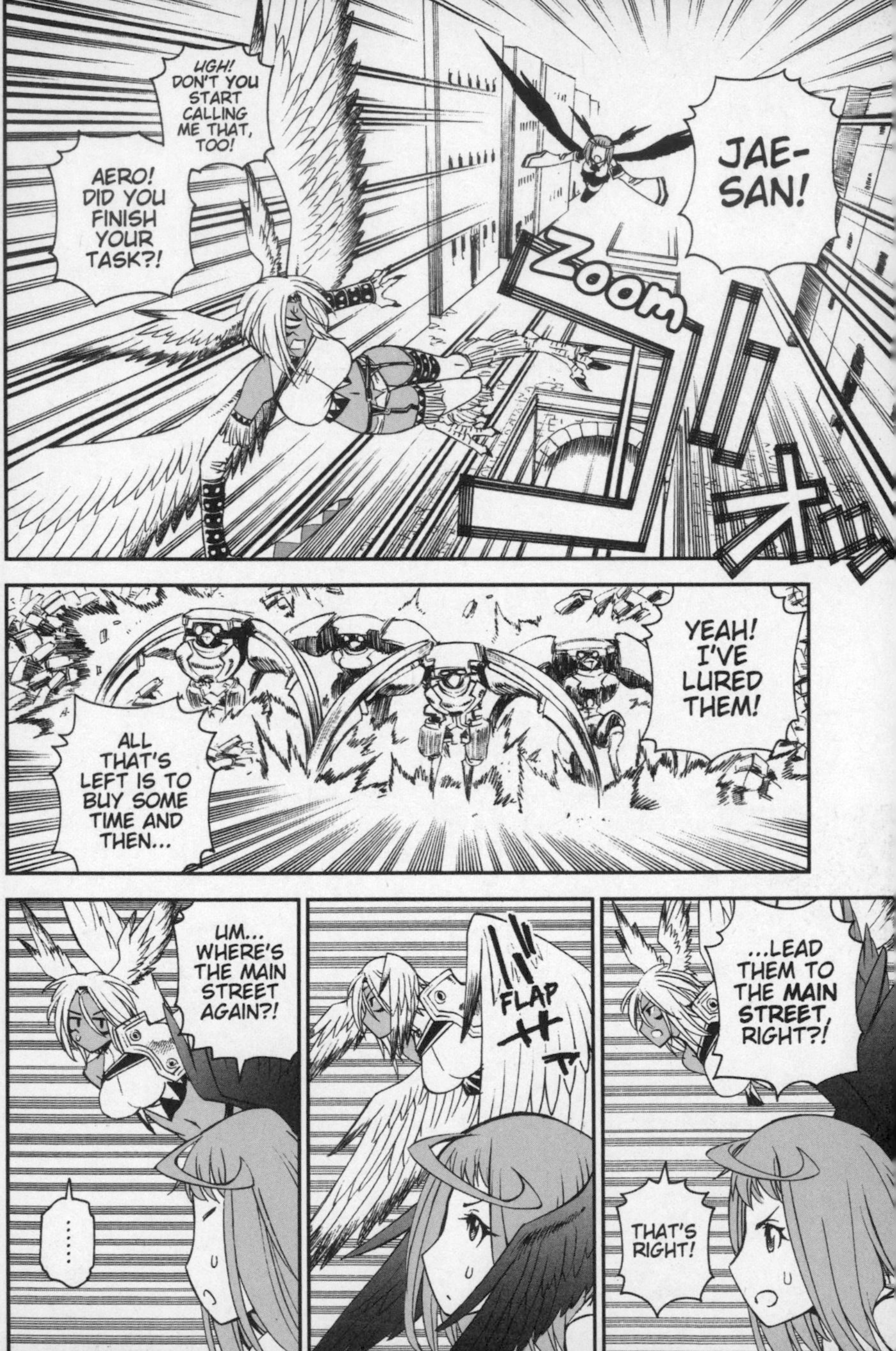
JAE-SAN!
UGH! DON'T YOU START CALLING ME THAT, TOO!
AERO! DID YOU FINISH YOUR TASK?!
ZOOM
YEAH! I'VE LURED THEM!
ALL THAT'S LEFT IS TO BUY SOME TIME AND THEN...
...LEAD THEM TO THE MAIN STREET, RIGHT?!
THAT'S RIGHT!
FLAP
UM... WHERE'S THE MAIN STREET AGAIN?!
......

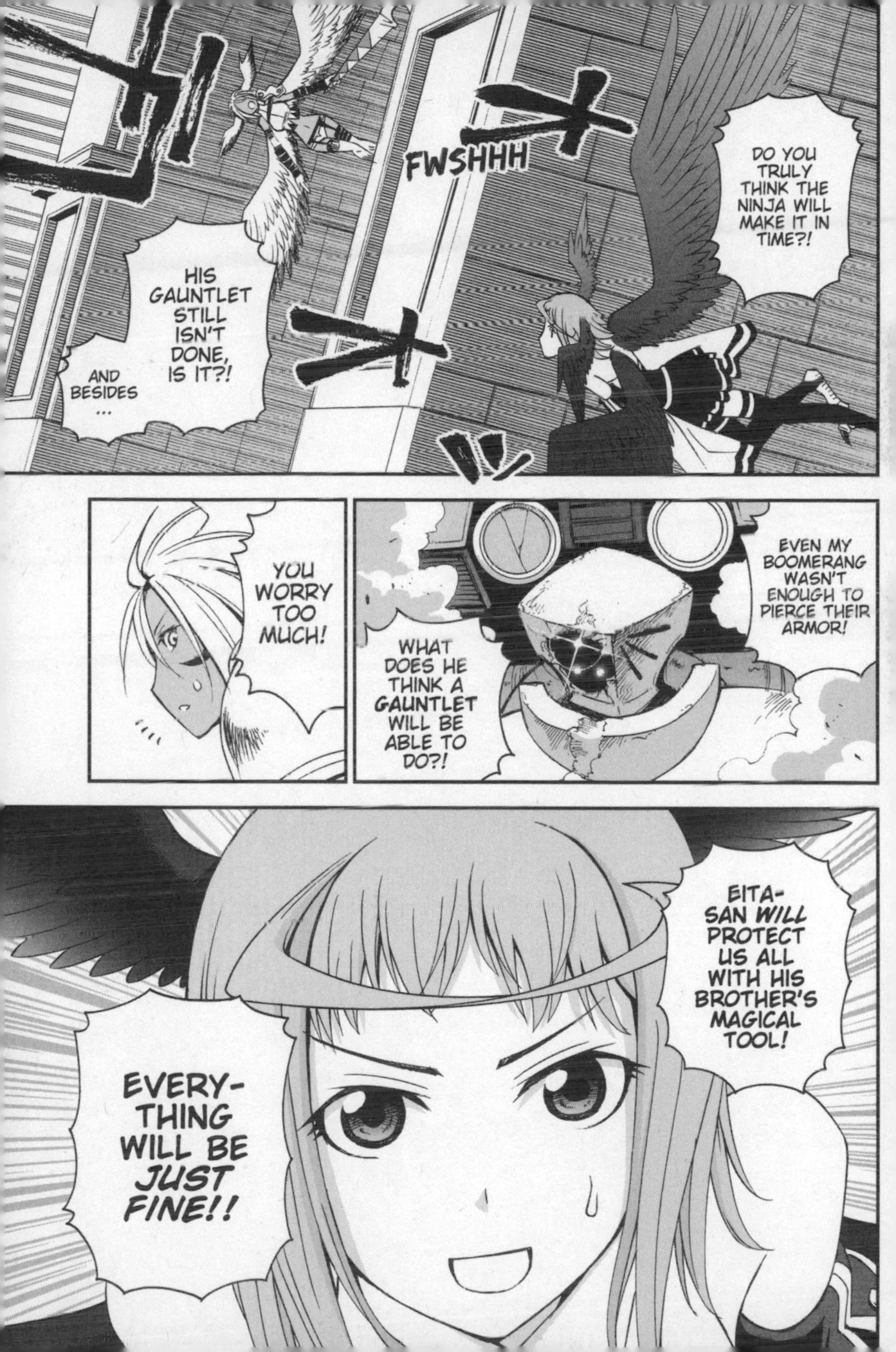
DO YOU TRULY THINK THE NINJA WILL MAKE IT IN TIME?!
FWSHHH
HIS GAUNTLET STILL ISN'T DONE, IS IT?!
AND BESIDES ...
EVEN MY BOOMERANG WASN'T ENOUGH TO PIERCE THEIR ARMOR!
WHAT DOES HE THINK A GAUNTLET WILL BE ABLE TO DO?!
YOU WORRY TOO MUCH!
EITA-SAN *WILL* PROTECT US ALL WITH HIS BROTHER'S MAGICAL TOOL!
EVERY-THING WILL BE *JUST FINE!!*

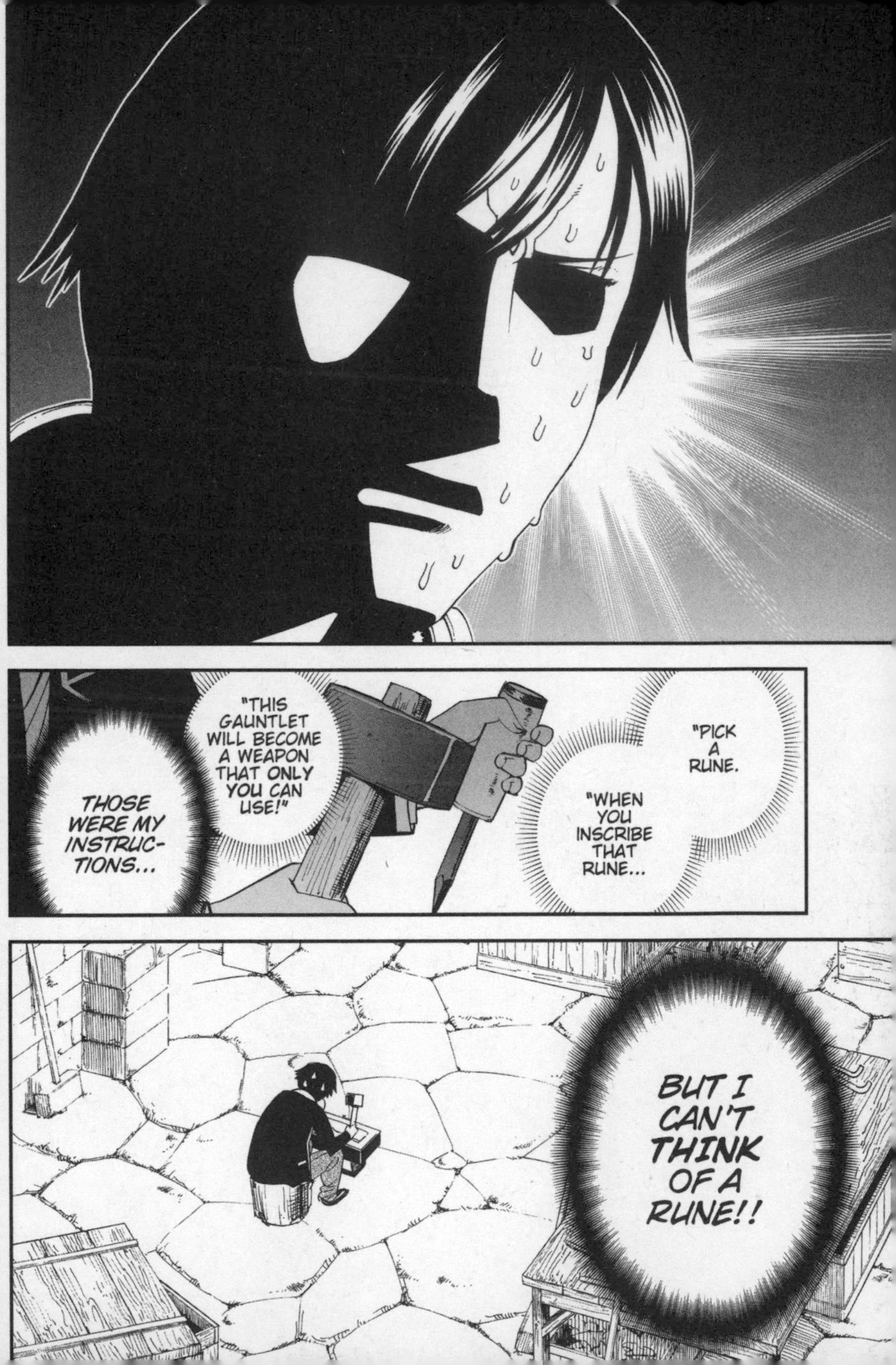
"PICK A RUNE.
"WHEN YOU INSCRIBE THAT RUNE...
"THIS GAUNTLET WILL BECOME A WEAPON THAT ONLY YOU CAN USE!"
THOSE WERE MY INSTRUC-TIONS...
BUT I CAN'T THINK OF A RUNE!!

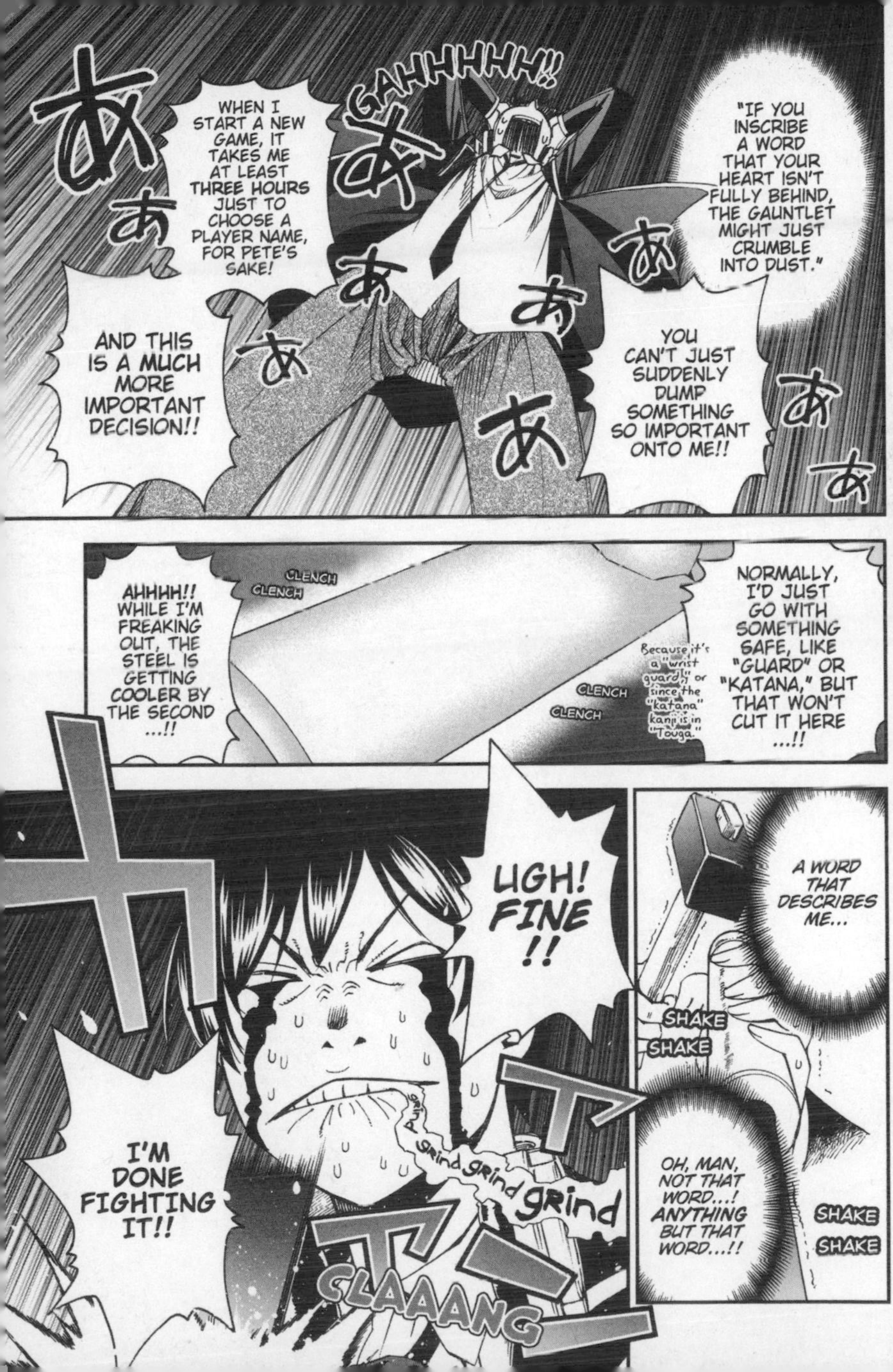
"IF YOU INSCRIBE A WORD THAT YOUR HEART ISN'T FULLY BEHIND, THE GAUNTLET MIGHT JUST CRUMBLE INTO DUST."
YOU CAN'T JUST SUDDENLY DUMP SOMETHING SO IMPORTANT ONTO ME!!
GAHHHHH!!
WHEN I START A NEW GAME, IT TAKES ME AT LEAST THREE HOURS JUST TO CHOOSE A PLAYER NAME, FOR PETE'S SAKE!
AND THIS IS A MUCH MORE IMPORTANT DECISION!!
NORMALLY, I'D JUST GO WITH SOMETHING SAFE, LIKE "GUARD" OR "KATANA," BUT THAT WON'T CUT IT HERE ...!!
Because it's a "wrist guard," or since the "katana" kanji is in "Touga."
CLENCH
CLENCH
CLENCH
CLENCH
AHHHH!! WHILE I'M FREAKING OUT, THE STEEL IS GETTING COOLER BY THE SECOND ...!!
A WORD THAT DESCRIBES ME...
SHAKE
SHAKE
OH, MAN, NOT THAT WORD...! ANYTHING BUT THAT WORD...!!
SHAKE
SHAKE
UGH! FINE!!
I'M DONE FIGHTING IT!!
grind grind grind
CLAAAANG

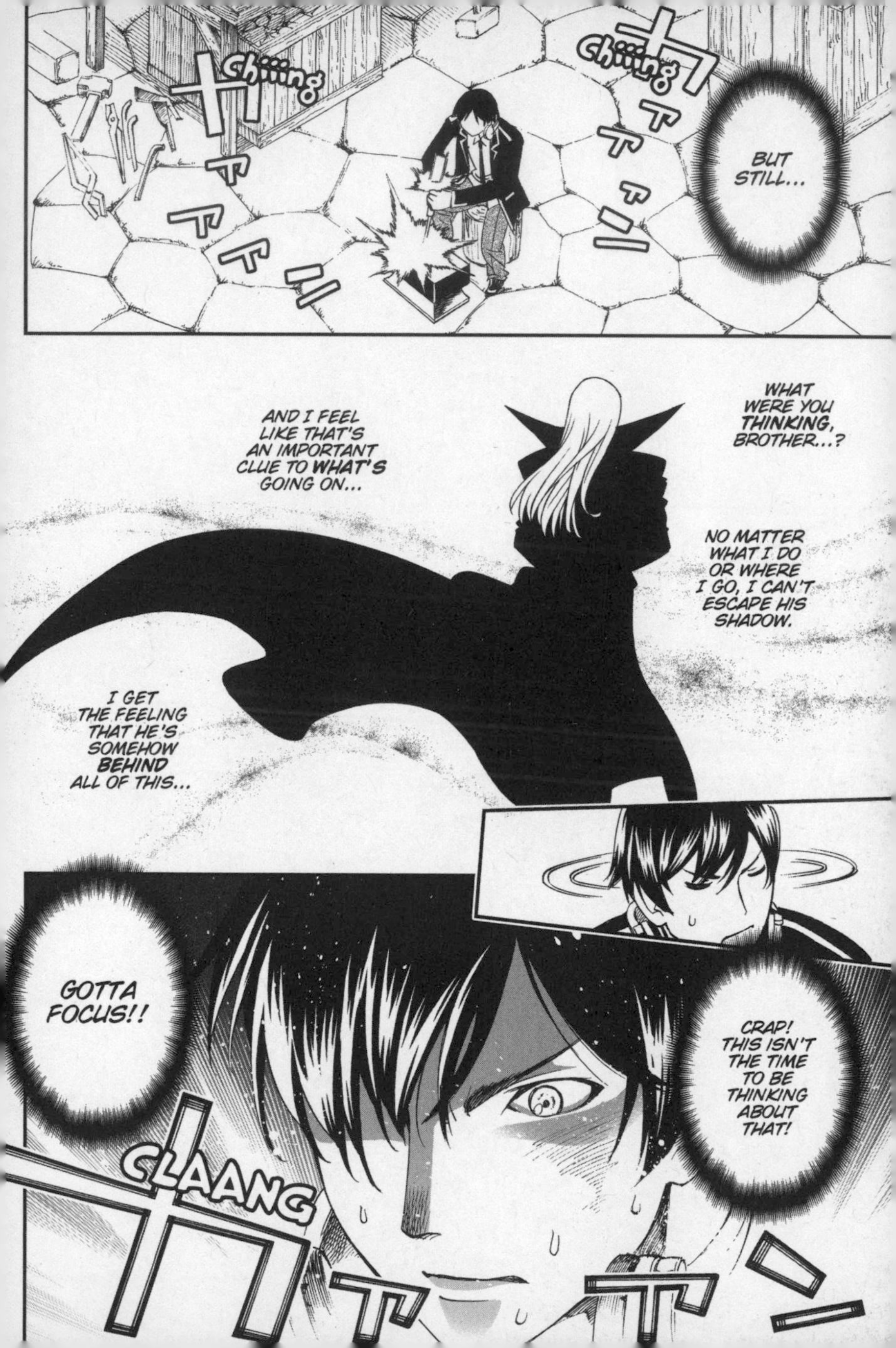
BUT STILL...
Chiiing
Chiiing
WHAT WERE YOU THINKING, BROTHER...?
AND I FEEL LIKE THAT'S AN IMPORTANT CLUE TO WHAT'S GOING ON...
NO MATTER WHAT I DO OR WHERE I GO, I CAN'T ESCAPE HIS SHADOW.
I GET THE FEELING THAT HE'S SOMEHOW BEHIND ALL OF THIS...
CRAP! THIS ISN'T THE TIME TO BE THINKING ABOUT THAT!
GOTTA FOCUS!!
CLAANG

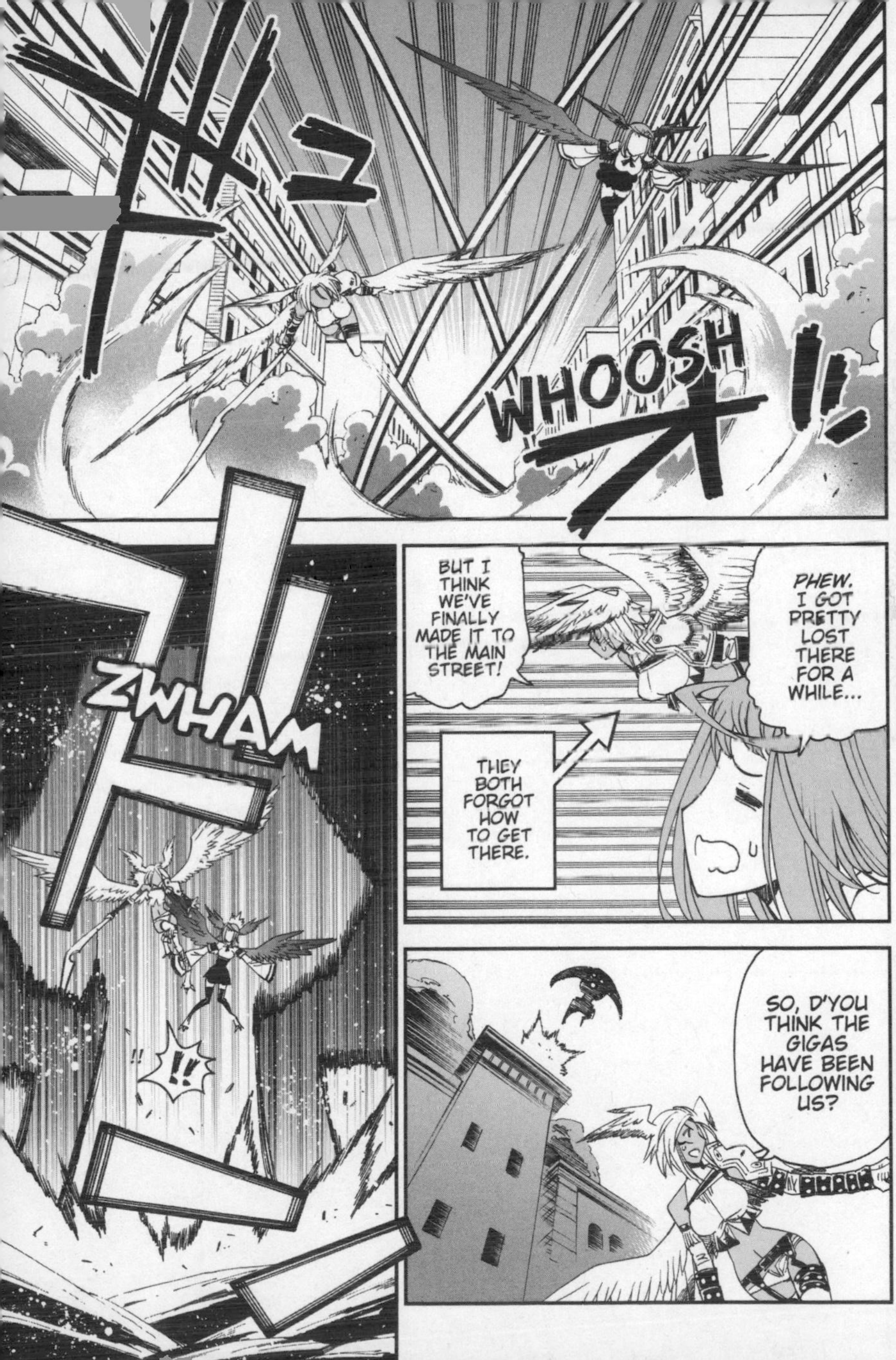
WHOOSH !!
PHEW. I GOT PRETTY LOST THERE FOR A WHILE...
BUT I THINK WE'VE FINALLY MADE IT TO THE MAIN STREET!
THEY BOTH FORGOT HOW TO GET THERE.
SO, D'YOU THINK THE GIGAS HAVE BEEN FOLLOWING US?
ZWHAM
!!
!!

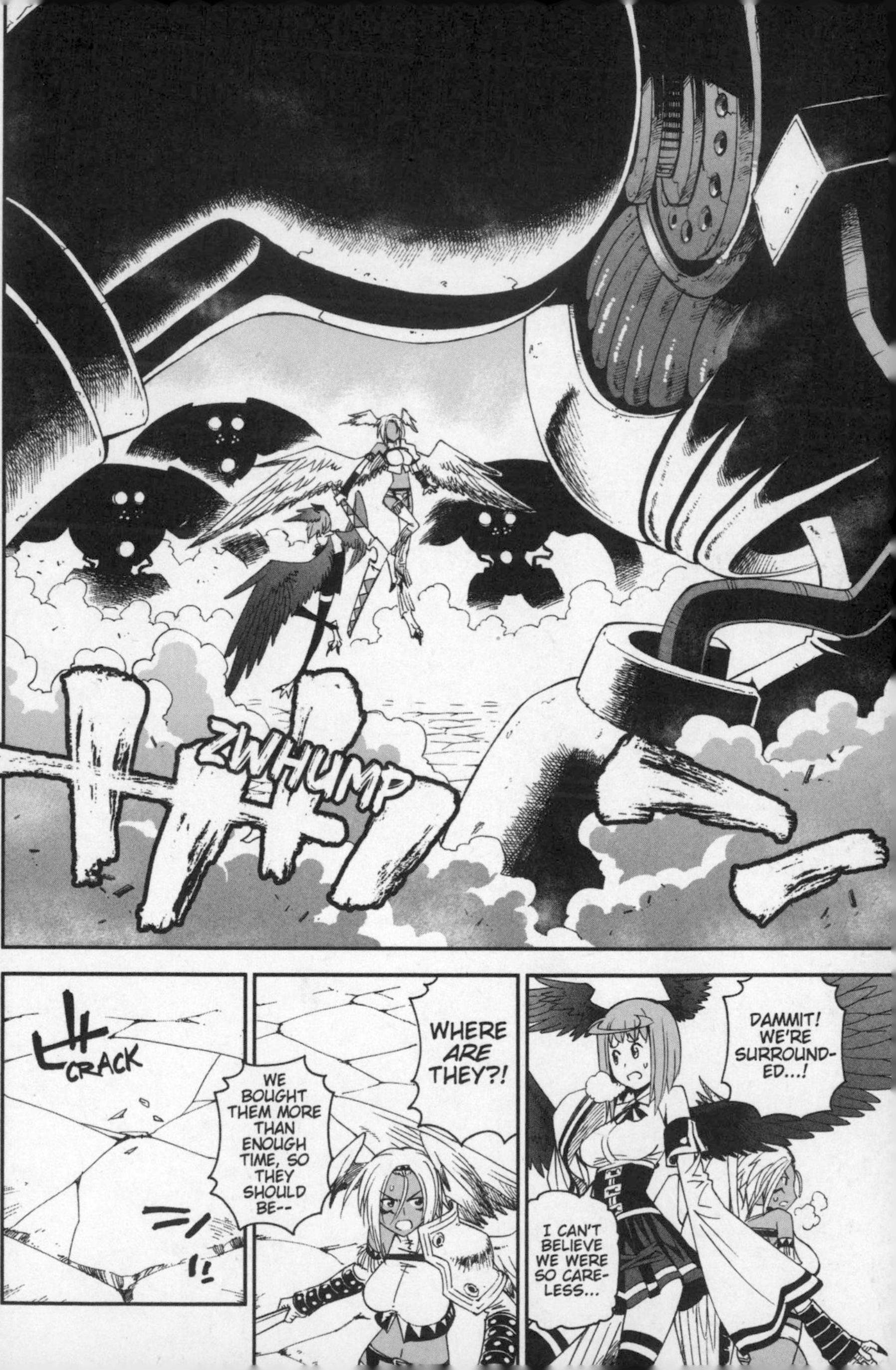
ZWHUMP
DAMMIT! WE'RE SURROUND-ED...!
I CAN'T BELIEVE WE WERE SO CARE-LESS...
WHERE ARE THEY?!
WE BOUGHT THEM MORE THAN ENOUGH TIME, SO THEY SHOULD BE--
CRACK

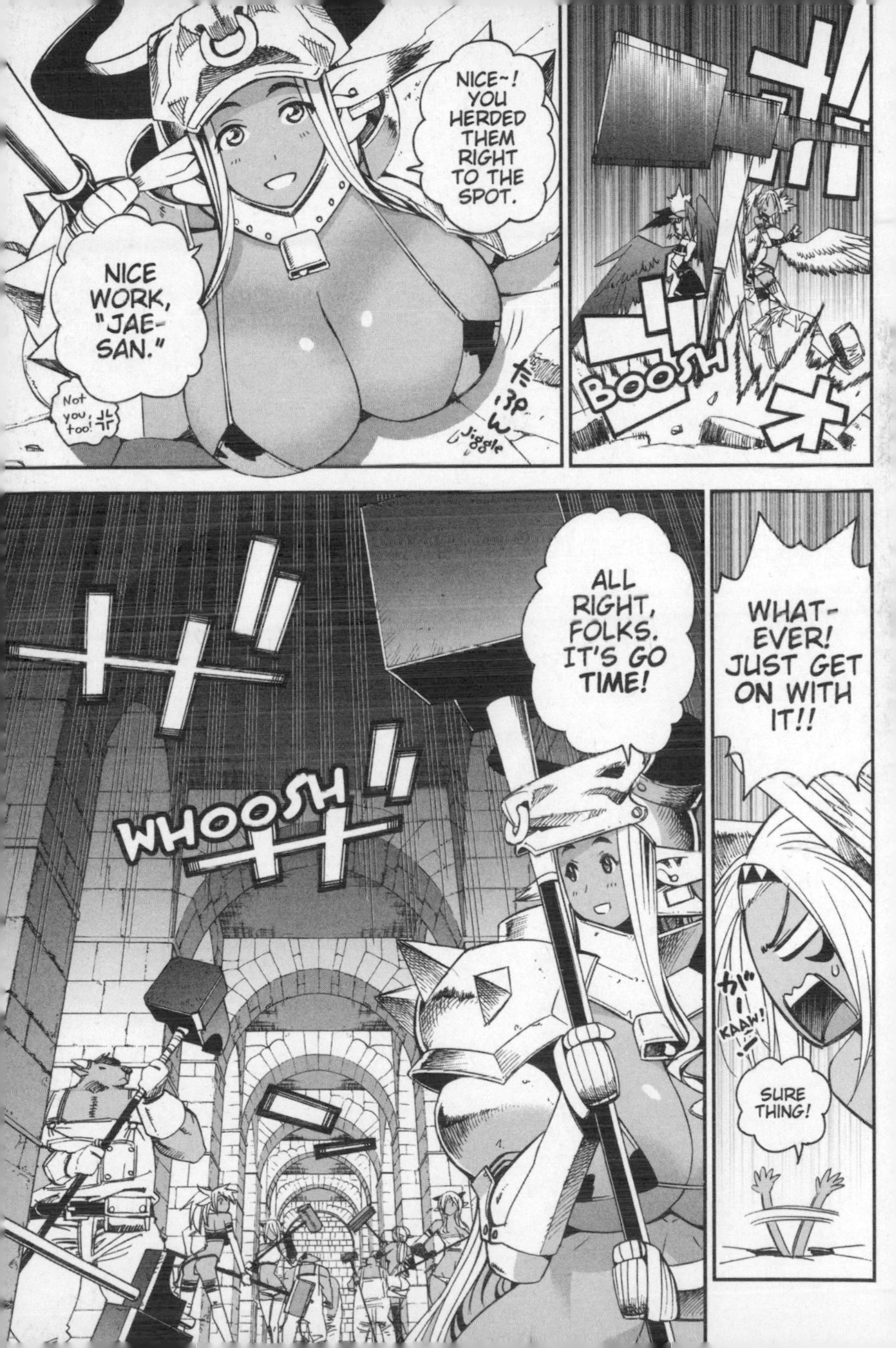
BOOSH
NICE~! YOU HERDED THEM RIGHT TO THE SPOT.
Jiggle
NICE WORK, "JAE-SAN."
Not you, too!
WHAT-EVER! JUST GET ON WITH IT!!
KAAW!
SURE THING!
ALL RIGHT, FOLKS. IT'S GO TIME!
WHOOSH

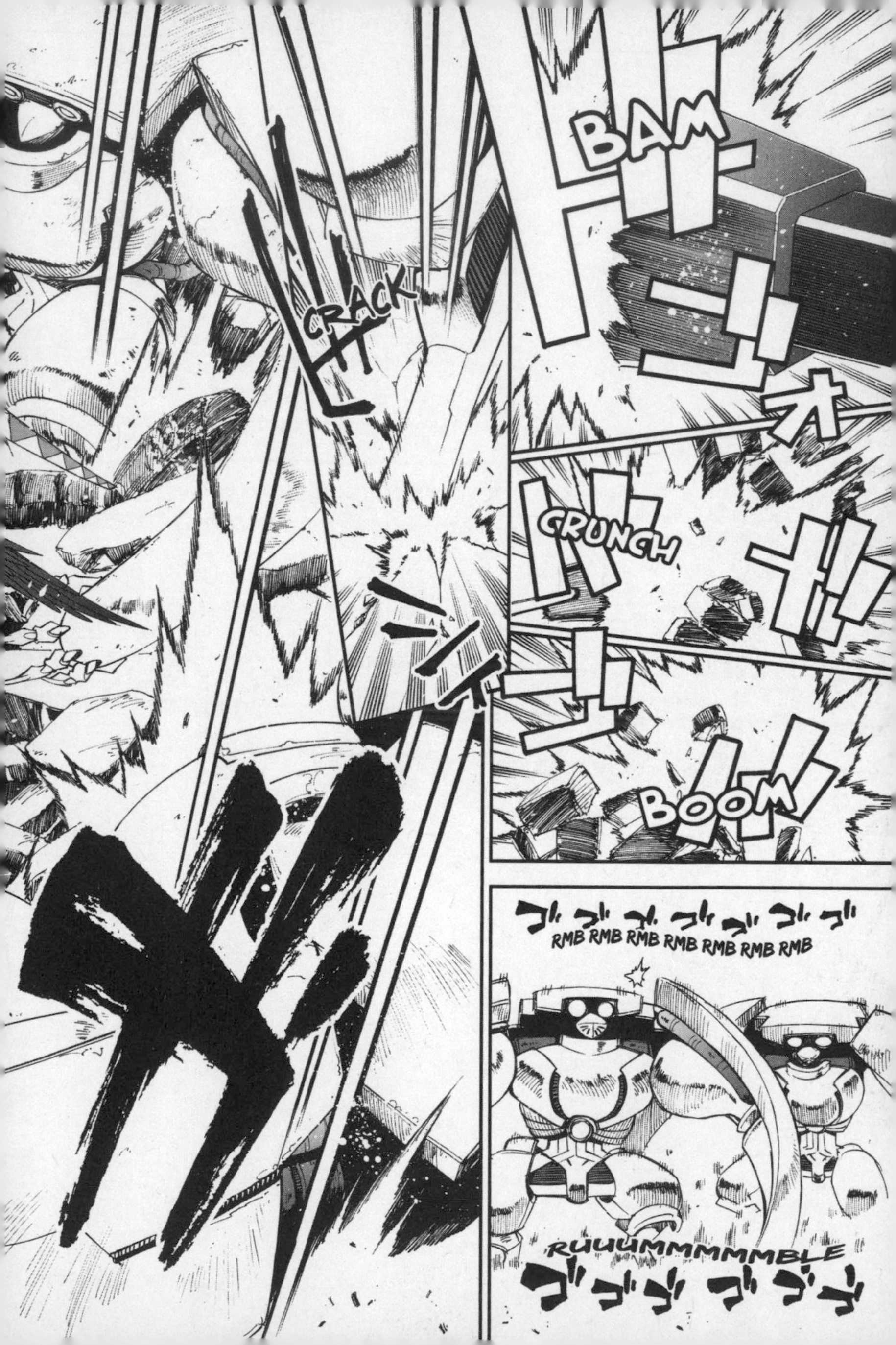
BAM
CRUNCH
BOOM
RMB RMB RMB RMB RMB RMB RMB
RUUUMMMMMBLE
CRACK

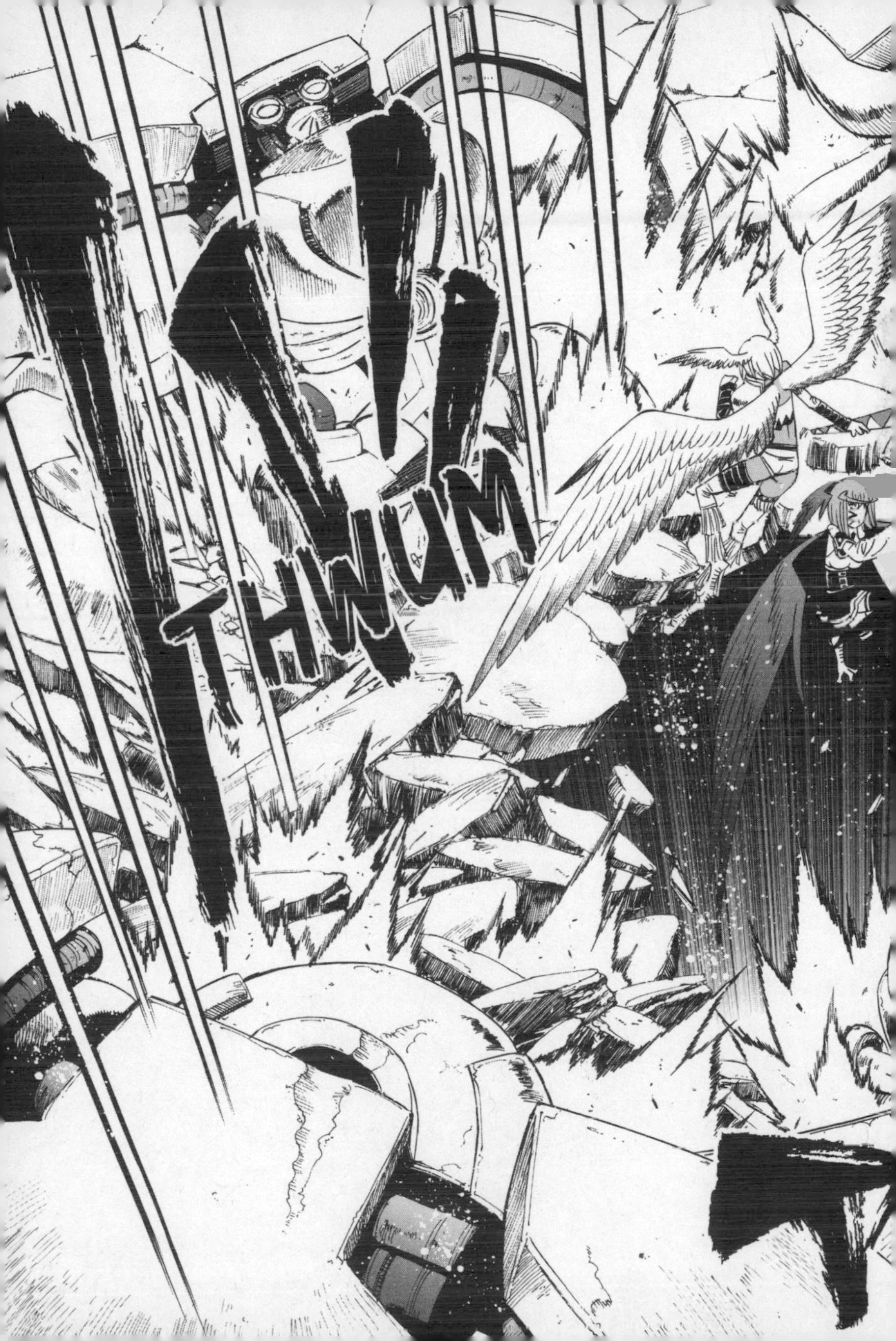
THWUM

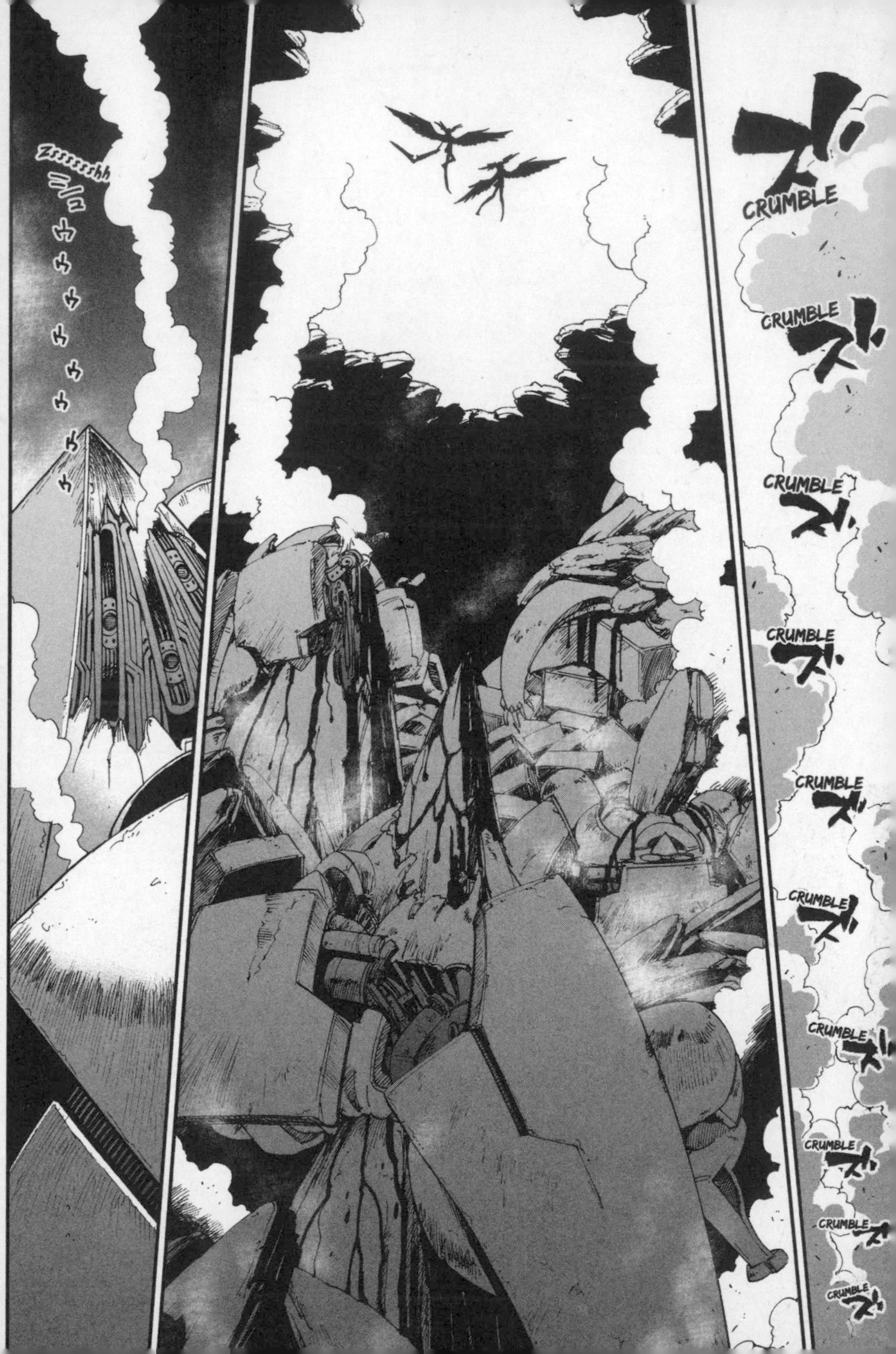
CRUMBLE
CRUMBLE
CRUMBLE
CRUMBLE
CRUMBLE
CRUMBLE
CRUMBLE
CRUMBLE
CRUMBLE
CRUMBLE
Zssssssshh

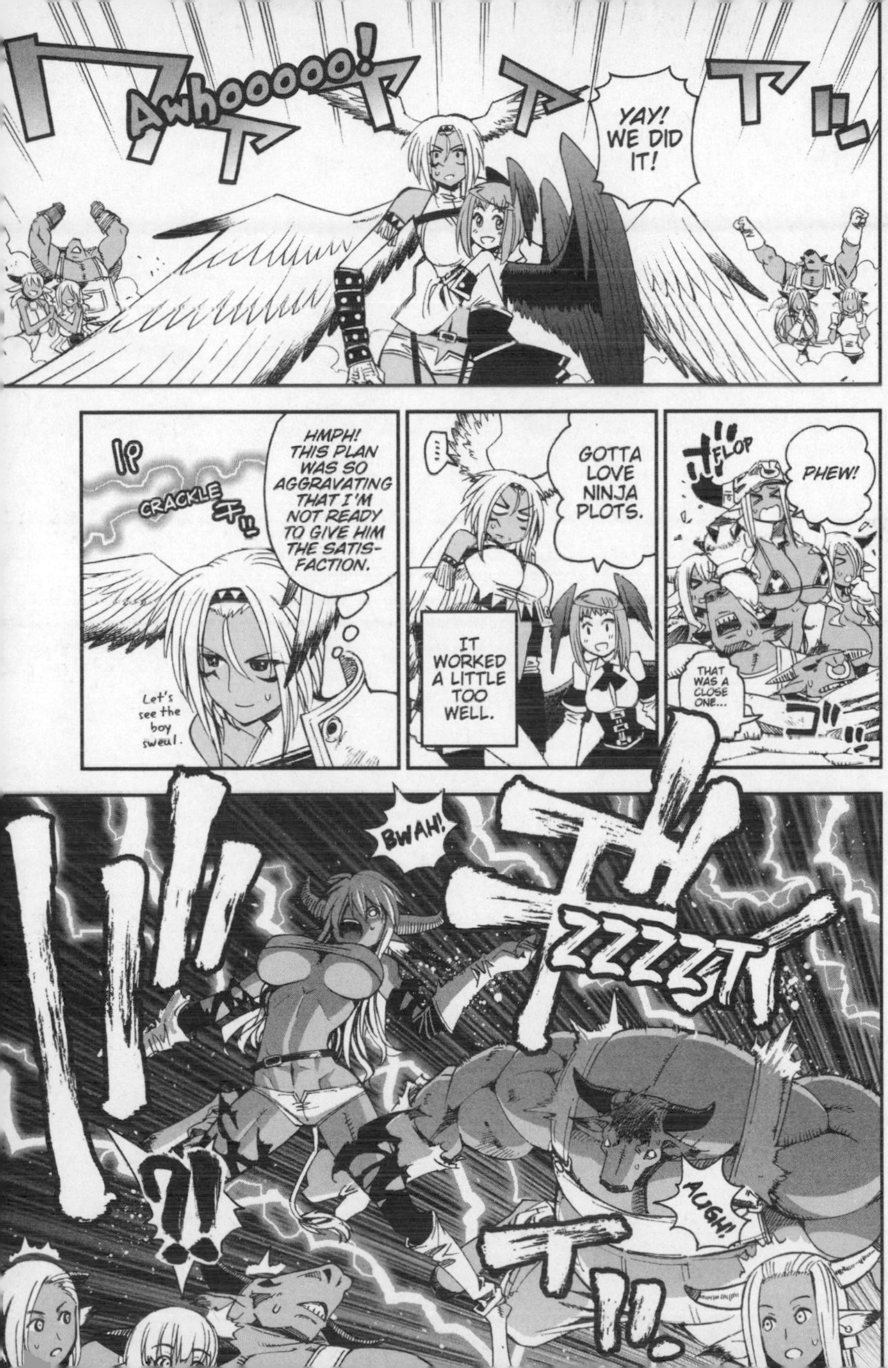
Awhooooo!
YAY! WE DID IT!
FLOP
PHEW!
THAT WAS A CLOSE ONE...
...
GOTTA LOVE NINJA PLOTS.
IT WORKED A LITTLE TOO WELL.
HMPH! THIS PLAN WAS SO AGGRAVATING THAT I'M NOT READY TO GIVE HIM THE SATISFACTION.
CRACKLE
Let's see the boy sweat.
BWAH!
ZZZZZT
AUGH!
?!

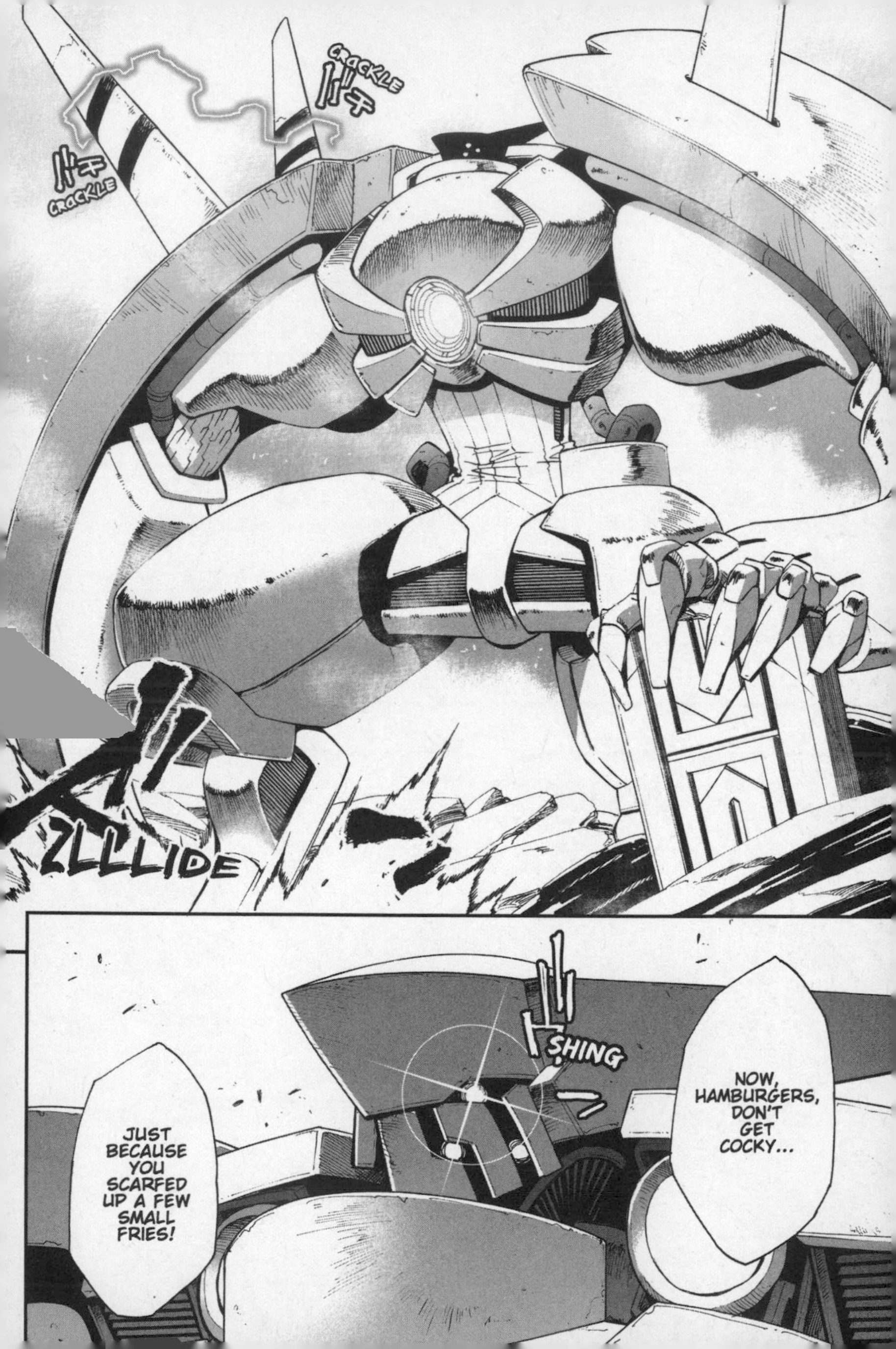
CRACKLE
CRACKLE
ZLLLIDE
SHING
NOW, HAMBURGERS, DON'T GET COCKY...
JUST BECAUSE YOU SCARFED UP A FEW SMALL FRIES!

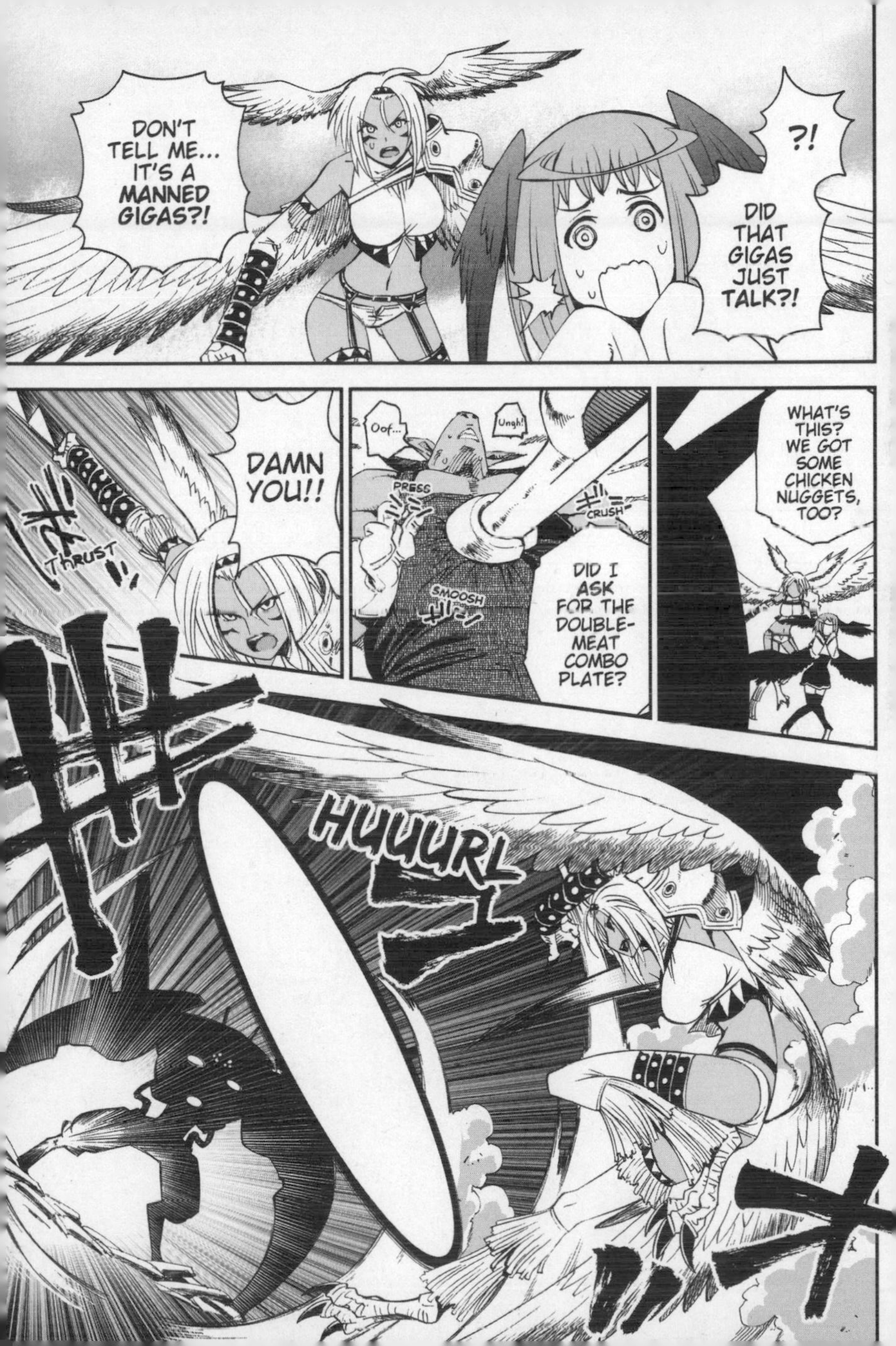
?!
DID THAT GIGAS JUST TALK?!
DON'T TELL ME... IT'S A MANNED GIGAS?!
WHAT'S THIS? WE GOT SOME CHICKEN NUGGETS, TOO?
Ungh!
Oof...
CRUSH
PRESS
DID I ASK FOR THE DOUBLE-MEAT COMBO PLATE?
SMOOSH
DAMN YOU!!
THRUST
HUUURL

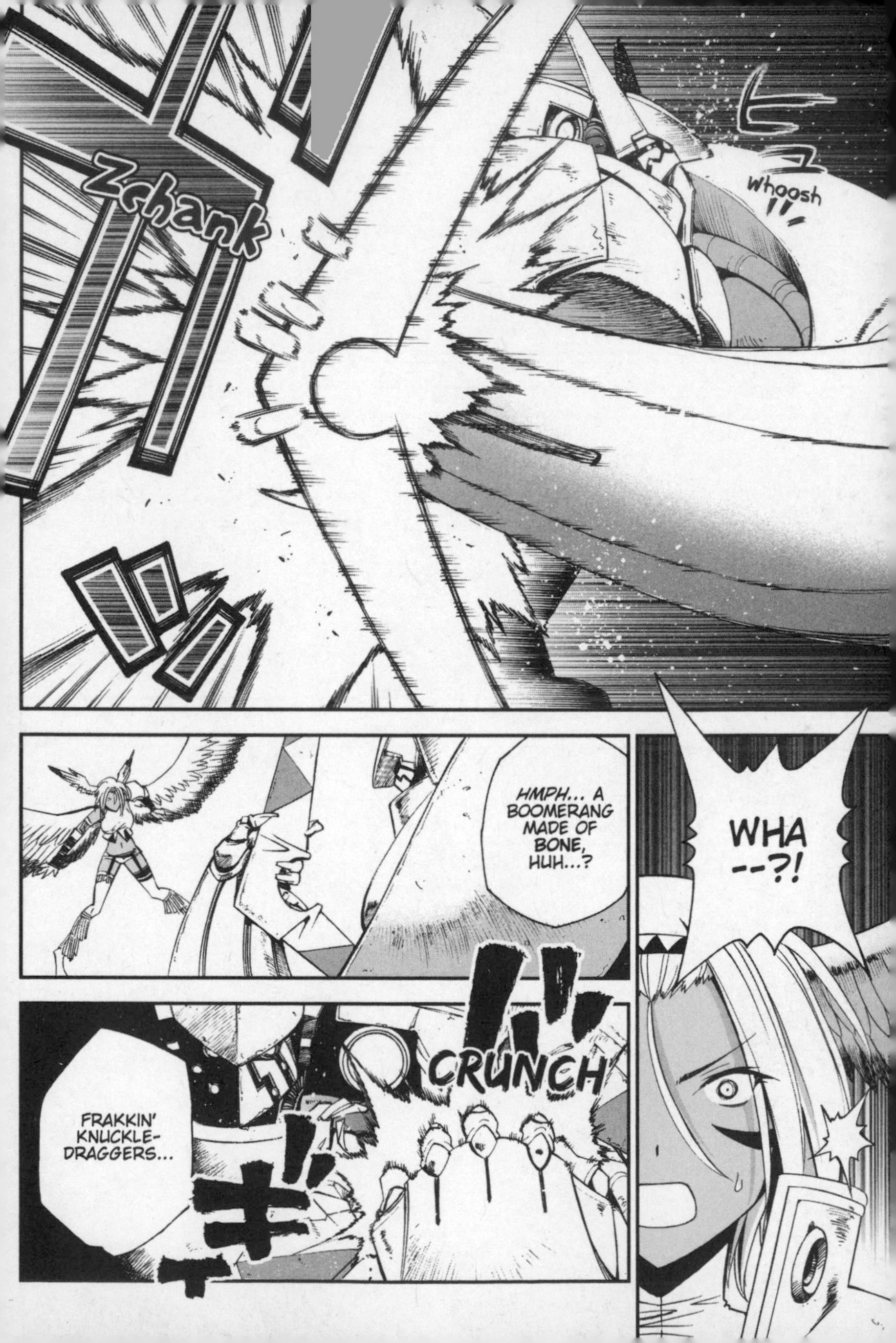
Whoosh
Zchank
WHA--?!
HMPH... A BOOMERANG MADE OF BONE, HUH...?
CRUNCH
FRAKKIN' KNUCKLE-DRAGGERS...

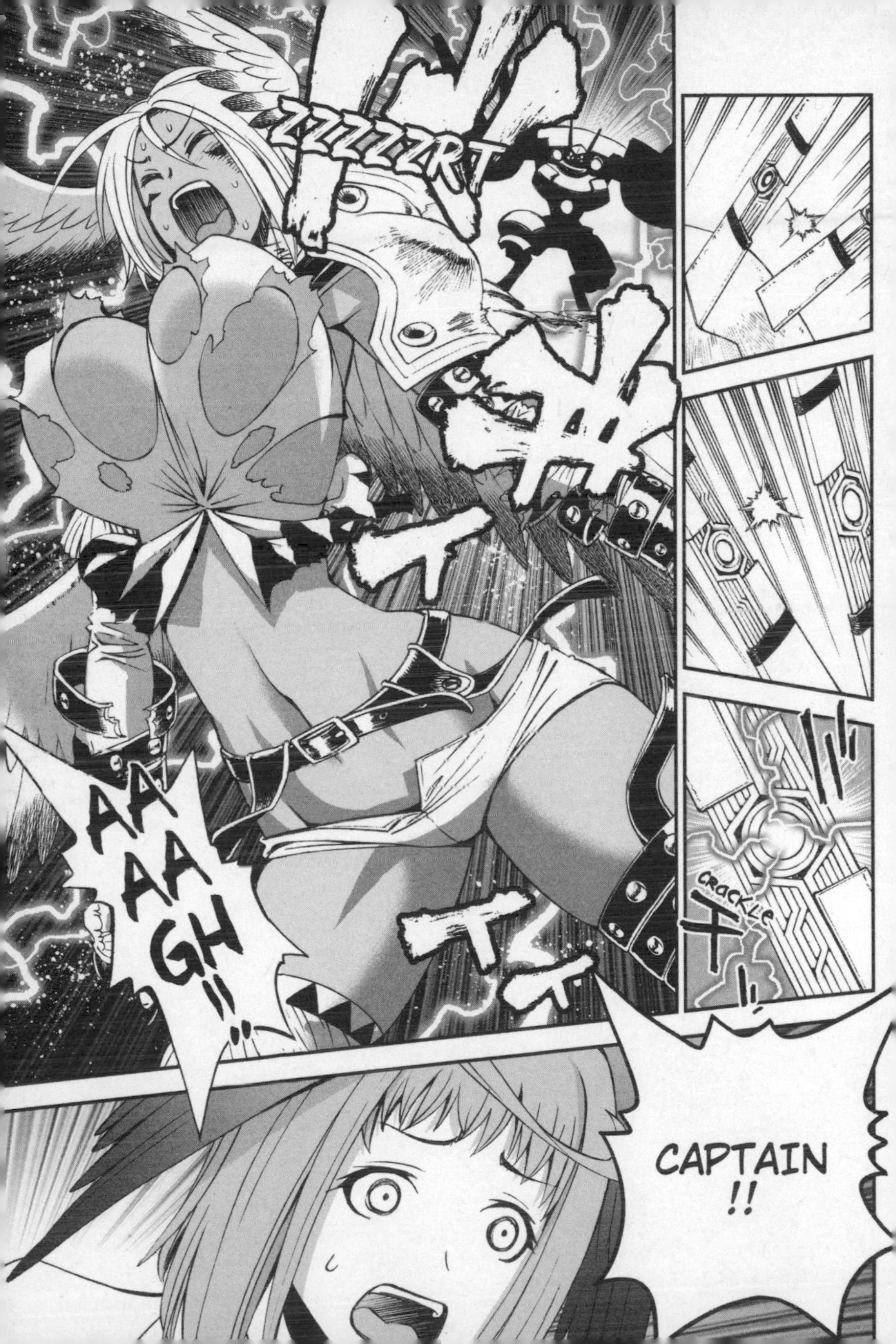
CRACKLE
ZZZZZRT
AAAAGH!!
CAPTAIN!!

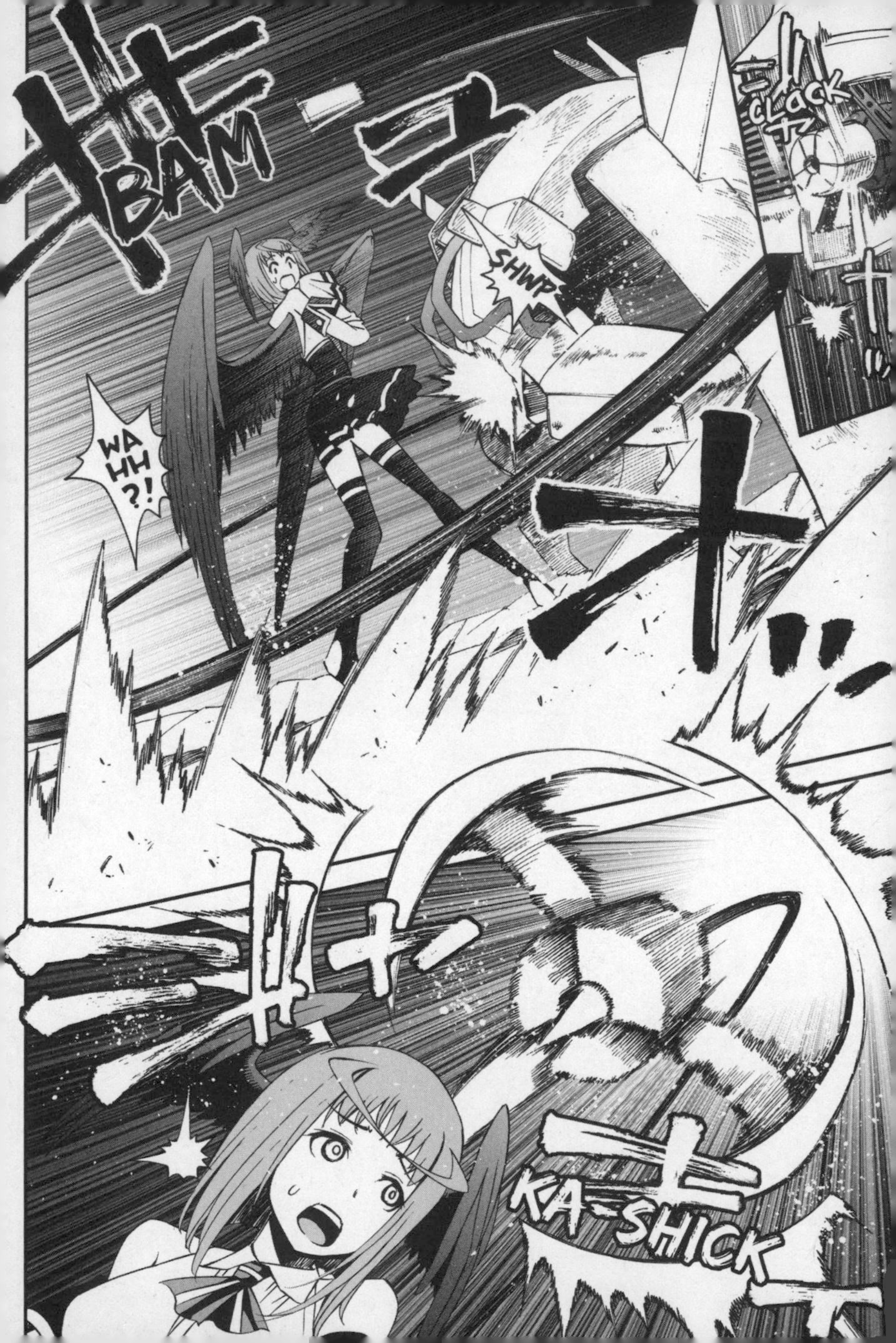
CLACK
BAM
SHWP
WAHH?!
KA-SHICK

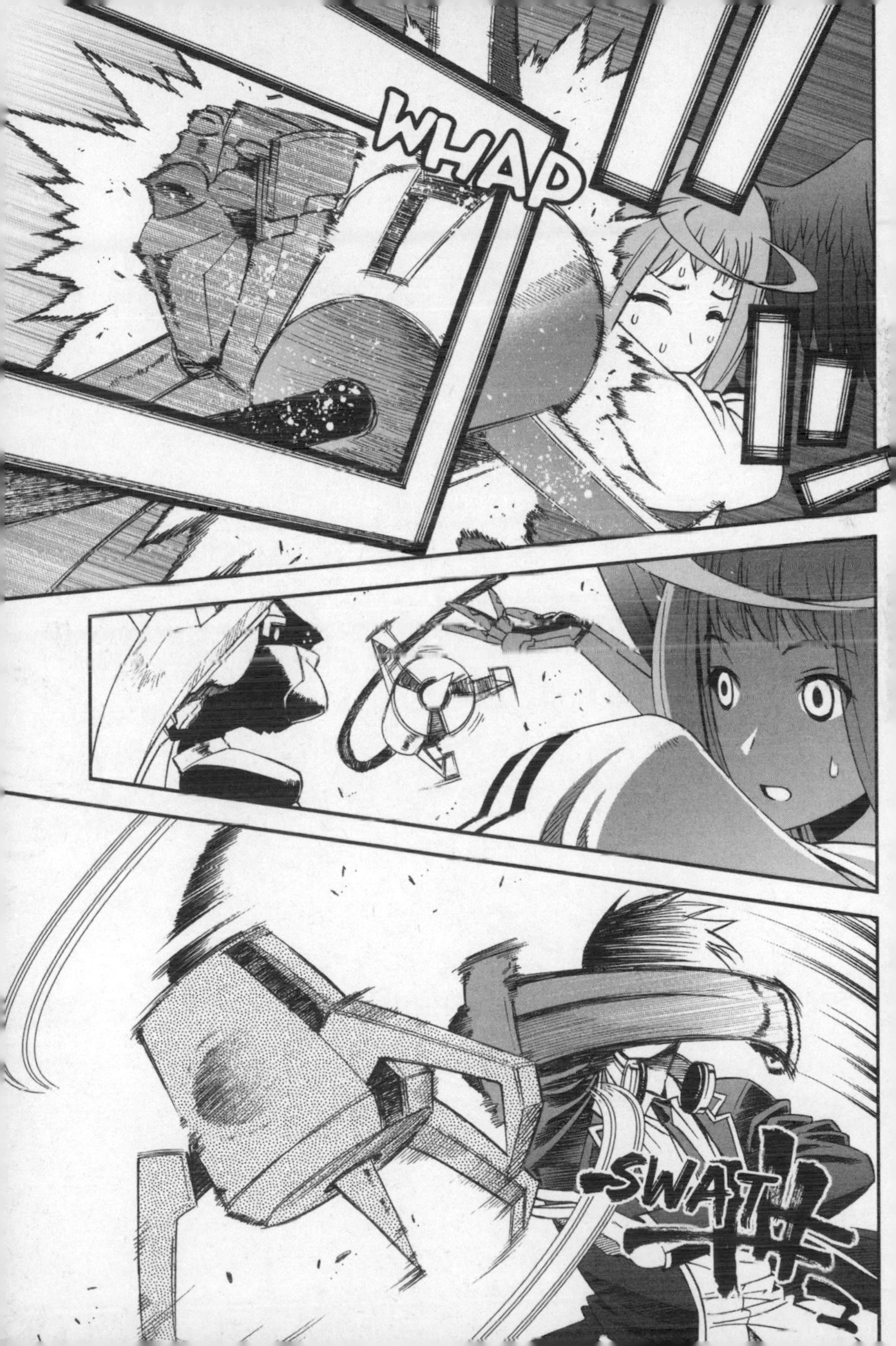
WHAP
SWATH

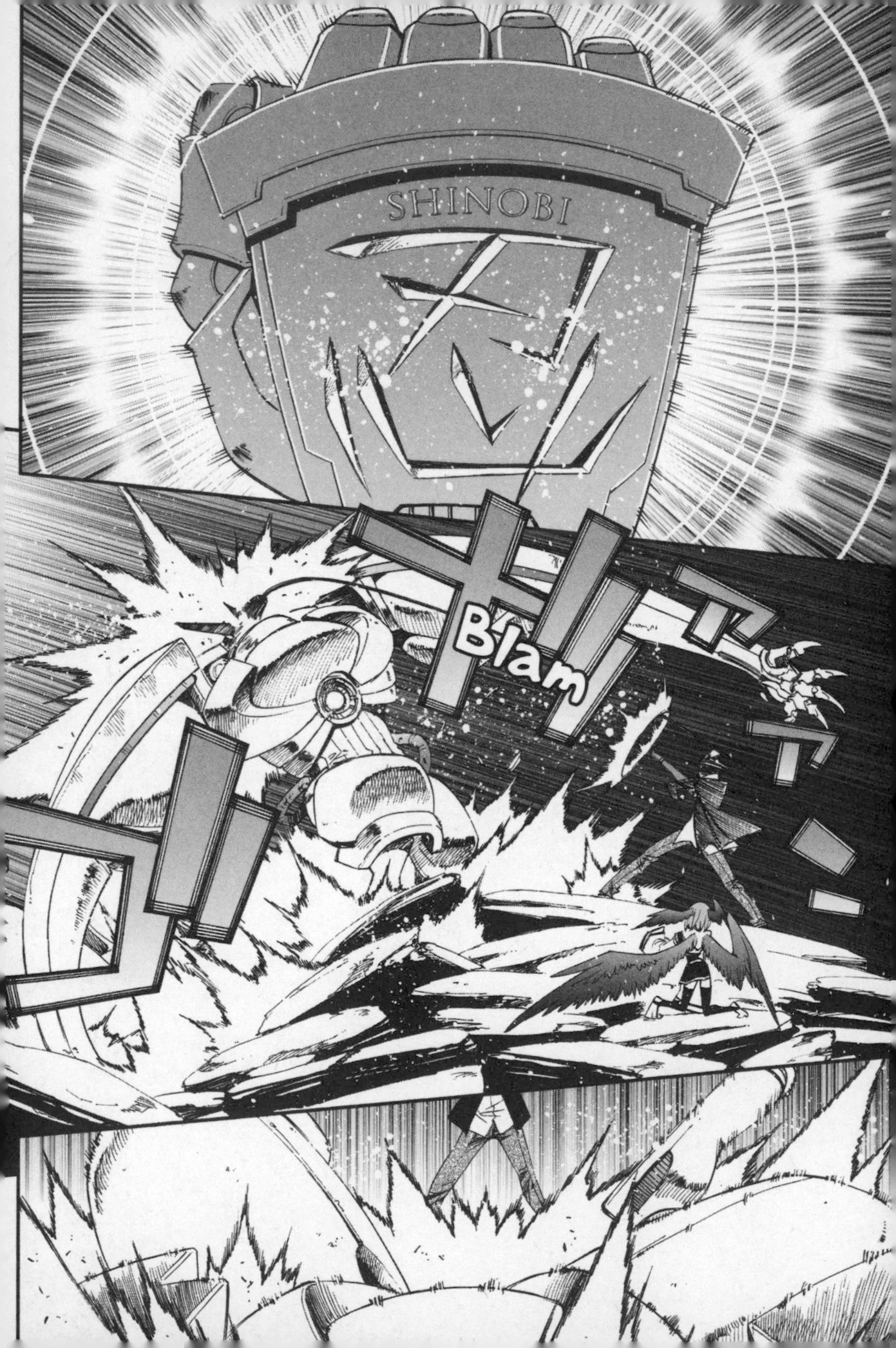
SHINOBI
Blam

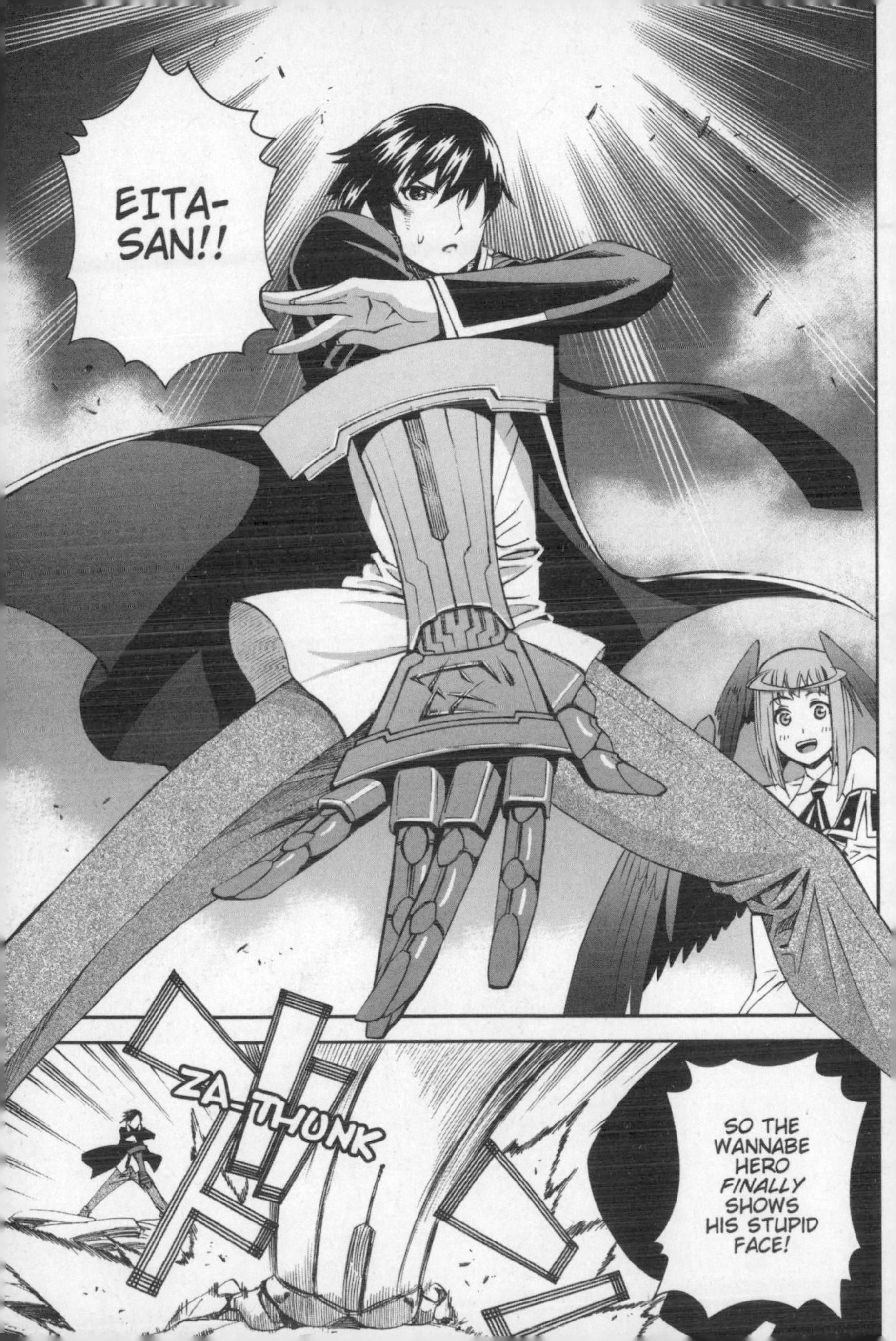
EITA-SAN!!
ZA-THUNK
SO THE WANNABE HERO *FINALLY* SHOWS HIS STUPID FACE!

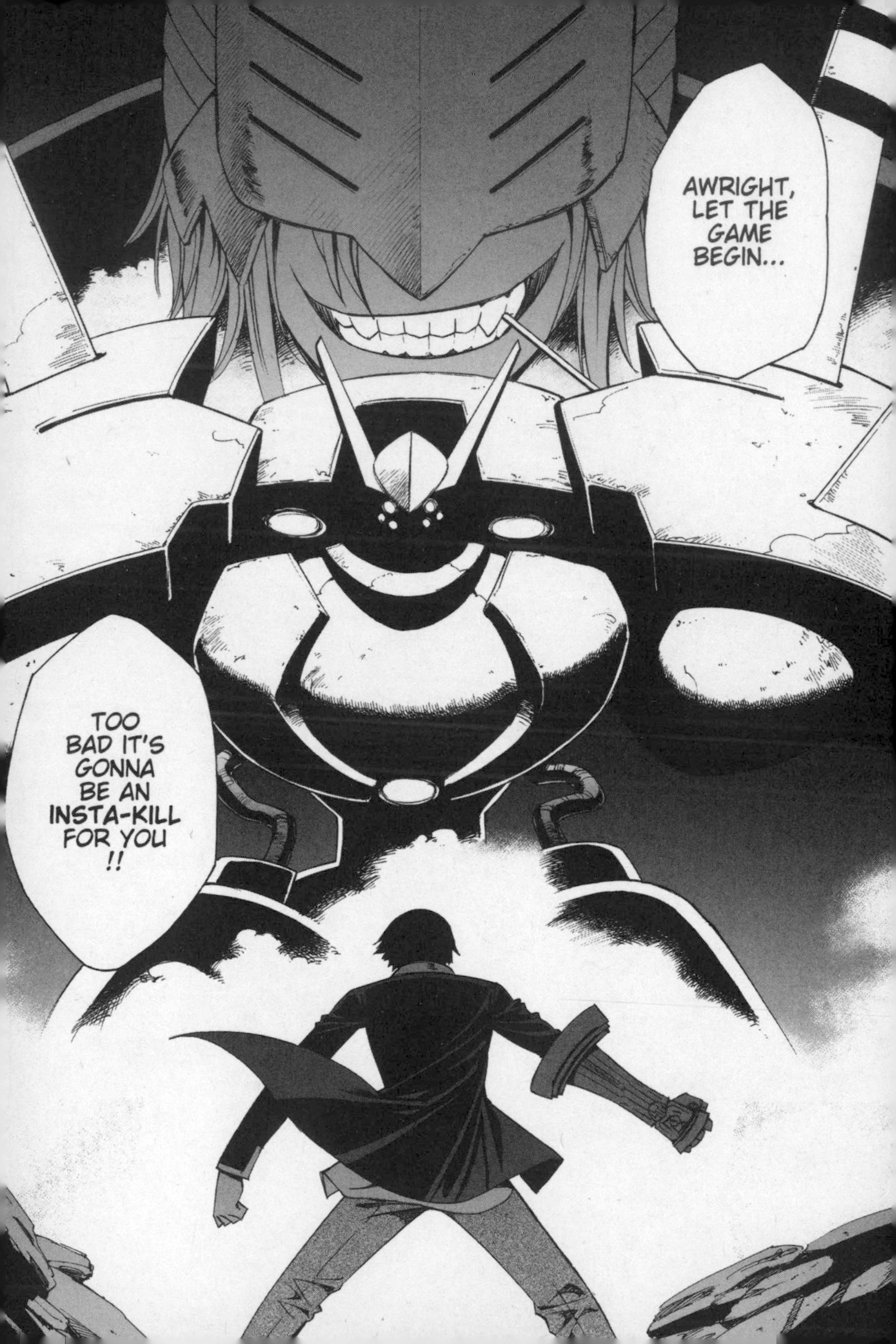
AWRIGHT, LET THE GAME BEGIN...
TOO BAD IT'S GONNA BE AN INSTA-KILL FOR YOU !!

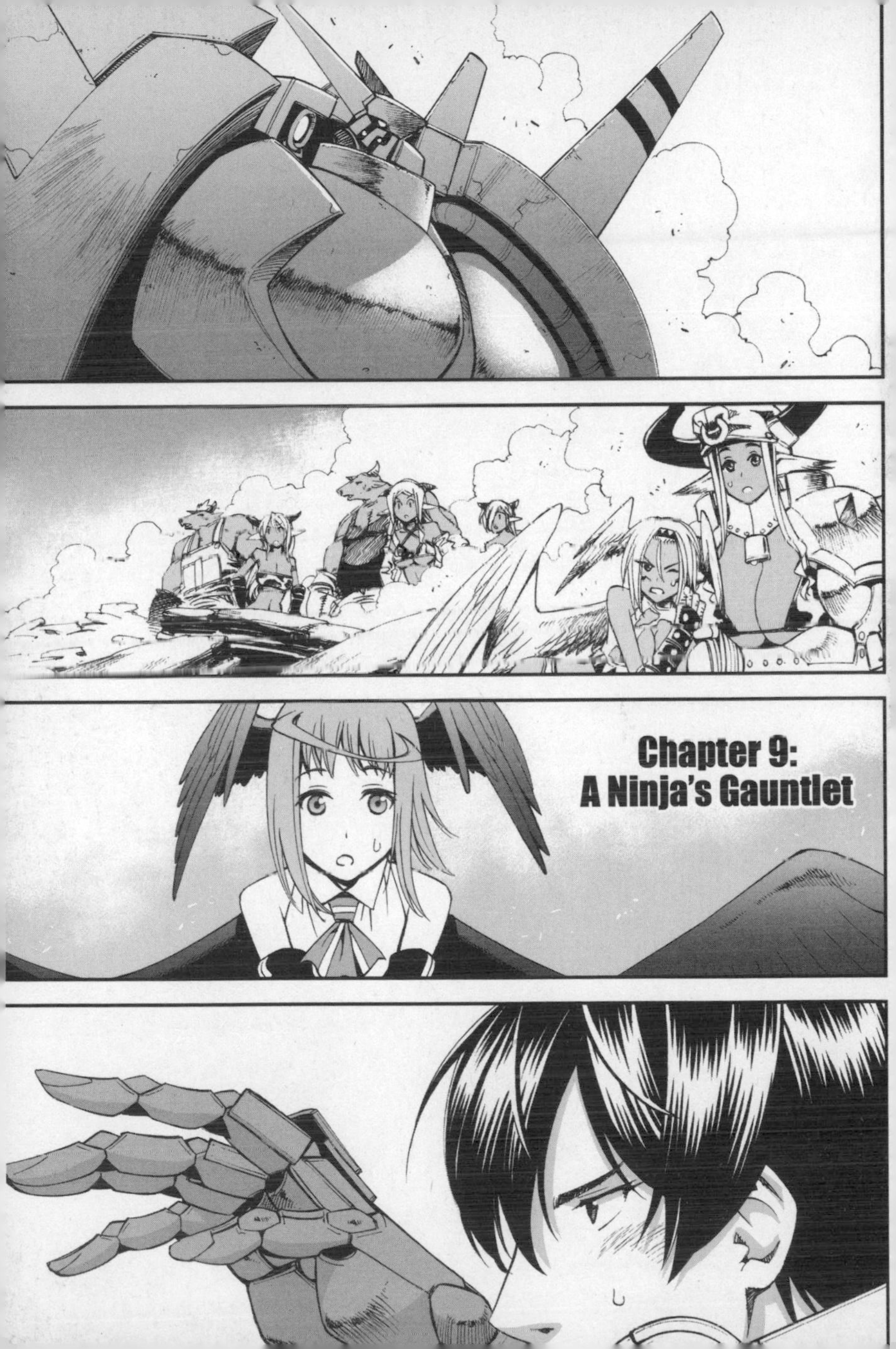
Chapter 9:
A Ninja's Gauntlet

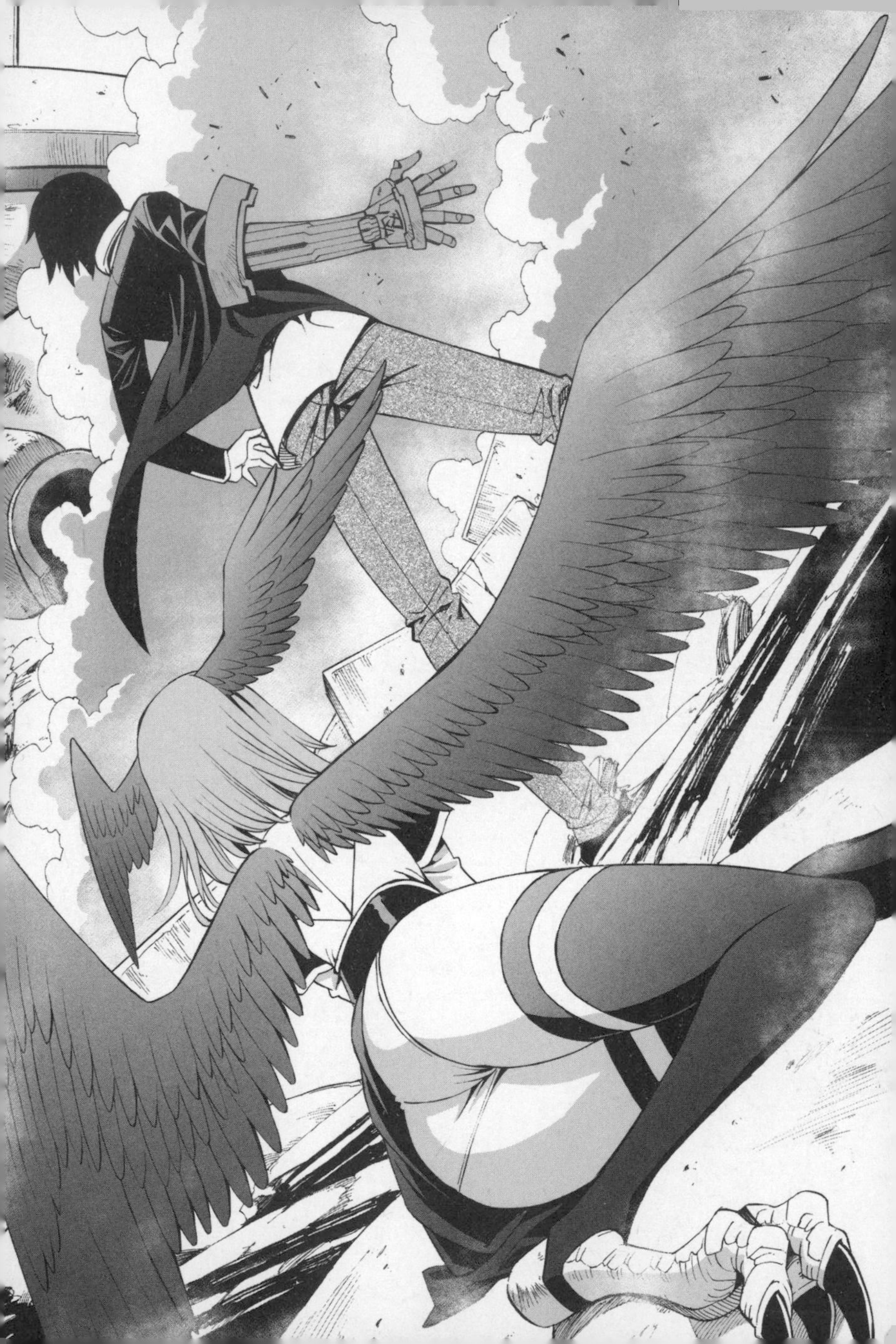

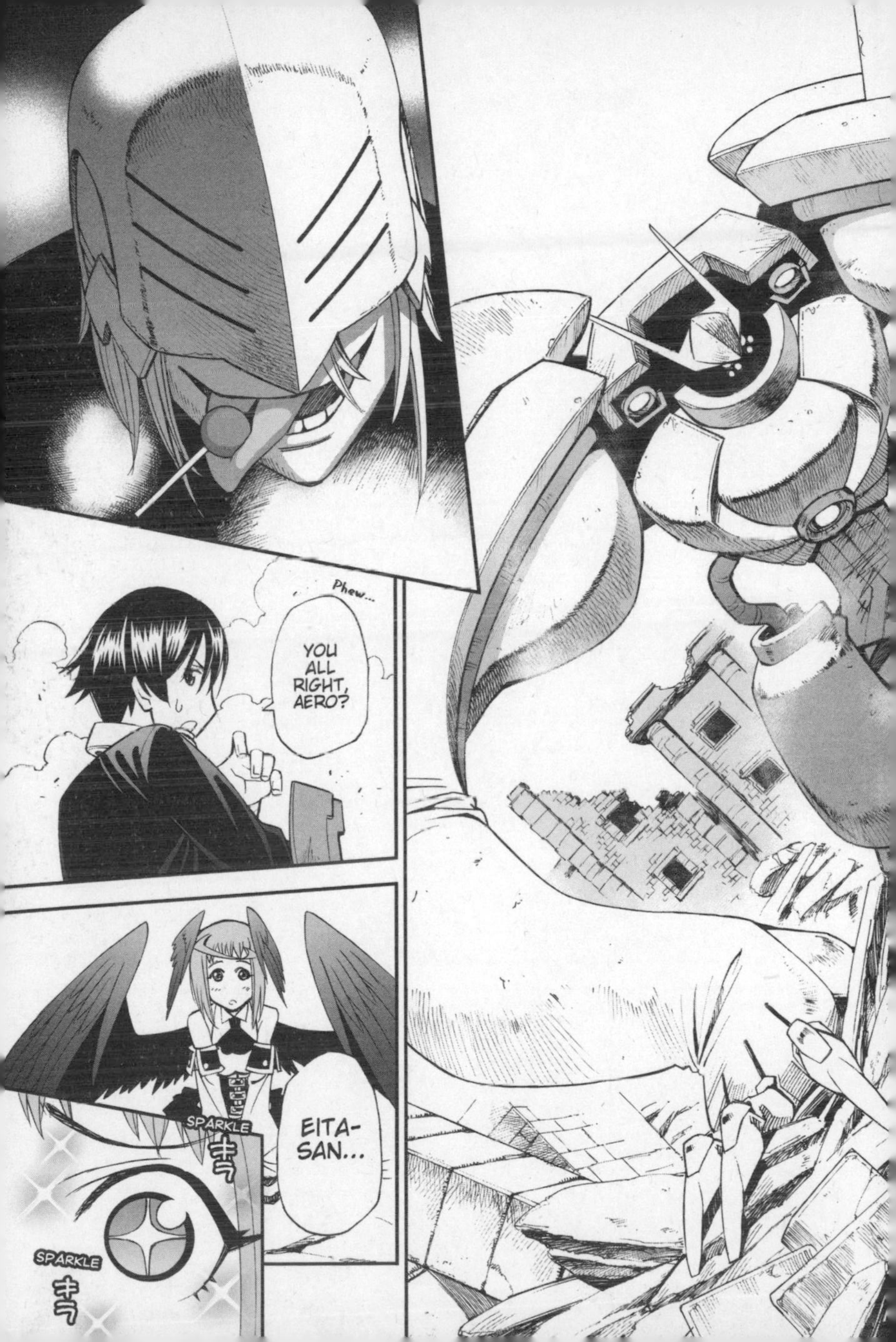
Phew...
YOU ALL RIGHT, AERO?
EITA-SAN...
SPARKLE
キラ
SPARKLE
キラ

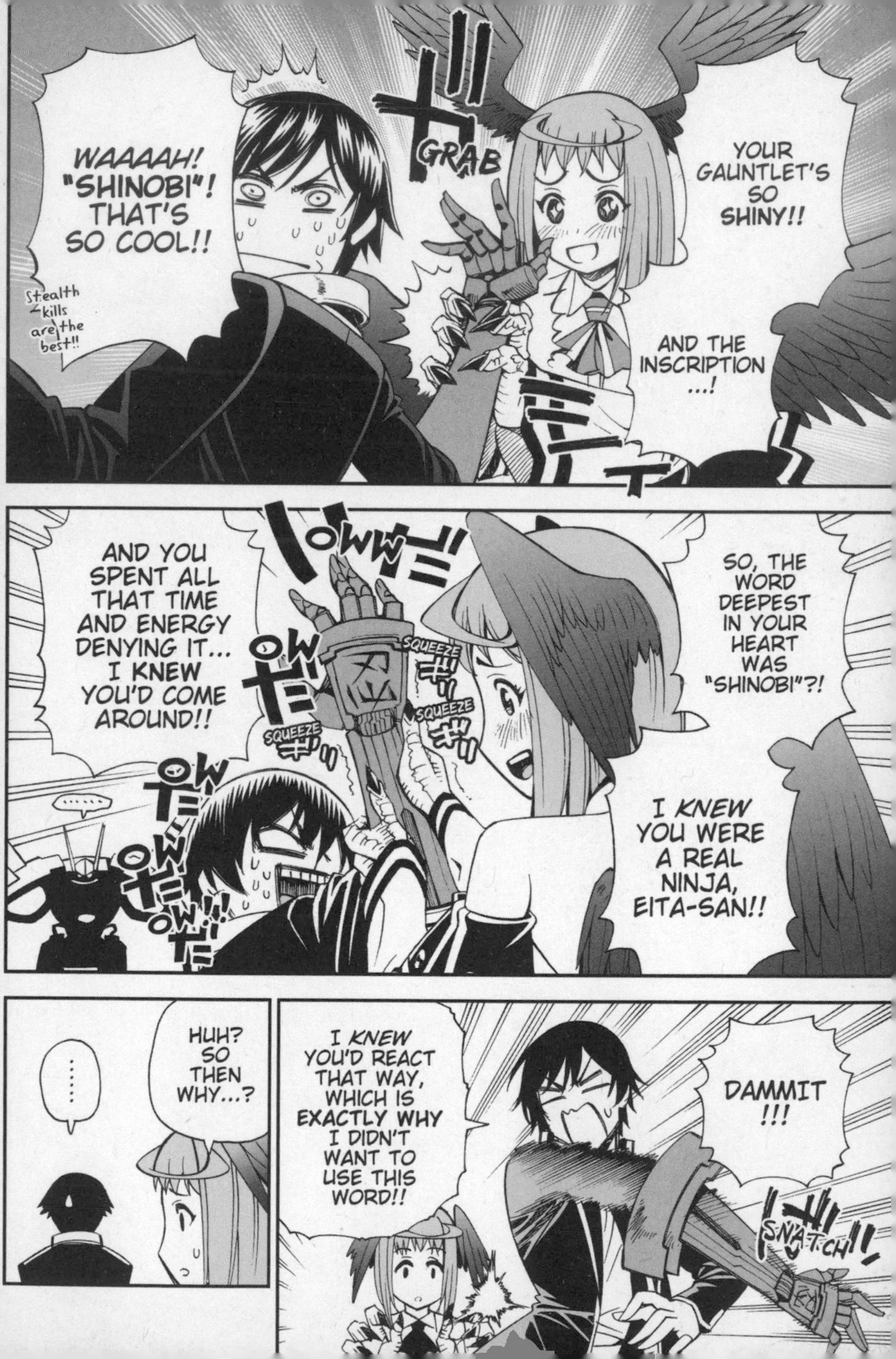
YOUR GAUNTLET'S SO SHINY!!
GRAB
AND THE INSCRIPTION ...!
WAAAAH! "SHINOBI"! THAT'S SO COOL!!
Stealth kills are the best!!
SO, THE WORD DEEPEST IN YOUR HEART WAS "SHINOBI"?!
I KNEW YOU WERE A REAL NINJA, EITA-SAN!!
SQUEEZE
SQUEEZE
AND YOU SPENT ALL THAT TIME AND ENERGY DENYING IT... I KNEW YOU'D COME AROUND!!
OW
SQUEEZE
OW
OW
OW!!
......
DAMMIT!!!
SNATCH
I KNEW YOU'D REACT THAT WAY, WHICH IS EXACTLY WHY I DIDN'T WANT TO USE THIS WORD!!
HUH? SO THEN WHY...?
......

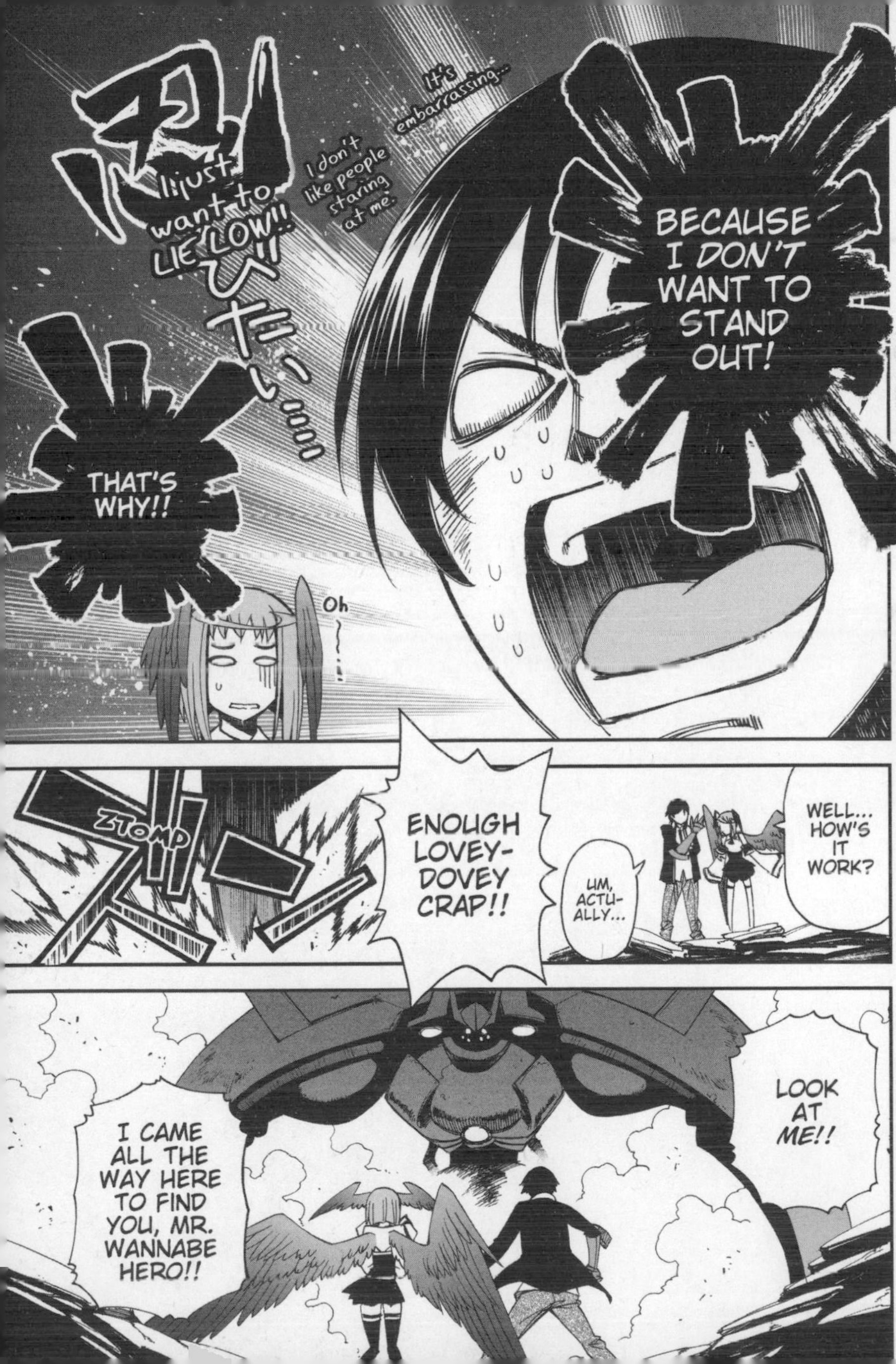
BECAUSE I DON'T WANT TO STAND OUT!
It's embarrassing...
I don't like people staring at me.
I-I just want to LIE LOW!!
THAT'S WHY!!
Oh ~...!
WELL... HOW'S IT WORK?
UM, ACTU-ALLY...
ENOUGH LOVEY-DOVEY CRAP!!
ZTOMP
LOOK AT ME!!
I CAME ALL THE WAY HERE TO FIND YOU, MR. WANNABE HERO!!

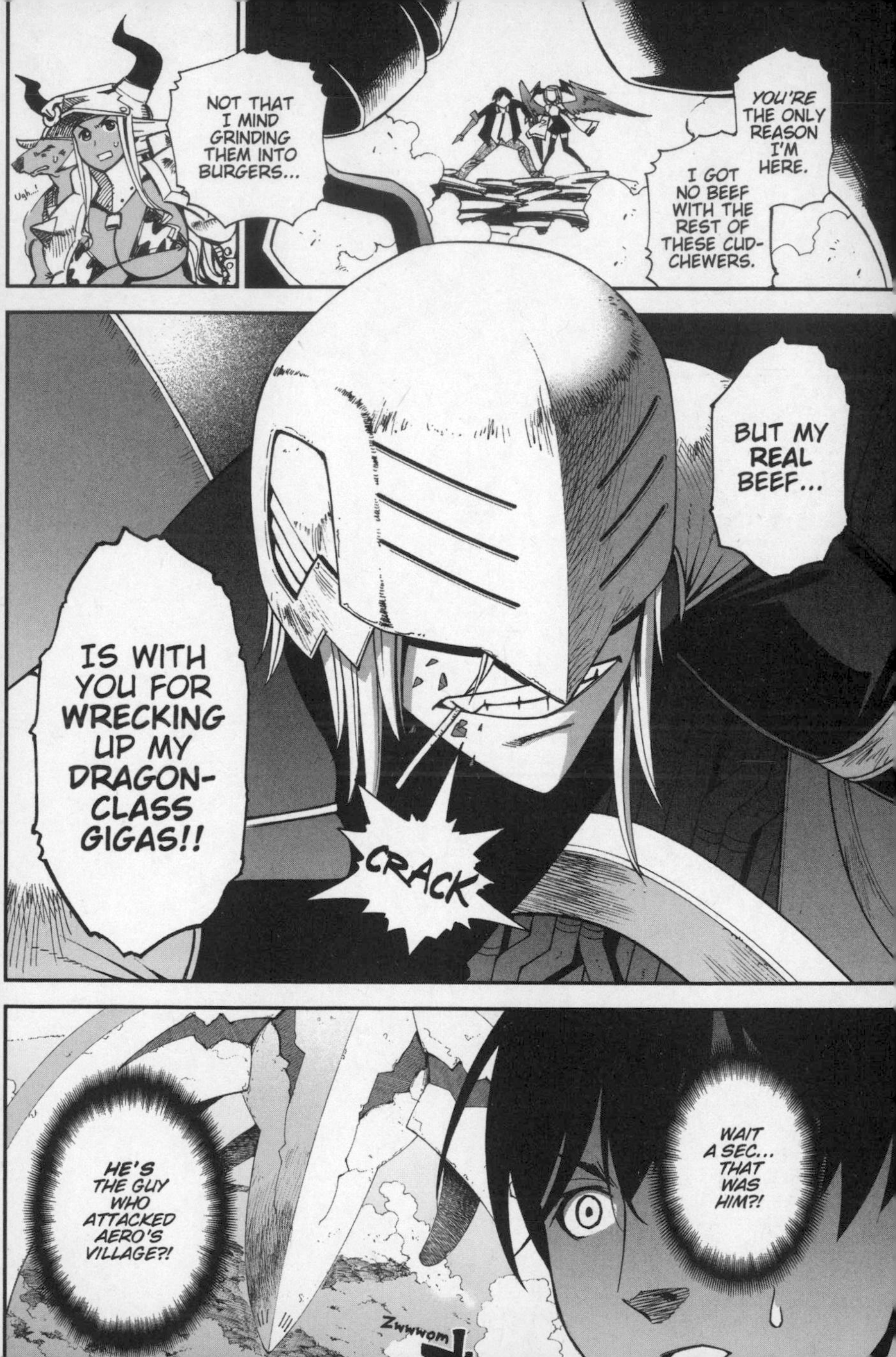
YOU'RE THE ONLY REASON I'M HERE.
I GOT NO BEEF WITH THE REST OF THESE CUD-CHEWERS.
NOT THAT I MIND GRINDING THEM INTO BURGERS...
Ugh...!
BUT MY REAL BEEF...
IS WITH YOU FOR WRECKING UP MY DRAGON-CLASS GIGAS!!
CRACK
WAIT A SEC... THAT WAS HIM?!
HE'S THE GUY WHO ATTACKED AERO'S VILLAGE?!
Zwwwom

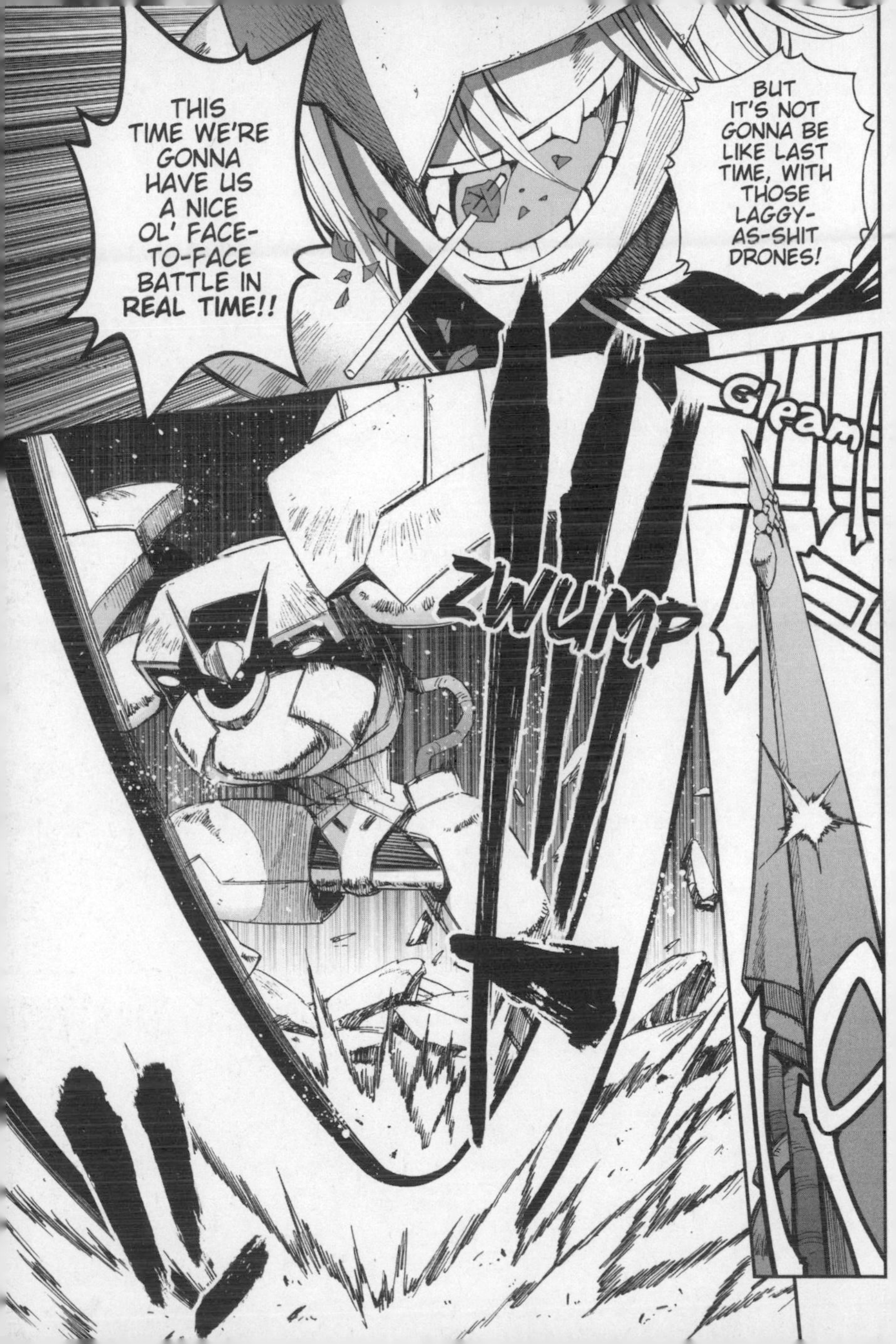
BUT IT'S NOT GONNA BE LIKE LAST TIME, WITH THOSE LAGGY-AS-SHIT DRONES!
THIS TIME WE'RE GONNA HAVE US A NICE OL' FACE-TO-FACE BATTLE IN REAL TIME!!
Gleam
ZWUMP

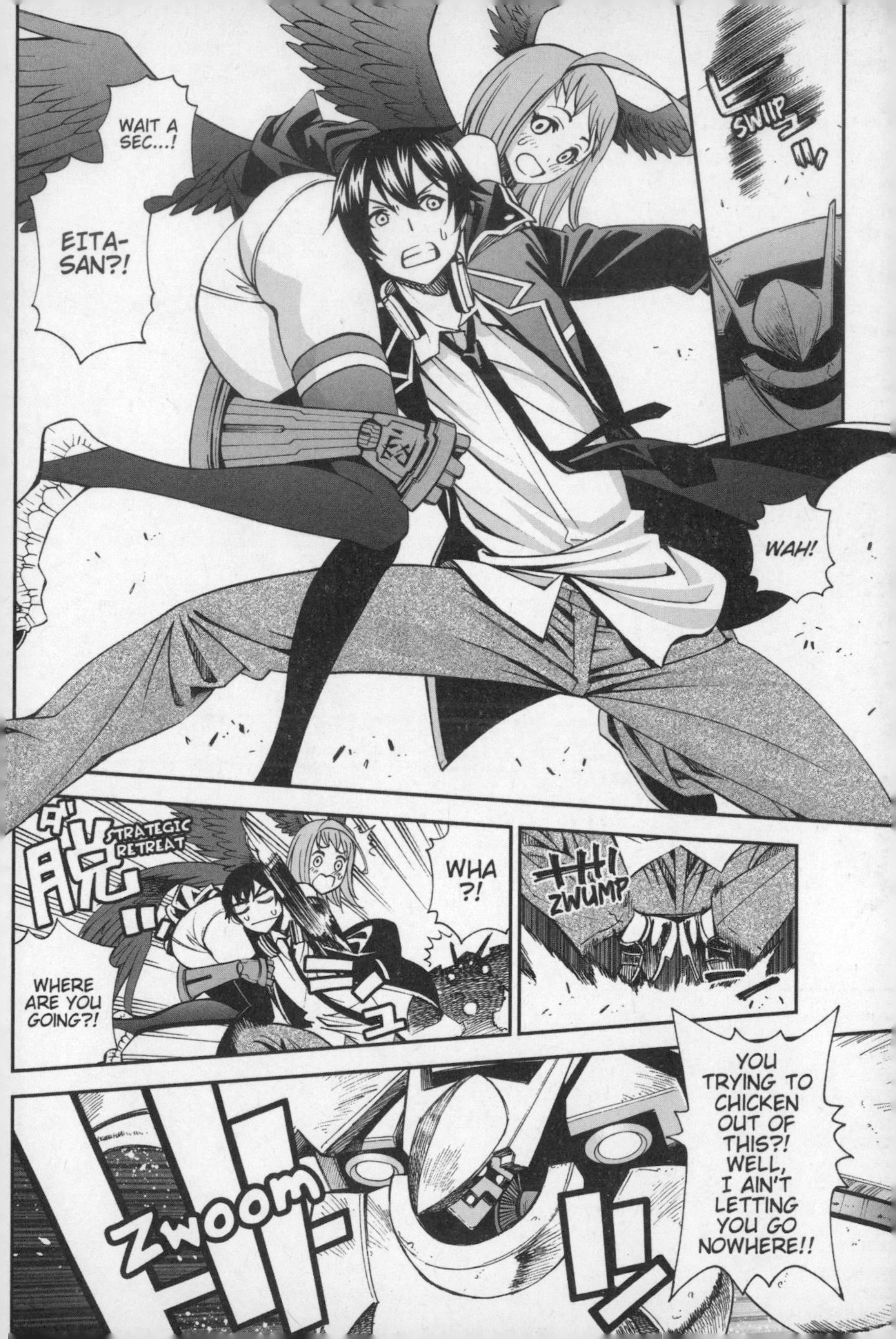
SWIIP
WAIT A SEC...!
EITA-SAN?!
WAH!
ZWUMP
STRATEGIC RETREAT
WHA?!
WHERE ARE YOU GOING?!
YOU TRYING TO CHICKEN OUT OF THIS?! WELL, I AIN'T LETTING YOU GO NOWHERE!!
Zwoom

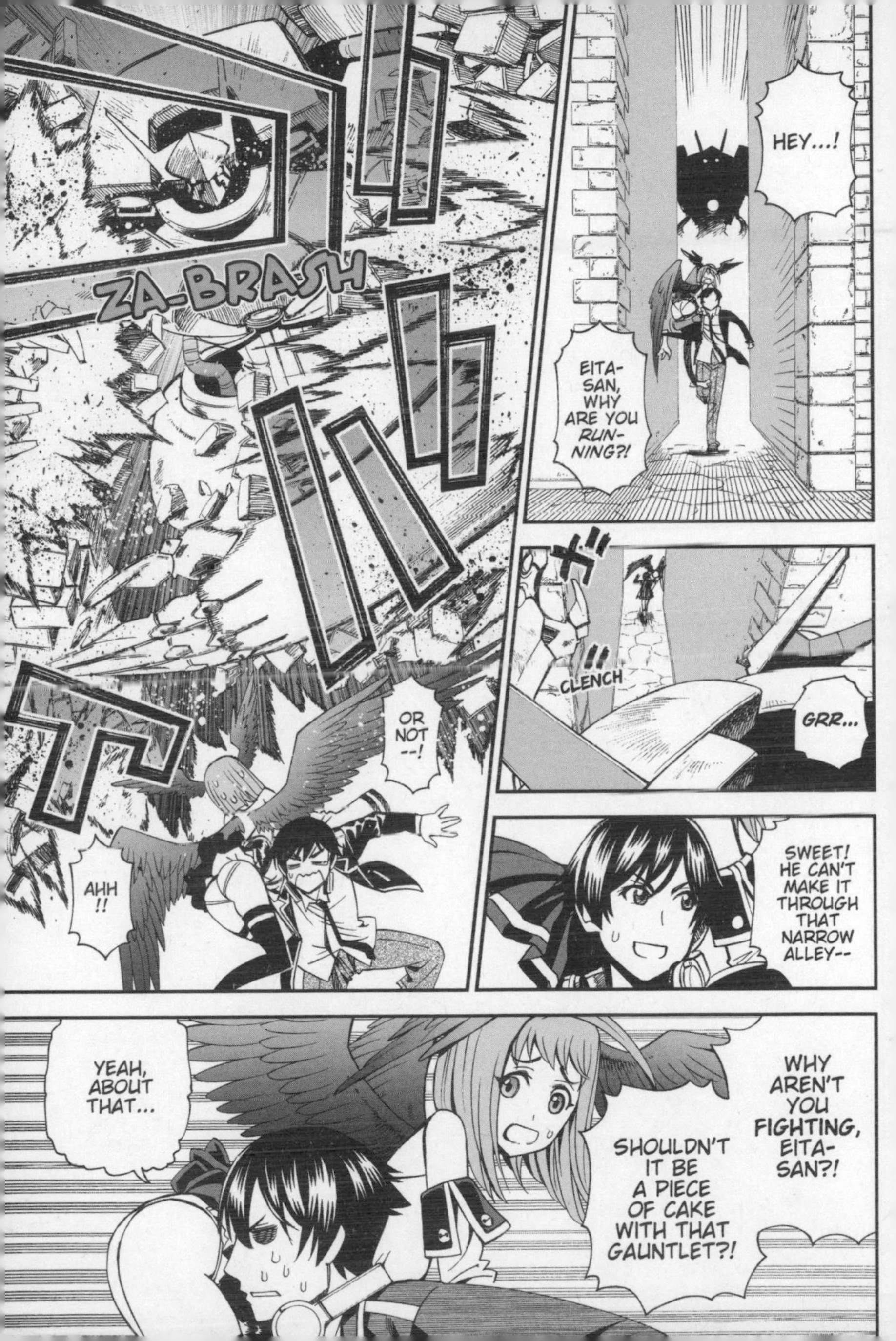

HEY...!
EITA-SAN, WHY ARE YOU RUN-NING?!
CLENCH
GRR...
SWEET! HE CAN'T MAKE IT THROUGH THAT NARROW ALLEY--
ZA-BRASH
OR NOT --!
AHH !!
WHY AREN'T YOU FIGHTING, EITA-SAN?!
SHOULDN'T IT BE A PIECE OF CAKE WITH THAT GAUNTLET?!
YEAH, ABOUT THAT...

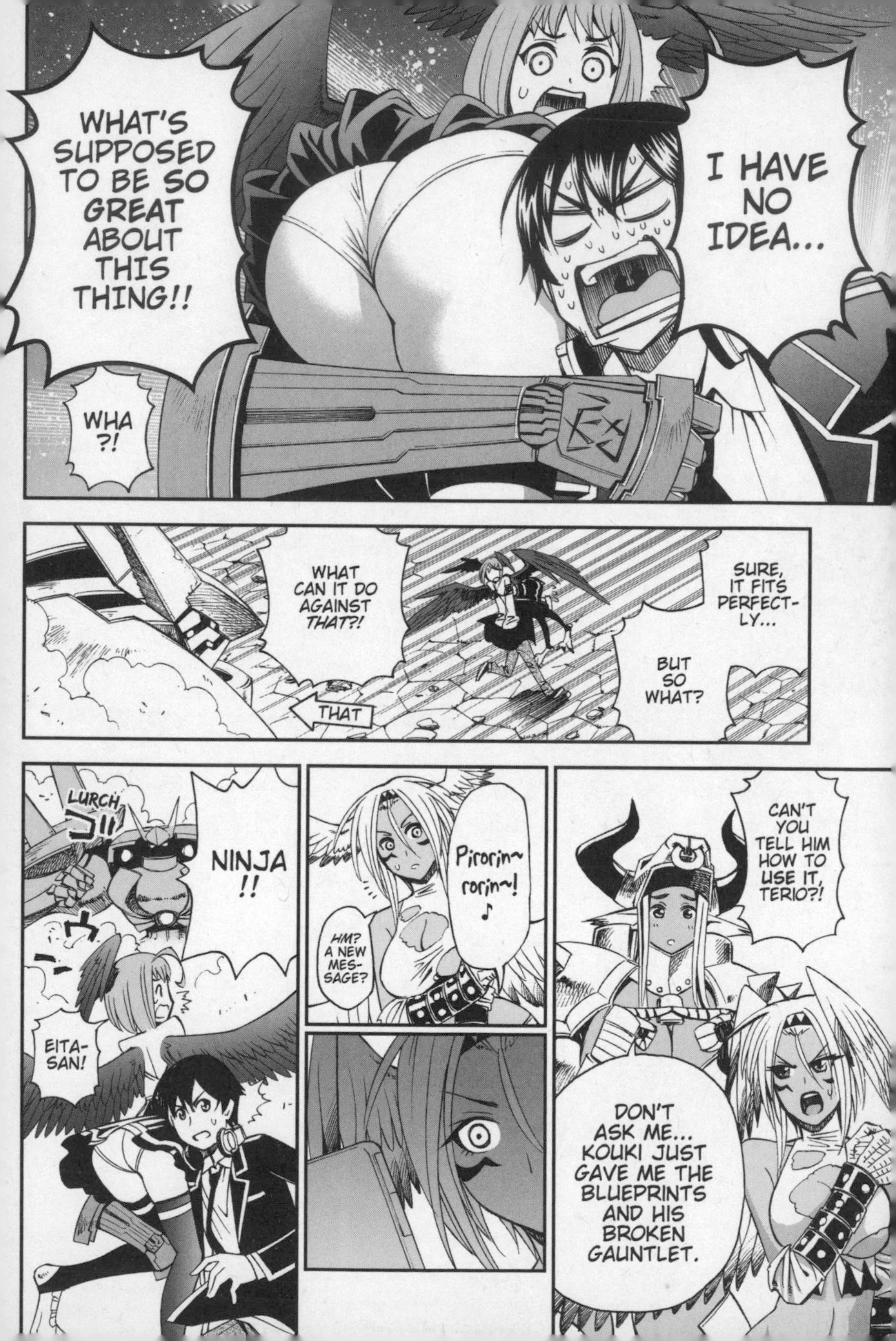
I HAVE NO IDEA...
WHAT'S SUPPOSED TO BE SO GREAT ABOUT THIS THING!!
WHA ?!
SURE, IT FITS PERFECT-LY...
BUT SO WHAT?
WHAT CAN IT DO AGAINST THAT?!
THAT
CAN'T YOU TELL HIM HOW TO USE IT, TERIO?!
DON'T ASK ME... KOUKI JUST GAVE ME THE BLUEPRINTS AND HIS BROKEN GAUNTLET.
Pirorin~ rorin~! ♪
HM? A NEW MES-SAGE?
LURCH
NINJA !!
EITA-SAN!

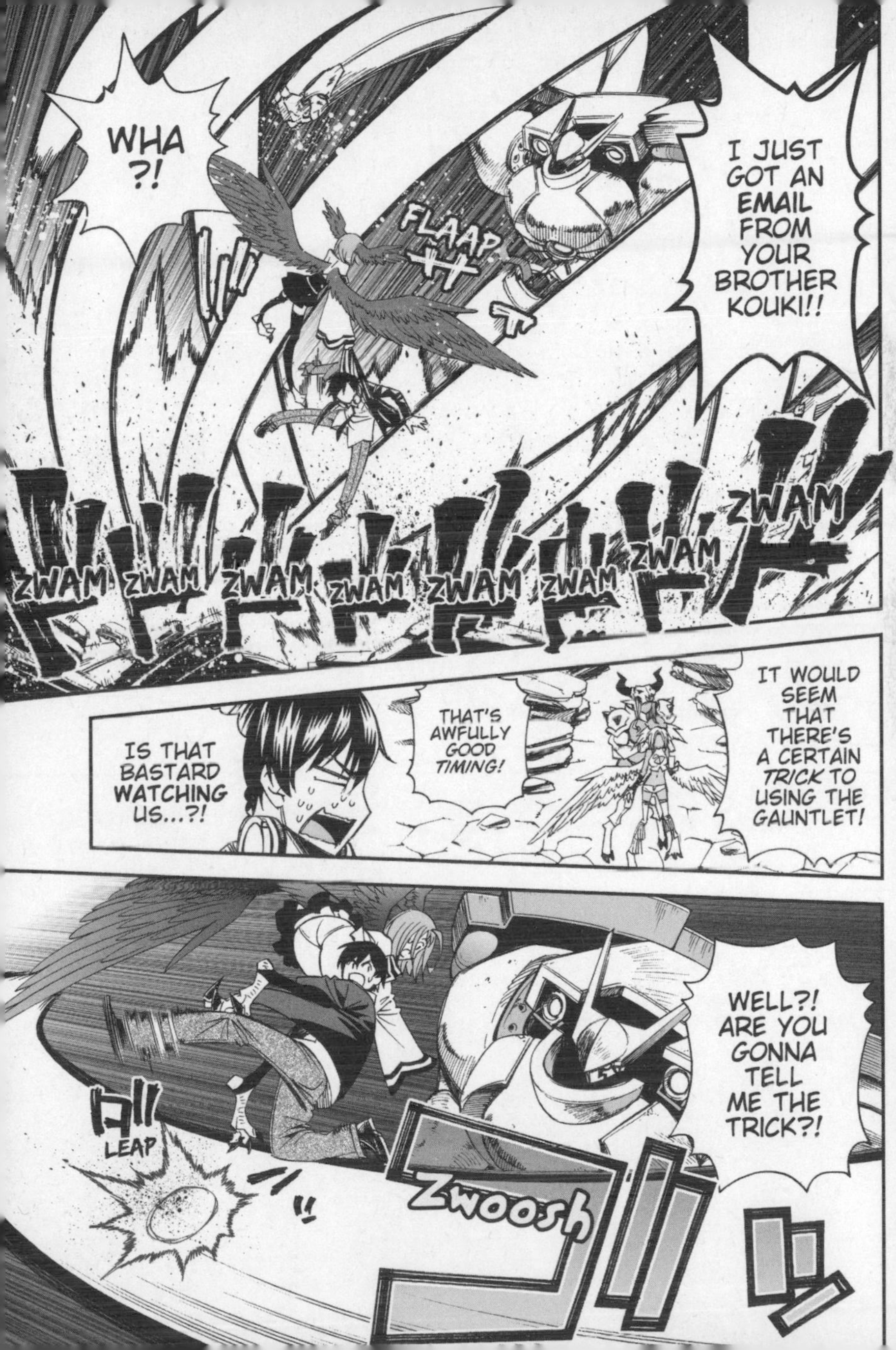
I JUST GOT AN EMAIL FROM YOUR BROTHER KOUKI!!
WHA ?!
FLAAP
ZWAM ZWAM ZWAM ZWAM ZWAM ZWAM ZWAM ZWAM ZWAM
IT WOULD SEEM THAT THERE'S A CERTAIN *TRICK* TO USING THE GAUNTLET!
THAT'S AWFULLY GOOD *TIMING*!
IS THAT BASTARD WATCHING US...?!
WELL?! ARE YOU GONNA TELL ME THE TRICK?!
Zwoosh
LEAP
!!

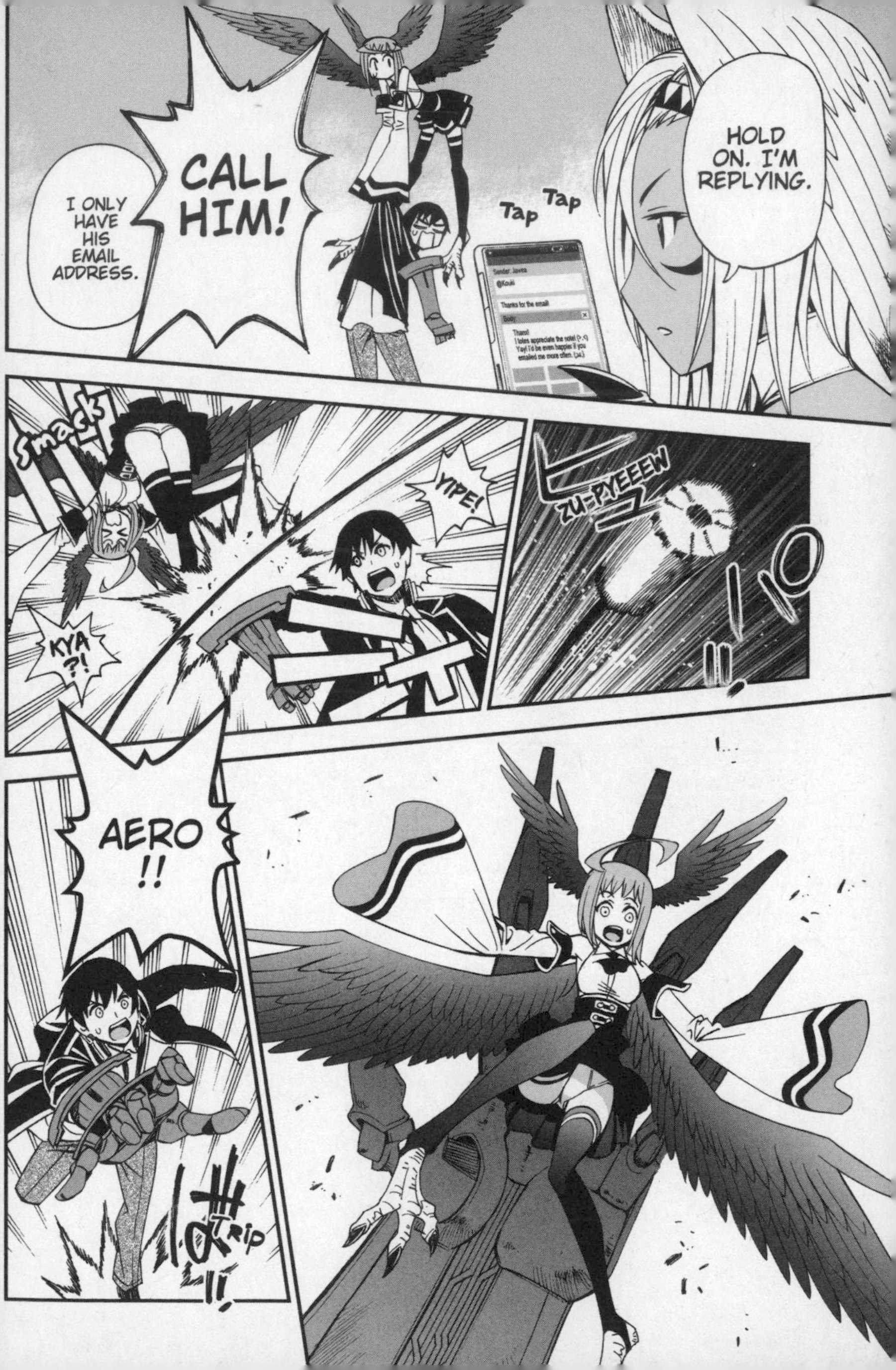
HOLD ON. I'M REPLYING.
Tap Tap
@Kouki
Thanks for the email
Body
I totes appreciate the note!
Yay! I'd be even happier if you emailed me more often.
CALL HIM!
I ONLY HAVE HIS EMAIL ADDRESS.
ZU-PYEEEW
!!
YIPE!
Smack
KYA ?!
...!
AERO !!
Trip

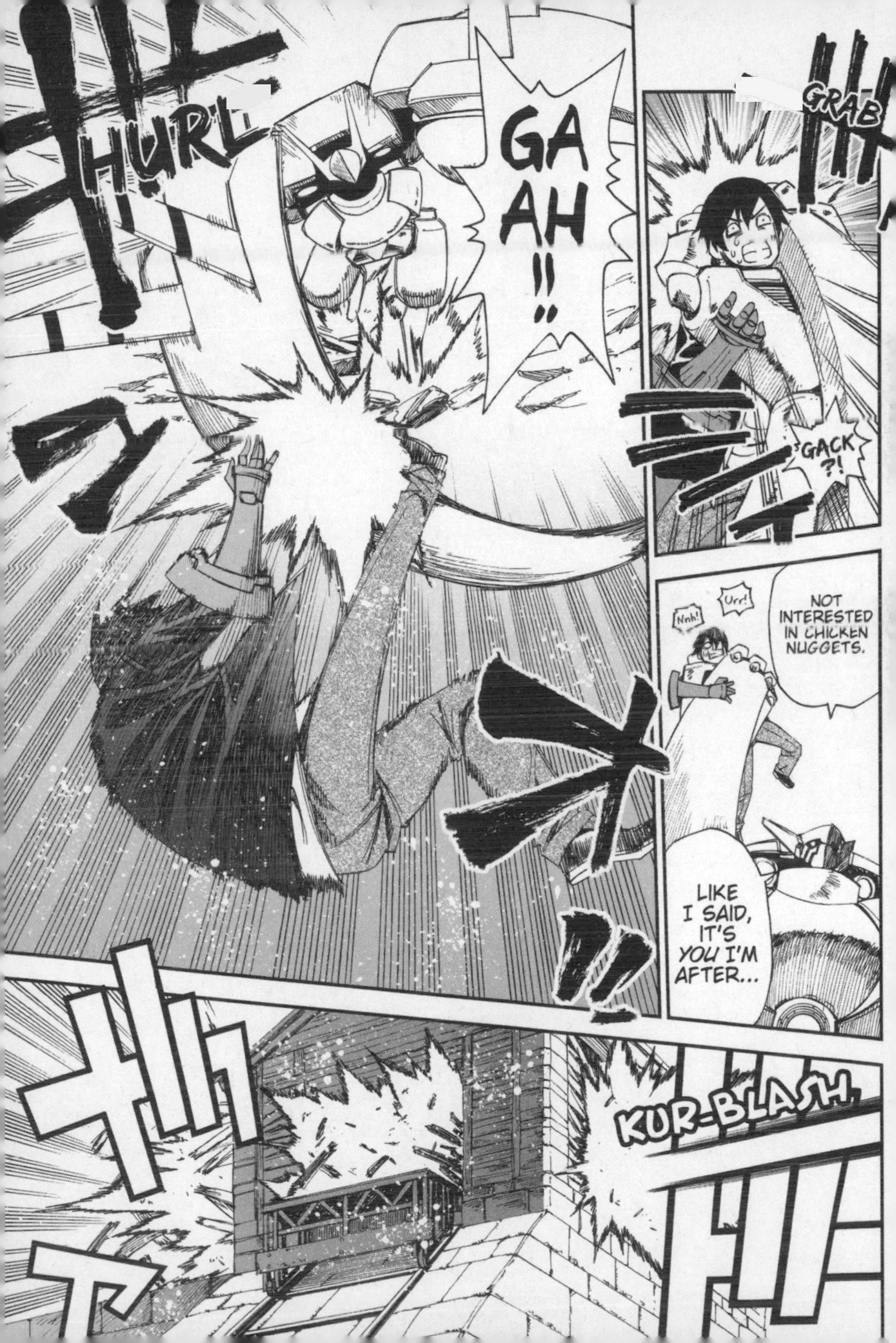
GRAB
GACK ?!
Nnh!
Urr!
NOT INTERESTED IN CHICKEN NUGGETS.
LIKE I SAID, IT'S *YOU* I'M AFTER...
HURL
GAAH!!
KUR-BLASH

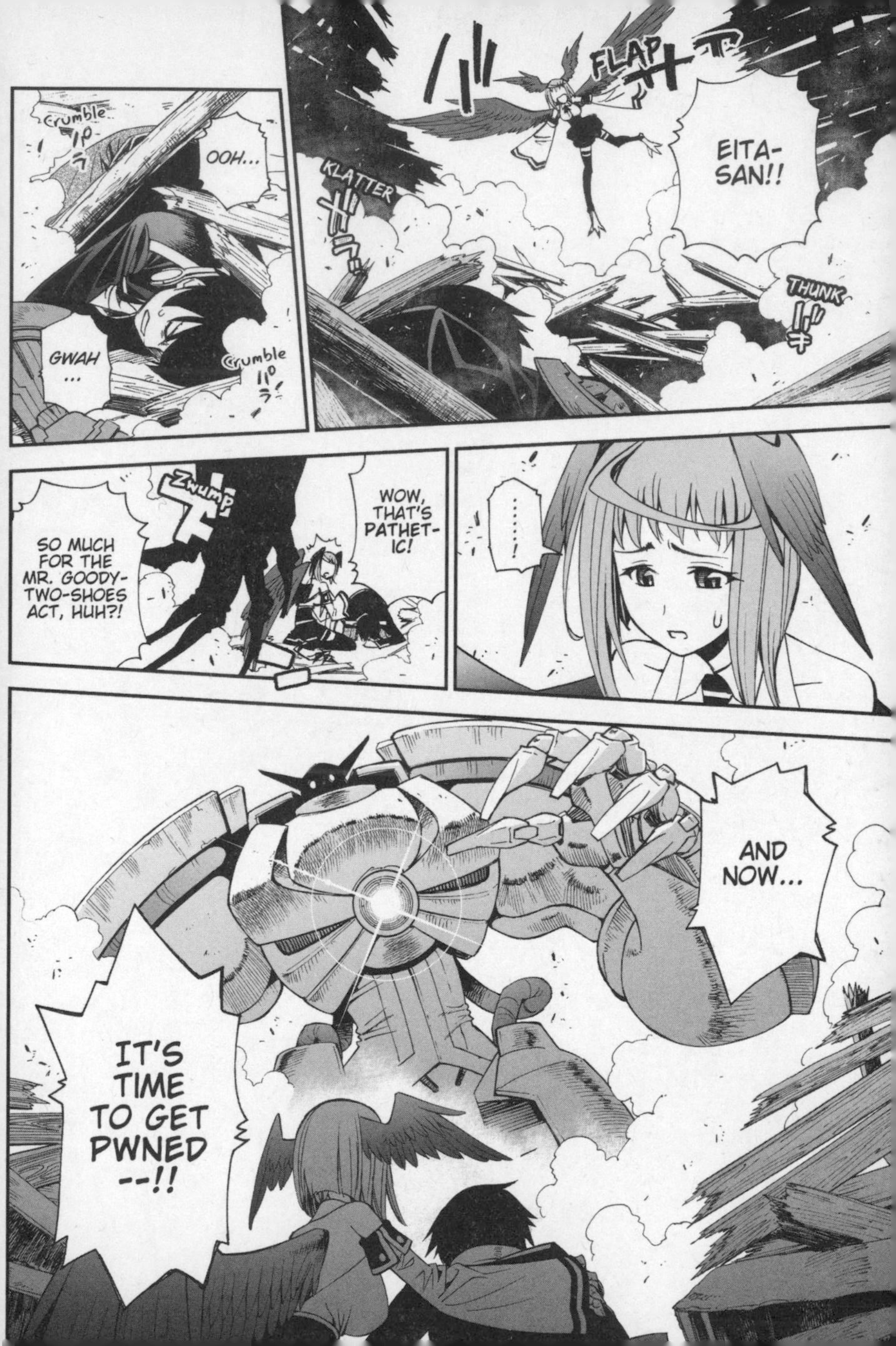
FLAP
EITA-SAN!!
KLATTER
THUNK
crumble
OOH...
GWAH ...
crumble
......!
WOW, THAT'S PATHET-IC!
Zwump
SO MUCH FOR THE MR. GOODY-TWO-SHOES ACT, HUH?!
AND NOW...
IT'S TIME TO GET PWNED --!!

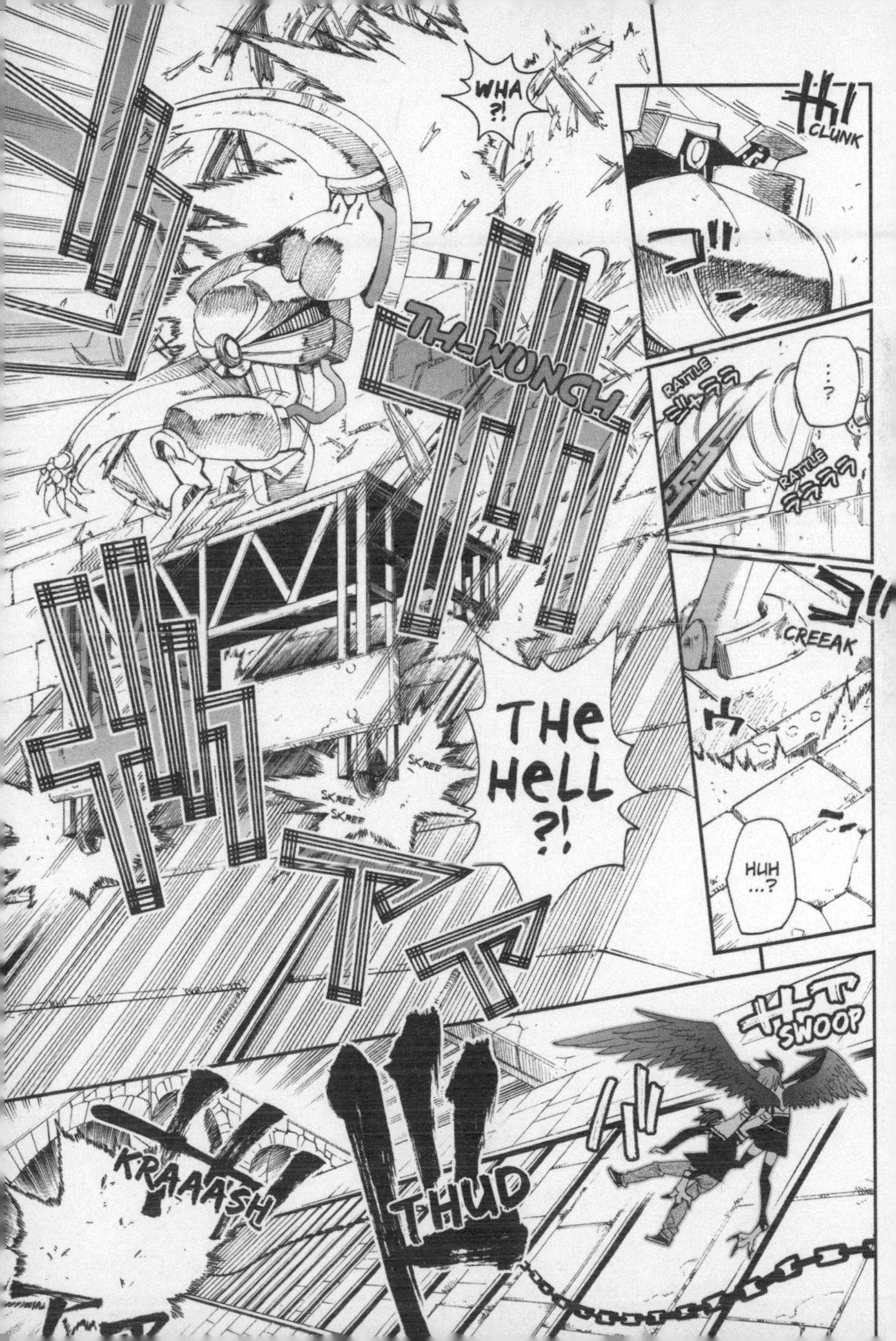
CLUNK
...?
RATTLE
RATTLE
CREEAK
HUH ...?
WHA ?!
TH-WONCH
THE HELL ?!
SKREE
SKREE
SKREE
SWOOP
THUD
KRAAASH

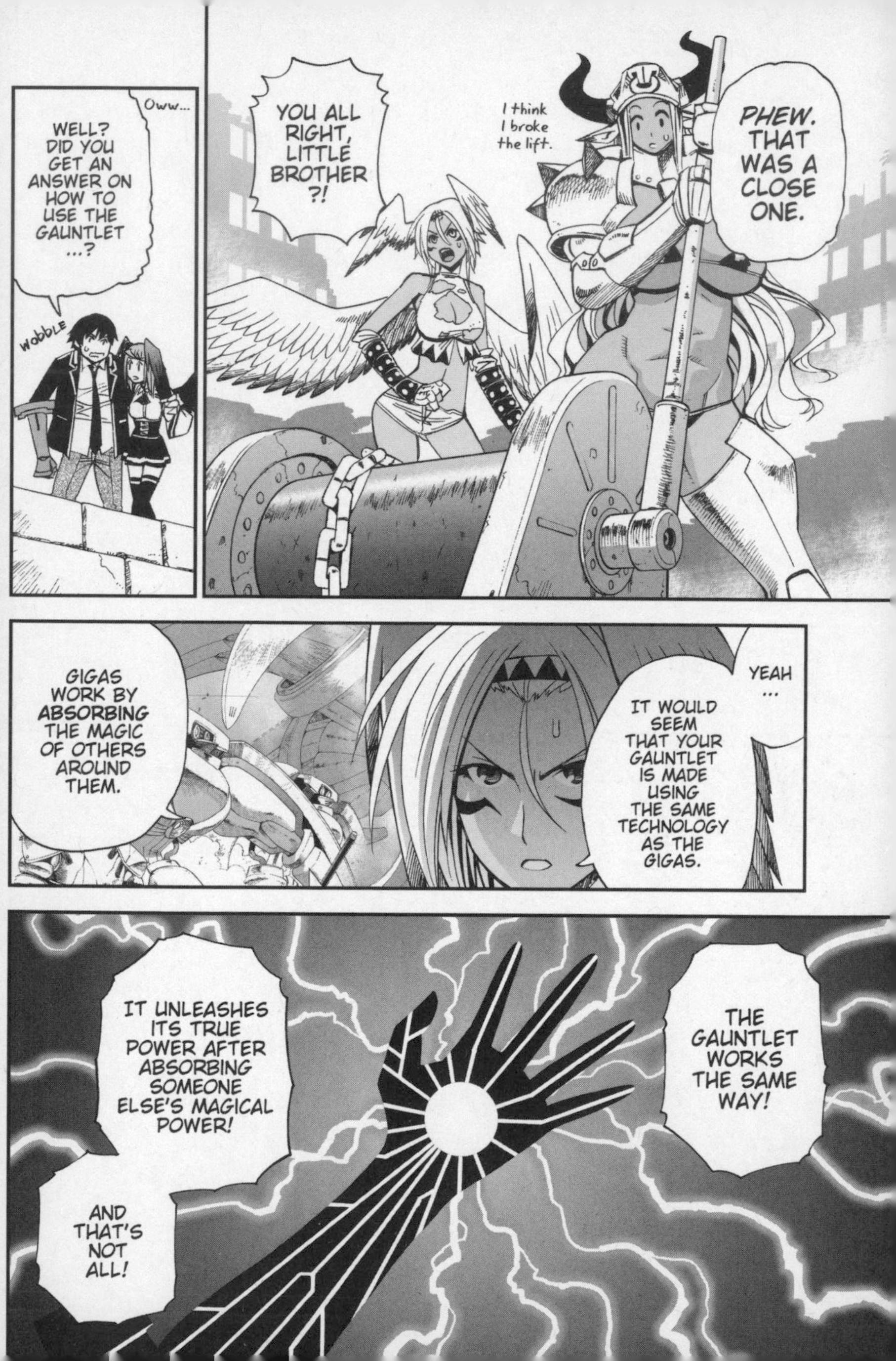
PHEW. THAT WAS A CLOSE ONE.
I think I broke the lift.
YOU ALL RIGHT, LITTLE BROTHER ?!
Oww...
WELL? DID YOU GET AN ANSWER ON HOW TO USE THE GAUNTLET ...?
WOBBLE
YEAH ...
IT WOULD SEEM THAT YOUR GAUNTLET IS MADE USING THE SAME TECHNOLOGY AS THE GIGAS.
GIGAS WORK BY ABSORBING THE MAGIC OF OTHERS AROUND THEM.
THE GAUNTLET WORKS THE SAME WAY!
IT UNLEASHES ITS TRUE POWER AFTER ABSORBING SOMEONE ELSE'S MAGICAL POWER!
AND THAT'S NOT ALL!

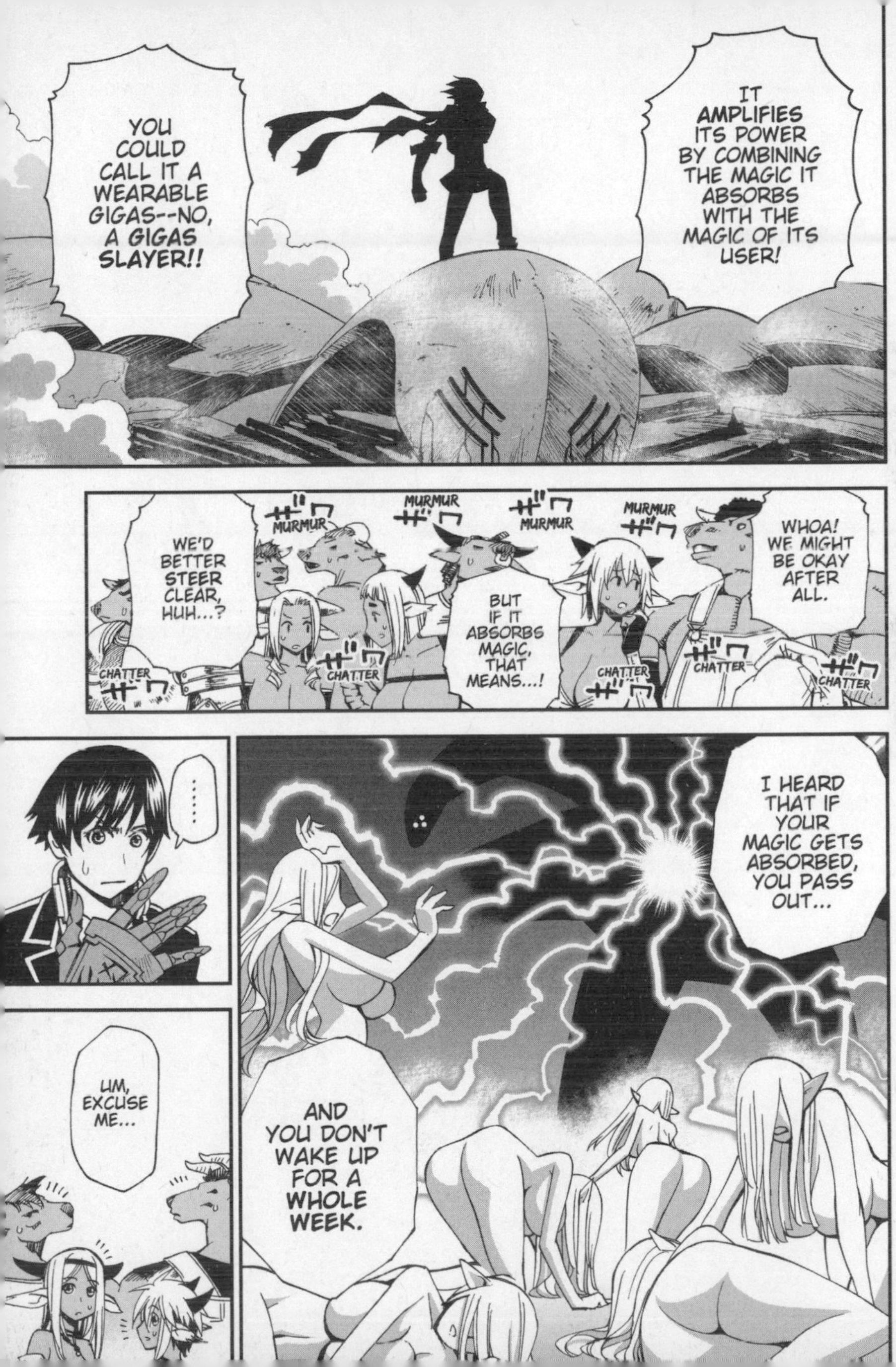
IT AMPLIFIES ITS POWER BY COMBINING THE MAGIC IT ABSORBS WITH THE MAGIC OF ITS USER!
YOU COULD CALL IT A WEARABLE GIGAS--NO, A GIGAS SLAYER!!
WHOA! WE MIGHT BE OKAY AFTER ALL.
MURMUR
MURMUR
MURMUR
MURMUR
CHATTER
CHATTER
CHATTER
BUT IF IT ABSORBS MAGIC, THAT MEANS...!
CHATTER
CHATTER
WE'D BETTER STEER CLEAR, HUH...?
I HEARD THAT IF YOUR MAGIC GETS ABSORBED, YOU PASS OUT...
AND YOU DON'T WAKE UP FOR A WHOLE WEEK.
......
UM, EXCUSE ME...

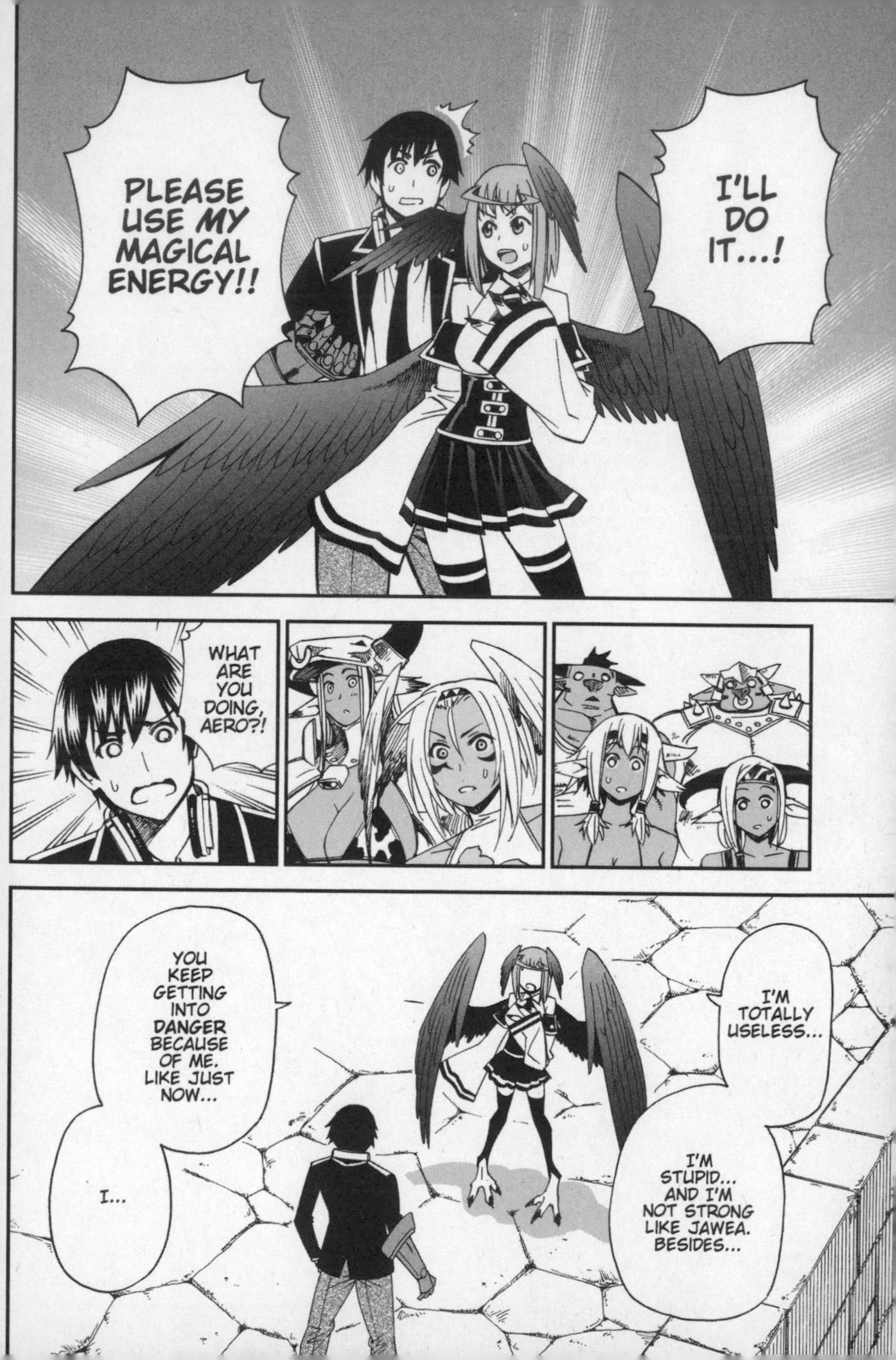
I'LL DO IT...!
PLEASE USE MY MAGICAL ENERGY!!
WHAT ARE YOU DOING, AERO?!
I'M TOTALLY USELESS...
I'M STUPID... AND I'M NOT STRONG LIKE JAWEA. BESIDES...
YOU KEEP GETTING INTO DANGER BECAUSE OF ME. LIKE JUST NOW...
I...

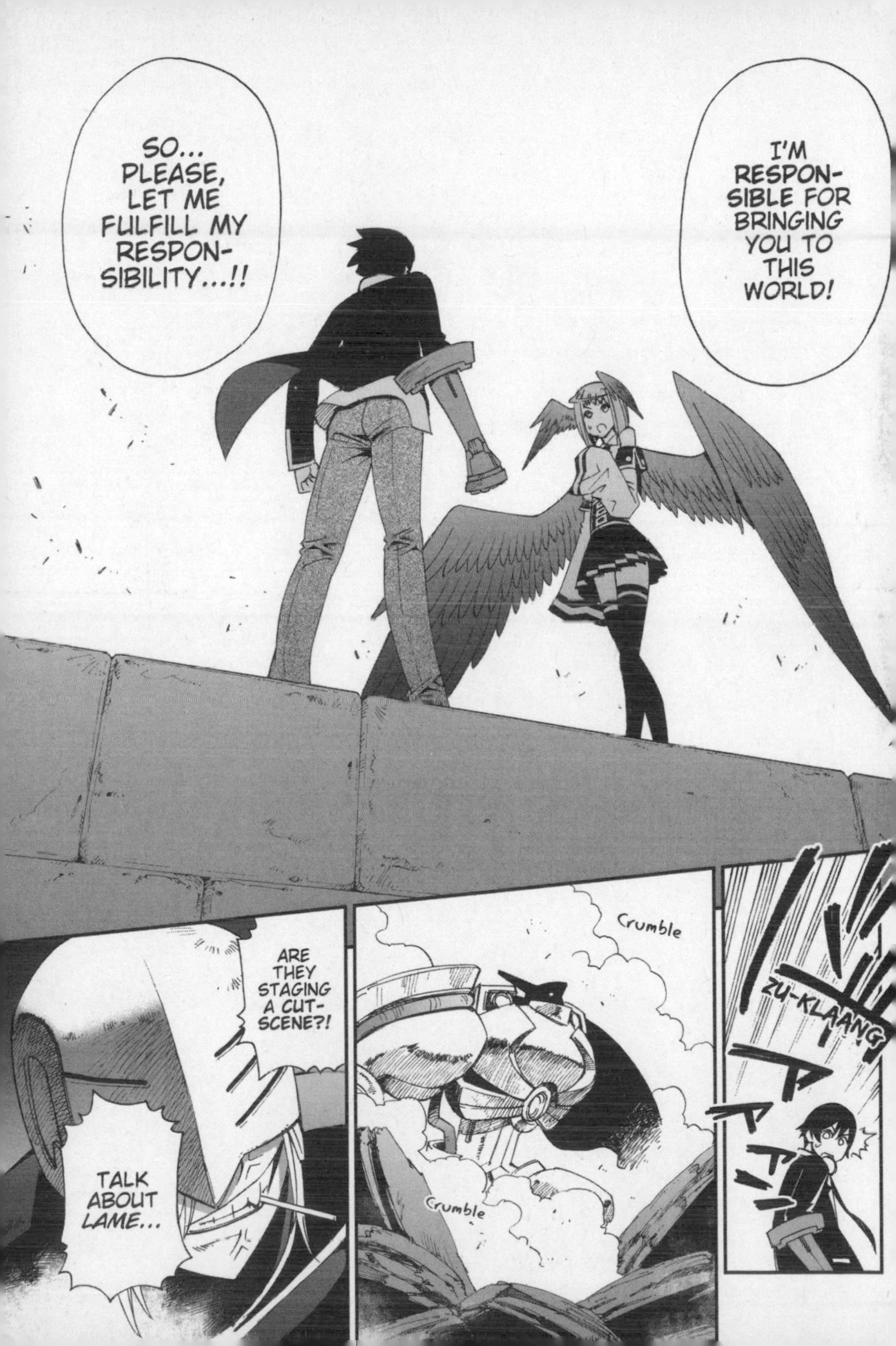
I'M RESPONSIBLE FOR BRINGING YOU TO THIS WORLD!
SO... PLEASE, LET ME FULFILL MY RESPONSIBILITY...!!
ZU-KLAANG
Crumble
Crumble
ARE THEY STAGING A CUT-SCENE?!
TALK ABOUT LAME...

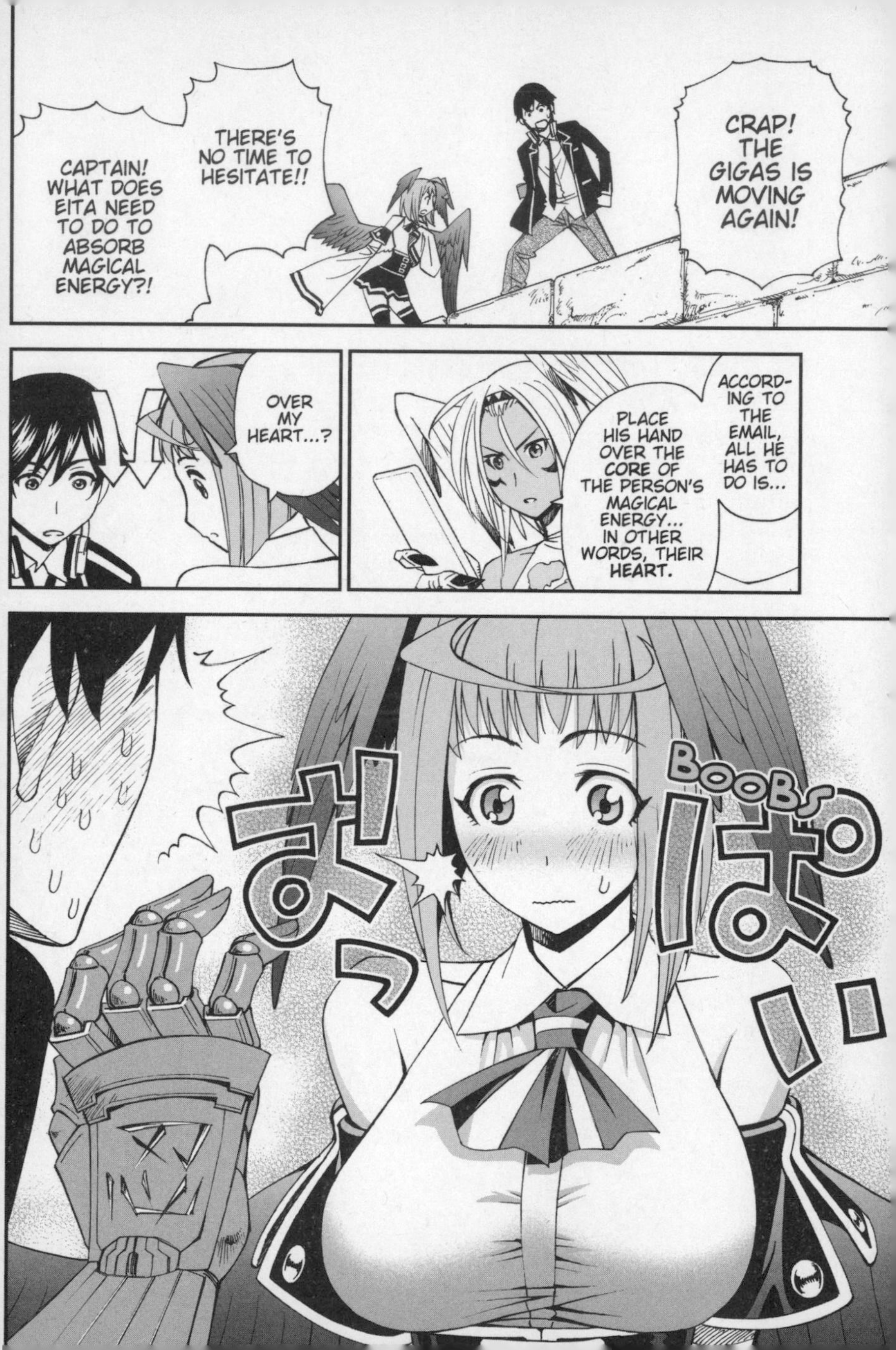
CRAP! THE GIGAS IS MOVING AGAIN!
THERE'S NO TIME TO HESITATE!!
CAPTAIN! WHAT DOES EITA NEED TO DO TO ABSORB MAGICAL ENERGY?!
ACCORD-ING TO THE EMAIL, ALL HE HAS TO DO IS...
PLACE HIS HAND OVER THE CORE OF THE PERSON'S MAGICAL ENERGY... IN OTHER WORDS, THEIR HEART.
OVER MY HEART...?
おっぱい
BOOBS

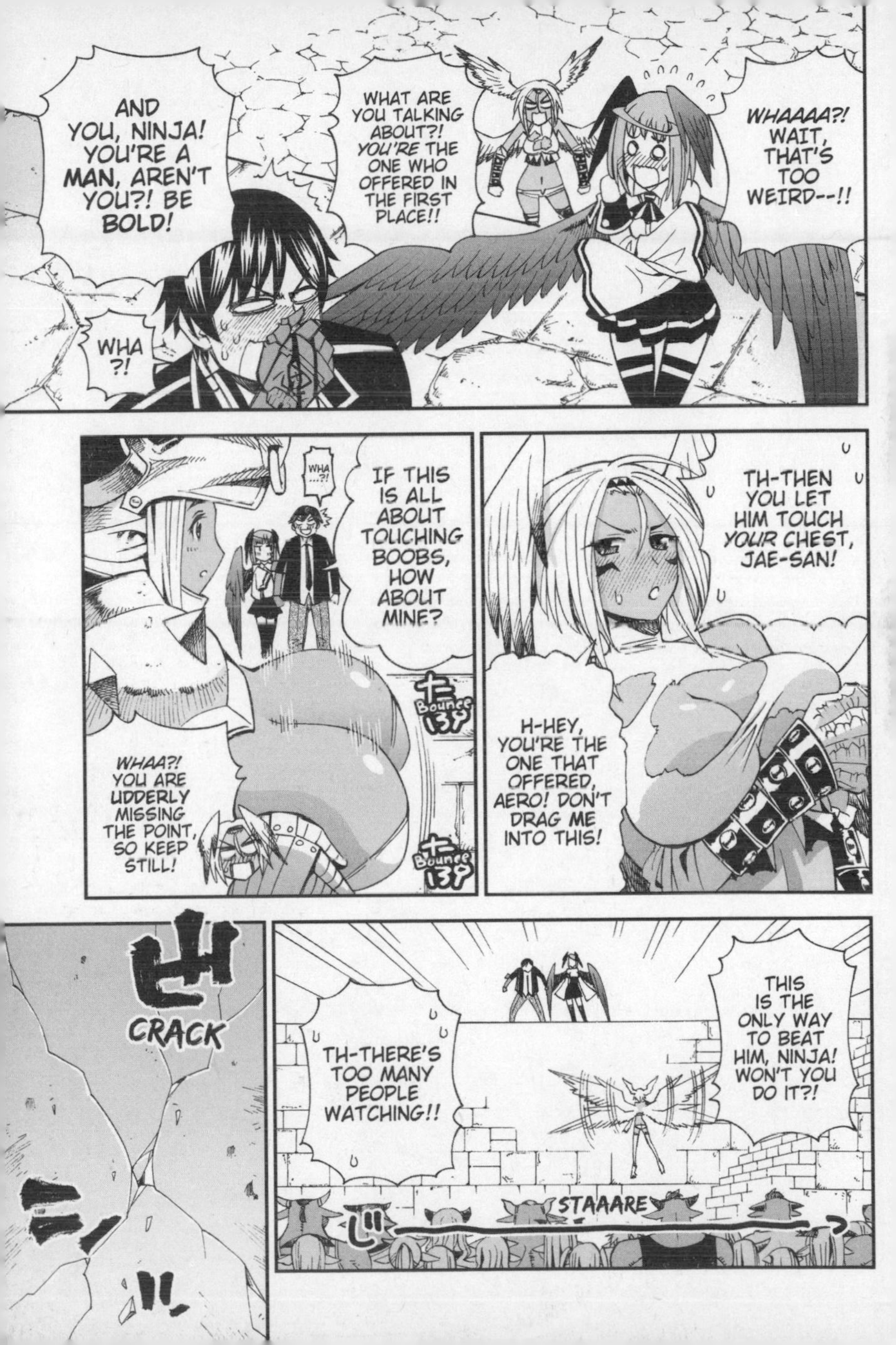

WHAAAA?! WAIT, THAT'S TOO WEIRD--!!
WHAT ARE YOU TALKING ABOUT?! YOU'RE THE ONE WHO OFFERED IN THE FIRST PLACE!!
AND YOU, NINJA! YOU'RE A MAN, AREN'T YOU?! BE BOLD!
WHA ?!
TH-THEN YOU LET HIM TOUCH YOUR CHEST, JAE-SAN!
H-HEY, YOU'RE THE ONE THAT OFFERED, AERO! DON'T DRAG ME INTO THIS!
IF THIS IS ALL ABOUT TOUCHING BOOBS, HOW ABOUT MINE?
WHA ...?!
Bounce
WHAA?! YOU ARE UDDERLY MISSING THE POINT, SO KEEP STILL!
Bounce
THIS IS THE ONLY WAY TO BEAT HIM, NINJA! WON'T YOU DO IT?!
TH-THERE'S TOO MANY PEOPLE WATCHING!!
STAAARE
CRACK

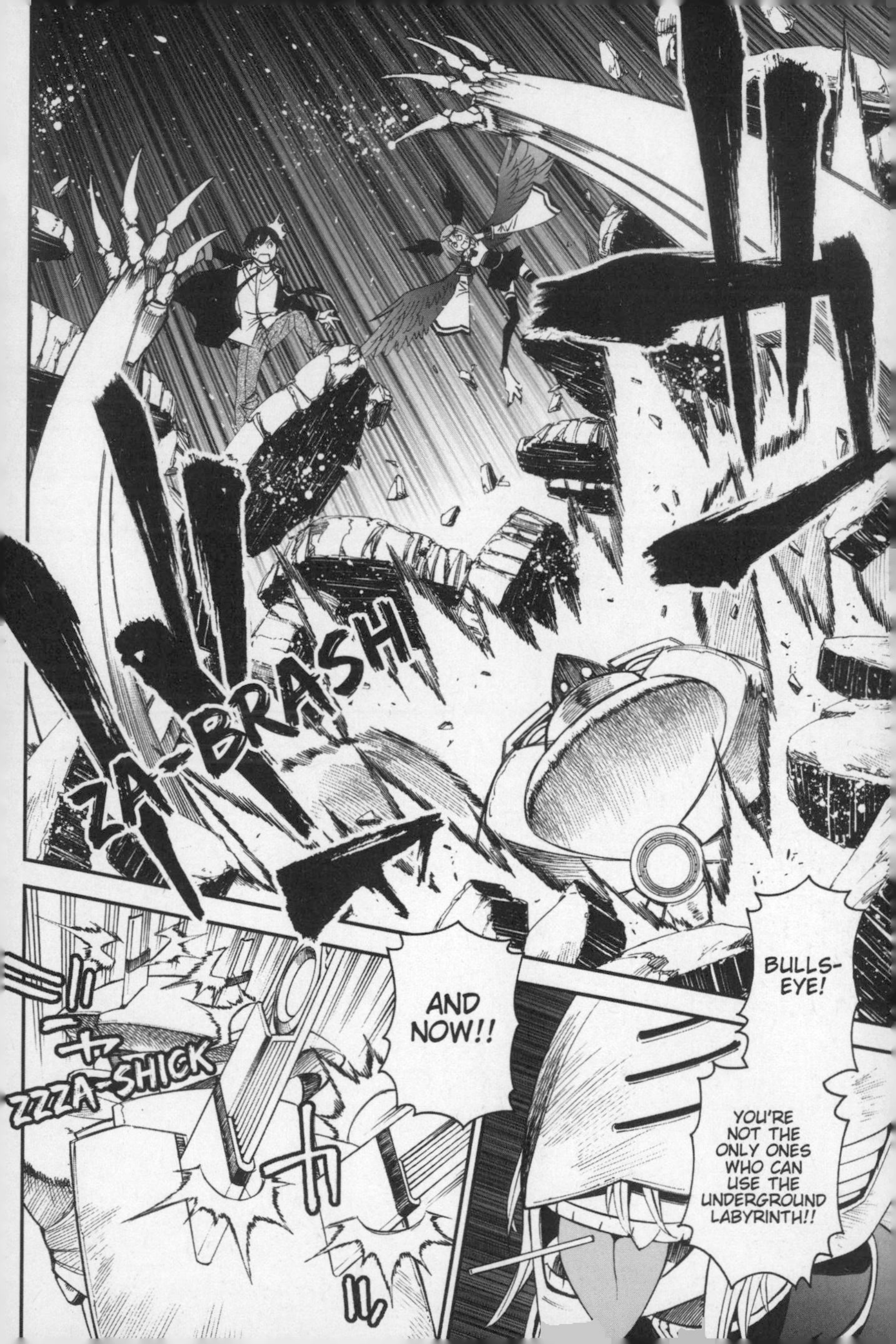
ZA-BRASH
BULLS-EYE!
AND NOW!!
YOU'RE NOT THE ONLY ONES WHO CAN USE THE UNDERGROUND LABYRINTH!!
ZZZA-SHICK

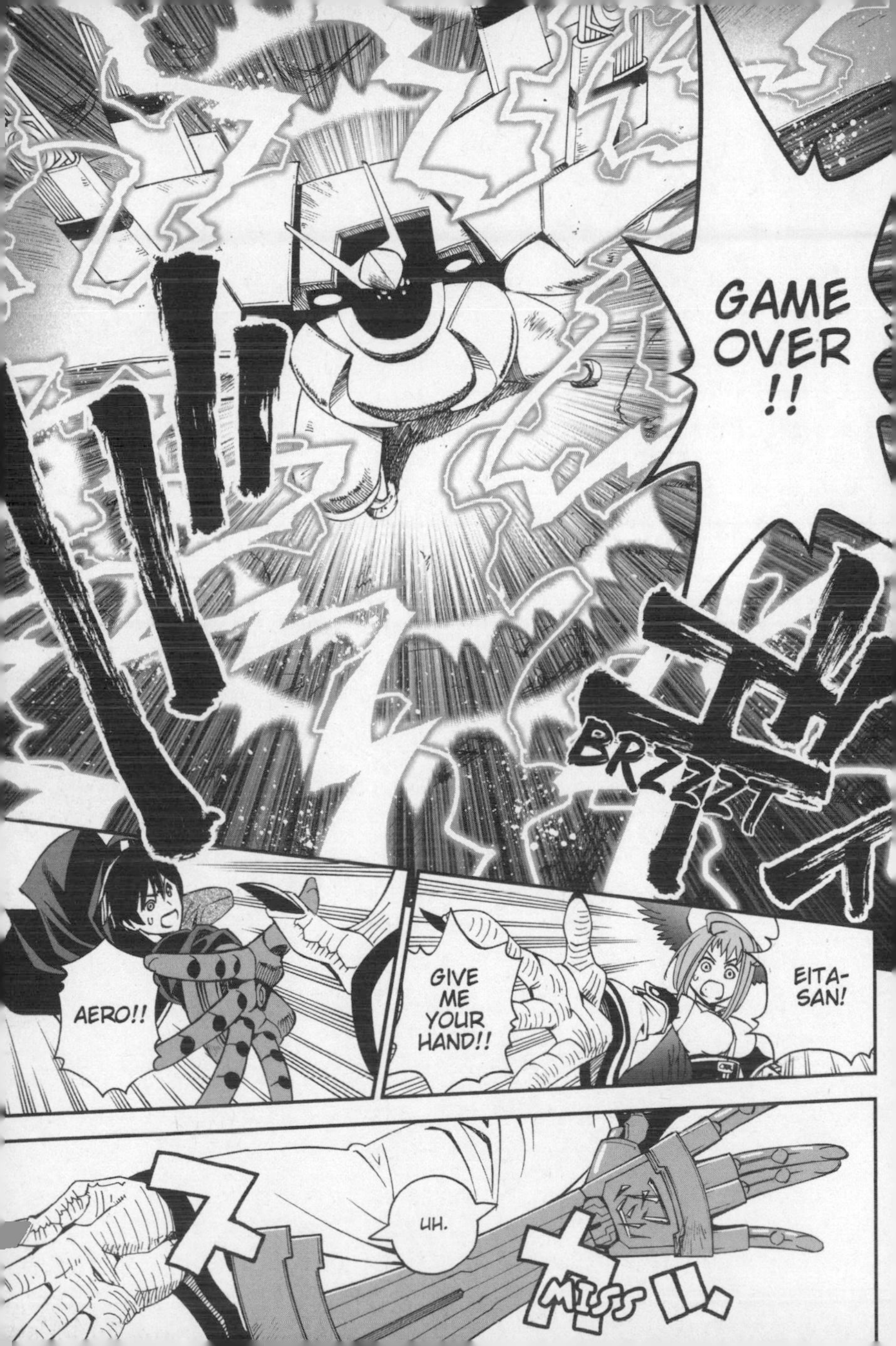
GAME OVER!!
BRZZZT
EITA-SAN!
GIVE ME YOUR HAND!!
AERO!!
UH.
MISS

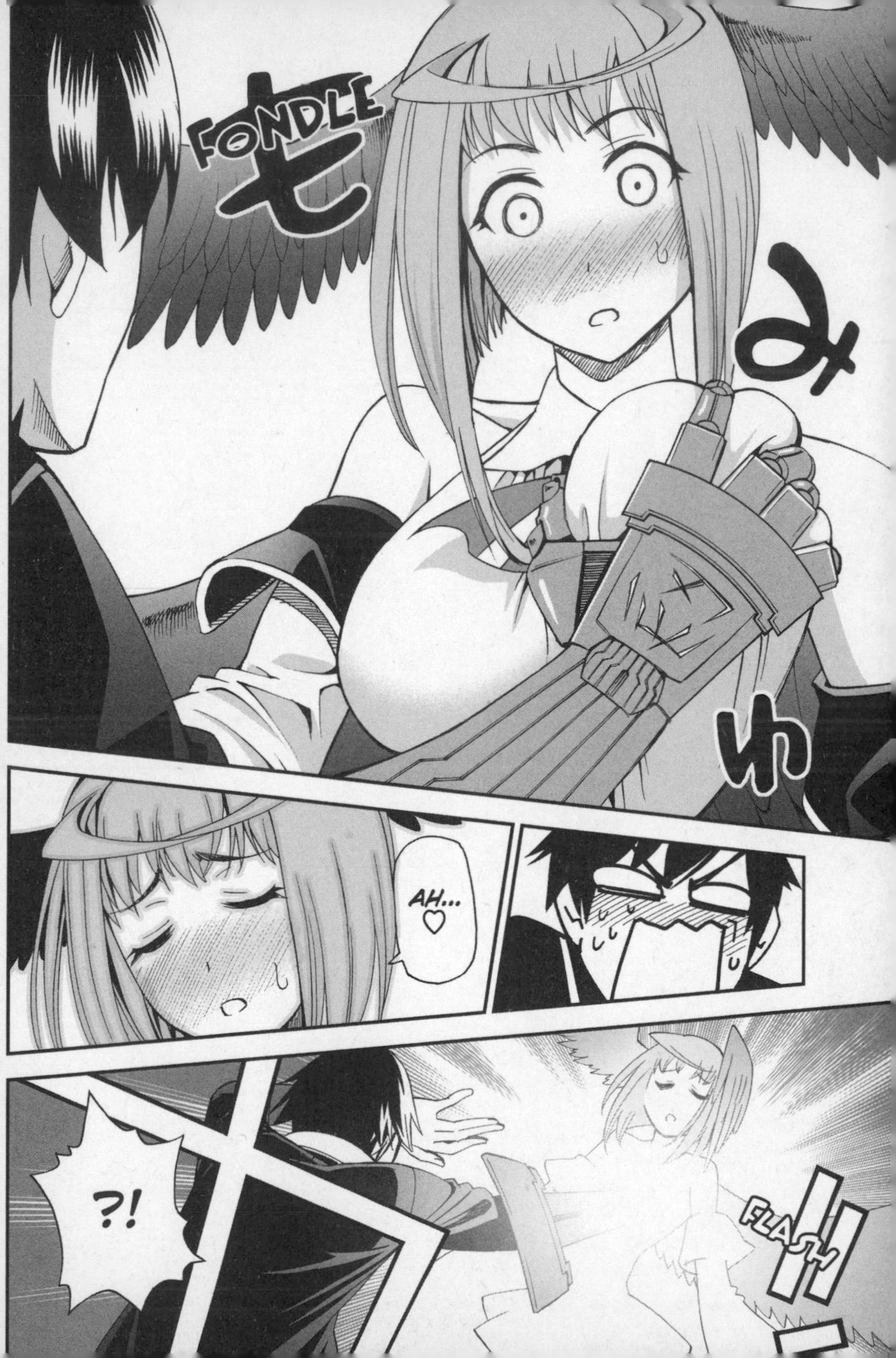
FONDLE
も
み
ゅ
AH... ♡
FLASH
?!

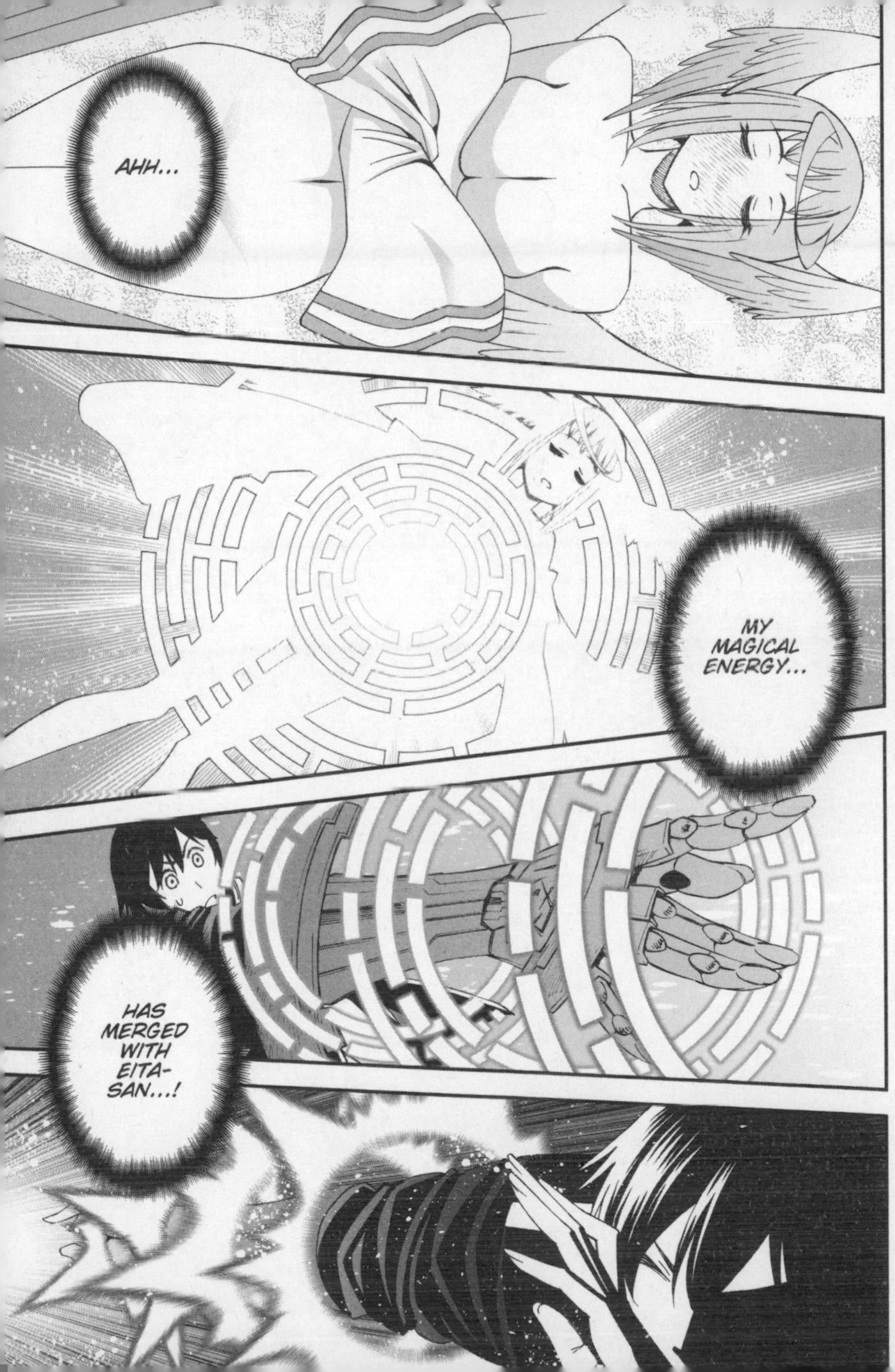
AHH...
MY MAGICAL ENERGY...
HAS MERGED WITH EITA-SAN...!

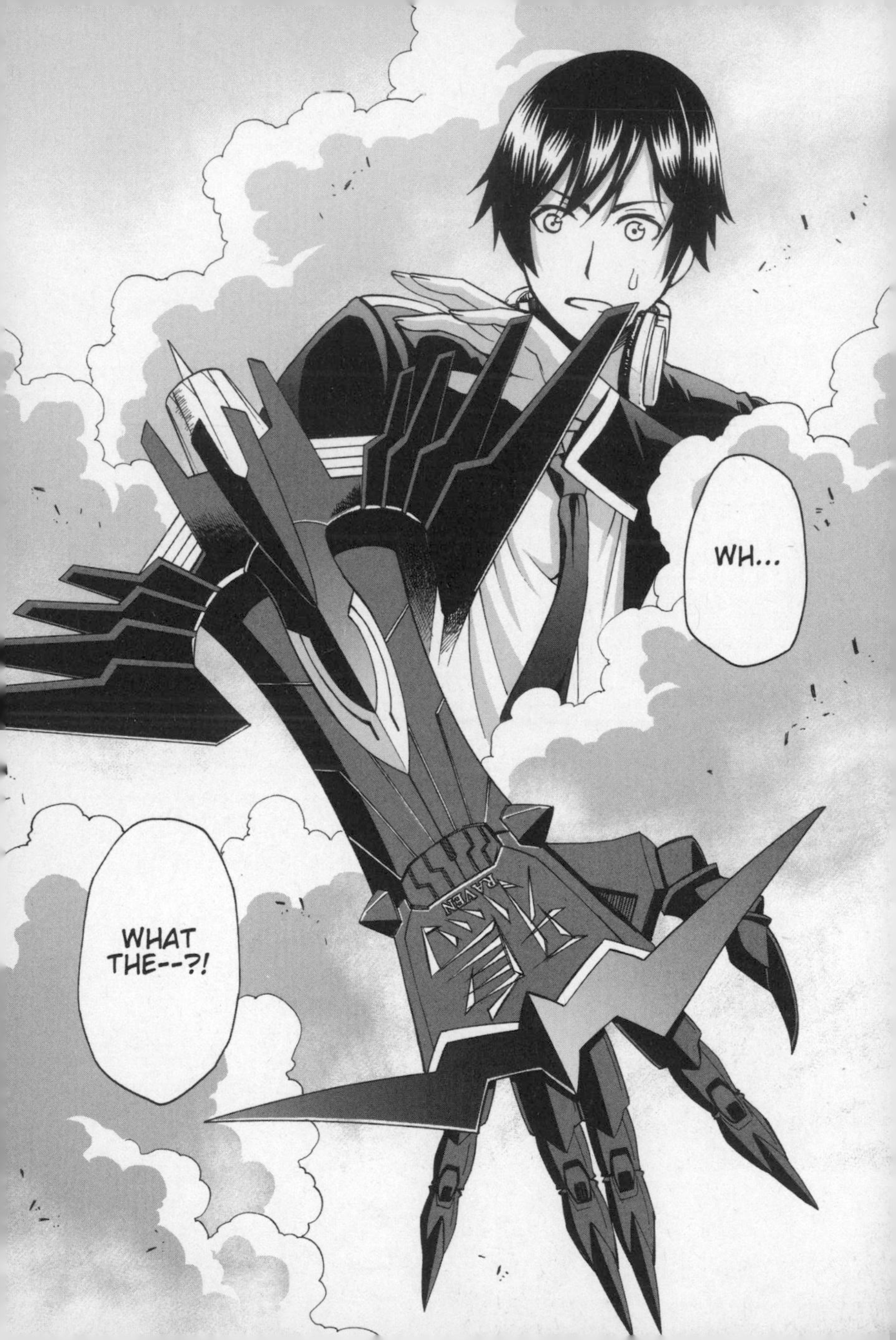
WH...
WHAT THE--?!
RAVEN

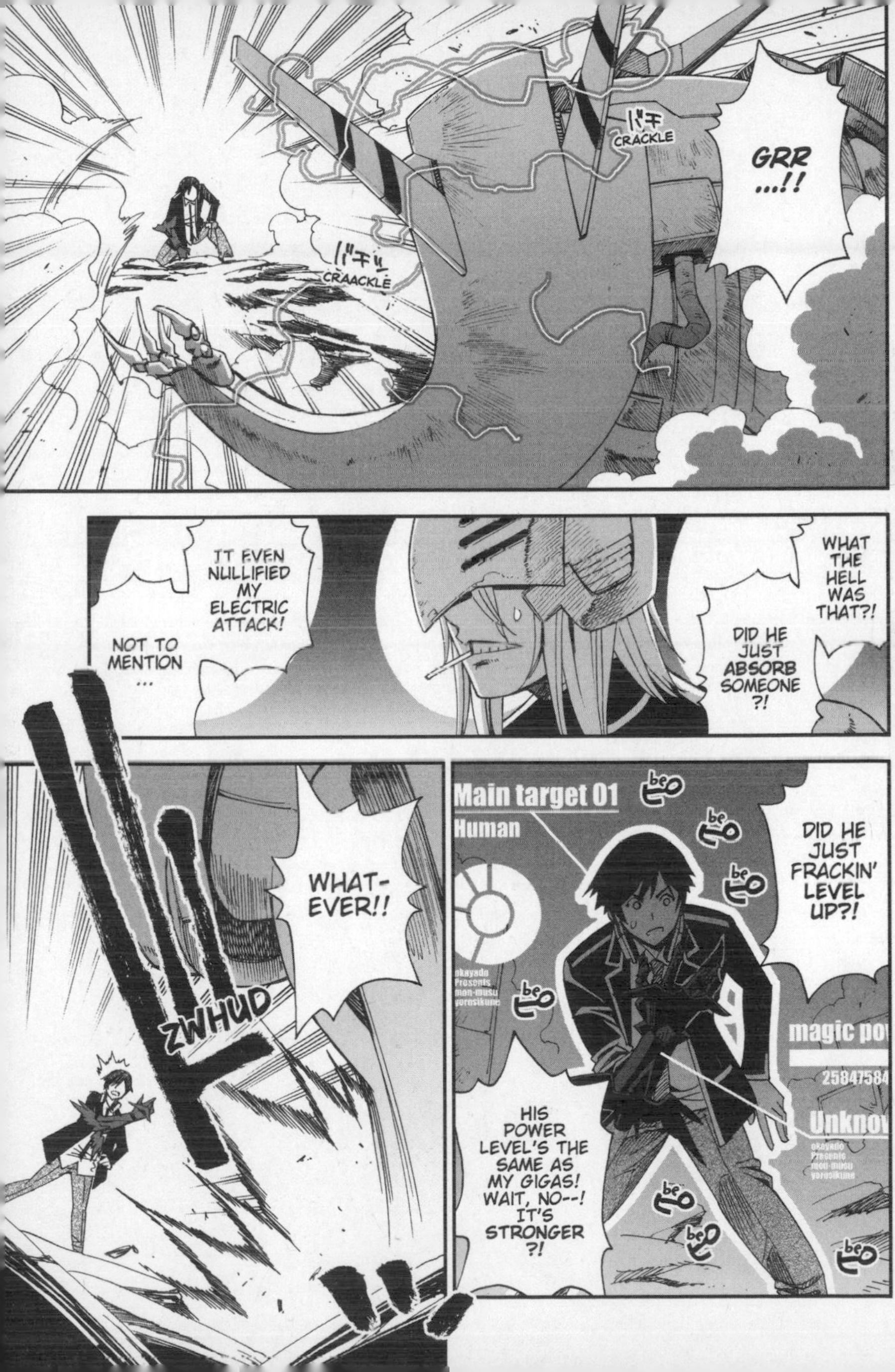
GRR ...!!
バチ
CRACKLE
バチッ
CRAACKLE
WHAT THE HELL WAS THAT?!
DID HE JUST ABSORB SOMEONE ?!
IT EVEN NULLIFIED MY ELECTRIC ATTACK!
NOT TO MENTION ...
Main target 01
Human
beピ
beピ
DID HE JUST FRACKIN' LEVEL UP?!
beピ
beピ
magic pow
25847584
Unknow
HIS POWER LEVEL'S THE SAME AS MY GIGAS! WAIT, NO--! IT'S STRONGER ?!
beピ
beピ
beピ
WHAT-EVER!!
ZWHUD

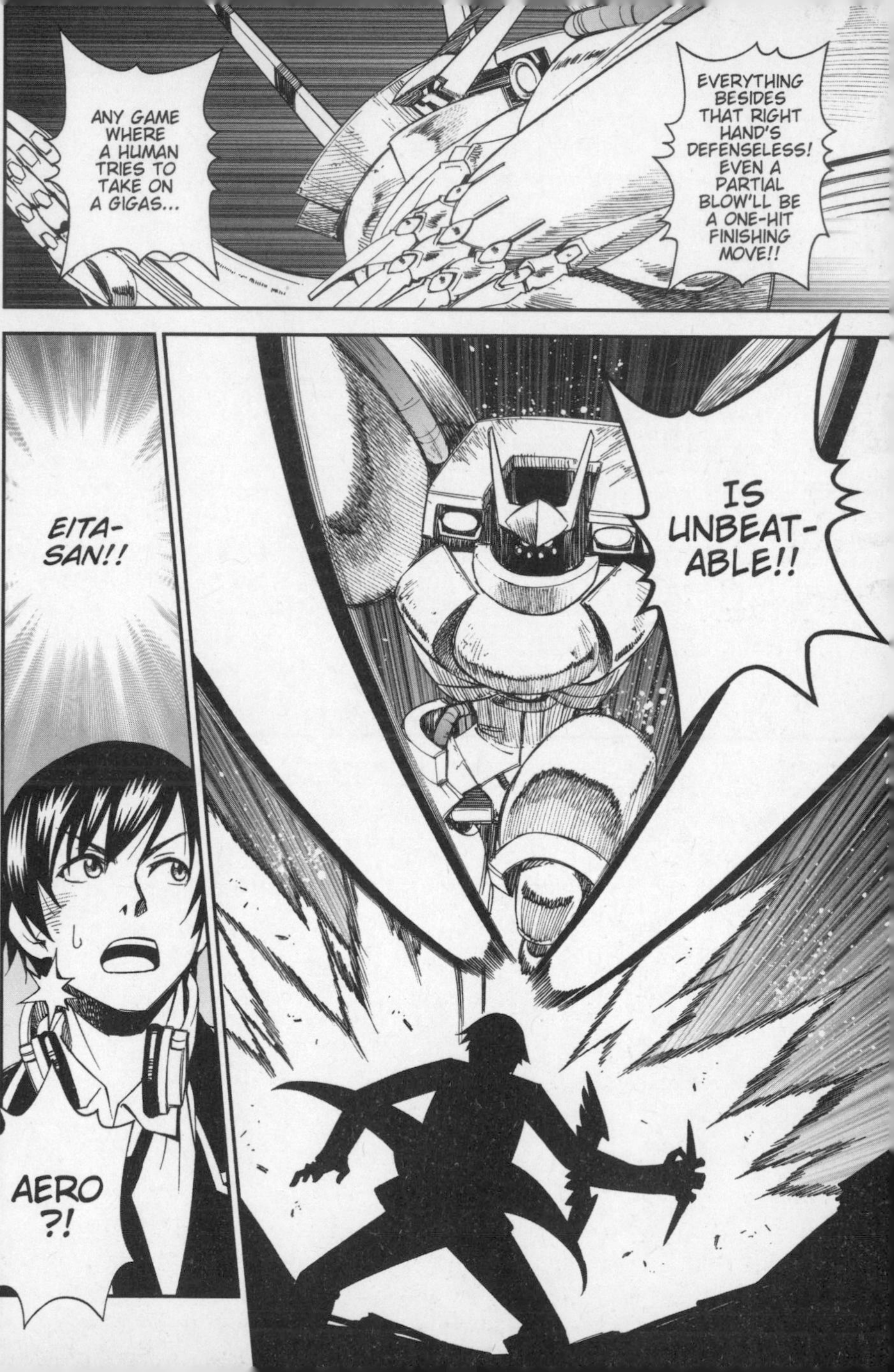
EVERYTHING BESIDES THAT RIGHT HAND'S DEFENSELESS! EVEN A PARTIAL BLOW'LL BE A ONE-HIT FINISHING MOVE!!
ANY GAME WHERE A HUMAN TRIES TO TAKE ON A GIGAS...
IS UNBEAT-ABLE!!
EITA-SAN!!
AERO ?!

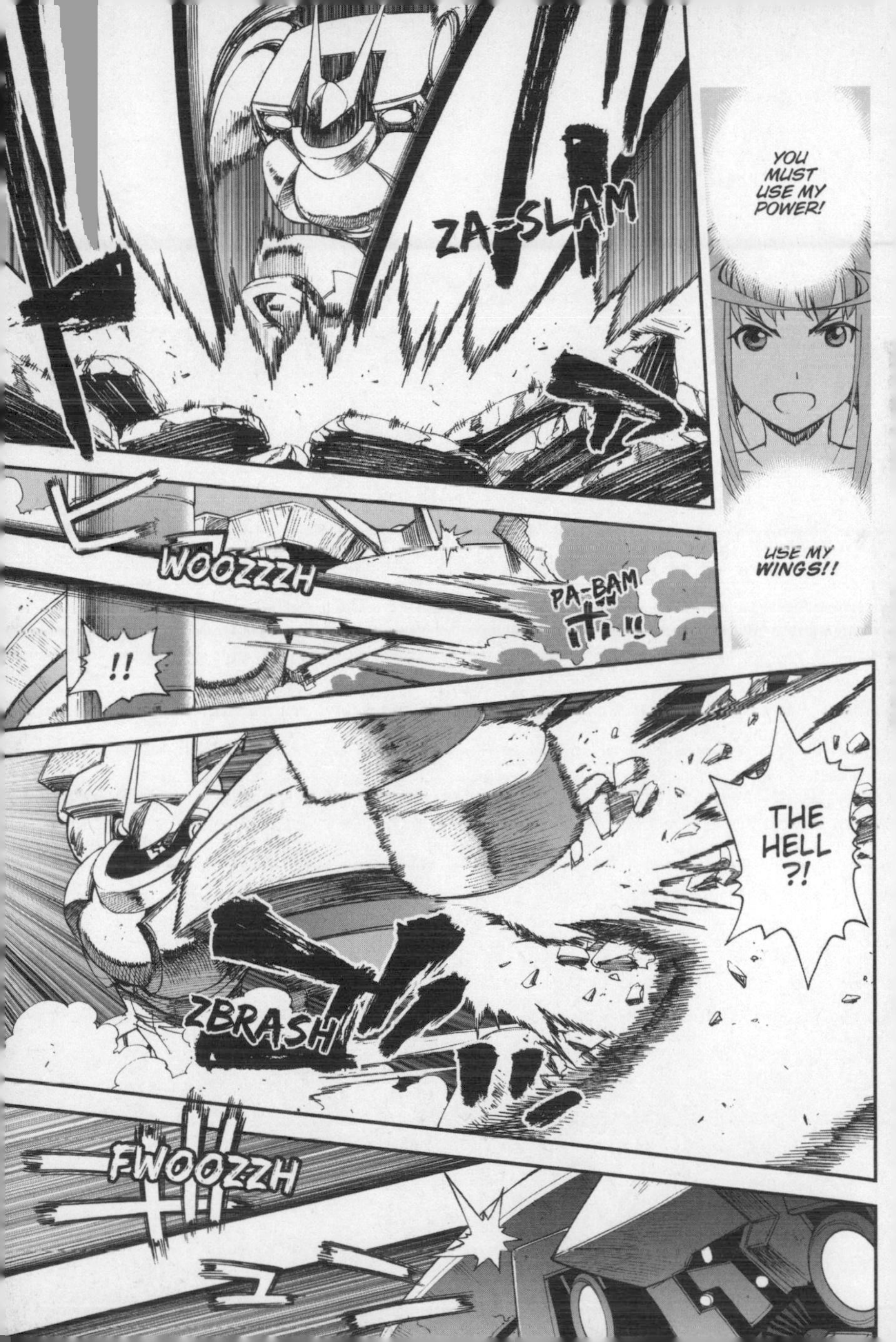
YOU MUST USE MY POWER!
USE MY WINGS!!
ZA-SLAM
PA-BAM
WOOZZZH
!!
THE HELL ?!
ZBRASH
FWOOZZH

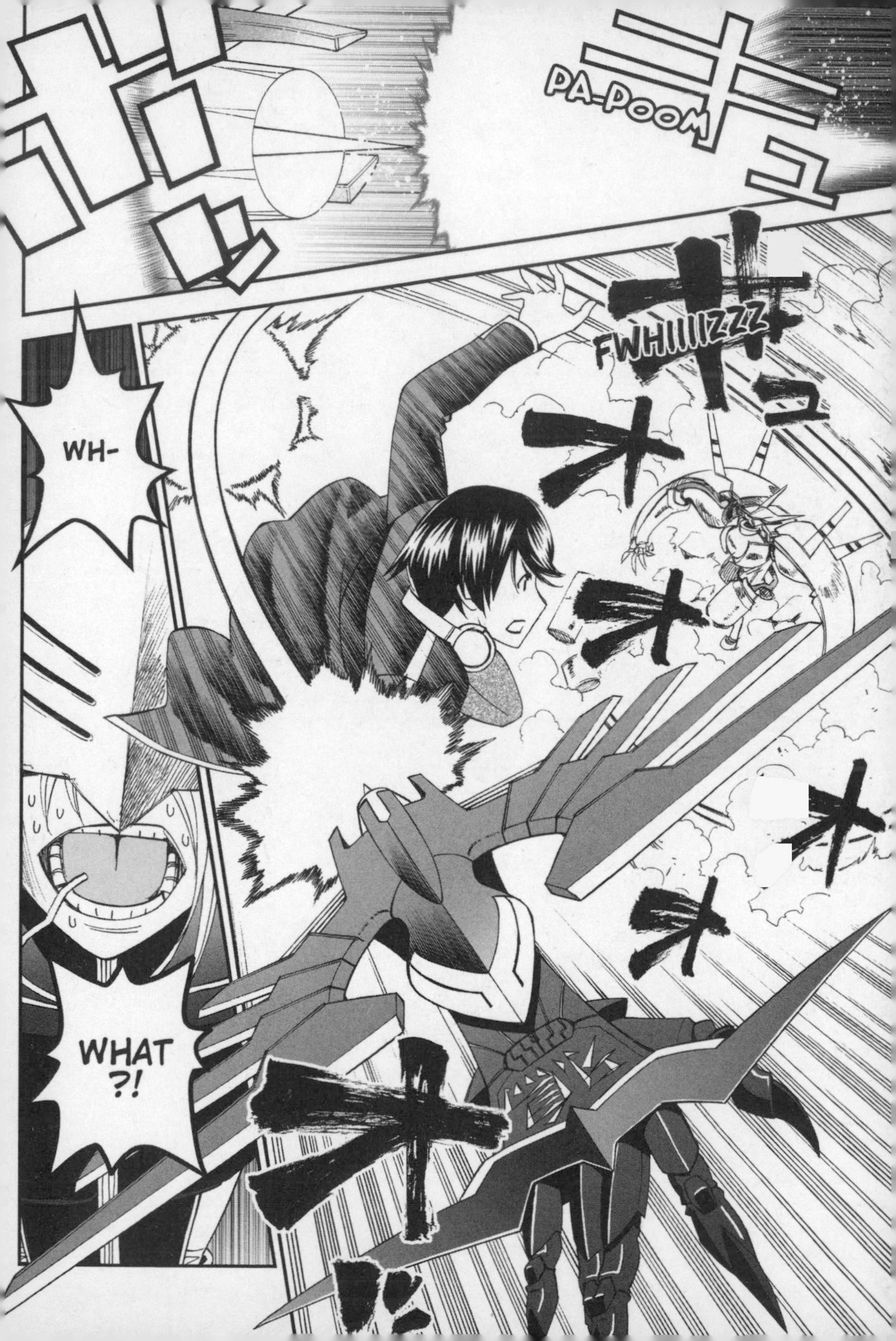
PA-POOM
FWHIIIIIZZZ
WH-
WHAT ?!

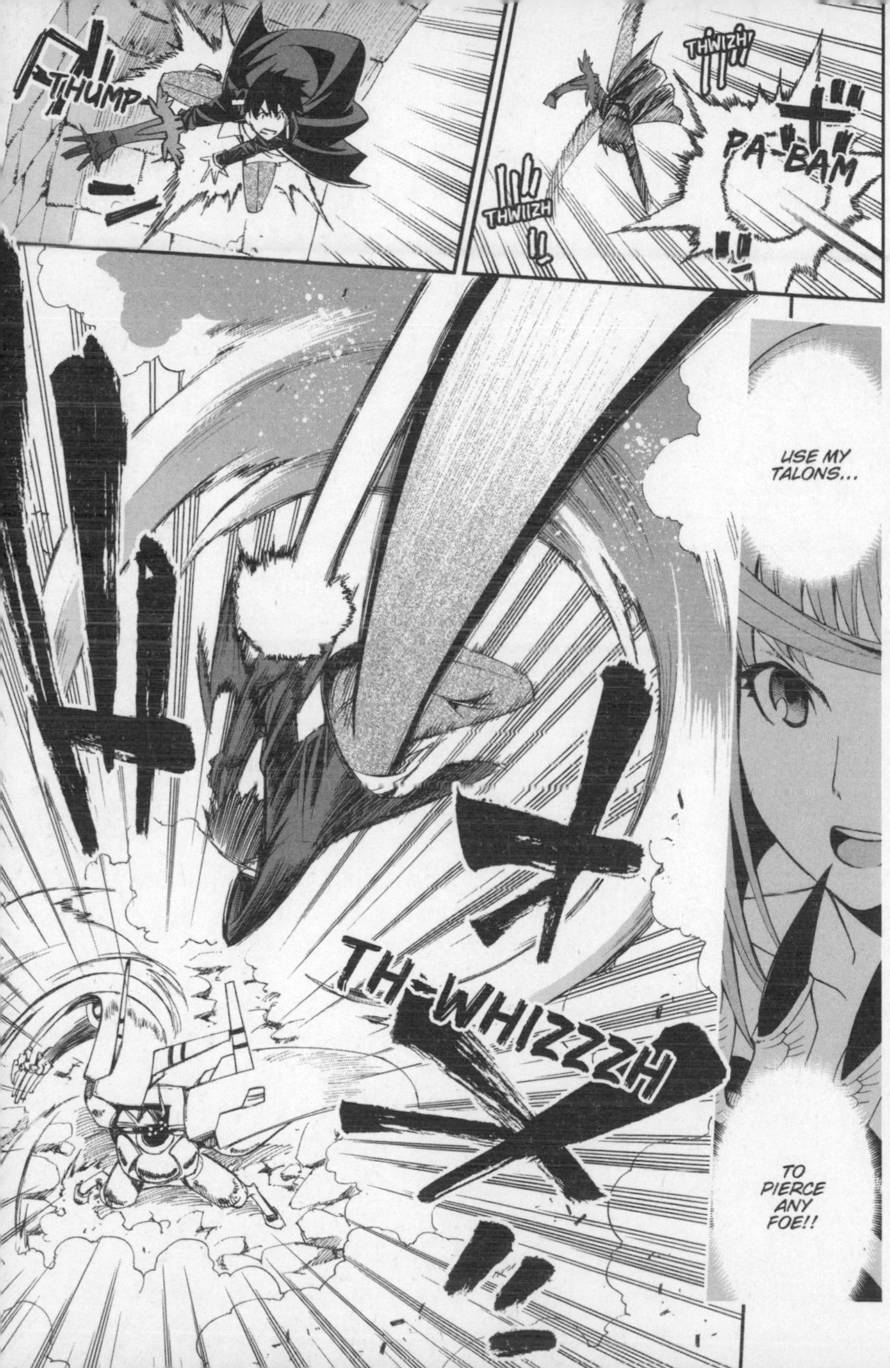
THWIZH
PA-BAM
THWIIZH
THUMP
USE MY TALONS...
TO PIERCE ANY FOE!!
TH-WHIZZZH

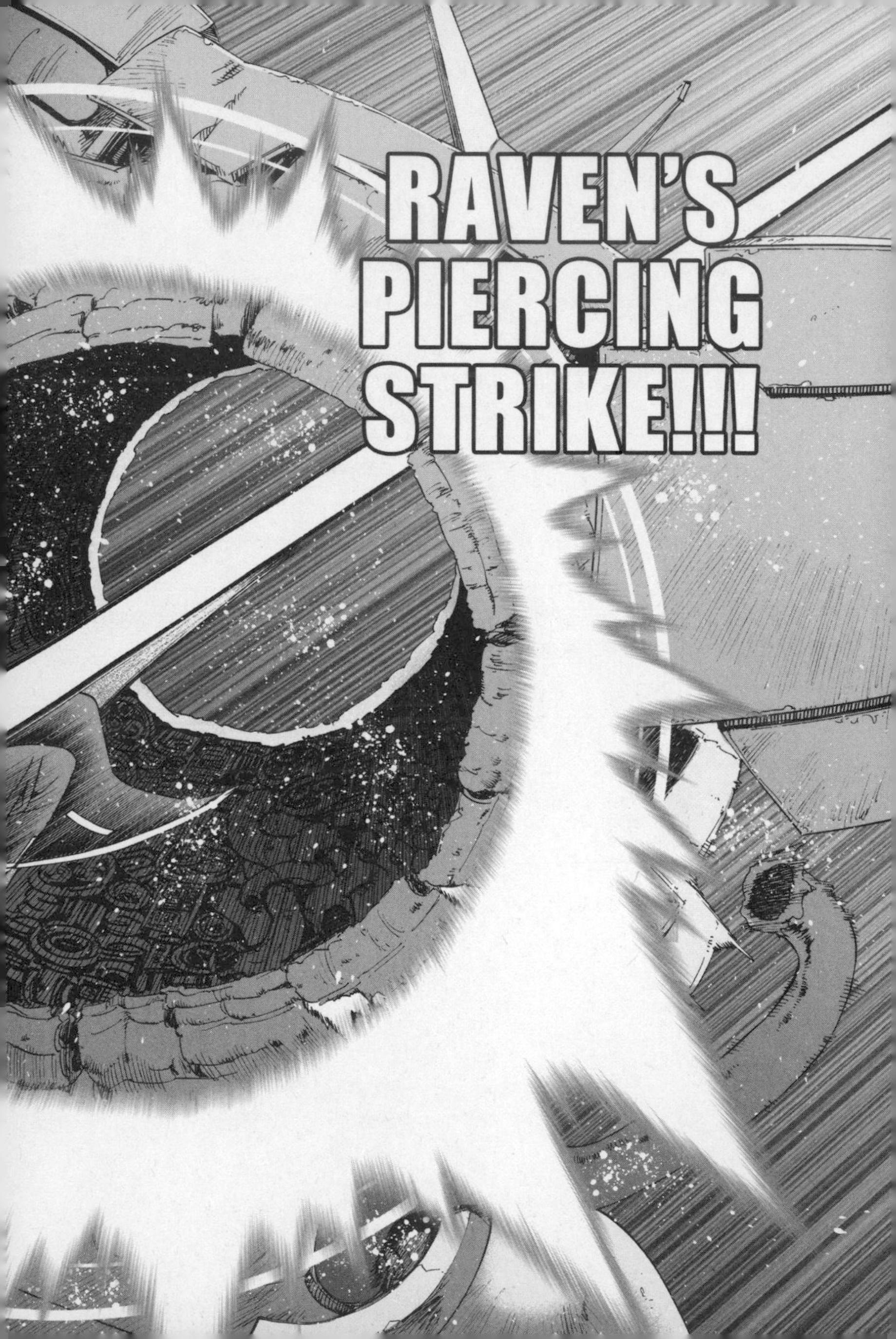
RAVEN'S PIERCING STRIKE!!!

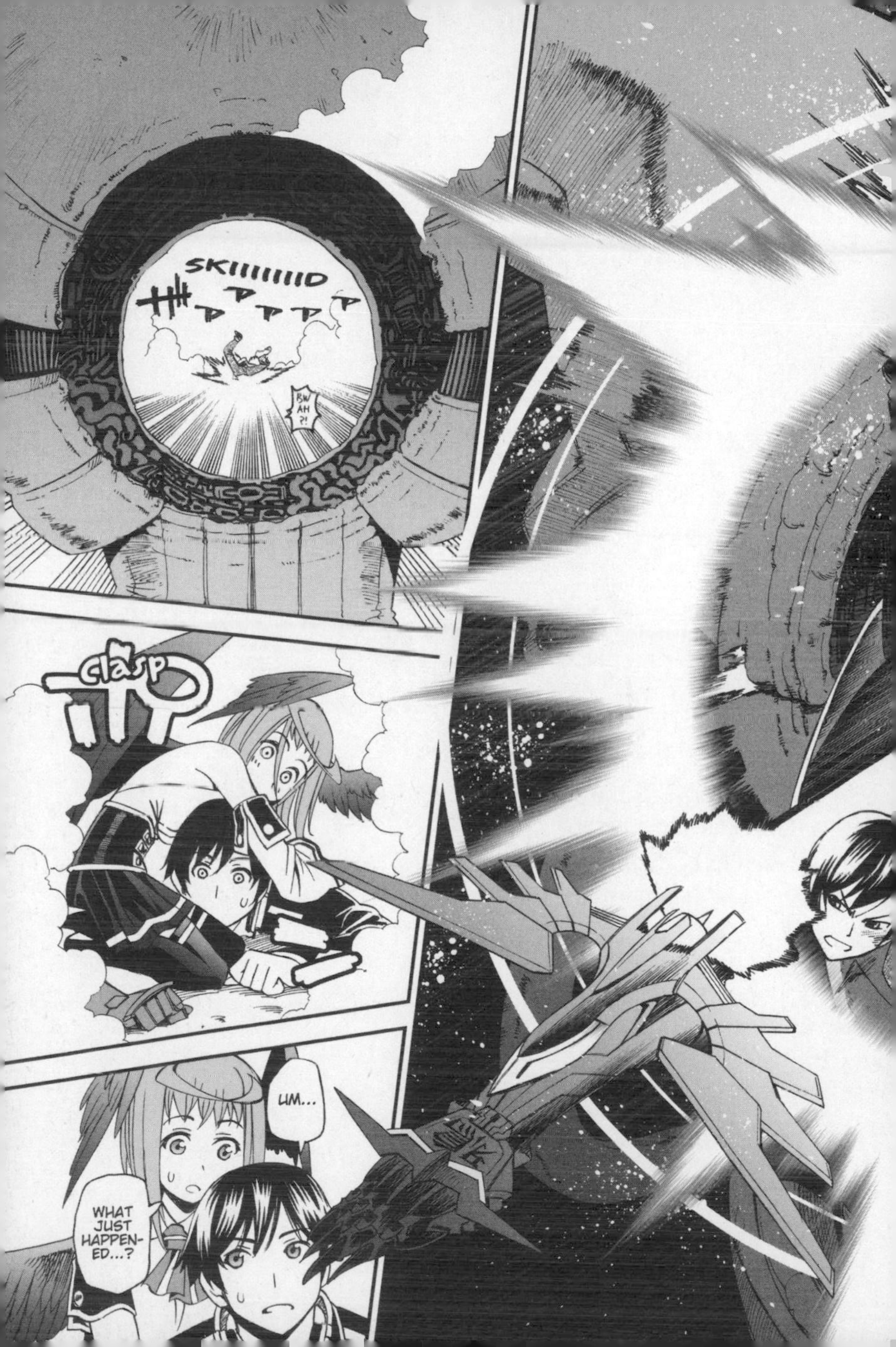
SKIIIIIIID
BWAH?!
CLASP
UM...
WHAT JUST HAPPENED...?

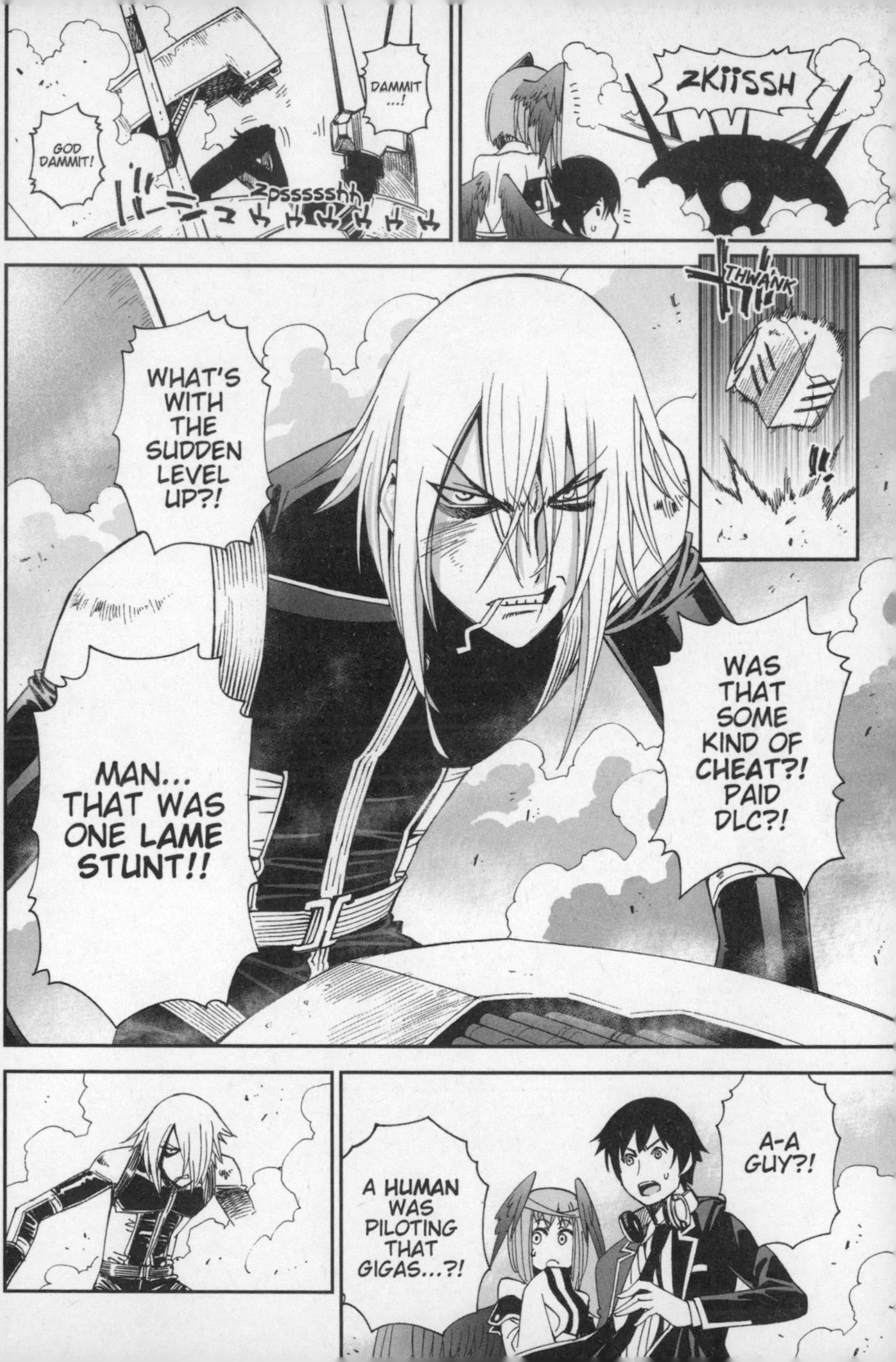
ZKIISSH
DAMMIT ...!
GOD DAMMIT!
Zpssssshh
THWANK
WHAT'S WITH THE SUDDEN LEVEL UP?!
WAS THAT SOME KIND OF CHEAT?! PAID DLC?!
MAN... THAT WAS ONE LAME STUNT!!
A-A GUY?!
A HUMAN WAS PILOTING THAT GIGAS...?!

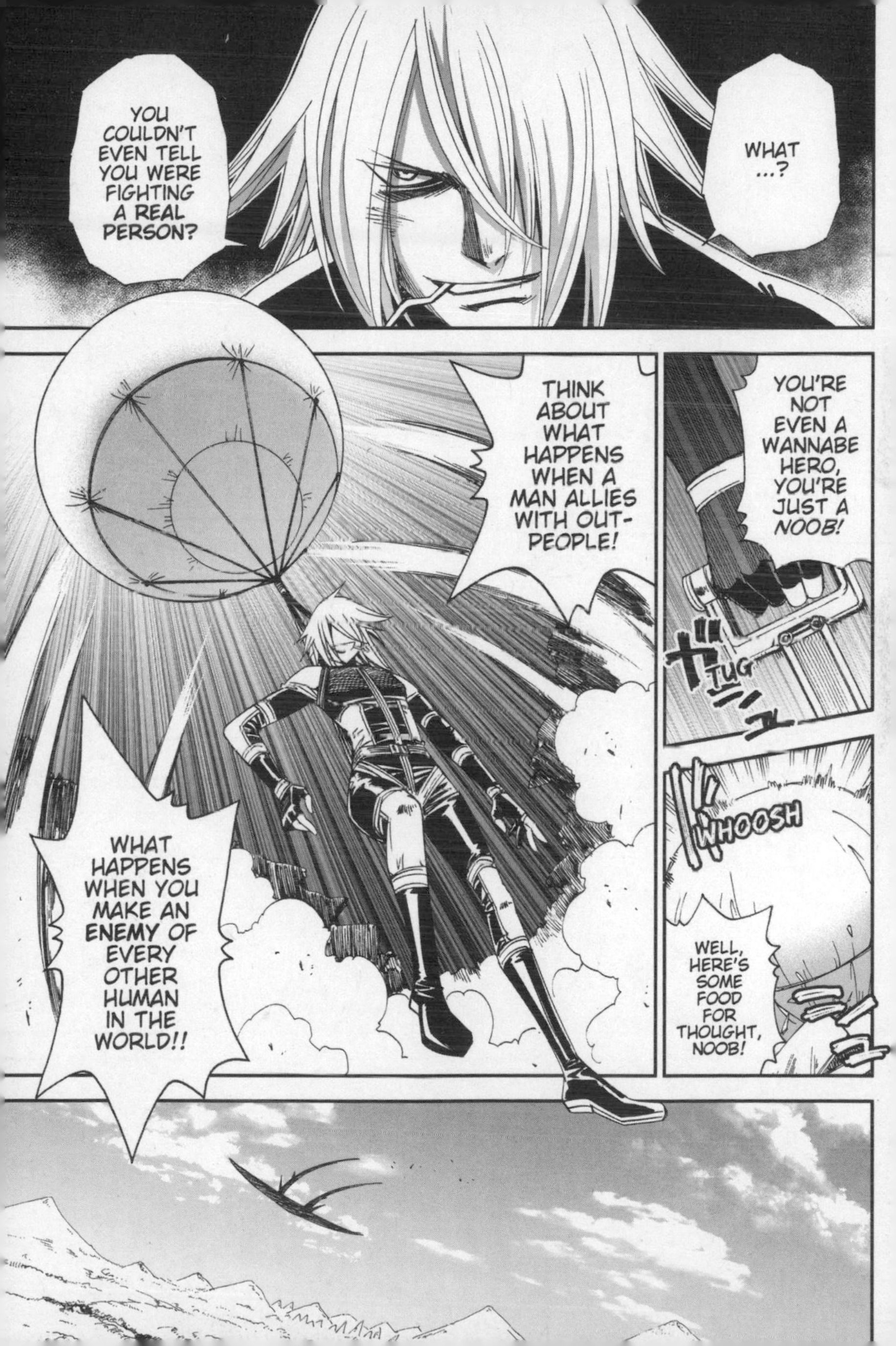

WHAT ...?
YOU COULDN'T EVEN TELL YOU WERE FIGHTING A REAL PERSON?
YOU'RE NOT EVEN A WANNABE HERO, YOU'RE JUST A *NOOB!*
TUG
WHOOSH
WELL, HERE'S SOME FOOD FOR THOUGHT, NOOB!
THINK ABOUT WHAT HAPPENS WHEN A MAN ALLIES WITH OUT-PEOPLE!
WHAT HAPPENS WHEN YOU MAKE AN **ENEMY** OF EVERY OTHER HUMAN IN THE WORLD!!

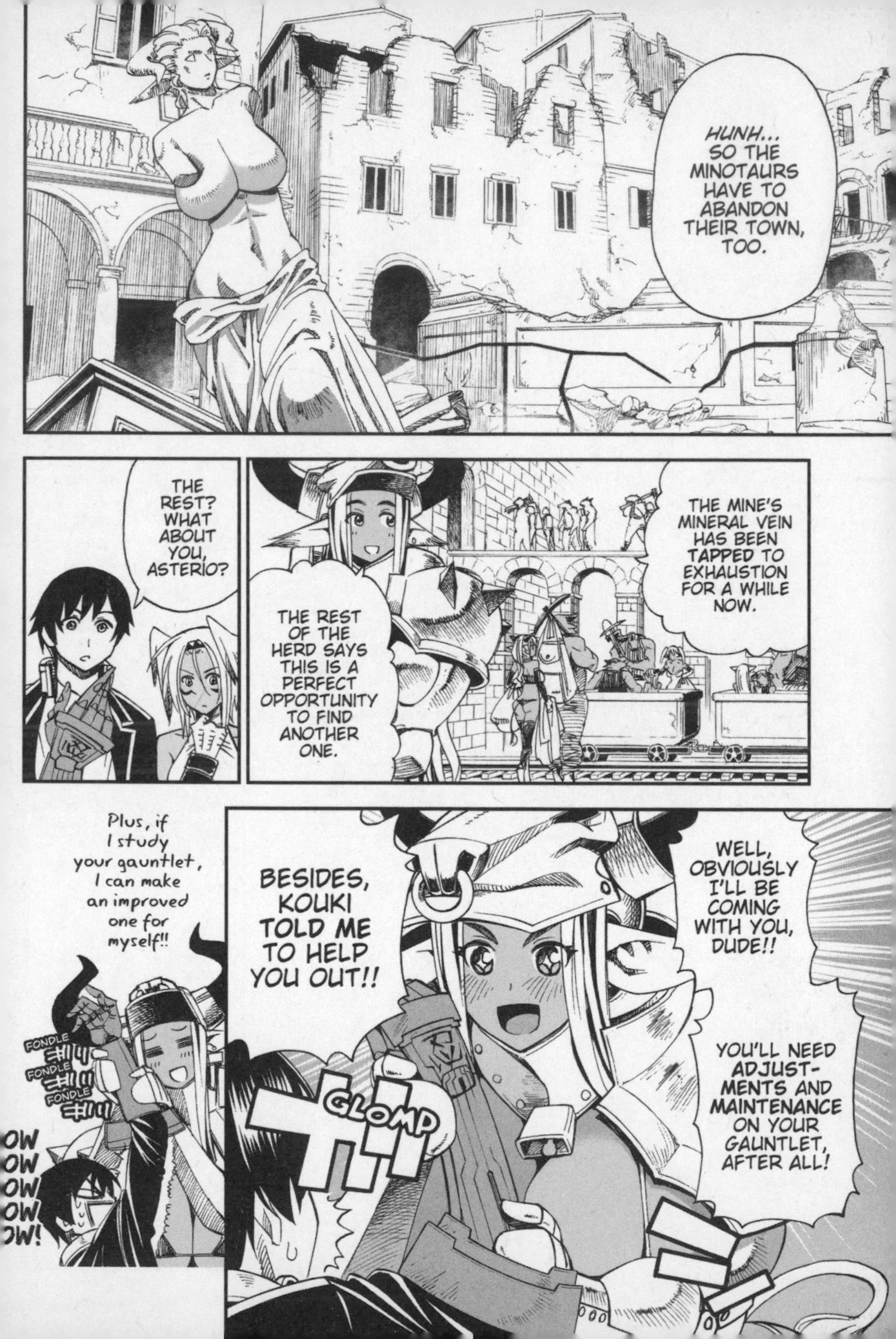
HUNH... SO THE MINOTAURS HAVE TO ABANDON THEIR TOWN, TOO.
THE MINE'S MINERAL VEIN HAS BEEN TAPPED TO EXHAUSTION FOR A WHILE NOW.
THE REST OF THE HERD SAYS THIS IS A PERFECT OPPORTUNITY TO FIND ANOTHER ONE.
THE REST? WHAT ABOUT YOU, ASTERIO?
WELL, OBVIOUSLY I'LL BE COMING WITH YOU, DUDE!!
YOU'LL NEED ADJUSTMENTS AND MAINTENANCE ON YOUR GAUNTLET, AFTER ALL!
BESIDES, KOUKI TOLD ME TO HELP YOU OUT!!
GLOMP
Plus, if I study your gauntlet, I can make an improved one for myself!!
FONDLE
FONDLE
FONDLE
OW OW OW OW OW!

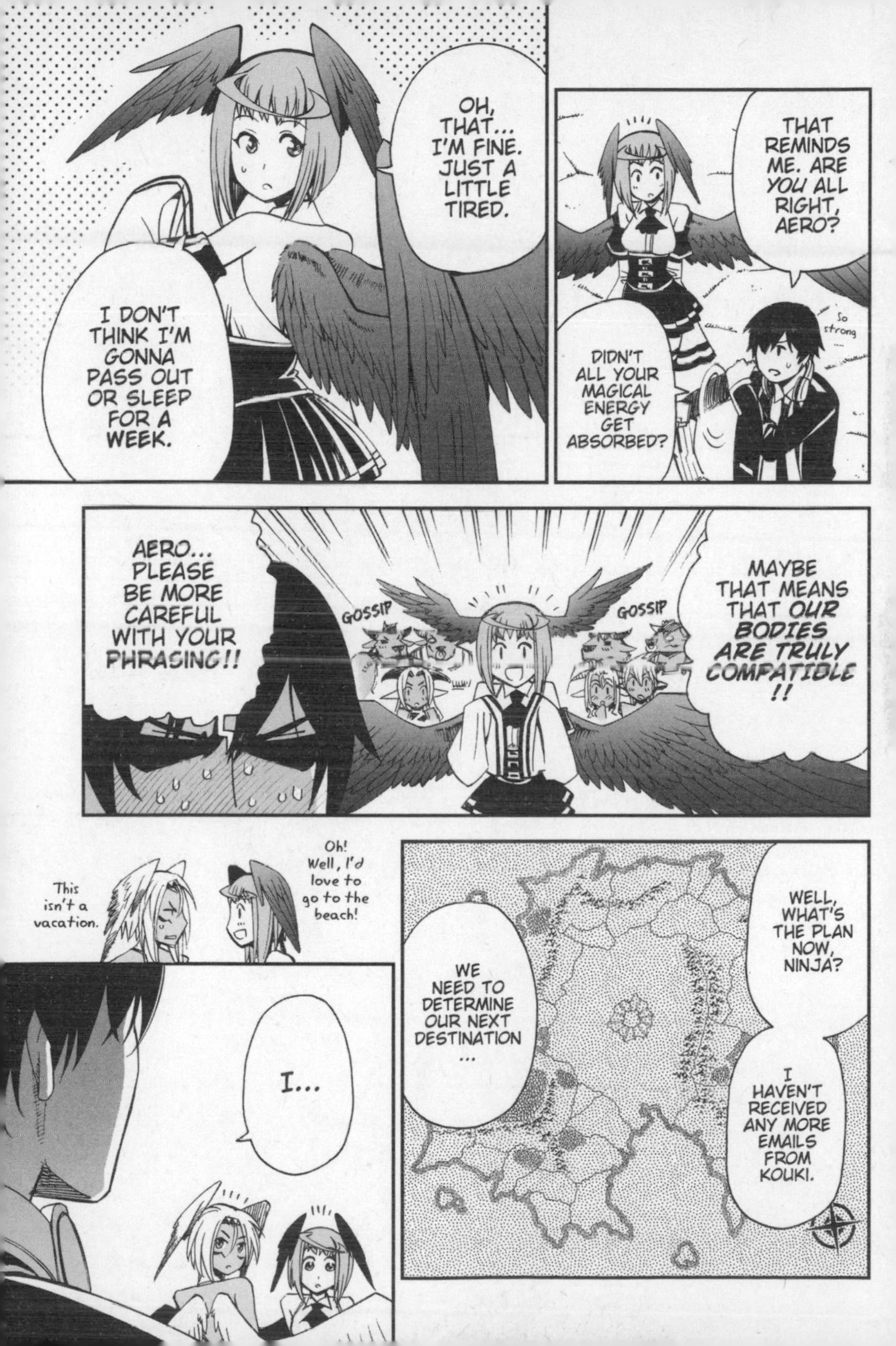
THAT REMINDS ME. ARE YOU ALL RIGHT, AERO?
So strong ...
DIDN'T ALL YOUR MAGICAL ENERGY GET ABSORBED?
OH, THAT... I'M FINE. JUST A LITTLE TIRED.
I DON'T THINK I'M GONNA PASS OUT OR SLEEP FOR A WEEK.
MAYBE THAT MEANS THAT OUR BODIES ARE TRULY COMPATIBLE !!
GOSSIP
GOSSIP
AERO... PLEASE BE MORE CAREFUL WITH YOUR PHRASING!!
WELL, WHAT'S THE PLAN NOW, NINJA?
I HAVEN'T RECEIVED ANY MORE EMAILS FROM KOUKI.
WE NEED TO DETERMINE OUR NEXT DESTINATION ...
Oh! Well, I'd love to go to the beach!
This isn't a vacation.
I...

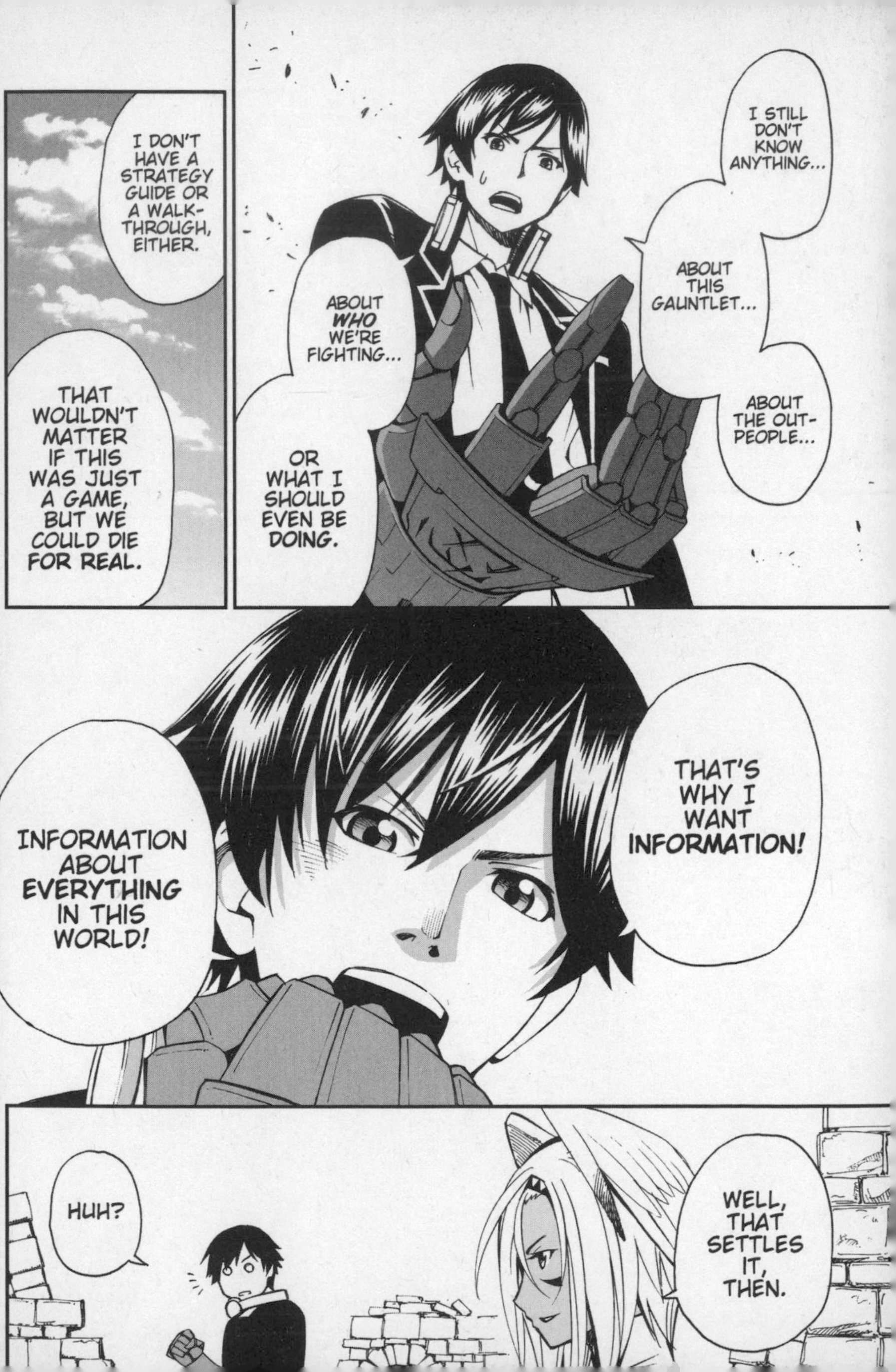
I STILL DON'T KNOW ANYTHING...
ABOUT THIS GAUNTLET...
ABOUT THE OUT-PEOPLE...
ABOUT *WHO* WE'RE FIGHTING...
OR WHAT I SHOULD EVEN BE DOING.
I DON'T HAVE A STRATEGY GUIDE OR A WALK-THROUGH, EITHER.
THAT WOULDN'T MATTER IF THIS WAS JUST A GAME, BUT WE COULD DIE FOR REAL.
THAT'S WHY I WANT INFORMATION!
INFORMATION ABOUT EVERYTHING IN THIS WORLD!
WELL, THAT SETTLES IT, THEN.
HUH?

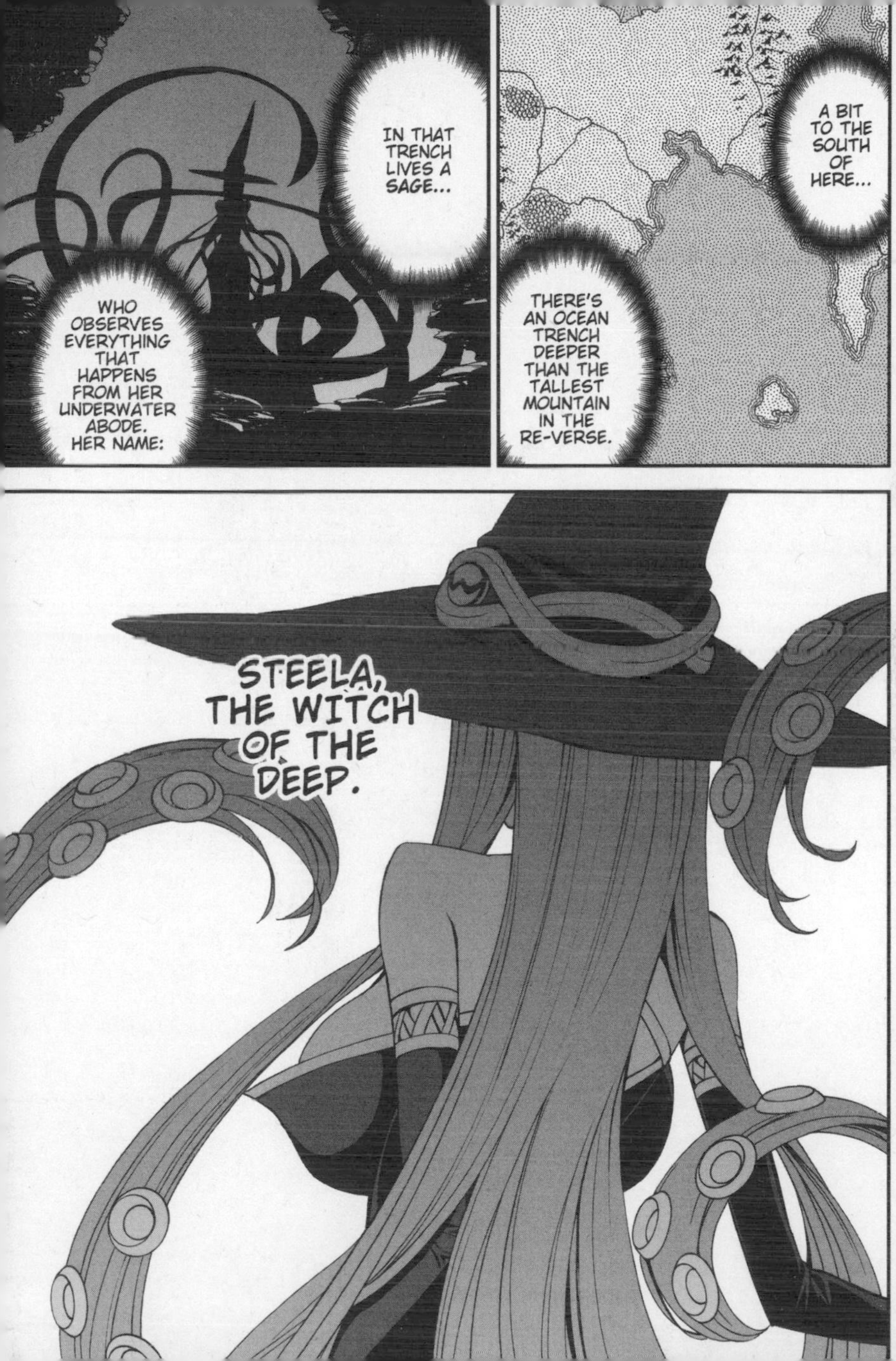
A BIT TO THE SOUTH OF HERE...
THERE'S AN OCEAN TRENCH DEEPER THAN THE TALLEST MOUNTAIN IN THE RE-VERSE.
IN THAT TRENCH LIVES A SAGE...
WHO OBSERVES EVERYTHING THAT HAPPENS FROM HER UNDERWATER ABODE. HER NAME:
STEELA, THE WITCH OF THE DEEP.

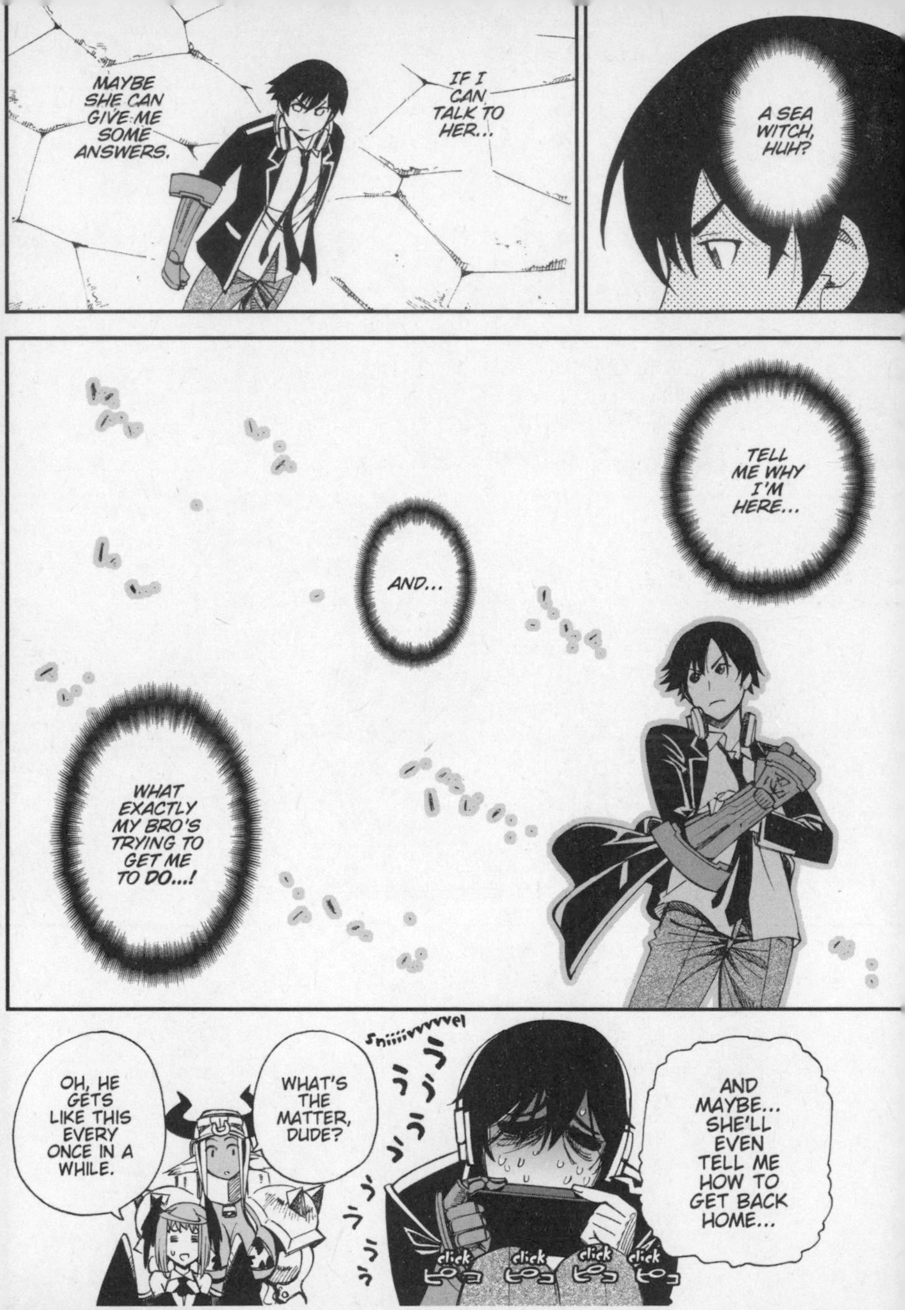
A SEA WITCH, HUH?
IF I CAN TALK TO HER...
MAYBE SHE CAN GIVE ME SOME ANSWERS.
TELL ME WHY I'M HERE...
AND...
WHAT EXACTLY MY BRO'S TRYING TO GET ME TO DO...!
AND MAYBE... SHE'LL EVEN TELL ME HOW TO GET BACK HOME...
click click click click
Sniiiivvvvvel
WHAT'S THE MATTER, DUDE?
OH, HE GETS LIKE THIS EVERY ONCE IN A WHILE.

TO BE CONTINUED

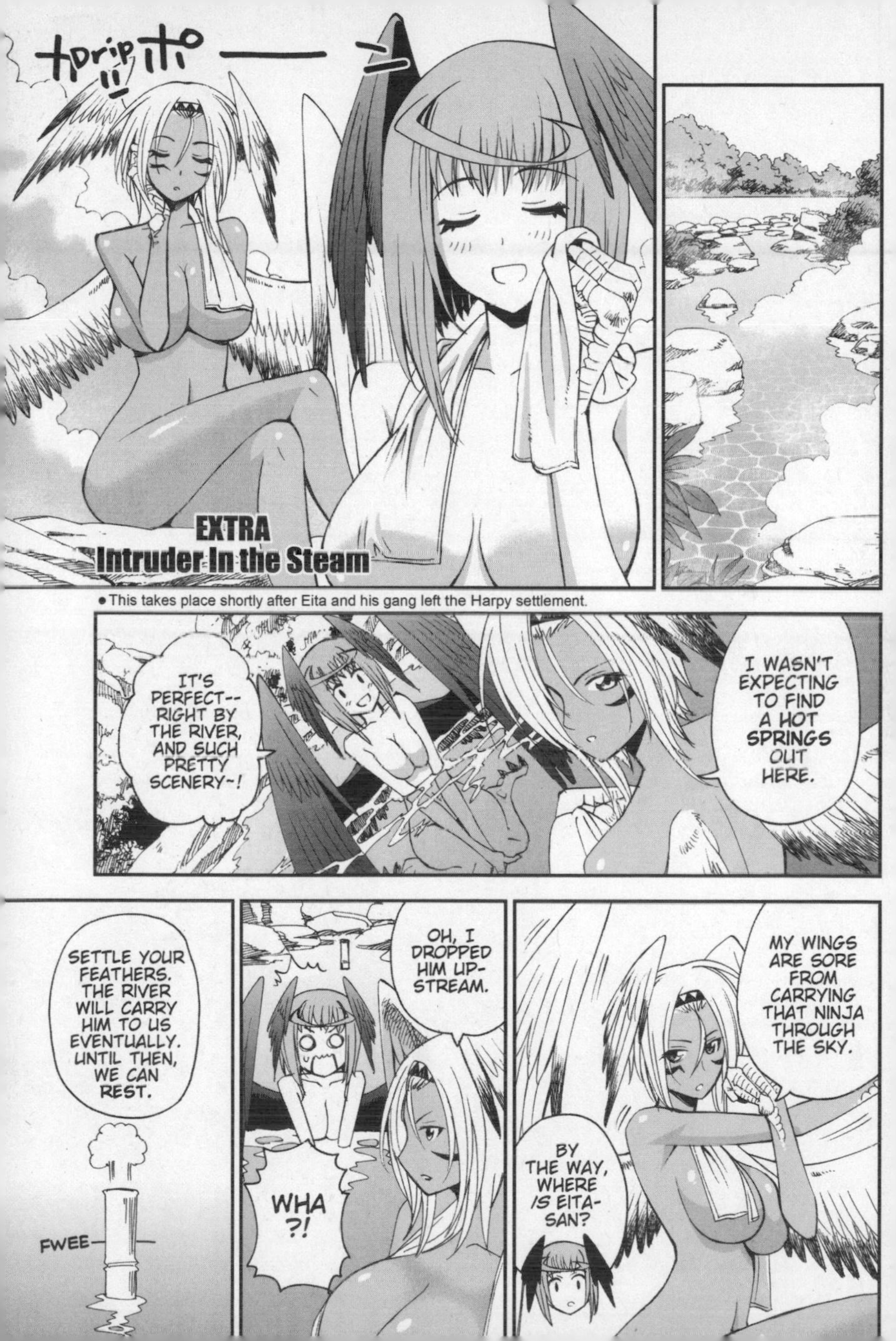
drip
EXTRA
Intruder In the Steam
● This takes place shortly after Eita and his gang left the Harpy settlement.
I WASN'T EXPECTING TO FIND A HOT SPRINGS OUT HERE.
IT'S PERFECT-- RIGHT BY THE RIVER, AND SUCH PRETTY SCENERY~!
MY WINGS ARE SORE FROM CARRYING THAT NINJA THROUGH THE SKY.
BY THE WAY, WHERE IS EITA-SAN?
OH, I DROPPED HIM UP-STREAM.
WHA?!
SETTLE YOUR FEATHERS. THE RIVER WILL CARRY HIM TO US EVENTUALLY. UNTIL THEN, WE CAN REST.
FWEE

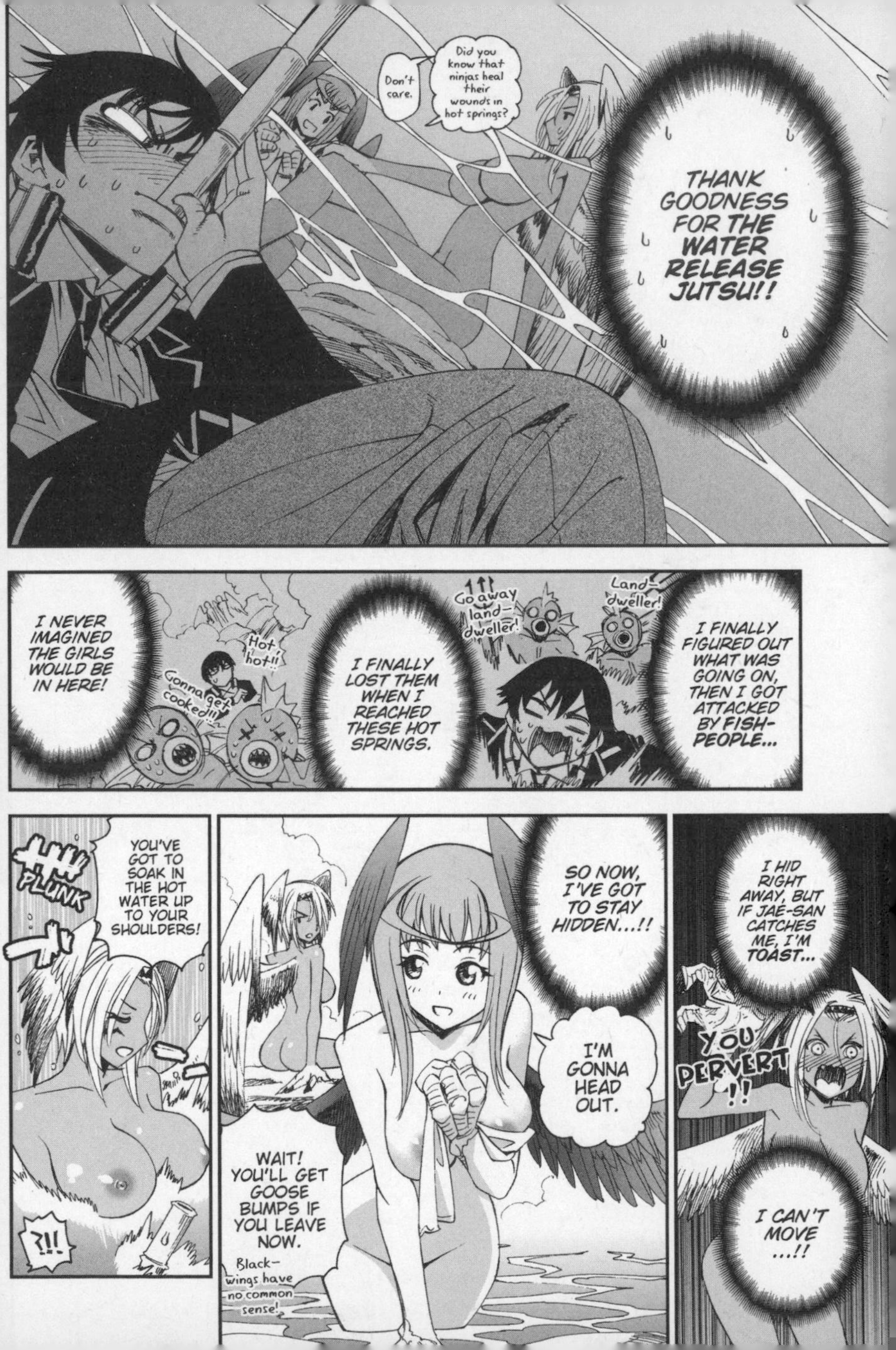
THANK GOODNESS FOR THE WATER RELEASE JUTSU!!
Did you know that ninjas heal their wounds in hot springs?
Don't care.
I FINALLY FIGURED OUT WHAT WAS GOING ON, THEN I GOT ATTACKED BY FISH-PEOPLE...
Land-dweller!
Go away land-dweller!
I FINALLY LOST THEM WHEN I REACHED THESE HOT SPRINGS.
Hot hot!!
Gonna get cooked!!!
I NEVER IMAGINED THE GIRLS WOULD BE IN HERE!
I HID RIGHT AWAY, BUT IF JAE-SAN CATCHES ME, I'M TOAST...
YOU PERVERT!!
I CAN'T MOVE...!!
SO NOW, I'VE GOT TO STAY HIDDEN...!!
I'M GONNA HEAD OUT.
WAIT! YOU'LL GET GOOSE BUMPS IF YOU LEAVE NOW.
Black-wings have no common sense!
YOU'VE GOT TO SOAK IN THE HOT WATER UP TO YOUR SHOULDERS!
PLUNK
?!!

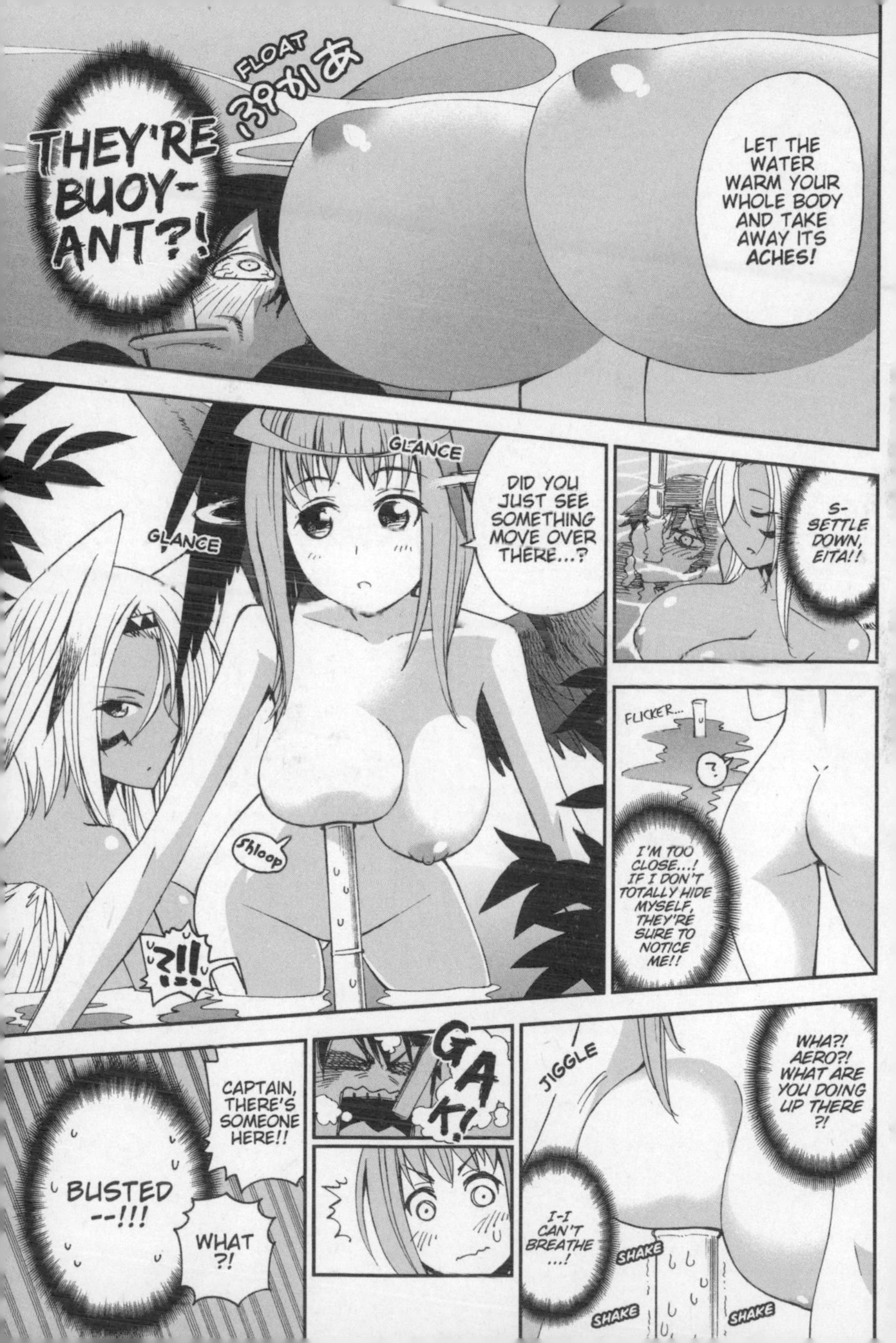
LET THE WATER WARM YOUR WHOLE BODY AND TAKE AWAY ITS ACHES!
FLOAT
ぷかぁ
THEY'RE BUOY-ANT?!
S-SETTLE DOWN, EITA!!
FLICKER...
?
I'M TOO CLOSE...! IF I DON'T TOTALLY HIDE MYSELF, THEY'RE SURE TO NOTICE ME!!
GLANCE
DID YOU JUST SEE SOMETHING MOVE OVER THERE...?
GLANCE
Shloop
?!!
WHA?! AERO?! WHAT ARE YOU DOING UP THERE?!
JIGGLE
I-I CAN'T BREATHE...!
SHAKE
SHAKE
SHAKE
GAK!
CAPTAIN, THERE'S SOMEONE HERE!!
BUSTED--!!!
WHAT?!

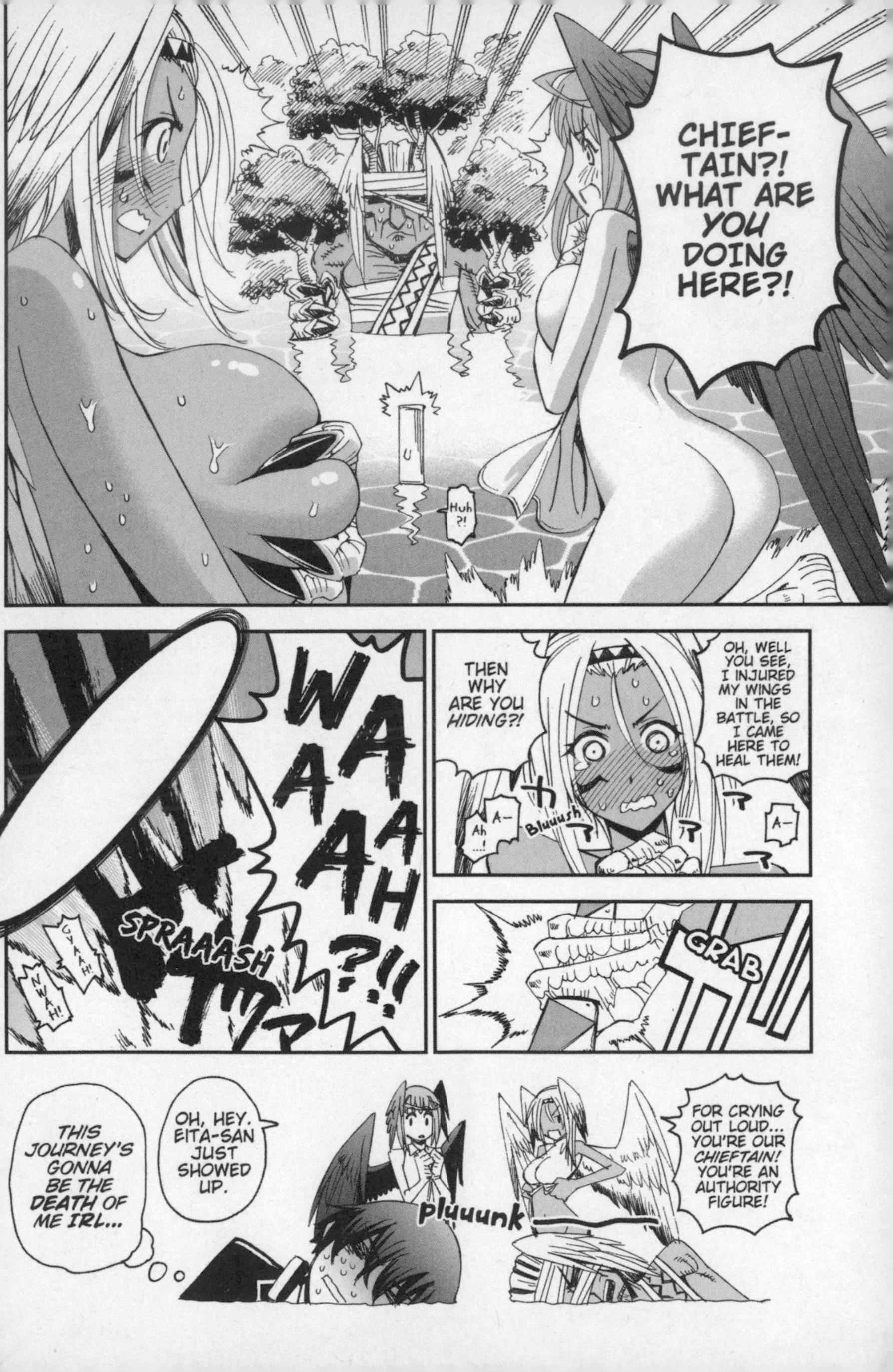
CHIEF-TAIN?! WHAT ARE *YOU* DOING HERE?!
Huh?!
OH, WELL YOU SEE, I INJURED MY WINGS IN THE BATTLE, SO I CAME HERE TO HEAL THEM!
THEN WHY ARE YOU *HIDING*?!
A—
Bluuush
A—
Ah ...!
GRAB
WAAAAAH?!!
SPRAAAASH
GYAAH!
NWAH!
FOR CRYING OUT LOUD... YOU'RE OUR *CHIEFTAIN*! YOU'RE AN AUTHORITY FIGURE!
OH, HEY. EITA-SAN JUST SHOWED UP.
pluuunk
THIS JOURNEY'S GONNA BE THE *DEATH* OF ME IRL...

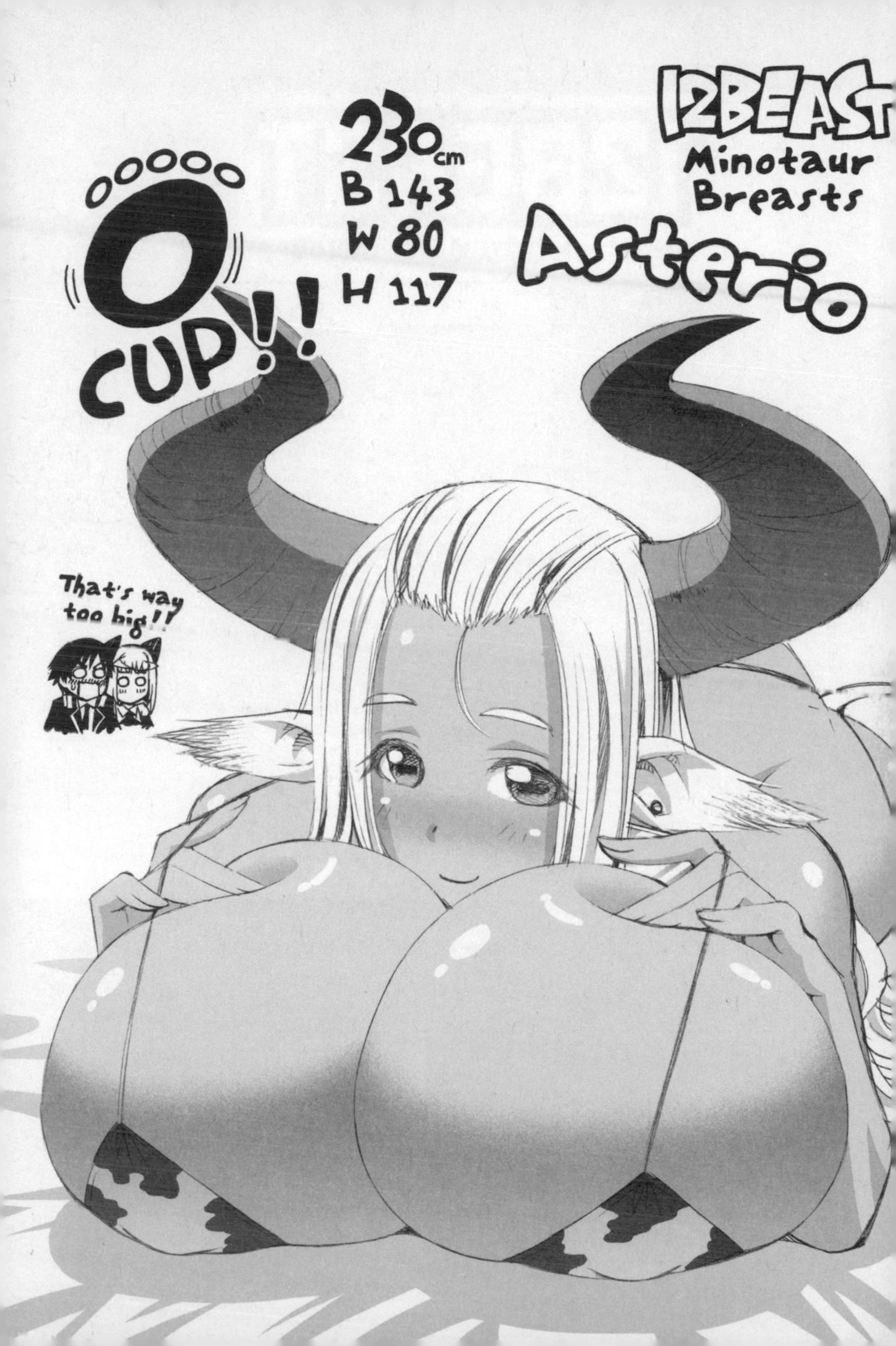
12BEAST
Minotaur
Breasts
Asterio
230cm
B 143
W 80
H 117
ooooo
O
CUP!!!
That's way too big!!

SEVEN SEAS ENTERTAINMENT PRESENTS

TRANSLATION
Ryan Peterson

ADAPTATION
Shanti Whitesides

LETTERING AND LAYOUT
Ma. Victoria Robado

COVER DESIGN
Nicky Lim

PROOFREADER
Janet Houck
Lee Otter

ASSISTANT EDITOR
Lissa Pattillo

MANAGING EDITOR
Adam Arnold

PUBLISHER
Jason DeAngelis

12BEAST VOLUME 2
© OKAYADO 2014
Edited by FUJIMISHOBO.
First published in Japan in 2014 by KADOKAWA CORPORATION, Tokyo.
English translation rights arranged with KADOKAWA CORPORATION, Tokyo
through TOHAN CORPORATION, Tokyo.

Seven Seas books may be purchased in bulk for educational, business, or
promotional use. For information on bulk purchases, please contact Macmillan
Corporate & Premium Sales Department at 1-800-221-7945 (ext 5442)
or write specialmarkets@macmillan.com.

Seven Seas and the Seven Seas logo are trademarks of
Seven Seas Entert

ISBN: 978-1-6269

Printed in Canada

First Printing: July

10 9 8 7 6 5 4

FOLLOW US ONLINE: *www.gomanga.com*

READING DIRECTIONS

This book reads from *right to left*, Japanese style.
If this is your first time reading manga, you start
reading from the top right panel on each page and
take it from there. If you get lost, just follow the
numbered diagram here. It may seem backwards at
first, but you'll get the hang of it! Have fun!!

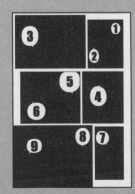